The Pragmatic
TypeScript
Programmer

Reshaping Modern JavaScript

Mike Zephalon

About Author

Mike Zephalon was born in Toronto, Canada, and developed a passion for technology and programming at an early age. His journey into the world of coding began when he was just a teenager, experimenting with simple scripts and exploring the vast possibilities of web development. Mike pursued his studies at the University of Toronto, where he majored in Computer Science. During his time at university, he became deeply interested in JavaScript, captivated by its versatility and power in building dynamic, interactive web applications.

Over the years, Mike has worked with several tech startups and companies, where he honed his skills as a front-end developer. His dedication to mastering JavaScript and its frameworks has made him a respected voice in the developer community. Through his books and tutorials, Mike aims to empower new and experienced developers alike, helping them unlock the full potential of JavaScript in their projects.

Table of Contents

1. Introduction to TypeScript, Installation and Setup

Introduction to TypeScript

What is TypeScript?

TypeScript is a **typed superset of JavaScript** developed and maintained by Microsoft. It is designed to enhance JavaScript by introducing optional static typing, modern JavaScript features, and tools that help developers catch errors early in the development process. TypeScript compiles to plain JavaScript, making it compatible with any environment where JavaScript runs, such as browsers, Node.js, and mobile applications.

Key characteristics include:

Static Typing: Adds optional type annotations to variables, functions, and properties.
Object-Oriented Features: Provides interfaces, classes, and inheritance.
Tooling Support: Integrates well with popular code editors like Visual Studio Code, offering autocompletion, refactoring, and error-checking.
Backwards Compatibility: Supports all JavaScript frameworks and libraries.

Why Use TypeScript?

Improved Code Quality:

Catch errors at compile time rather than runtime.
Provides better IDE support with autocompletion and real-time error detection.

Readability and Maintainability:

Explicit types make the codebase easier to understand and maintain.
Enhances collaboration in teams by clearly defining how functions and components work.

Scalability:

Well-suited for large projects where maintaining JavaScript code can be challenging.

Ecosystem and Compatibility:

Integrates seamlessly with JavaScript libraries and frameworks like React, Angular, and Vue.js.

Key Features of TypeScript

Optional Static Typing:

```
let message: string = "Hello, TypeScript!";
```

Interfaces and Classes:

```
interface User {
    id: number;
    name: string;
}

class Employee implements User {
    constructor(public id: number, public name: string) {}
}
```

Advanced Type Features:

Union and Intersection Types
Type Aliases and Generics
Type Inference

Modern JavaScript Support:

Includes ES6+ features such as modules, arrow functions, destructuring, etc.

Installation and Setup

Getting started with TypeScript requires a few simple steps. Below, we will walk through installing TypeScript, setting up your development environment, and writing your first TypeScript program.

Prerequisites

Before installing TypeScript, ensure that:
You have **Node.js** and **npm** installed.
Download and install from Node.js official website.

Verify installation:
node -v
npm -v
You have a code editor like **Visual Studio Code (VS Code)** for a smooth development experience.

Installing TypeScript

There are multiple ways to install TypeScript. The most common is via npm.

Global Installation

To use TypeScript across multiple projects:
npm install -g typescript

Verify the installation:
tsc -v
This command checks the installed TypeScript version.

Local Installation

For project-specific TypeScript installations:
npm install --save-dev typescript

This installs TypeScript as a development dependency, isolating it within your project.

Setting Up TypeScript

Step 1: Create a New Project

Open your terminal and create a new directory:
mkdir typescript-project
cd typescript-project

Initialize a new Node.js project:
npm init -y

This generates a package.json file with default configurations.

Step 2: Install TypeScript Locally

Install TypeScript as a development dependency:

npm install --save-dev typescript

Step 3: Configure the TypeScript Compiler

Create a **TypeScript configuration file (tsconfig.json)**:

tsc --init
A tsconfig.json file will be created. It includes default options for compiling TypeScript. You can customize settings as per your needs. Common configurations include:

```
{
  "compilerOptions": {
    "target": "ES6",            // Target JavaScript version
    "module": "commonjs",         // Module system
    "outDir": "./dist",          // Output directory for compiled files
    "strict": true,            // Enable strict type-checking
    "esModuleInterop": true       // Ensure compatibility with CommonJS modules
  },
  "include": ["src/**/*"],         // Include files
  "exclude": ["node_modules"]       // Exclude files
}
```

Step 4: Organize Your Project Structure

A common directory structure for TypeScript projects:

typescript-project/

```
├── src/             // Source code
│   └── index.ts        // Main TypeScript file

├── dist/             // Compiled JavaScript files
```

```
└── index.js
├── tsconfig.json      // TypeScript configuration
├── package.json       // Project metadata and dependencies
```

Step 5: Write Your First TypeScript Program

Create a new src/index.ts file:

```
const greet = (name: string): string => {
   return `Hello, ${name}!`;
};
```

```
console.log(greet("TypeScript"));
```

Compile the file:
Tsc

By default, the tsc command compiles files based on the tsconfig.json configuration.

Run the compiled JavaScript file:
node dist/index.js

Using TypeScript with Build Tools

For larger projects, you may want to integrate TypeScript with build tools like Webpack, Babel, or Vite.

Using Webpack with TypeScript

Install Webpack and related dependencies:
npm install --save-dev webpack webpack-cli ts-loader

Configure webpack.config.js:
```
const path = require('path');
module.exports = {
   entry: './src/index.ts',
   output: {
      filename: 'bundle.js',
      path: path.resolve(__dirname, 'dist'),
   },
   resolve: {
      extensions: ['.ts', '.js'],
   },
   module: {
      rules: [
         {
            test: /\.ts$/,
            use: 'ts-loader',
            exclude: /node_modules/,
         },
      ],
   },
```

```
};
```

Run Webpack:
npx webpack

Development Environment Recommendations

1. Visual Studio Code (VS Code):

Install the **TypeScript Language Features** extension.
Features include IntelliSense, autocompletion, and error detection.

2. ESLint and Prettier:

For consistent code formatting and linting:

npm install --save-dev eslint prettier eslint-config-prettier eslint-plugin-prettier
Configure. eslintrc.json:
```
{
   "parser": "@typescript-eslint/parser",
   "plugins": ["@typescript-eslint"],
   "extends": ["plugin:@typescript-eslint/recommended"]
}
```

3. Debugging in VS Code:

Use the built-in debugger for TypeScript files.

Configure .vscode/launch.json:
```
{
   "version": "0.2.0",
   "configurations": [
      {
         "type": "node",
         "request": "launch",
         "name": "Launch Program",
         "skipFiles": ["<node_internals>/**"],
         "program": "${workspaceFolder}/src/index.ts",
         "preLaunchTask": "tsc: build - tsconfig.json"
      }
   ]
}
```

Common Commands for TypeScript Development

Compile all TypeScript files:
Tsc

Compile a single file:
tsc src/file.ts

Watch mode for development:

```
tsc –watch
```

Clean output directory:
```
rm -rf dist
```

TypeScript is a programming language that extends JavaScript by adding static types on top of it. Created by Microsoft developer Anders Hejlsberg, TypeScript was released in 2012 as an open-source project.

Brief overview of TypeScript

TypeScript provides the ability to write scalable and maintainable applications while leveraging the features and versatility of JavaScript. As a superset of JavaScript, TypeScript is compatible with any valid JavaScript code, allowing developers to gradually adopt it in their existing projects without the need for a complete rewrite. It enables developers to specify the type of variables, function parameters, and return types. This allows for catching errors at compile-time rather than runtime, resulting in improved code quality, maintainability, readability, and fewer bugs in production. Additionally, it can result in fewer lines of code, as values do not need to be explicitly checked for type.

TypeScript also introduces a range of advanced features such as interfaces and generics. These features enhance the development experience by providing a way to define contracts, organize code into reusable components, and enforce type safety across the application. Through this last decade, TypeScript has gained significant popularity in the web development community due to its ability to address many challenges faced by JavaScript developers.

It is becoming the preferred choice for large-scale applications and has been widely adopted by notable companies like Microsoft, Google, Airbnb, and Slack. With a growing community and support from major industry players, TypeScript's future is bright for years to come!

Community-driven projects like **DefinitelyTyped** provide TypeScript definitions for popular JavaScript libraries, making it easier for developers to leverage existing code while enjoying the benefits of TypeScript's type system on the web browser, NodeJS or any JavaScript runtime.

The motivation behind creating TypeScript

TypeScript was created to address the limitations and challenges faced by JavaScript developers when working on large-scale applications. As web applications grows both in size and complexity, the flexibility of JavaScript's dynamic typing becomes a double-edged sword, leading to runtime errors, maintainability issues, and difficulty scaling codebases.

One of the primary motivations behind creating TypeScript was to introduce static typing to JavaScript, enabling developers to catch errors at compile time instead of runtime. This would result in more robust, maintainable, and scalable applications. Since TypeScript is a superset of JavaScript, it allows developers to gradually adopt its features without having to rewrite their entire codebase.

Another motivation was to improve tooling and editor support. With static typing, editors can provide better code navigation, autocompletion, and refactoring capabilities, ultimately improving developer productivity. The type information also enables better documentation and code understanding, making it easier for teams to collaborate and maintain their projects.

TypeScript also enables better code organization and scalability through the introduction of features like classes, modules, and interfaces. These language constructs allow developers to structure their code in a more modular and maintainable manner, facilitating code reuse and separation of concerns.

TypeScript's relationship with JavaScript

TypeScript is a superset of JavaScript, which means that any valid JavaScript code is also valid TypeScript code. TypeScript extends JavaScript by adding optional static typing and a host of other features that make it easier to develop, maintain, and scale large web applications.

Developers can start by writing JavaScript code and then gradually introduce type annotations to enhance the code with static typing. This allows projects to transition to TypeScript at their own pace, without the need for a complete rewrite to start using it.

One of the key benefits of TypeScript's relationship with JavaScript is its ability to leverage its vast ecosystem. TypeScript can use existing JavaScript libraries, frameworks, and tools seamlessly, enabling developers to utilize popular JavaScript libraries like React or Express in their TypeScript projects without any issues.

The TypeScript compiler converts TypeScript into JavaScript code that can be executed in any JavaScript runtime environment. This compilation process ensures that TypeScript code is transformed into its equivalent JavaScript representation, maintaining compatibility with existing JavaScript tools and platforms.

TypeScript's close relationship with JavaScript also ensures that it stays up to date with the latest ECMAScript standards. As new features are introduced to JavaScript, they are often incorporated into TypeScript, allowing developers to use cutting-edge language features while still benefiting from TypeScript's type system and tooling support.

In summary, TypeScript and JavaScript share a symbiotic relationship of enhancement and extension. TypeScript builds upon the foundation laid by JavaScript, adding static typing and other features that make it easier to develop and maintain large applications. This allows developers to seamlessly transition between the two languages and ensures that TypeScript stays updated with the evolving JavaScript ecosystem.

Microsoft and TypeScript

Microsoft's involvement in TypeScript development has been pivotal in shaping the language's trajectory and overall success. Development was started in 2010 by Anders Hejlsberg, who is also known for his work on other programming languages like **C#**, **TurboPascal** and **Delphi**. It was released as an open-source project by Microsoft in 2012 and the company has continued to play an active role in its development, maintenance, and promotion.

The backing from a tech giant like Microsoft has provided TypeScript with the necessary resources for its growth and evolution, along with the open-source community support has enabled it to become a powerful and feature-rich language that addresses many challenges faced by JavaScript developers. The company has been actively involved in maintaining and advancing TypeScript through its dedicated development team. They regularly release updates, add new features, improve performance, and address community feedback. Microsoft also provides extensive documentation, tutorials, and resources for developers to learn and use TypeScript effectively.

Microsoft's commitment to TypeScript is evident in its integration with popular Microsoft tools like Visual Studio Code, a widely used open-source code editor. It has built-in support for TypeScript, offering features like syntax highlighting, code completion, and error checking. This integration has significantly eased the process of working with TypeScript, further boosting its adoption by developers.

Moreover, Microsoft has fostered a thriving community around TypeScript by being responsive to the needs of developers, actively engaging in discussions through forums and GitHub repositories, and collaborating with other companies and organizations in the tech industry to improve TypeScript's interoperability with various tools, frameworks, and libraries.

Visual Studio Code as a TypeScript editor

Developed by Microsoft in 2015, VS Code quickly became one of the most popular editors among TypeScript developers. It provides a seamless coding experience and offers a wide range of features and extensions for TypeScript development; besides providing native support with intelligent code completion, syntax highlighting, and error detection.

One of the standout features of VS Code is its rich debugging capabilities. It allows developers to set breakpoints, inspect variables, and step through their TypeScript code during runtime, helping to identify and fix bugs effectively. Additionally, the Visual Studio Code Marketplace offers a wide range of TypeScript-related extensions that provide additional functionalities and tools to enhance development, like managing imports, code snippets and an ever-growing number of specialized features.

The strong integration between TypeScript and VS Code extends beyond the editor itself. VS Code integrates with the TypeScript compiler, enabling developers to compile and build TypeScript projects directly from the editor. It provides build tasks and configuration options to customize the compilation process, making it convenient for developers to manage their TypeScript projects seamlessly.

VSCode's IntelliSense feature plays a crucial role in enhancing TypeScript development. It offers intelligent code suggestions based on the project's context, allowing developers to write code more quickly and accurately. By understanding TypeScript's static types, IntelliSense can provide precise and relevant suggestions, reducing the likelihood of errors and improving overall code quality.

Besides VS Code, there are TypeScript plugins for pretty much any popular text editors and IDEs like **Vim**, **Emacs**, **Notepad++**, **Webstorm**, and so on. For convenience we will be using VS Code for the rest of the examples in this book, but feel free to explore the TypeScript toolset of your favourite editor, whatever it may be. Please refer to the following figure:

Figure: Welcome screen for Visual Studio Code

The TypeScript ecosystem

The TypeScript ecosystem is extensive and versatile, offering a wide variety of libraries, plugins, and frameworks that help developers create powerful, scalable, and maintainable applications. These resources enhance the development experience, streamline workflows, and facilitate the adoption of best practices in the development process.

Angular, developed and maintained by Google, is a powerful web application framework built with TypeScript baked into it. React and Vue, both widely used JavaScript libraries for building user interfaces, also have excellent TypeScript support, enabling developers to build robust and maintainable UI applications.

Plugins

Plugins expand the functionality of the language and its associated development environments, such as Visual Studio Code. Notable examples include **TSLint** for enforcing coding style and best practices, **Prettier** for automatically maintaining a consistent coding style across a project, and various plugins for intelligent code completion, error detection, and navigation features tailored for TypeScript development.

Libraries

Libraries play a crucial role in the TypeScript ecosystem as pre-written code packages that developers can incorporate into their projects to manage specific tasks or functionalities. Several libraries natively support TypeScript, meaning they are written in TypeScript and provide type definitions out of the box. This simplifies the development process as developers can directly import and utilize these libraries without the need for external type definitions.

One of the most significant advantages TypeScript offers is the ability to work with JavaScript libraries through type definition files. The **DefinitelyTyped** project is a community-driven repository that hosts TypeScript type definitions for thousands of popular JavaScript libraries. By using the **@types** organization, developers can quickly obtain type definitions for a specific library, ensuring accurate type checking and code completion in their TypeScript projects.

To install a type definition for a specific library, you can use the following command: **npm install -- save-dev @types/library-name**

Once installed, TypeScript will automatically recognize the types provided by the type definition file, enabling seamless integration with the library in question. This allows developers to take advantage of TypeScript's features, such as type checking, autocompletion, and code navigation, even when working with third-party JavaScript libraries. By utilizing these type definitions, developers can harness the full power of TypeScript's type system while leveraging the vast ecosystem of JavaScript libraries.

TypeScript also has a strong presence in the testing landscape, with testing frameworks like Jest and Jasmine offering extensive TypeScript support. Build tools like **webpack** and **Rollup** also have excellent TypeScript integration, enabling developers to bundle and optimize TypeScript code for production.

What is a type system and why it matters?

A type system plays an integral role in programming languages, enforcing rules and protocols to help developers write clean, reliable code. It classifies data into categories such as numbers, strings, Booleans, or even user-defined types, defining the permissible operations on them. Among various type systems, static and dynamic typing are two prevalent paradigms.

Static and dynamic typing

In programming languages, the concept of typing refers to how variables and expressions are associated with certain types of data. A type system categorizes values into different types, such as numbers, strings, Booleans, and so on, or custom types. It defines rules for how these types interact and what operations can be performed on them. Static typing and dynamic typing are two contrasting approaches to type systems, each with its own characteristics and advantages.

Static typing

In a statically typed language, the data type of a variable is determined at compile-time, meaning that the type information is checked and enforced before the program is run. Languages like Java, C++ and TypeScript are statically typed. Static typing offers several benefits, including early detection of type errors, improved code readability, better tool support like code completion and refactoring, and more robust and reliable code, reducing the chances of unexpected runtime errors.

Dynamic typing

Dynamic typing, on the other hand, means that a variable's data type is determined at runtime. Languages like JavaScript, Python, and Ruby are dynamically typed. This approach allows for greater flexibility, as variables can change their types during the execution of a program. Dynamic typing allows for easier to write and more concise code, faster development, and rapid prototyping. However, this flexibility can also introduce challenges in terms of debugging and maintaining code, as type-related errors might not be apparent until the code is executed.

Static versus dynamic typing

Each typing approach has its pros and cons. Statically typed languages generally lead to more reliable and maintainable code, particularly beneficial in large-scale projects or when collaborating with other developers. Dynamic typing allows for more flexibility and may be better suited for smaller projects or rapid prototyping, but the lack of type information can make it more challenging to understand and maintain code, especially in larger projects.

Aspect	Static typing	Dynamic typing
Type checking	Performed at compile time	Performed at run time
Type declaration	Required or inferred	Not required
Type errors	Detected early by the compiler	Detected late by the interpreter
Advantages	More reliable, readable, and performant	More flexible, expressive, and productive
Disadvantages	More verbose, rigid, and complex	More prone to bugs, ambiguity, and inefficiency
Examples	Java, C, C++, Go, Scala	Python, JavaScript, PHP, Ruby

Table: Comparison of static and dynamic typed languages

In essence, the choice between static and dynamic typing depends on the project size and requirements.

TypeScript, as a statically typed superset of JavaScript, offers the best of both worlds by providing a robust type system on top of the existing dynamic nature of JavaScript. This enables developers to leverage the benefits of static typing while retaining the flexibility and expressiveness of JavaScript.

Historical context and implications of JavaScript

During the constraints of mere ten days in September of 1995, JavaScript was created by Brendan Eich at Netscape to enable users to create more interactive and dynamic web pages. It was designed to be easy to learn and use, with a focus on providing a lightweight and flexible language that could be quickly integrated into HTML pages.

Consequently, JavaScript adopted dynamic typing as one of its core features to cater to these needs. In the context of JavaScript's historical development, dynamic typing made sense. Web development in the mid1990s was relatively simple, and developers needed a language that allowed for rapid development cycles and quick iterations. Dynamic typing provided this flexibility, enabling developers to write code without being burdened by explicit type annotations or compile-time type checking. This was crucial at the time since each browser had different implementations of JavaScript, as it enabled developers to adapt their code using different runtime checks.

However, as the web evolved and web applications grew in complexity, the limitations of JavaScript's dynamic typing became more apparent. The lack of type information made it difficult to maintain and understand larger codebases, as developers had to rely on comments, documentation, or runtime testing to deduce the expected types of variables and function arguments.

Additionally, the absence of compile-time type checking means that type-related errors can easily slip into production, leading to runtime failures and making it hard to debug these hidden issues. The implications of JavaScript's dynamic typing also affect tooling and code analysis. Without the ability to infer types at compile-time, tools like code editors and linters face limitations in providing accurate code completion, refactoring support, and error detection.

To address these challenges and improve code quality, TypeScript emerged as a statically typed superset of JavaScript. By introducing static typing to JavaScript, TypeScript provides developers with the ability to catch type errors during the development phase before the code is executed. TypeScript's static typing enhances code reliability and maintainability by allowing developers to explicitly declare types and enforce stricter type checks, while also retaining JavaScript's flexibility by offering optional typing.

It is worth noting that TypeScript is not the first project that attempted to do this. For example, Haxe introduced similar capabilities as far back as 2006, though it did not gain the same traction and widespread adoption as TypeScript has.

A Brief history of TypeScript

TypeScript's journey began with the recognition that the dynamic nature of JavaScript, while having its advantages, could hinder development efficiency and code maintainability in large-scale projects. In October 2012, Microsoft introduced TypeScript to the world, a statically typed superset of JavaScript designed to address these challenges.

It was started by Anders Hejlsberg, a renowned software engineer with an impressive track record that includes helping the creation of **Turbo Pascal**, **Delphi**, and **C#**. Alongside his team at Microsoft, Hejlsberg aimed to create a language that would be easily adopted by the vast JavaScript developer community while enhancing the language with static typing capabilities.

TypeScript's development took a pragmatic approach, ensuring that any valid JavaScript code was also valid
TypeScript code. This decision allowed developers to incrementally adopt TypeScript features into their existing JavaScript projects, making the transition smoother and less daunting. TypeScript also embraced the rapidly evolving ECMAScript standard, adopting new features and syntax additions as they emerged.

Over the years, TypeScript has seen significant growth in popularity and adoption. With each release, the language has become more refined and feature-rich, backed by a strong community and industry support. According to Github's blog, Octoverse, TypeScript has become the fourth most used language since 2020 and on.

Please refer to the following figure:

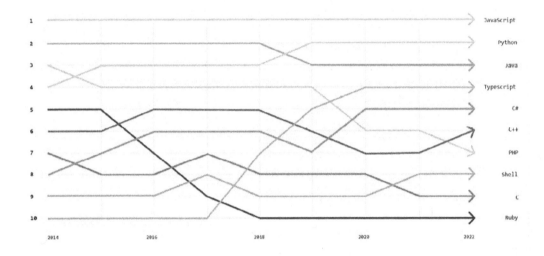

Figure: TypeScript has quickly become the fourth most popular language on Github

Today, TypeScript is widely recognized as a powerful tool for developing large-scale, complex web applications, helping developers write safer, more maintainable, and efficient code.

TypeScript's key features

In this section, we will discuss some important TypeScript key features.

Type annotation

One of the foundational features of TypeScript is its type annotation system.
 Type annotations enable developers to explicitly specify the types of variables, function parameters, and return values. By declaring these types, developers provide a blueprint for how the code should behave, which can significantly improve the readability and maintainability of the code.

 TypeScript uses these annotations to perform compile-time type checking, ensuring that the code adheres to the specified types. When the TypeScript compiler encounters a type mismatch, it raises a compilation error, alerting the developer to potential issues before the code is executed. This process helps catch common programming errors early, reducing the likelihood of runtime errors and making it easier to identify and fix issues during development.

Compile-time type checking

The compile-time type checking process offers several advantages for developers.

The compile-time type checking is made possible by TypeScript's transpiler, which converts TypeScript code into equivalent JavaScript code. During this conversion, the type information is stripped away, resulting in type-erased JavaScript code that can be executed in any JavaScript runtime environment. The transpiler is also responsible for transforming TypeScript-specific language features into equivalent JavaScript constructs, ensuring compatibility across different JavaScript engines.

TypeScript's type annotation and compile-time type checking system helps enforce code contracts, making it easier to reason about the behaviour of the code and the relationships between different parts of the application. Additionally, they provide a form of documentation that remains in sync with the code as it evolves. This self-documenting nature of TypeScript code can be particularly valuable in large-scale projects, where team collaboration and knowledge sharing are crucial to the success of the project.

Type inference

Type inference is an important feature of TypeScript that complements type annotations, providing a powerful and flexible type-checking system.

While type annotations allow developers to explicitly specify types, type inference enables the TypeScript compiler to automatically deduce types based on the context in which variables and functions are used.

TypeScript's type inference mechanism is intelligent and can infer types in various situations. For example, when a variable is initialized with a value, the compiler can infer the type of the variable from the value's type. Similarly, when a function is defined with parameters and a return value, the compiler can infer the types of the parameters and the return value based on the function's implementation.

Inference also plays a key role when working with generic types. For instance, when a developer uses a generic function or class without explicitly specifying the type arguments, TypeScript can often infer the correct types based on the context in which the generic function or class is used. This makes the code more concise and readable without sacrificing type safety.

Type inference offers several benefits to developers:

First, it reduces the amount of type annotation required, making the code less verbose and more readable. This can be particularly helpful in situations where the types are obvious from the context and adding explicit annotations would be redundant.

Second, type inference can help catch errors that might otherwise go unnoticed. For example, if the TypeScript compiler infers an unexpected type, it may indicate a logic error in the code.

However, it is important to note that type inference has its limitations. In some cases, the TypeScript compiler may not be able to deduce the correct types, and explicit type annotations will be necessary. Additionally, relying too heavily on type inference can lead to less self-documenting code, making it harder for developers to understand and maintain these codes.

Type erasure

TypeScript employs a process called **type erasure** during the compilation phase, which refers to the removal of type information from TypeScript code as it is transformed into JavaScript.

Type erasure ensures that the type annotations present in TypeScript code have no runtime impact and allows the compiled JavaScript code to be executed in any JavaScript runtime environment.

The primary purpose of type erasure is to maintain compatibility with JavaScript, a dynamically typed language without a built-in type system. By erasing type information during compilation, TypeScript generates JavaScript code that adheres to this typeless nature, ensuring seamless integration with existing JavaScript libraries, frameworks, and tools.

Although type erasure removes type information at runtime, type checking and static type analysis still occur during the compilation process. The TypeScript compiler analyses the code, performs type checking, and verifies type correctness at compile time, reporting any type errors or mismatches as compilation errors.

Type erasure has several implications for developers:

First, it means that TypeScript's type checks are performed exclusively at compile time, with no runtime type checking. This emphasizes the importance of writing accurate type annotations and leveraging TypeScript's type-checking features to catch errors during the development process.

Second, due to type erasure, developers cannot rely on TypeScript's type information for runtime behaviour. For example, type guards must be based on values or properties that exist at runtime, not solely on TypeScript types.

Lastly, type erasure reinforces the fact that TypeScript is a strict superset of JavaScript, meaning that any valid JavaScript code is also a valid TypeScript code. This compatibility allows TypeScript developers to use the vast JavaScript ecosystem while still benefiting from static type checking and type analysis during development.

In summary, type erasure is a crucial aspect of TypeScript's design that enables the language to maintain compatibility with JavaScript while still providing a robust and comprehensive type system at compile time. Understanding type erasure and its implications can help developers write more effective and efficient TypeScript code.

Other features

TypeScript enhances JavaScript development by incorporating key features from ECMAScript 2015 (ES6) and subsequent versions, as well as introducing TypeScript-specific features. These include interfaces, enumerated types (enums), generics, namespaces, tuples, async/await, classes, modules, and arrow functions.

Namespaces: Helps organize and encapsulate code, providing better modularity and preventing naming collisions.

Tuples: Represent fixed-length arrays with elements of different types, adding type safety and clarity to compound values.

Arrow functions: Introduced in ECMAScript 2015, arrow functions offer a more concise syntax for anonymous functions, automatically bind the value of **this**, and support lexical scoping, making them a popular choice for writing modern JavaScript code.

Async/await: TypeScript fully supports async/await from ECMAScript 2017, simplifying asynchronous programming and making it easier to work with promises and write clean, readable asynchronous code.

Classes: TypeScript enhances ECMAScript 2015 classes with features like access modifiers, abstract classes, and decorators, bringing traditional object-oriented programming concepts to JavaScript and making it more powerful for building complex applications.

Interfaces: TypeScript interfaces define custom types based on the shape of an object, creating contracts that objects must adhere to. This promotes code consistency, interoperability, and improved type checking.

Enumerated types: Enums represent a set of named constants, improving code readability, expressiveness, and reducing the likelihood of errors.

Generics: Enables the creation of reusable, type-safe code components that work with multiple types, enhancing code flexibility, maintainability, and performance.

Modules: TypeScript supports the ES6 module syntax, providing a way to encapsulate code and manage dependencies between different parts of an application, promoting modularity and code sharing.

These features make TypeScript a powerful and versatile language for building complex web applications. By combining the best of JavaScript with additional enhancements, TypeScript offers developers a rich set of tools for creating scalable, maintainable, and type-safe code.

Differences between TypeScript and JavaScript

A primary difference between TypeScript and JavaScript is the introduction of type annotations in TypeScript. Type annotations are a way for developers to explicitly specify the expected data types of variables, function parameters, and return values. By adding type annotations, developers can leverage TypeScript's powerful type checking capabilities, catching potential errors during compile time rather than runtime.

In TypeScript, type annotations are added using a colon (:) followed by the type,
such as: **let age: number = 25**

In contrast, in JavaScript, variables can be declared without explicitly specifying their types, such as:
let age = 25.

JavaScript relies on type inference to determine the type of variables based on their assigned values. Type annotations can also be used with function parameters and return values. For instance, consider the following TypeScript function that takes two numbers as arguments and returns their sum:

```
function add(a: number, b: number): number {   return a + b;
}
```

In JavaScript, the same function would be written without type annotations:

```
function add(a, b) {   return a + b;
}
```

Type annotations enhance code documentation, making it easier for developers to understand the expected types and usage of variables, functions, and objects. They improve code maintainability and reliability by providing clear expectations for inputs and outputs, reducing potential bugs. Additionally, TypeScript supports more advanced types, such as interfaces, enums, and generics, which can be used in type annotations to create more complex and expressive type definitions.

While the syntax for type annotations is unique to TypeScript, the rest of the TypeScript syntax is a superset of JavaScript, meaning any valid JavaScript code is also a valid TypeScript code. This makes it easy for developers to transition from JavaScript to TypeScript. However, TypeScript adds several new features and enhancements, particularly when it comes to working with types, making it more powerful and expressive than JavaScript.

Performance implications and trade-offs

When comparing TypeScript and JavaScript, it is essential to consider the performance implications and trade-offs associated with each language. TypeScript introduces benefits such as static typing and improved tooling, but it also comes with some overhead in terms of compilation time and complexity.

One performance implication of using TypeScript is the need for a compilation step. TypeScript code must be transpiled to JavaScript before it can be executed in a browser or a Node.js environment. This additional step can result in longer build times compared to working with JavaScript directly. However, modern build tools and incremental compilation have significantly reduced this overhead, making it less of a concern for many projects.

 Another trade-off to consider when using TypeScript is the potential impact on runtime performance. TypeScript is a superset of JavaScript and introduces additional features, such as interfaces and generics. However, TypeScript undergoes a process called **type erasure** during compilation, removing all type information from the generated JavaScript code. As a result, the runtime performance of TypeScript and JavaScript should be nearly identical.

 In addition to performance considerations, TypeScript can introduce some complexity in terms of tooling and learning curve. Developers may need to familiarize themselves with TypeScript-specific tools, such as type checkers, linters, and IDE integrations. However, many popular development tools, like Visual Studio Code, provide excellent TypeScript support out of the box, which can help mitigate this learning curve.

Despite these trade-offs, the benefits of using TypeScript often outweigh the drawbacks for many projects. TypeScript's type system can help catch errors during compile time, leading to fewer runtime bugs and improved code maintainability. Furthermore, TypeScript's static typing enhances the developer experience by providing better autocompletion, refactoring, and code navigation capabilities in IDEs.

Team collaboration benefits with TypeScript

TypeScript offers several benefits that enhance collaboration, communication, and code maintainability in a team environment. These advantages stem from TypeScript's type system, providing better code readability, stricter error checking, and improved tooling support.

Code readability: TypeScript's type annotations improve code readability, making it easier for team members to understand the intent and structure of the code. With explicit information about expected types for function parameters, return values, and object properties, developers can grasp the code's purpose and usage more easily. This enhanced readability reduces misunderstandings and miscommunications among team members, promoting more effective collaboration.

Code as documentation: The static typing features in TypeScript serve as a form of self-enforced documentation for the code. This is an added advantage for both maintaining the codebase and onboarding new developers, ensuring the guide lines are necessarily followed.

Code maintainability: TypeScript's static typing catches potential errors during development, resulting in stable and reliable code. This is particularly beneficial in a team setting, where multiple developers may work on different project aspects. TypeScript helps prevent errors caused by inconsistent data types, typos, or incorrect assumptions about the code's behaviour, leading to better code quality and reduced debugging time.

Tooling and IDE support: TypeScript's integration with popular IDEs, like Visual Studio Code, enables advanced features such as autocompletion, refactoring, and code navigation. These features significantly improve developer productivity and help maintain consistent coding styles across the team. Additionally, TypeScript's type information can be leveraged by linters and formatters to enforce coding standards and best practices, ensuring clean, organized, and maintainable code.

Onboarding new team members: TypeScript's type system serves as a form of documentation, helping new team members get up to speed more quickly. When joining a project, developers can rely on type information to understand how different codebase parts interact, making it easier to contribute to the project and reducing onboarding time.

TypeScript's additional build and compilation steps

TypeScript brings several benefits, such as type checking, improved tooling, and better code organization. However, it requires additional build and compilation steps compared to plain JavaScript. Since TypeScript is a superset of JavaScript, it must be compiled to JavaScript before running in a browser or a JavaScript runtime like Node.js.

The TypeScript compiler handles the compilation process. It takes TypeScript files as input, performs type checking, and outputs JavaScript files that can run in a browser or a Node.js environment. This step ensures that TypeScript's type system benefits are applied to the code before execution.

Developers may need to configure build tools like Webpack, Babel, or Rollup to work with TypeScript. These tools may require specific loaders or plugins to handle TypeScript files, such as **ts-loader** for **Webpack** or **@babel/preset-typescript** for **Babel**.

Despite these extra steps, the advantages of using TypeScript often outweigh the added complexity. Incorporating TypeScript into the development process allows developers to catch errors early, improve code maintainability, and utilize advanced language features. The additional build and compilation steps required for TypeScript are a small price to pay for the significant benefits it brings to JavaScript development.

Benefits of a type system in large-scale projects

Incorporating a type system into large-scale projects offers numerous advantages that can significantly improve the development process, code quality, and application stability. Some key benefits include:

Improved code quality and reliability: A type system enforces strict rules on how data is handled, reducing the likelihood of type-related errors, and promoting consistent usage of variables and functions. By catching errors at compile-time, developers can identify and fix issues before they become runtime problems, leading to more reliable and robust applications.

Enhanced maintainability and readability: Type information provides valuable context that can make codes easier to understand and modify. By explicitly specifying the expected types of variables, function parameters, and return values, developers can quickly grasp the purpose and behaviour of different code segments, leading to faster development and easier maintenance.

Better collaboration and code comprehension: In large projects with multiple developers, a type system can serve as a form of self-documentation, clarifying how various parts of the codebase interact. This shared understanding helps developers collaborate more effectively and reduces the risk of introducing bugs when modifying or extending existing code.

More efficient refactoring: Type systems enable powerful code analysis and refactoring features in **integrated development environments (IDEs)** and other development tools. By leveraging type information, these tools can accurately identify dependencies, detect potential issues, and perform safe automated refactoring that minimize the risk of breaking existing functionality.

Early error detection: The presence of a type system can help catch potential issues early in the development process, reducing the time and effort spent on debugging and testing. By addressing problems before they reach production, developers can deliver higher-quality applications with fewer defects and security vulnerabilities.

Potential performance optimizations: Static typing can provide opportunities for performance optimizations by enabling compilers and other tools to generate more efficient code. With detailed type information, these tools can make informed decisions about data representation, memory allocation, and function inlining, potentially leading to faster and more resource-efficient applications.

Reusable code: One of TypeScript's standout features is its support for generics, which allows you to write code that works over a variety of types, allowing developers to write more reusable code.

In summary, the benefits of a type system in large-scale projects are manifold, encompassing aspects like code quality, maintainability, collaboration, tooling support, and performance. By adopting a type system such as TypeScript, developers can better manage the complexity of their projects and deliver more stable, efficient, and maintainable web applications.

Better readability with type annotations and interfaces

TypeScript enhances readability using type annotations and interfaces, which provide explicit type information for variables, function parameters, and return values. This clarity makes the codebase more understandable and maintainable.

TypeScript's annotations and interfaces create clear contracts between functions and components, ensuring correct usage throughout the application and reducing unexpected behaviour or runtime errors. Enforcing contracts at compile-time improves maintainability and scalability, as developers can focus on implementation logic without worrying about type-related issues.

Clear contracts also simplify refactoring or updating the codebase, allowing changes to individual parts without inadvertently affecting other areas. This promotes code reuse, reduces potential errors, and enhances the development experience.

Improved code navigation and understanding are achieved through TypeScript's explicit annotations and interfaces. IDEs leverage TypeScript's type system to provide powerful navigation features like Go to Definition, Find All References, and IntelliSense. These tools enable efficient navigation, allowing developers to focus on implementing features or fixing issues.

Better code navigation and understanding also streamline onboarding new team members. Developers new to the project can quickly get up to speed, thanks to TypeScript's explicit contracts and intuitive navigation.

Maintainability benefits

TypeScript also provides many maintainability benefits. These are discussed in detail below.

Early error detection through static typing

TypeScript's static typing enables early error detection during development, reducing the likelihood of bugs in production. This results in a more robust and reliable application, as issues are addressed before affecting end-users.

Static typing also promotes accurate documentation and code structure, preventing misunderstandings within the development team and encouraging cleaner, more modular code. This enhances maintainability and makes updating code easier.

Refactoring support and safe code modifications

TypeScript enhances refactoring support and promotes safe code modifications, essential for maintaining JavaScript applications. With its static typing system, TypeScript offers better tooling and code analysis, allowing developers to confidently make changes.

IDEs with TypeScript support provides powerful refactoring tools that leverage type information for improved accuracy and effectiveness. This helps developers avoid pitfalls and minimizes the chance of introducing new bugs.

Encouraging best practices and design patterns

TypeScript promotes best practices and design patterns, contributing to the maintainability and robustness of JavaScript applications. Developers can write clean, modular, and reusable code using TypeScript's features.
TypeScript encourages the use of interfaces to define contracts and generics for reusable, type-safe code. Interfaces ensure predictable code structure, while generics enable flexible, maintainable code without duplicating logic.

By embracing modern JavaScript features like classes, modules, and arrow functions, TypeScript supports better code organization, encapsulation, separation of concerns, and the use of pure functions.

Modular architecture and namespace organization

TypeScript supports modular architecture and namespace organization, providing scalability advantages for largescale JavaScript applications. These features promote well-structured and organized code for easy scaling and maintenance.

Modular architecture encourages dividing code into smaller, self-contained units called **modules**. TypeScript's support for modules enables encapsulation, dependency management, code reusability, and separation of concerns.

Facilitating collaboration in large teams

TypeScript aids collaboration in large teams by offering a robust type system, clear interfaces, modular architecture, and enhanced tooling support. Type annotations and interfaces establish a contract between parts of an application, simplifying understanding and promoting teamwork. Developers can rely on TypeScript's type system to enforce consistency across the codebase.

TypeScript's support for modules and namespaces encourages separation of concerns, resulting in well-organized code. This allows developers to work concurrently without conflicts, while modular code promotes code reuse across different parts of the application or projects.

Supporting complex codebases and growing projects

TypeScript is valuable for managing complex codebases and growing projects, with benefits such as static typing, modular architecture, and advanced language features. Static typing helps catch errors early, reducing runtime issues and simplifying debugging, which is crucial for large, complex applications.

Modular architecture allows better organization and separation of concerns, enabling developers to divide the codebase into smaller units, improving maintainability and extensibility. Generics and interfaces promote code reuse and extensibility, creating flexible, type-safe components that adapt to different use cases, resulting in a more maintainable and scalable codebase.

Autocompletion and IntelliSense in Visual Studio Code

Autocompletion, also known as **code completion**, is a feature that helps developers write code more quickly and accurately by suggesting possible completions based on the context. As developers' type, VS Code analyzes the surrounding code and offers relevant suggestions, such as variable names, function names, or properties, that match the current input. This speeds up the coding process, reduces the likelihood of typos, and helps maintain consistent naming conventions throughout the project.

IntelliSense is another valuable feature in VS Code that enhances productivity by providing contextual information about the code as developers work. It offers real-time feedback on syntax errors, type information, and function signatures, among other things. By hovering over a symbol, developers can see its type, documentation, and other relevant details, making it easier to understand the code and its purpose. IntelliSense also displays type information and error messages as developers' type, allowing them to catch and fix issues early in the development process.

Additional benefits of using TypeScript

Embracing TypeScript extends your capabilities as a developer beyond the provision of static types. TypeScript's potent features and its wide acceptance across several popular frameworks bring a myriad of advantages that improve the development experience and enhance the resulting code quality. This section explores TypeScript's adoption across numerous frameworks like Angular, React, Vue, Svelte, and Next.js, and the unique benefits they offer when combined with TypeScript's powerful features.

Angular's adoption of TypeScript

TypeScript plays a significant role in the **Angular framework**, a popular web application framework developed by Google. Angular has embraced TypeScript as its primary language since the release of Angular 2, marking a substantial milestone in TypeScript's adoption in the web development community.

Angular leverages TypeScript's static typing to provide enhanced tooling support and an improved developer experience. The use of static types enables better code navigation, autocompletion, and error checking within Angular projects. Developers can take advantage of TypeScript's features, such as interfaces, classes, and decorators, to build more maintainable and scalable applications.

TypeScript's strong typing also enhances Angular's capabilities, allowing for robust dependency injection, modular architecture, and component-based development. The static type checking ensures that dependencies are correctly resolved, reducing runtime errors, and making it easier to manage complex applications.

The official Angular documentation and examples are primarily written in TypeScript, providing a comprehensive resource for developers using TypeScript with Angular. This integration has gained popularity among developers due to the improved development experience, code maintainability, and scalability it offers.

TypeScript support in React and other UI frameworks

TypeScript has gained significant support and adoption within various JavaScript frameworks used for building user interfaces, such as React, Vue, Svelte, and Next.js. Although TypeScript is not the default language for these frameworks, the tools and support available make it relatively easy for developers to adopt TypeScript in these environments.

React has excellent TypeScript support through the official **@types/react** package, which provides type definitions for React components, hooks, and other related APIs. This enables developers to write React applications with static typing, promoting code organization, maintainability, and scalability.

Similarly, **Vue**, a progressive JavaScript framework, has embraced TypeScript with official support and type declarations provided through the **@types/vue** package. This allows developers to write Vue applications using TypeScript, benefiting from the enhanced tooling support, code navigation, and type checking that TypeScript provides.

Svelte is a modern and lightweight UI framework that also supports TypeScript, enhancing the development experience with type safety and advanced language features. To use TypeScript in a Svelte project, developers can configure the Svelte preprocessor to understand TypeScript files, and then use type annotations and interfaces in their Svelte components.

Next.js, a popular framework for building React applications with server-side rendering and has built-in support for TypeScript. Developers can easily create TypeScript-based Next.js projects by adding a **tsconfig.json** file and installing the necessary dependencies.

TypeScript's integration with these UI frameworks enables developers to leverage the advantages of static typing, such as early error detection, improved code documentation, and better collaboration in large teams. It helps reduce potential bugs, improve code quality, and enhance the overall development experience when building complex UI components and applications.

TypeScript support in Node.js

TypeScript has emerged as a popular choice for backend development, thanks to its compatibility with Node.js, a widely used runtime environment for executing JavaScript on the server-side. Node.js leverages the power of TypeScript's static typing and advanced language features, resulting in an improved development experience, better code organization, and increased maintainability for server-side applications.

To set up a Node.js project with TypeScript, developers can use the **tsc** command to compile TypeScript files into JavaScript before running them on the Node.js runtime. By using TypeScript's **tsconfig.json** configuration file, they can specify the desired output format, module resolution, and other compiler options to suit their project requirements.

TypeScript's integration with Node.js promotes the use of interfaces and type annotations, which enforce clear contracts between different parts of the application. This makes it easier for developers to understand and manage complex backend architectures, especially when dealing with asynchronous operations, data processing, and third-party API integrations.

Moreover, TypeScript's extensive ecosystem offers numerous type definition packages for popular Node.js libraries and frameworks, such as **Express**, **Koa**, and **NestJS**, among others. These packages enable developers to leverage TypeScript's features while working with well-established tools and frameworks in the Node.js ecosystem.

Installation and Setup

Installing TypeScript

In this part of the book, we will guide you through the installation of TypeScript on Windows, MacOS, and Linux. As TypeScript relies on Node.js to run, each section includes steps to ensure Node.js is installed, followed by the TypeScript setup.

Installation on Windows

Installing TypeScript on a Windows machine is a straightforward process with few simple steps. TypeScript requires Node.js to run, so the first step is to ensure that you have it installed on your system. To download Node.js, visit the official Node.js website and look for the latest **Long Term Support (LTS)** version for Windows. This version is recommended because it provides stability and long-term support, making it suitable for most users. Once the installer is downloaded, run the executable file and follow the installation wizard.

Make sure to choose the option to add Node.js to the path during the installation process. After the installation is complete, open a **Command Prompt** or **PowerShell** window and run the following command to verify that Node.js is installed correctly:
node -v

This command should display the installed Node.js version. With Node.js installed, you can now install TypeScript using the **Node Package Manager (npm)**, is included with Node.js. Again, on a Command Prompt or PowerShell window run the following command:

npm install -g typescript

The **-g** flag indicates that TypeScript should be installed as a global package, making it accessible from any directory in your system. After TypeScript is installed, you can verify the installation by running the following command: tsc -v

This command should display the installed TypeScript version. If you need to update TypeScript to a newer version in the future, you can do so by running the following command:
npm update -g typescript

With TypeScript successfully installed on your Windows machine, you can now proceed to set up the development environment and start working with TypeScript projects.

Installation on MacOS

For MacOS, the procedure to install TypeScript remains largely similar due to the dependency on Node.js, start by confirming the presence of Node.js on your MacOS system. To install Node.js, visit the official Node.js website and download the latest LTS version for MacOS. Choosing the latest LTS version that guarantees stability and long-term support. Once the installer is downloaded, double-click the package file and follow the installation wizard.

Another way to install Node.js on Mac is using Homebrew, a package manager for MacOS. If you do not have Homebrew installed, you can install it by following the instructions on the official Homebrew website which instructs to install it via terminal:

Once Homebrew is installed, run the following command on a Terminal window to install the latest LTS version of Node.js:

brew install node@lts

The LTS version is recommended as it offers stability and long-term support, making it ideal for most users. After the installation is complete, you may need to add Node.js to your **PATH**. To do this, add the following line to your ~/**.zshrc** or ~/**.bashrc** file:

export PATH="/usr/local/opt/node@lts/bin:$PATH"

Then, restart your Terminal or run source ~/**.zshrc** or source ~/**.bashrc** to apply the changes. To verify that Node.js is installed correctly, run the following command:
node -v

This command should display the installed Node.js version. With Node.js installed, you can now install TypeScript using the npm, which comes bundled with Node.js. In the Terminal window, run the following command:

npm install -g typescript

The **-g** flag indicates that TypeScript should be installed as a global package, making it accessible from any directory in your system. After TypeScript is installed, you can verify the installation by running the following command: tsc -v

This command should display the installed TypeScript version. To update TypeScript to a newer version in the future, you can do so by running the following command:
npm update -g typescript

With TypeScript successfully installed on your MacOS machine, you can now proceed to set up your development environment and start working with TypeScript projects.

Installation on Linux

Installing TypeScript on a Linux machine involves a few simple steps, like the process for Windows and MacOS. As with the other platforms, TypeScript requires Node.js to run, so you must first ensure that Node.js is installed on your system.

To install Node.js on Linux, you can use the package manager for your specific distribution. For example, on Debian-based distributions like Ubuntu, open a Terminal window and run the following commands to update your package list and install Node.js:

sudo apt update sudo apt install nodejs

On Red Hat-based distributions like Fedora, you can use the following commands:

sudo dnf upgrade sudo dnf install nodejs

In any other distribution, use the corresponding package manager to install the package Node.js, which is how most packages are named, or on a few exceptions it can be just node. After the installation is complete, verify that Node.js is installed correctly by running the following command: **node -v**

This command should display the installed Node.js version. With Node.js installed, you can now install TypeScript using the npm, which comes bundled with Node.js. In the Terminal window, run the following command: **npm install -g typescript**

The **-g** flag indicates that TypeScript should be installed as a global package, making it accessible from any directory in your system. After TypeScript is installed, you can verify the installation by running the following command: **tsc -v**

This command should display the installed TypeScript version. To update TypeScript to a newer version in the future, you can do so by running the following command: **npm update -g typescript**

With TypeScript successfully installed on your Linux machine, you can now proceed to set up your development environment and start working with TypeScript projects.

Choosing a code editor

When working with TypeScript, selecting a suitable code editor is essential for a smooth development experience. Several code editors provide excellent support for TypeScript, including syntax highlighting, autocompletion, and error checking. Some popular options are Visual Studio Code, WebStorm, Sublime Text, Atom, Vim, and Emacs.

Visual Studio Code (VSCode): Developed by Microsoft, the same company behind TypeScript, VSCode is a free, open-source code editor that offers excellent TypeScript support out of the box. The built-in features of the code like IntelliSense, autocompletion, and debugging tools make it a popular choice among TypeScript developers.

WebStorm: WebStorm is a powerful, commercial IDE developed by JetBrains, known for its extensive TypeScript support. It includes built-in tools for refactoring, code navigation, and error checking. WebStorm also offers seamless integration with many popular web development tools and frameworks, making it a solid option for TypeScript development.

Sublime Text: Sublime Text is a popular, lightweight text editor that can be easily extended with plugins to support TypeScript. The TypeScript package for Sublime Text provides syntax highlighting, autocompletion, and error checking. While not as feature-rich as VSCode or WebStorm, Sublime Text is an excellent choice for developers who prefer a minimalist editor.

Atom: Atom is a free, open-source text editor developed by GitHub. It can be extended with a variety of packages to support TypeScript development. The atom-typescript package offers syntax highlighting, autocompletion, and error checking, making Atom a viable option for TypeScript developers.

Vim: Vim is a highly customizable, keyboard-driven text editor that has been around for decades. With the right plugins, such as **vim-typescript**, Vim can become a powerful TypeScript development environment. It supports syntax highlighting, autocompletion, and error checking.

Emacs: Emacs is another highly extensible and customizable text editor with a long history. To enable TypeScript support in Emacs, you can use the **typescript-mode** and **tide** packages, which provide syntax highlighting, autocompletion, and error checking capabilities.

There are just some examples, as there are infinite options, and most of them have plugins for TypeScript integration. Ultimately, the choice of code editor depends on your personal preferences and requirements. Each editor has its strengths and weaknesses, so it is essential to choose one that aligns with your development workflow and provides the necessary features for your projects.

Configuring your code editor for TypeScript

Once you have chosen a code editor, you will need to configure it for TypeScript development. In this section, we will provide a brief overview of setting up TypeScript support for some popular code editors.

Visual Studio Code (VSCode)

VSCode provides built-in TypeScript support, so no additional extensions are needed. To configure TypeScript, you can create a **tsconfig.json** file in your project's root directory. This file contains various compiler options and settings that help customize the behaviour of the TypeScript compiler. Here is a basic example of a **tsconfig.json** file:

```
{
  "compilerOptions": {
      "target": "es5",
      "module": "commonjs",
      "strict": true,
      "outDir": "./dist"
  },
  "include": ["./src/**/*.ts"],   "exclude": ["./node_modules"]
}
```

You can also configure VSCode settings specific to TypeScript by opening the **settings.json** file (**File** | **Preferences** | **Settings**) and adding or modifying the desired settings, such as:

```
{
  "typescript.updateImportsOnFileMove.enabled": "always",   "typescript.preferences.quoteStyle": "single"
}
```

WebStorm

WebStorm also includes built-in TypeScript support, so no additional plugins are required. Just like with VSCode, you can create a **tsconfig.json** file in your project's root directory to configure TypeScript compiler options. WebStorm will automatically recognize the **tsconfig.json** file and use the specified settings.

To further configure WebStorm for TypeScript development, navigate to **Preferences** | **Languages** and

Frameworks | TypeScript. Here, you can enable or disable TypeScript support, choose the TypeScript version, and configure various options, such as automatically compiling TypeScript files on save.

Sublime Text

To enable TypeScript support in Sublime Text, you need to install the **TypeScript** package using the **Package Control** package manager. To install Package Control, follow the instructions on the official Package Control website.

Once Package Control is installed, press Ctrl + Shift + P (or Cmd + Shift + P on macOS), type install package in the command palette, and hit Enter. In the package list, search for **TypeScript** and press Enter to install it.

Atom

For TypeScript support in Atom, you need to install the **atom-typescript** package. To do this, go to the **Atom menu | Preferences | Install**, search for **atom-typescript**, and click on the **Install** button.

Vim

To enable TypeScript support in Vim, you can use the **vim-typescript** plugin.

Emacs

For TypeScript support in Emacs, you need to install the **typescript-mode** and **tide** packages using the built-in package manager or any other Emacs package manager. Once installed, add the following to your Emacs configuration file (usually **.emacs** or **init.el**):

```
(require 'typescript-mode)
(require 'tide)

(defun setup-tide-mode ()
  (interactive)
  (tide-setup)
  (flycheck-mode +1) (setq flycheck-check-syntax-automatically '(save mode-enabled))
  (eldoc-mode +1)
  (tide-hl-identifier-mode +1)
  (company-mode +1))

(add-hook 'typescript-mode-hook #'setup-tide-mode)
```

With your chosen code editor configured for TypeScript, you are now ready to start writing and compiling TypeScript code. As we continue through this book, we will focus exclusively on VSCode for TypeScript development. VSCode is a widely popular and versatile code editor that offers extensive TypeScript support out of the box. Additionally, its extensive range of extensions and tight integration with TypeScript provide an exceptional development experience. By concentrating on VSCode, we aim to provide an in-depth and cohesive guide to setting up the TypeScript development environment, which will enable you to take full advantage of the powerful features this editor offers.

However, the principles discussed can still be applied to other editors, the examples and code instructions should work in any environment that has proper TypeScript set up, as explained in the previous sections.

Debugging your TypeScript code

Debugging TypeScript has an extra layer of complexity when compared to debugging regular JavaScript code, as it requires attention to both the TypeScript source code and the compiled JavaScript output. For ease and efficiency, most modern development environments and browsers provide source map support, which allows you to debug TypeScript code directly in your code editor or a web browser.

Debugging in VSCode

VSCode provides a powerful built-in debugger for TypeScript, allowing you to identify and fix issues in your code more efficiently. To set up debugging in VSCode, you will need to create a **launch.json** configuration file that specifies how the debugger should interact with your TypeScript project.

First, open your TypeScript project in VSCode, and then follow the given steps:

Click on the **Debug icon** in the **Activity Bar** on the side of the window.
At the top of the **Debug view**, click the **gear icon** to open the launch configuration dropdown menu.
Select **Node.js** from the dropdown menu. VSCode will automatically create a **launch.json** file with the default Node.js debugger configuration.

Here is a simple example of a **launch.json** configuration for debugging a TypeScript project with the built-in Node.js debugger:

```
{
 "version": "0.2.0",
 "configurations": [
        {
        "type": "node",
        "request": "launch",
        "name": "Launch Program",
        "skipFiles": ["<node_internals>/**"],
        "program": "${workspaceFolder}/src/index.ts",
        "preLaunchTask": "tsc: build - tsconfig.json", "outFiles": ["${workspaceFolder}/out/**/*.js"]
        }
 ]
}
```

This configuration instructs the debugger to launch the program specified in the **program** attribute, using the built-in Node.js debugger. The **preLaunchTask** attribute tells VSCode to run the TypeScript compiler before launching the debugger, ensuring your TypeScript files are compiled to JavaScript.

As an alternative, you can use the JavaScript Debugger (Nightly) extension, which offers some cutting-edge features and improvements over the built-in debugger. To use this extension, set the type attribute to **pwa-node** in your launch.json configuration. However, keep in mind that the nightly version might introduce instability or compatibility issues, so using the built-in Node.js debugger is recommended for most users.

Debugging in other code editors and browsers

In this section, we will briefly explore some alternatives for those who prefer to use a different development environment:

WebStorm: JetBrains' WebStorm is a popular **integrated development environment (IDE)** for JavaScript, TypeScript, and other web technologies. It provides a built-in debugger that works seamlessly with TypeScript projects. To start debugging in WebStorm, you will need to create a Run/Debug configuration for your TypeScript project and then launch the debugger using the Debug button in the top-right corner of the IDE.

Sublime Text: Sublime Text is another widely used text editor that supports TypeScript through the TypeScript plugin. To enable debugging for TypeScript in Sublime Text, you can install the Debugger extension from the Package Control. Once the extension is installed, you can create a debug configuration file (similar to VSCode's **launch.json**) and use the Debugger panel to start, stop, and control your debugging session.

Atom: The Atom text editor, developed by GitHub, supports TypeScript via the atom-typescript package. To debug TypeScript in Atom, you can use the **atom-ide-debugger-node** package, which provides a Node.js debugger for the Atom IDE. After installing the package, you can create a debug configuration file and start debugging using the Debugger panel.

Browser Debuggers: Modern web browsers like Google Chrome, Mozilla Firefox, and Microsoft Edge come with built-in developer tools, including powerful JavaScript debuggers. Although these debuggers are designed for JavaScript, they can be used to debug TypeScript code by leveraging **source maps**. When using the TypeScript compiler or a build tool like Webpack, make sure to generate source maps alongside the compiled JavaScript files. With source maps enabled, the browser's debugger can map the JavaScript code back to the original TypeScript, allowing you to set breakpoints, step through the code, and inspect variables directly in TypeScript.

While debugging support varies between different code editors and browsers, most of them offer the necessary tools to debug TypeScript code efficiently.

Working with the TypeScript compiler

The **TypeScript compiler (tsc)** is a crucial tool in the TypeScript development process, responsible for converting TypeScript code into JavaScript. In this section, we will explore the basics of working with the compiler, including it configuration, compile TypeScript files, and handle common compilation options.

Compiler configuration

The TypeScript compiler is highly configurable, and you can customize its behaviour using a configuration file called **tsconfig.json**. This file, usually placed at the root of your TypeScript project, contains various options that control the compilation process, such as the target JavaScript version, module system, and whether to generate source maps.

To create a **tsconfig.json** file, you can either manually create a new file at the root of your project and populate it with the necessary configuration options or use the **npx tsc --init** command to generate one with default settings. The npx command is a package runner tool included with npm that allows you to run CLI-based packages without having to install them globally. To automatically create a tsconfig.json file use the command: **npx tsc –init**

This command generates a **tsconfig.json** file with default settings in your project directory. The file will contain various compiler options with most of them in blocks of comments, meaning they would not be executed but allow you to easily customize the configuration by uncommenting or modifying the options as needed.

If you prefer to configure it manually, here is an example of a simple **tsconfig.json** file:

```
{
  "compilerOptions": {
      "target": "es5",
      "module": "commonjs",
      "sourceMap": true
  }
}
```

With the **tsconfig.json** file in place, you can now configure the TypeScript compiler to suit your project's needs. You can also configure your code editor to recognize the **tsconfig.json** file and adjust the settings accordingly providing a smooth development experience.

Common options for tsconfig.json

The configuration file has a list of options that change how the compiler works:

target: It determines the ECMAScript version your project will utilize. For instance, if you designate the target as ES2015 and employ class syntax, the code will be compiled into an equivalent ES5 constructor function. Available versions include ES3 (default), ES5, ES2015, ES2016, ES2017, ES2018, ES2019, ES2020, or ESNEXT.

module: It is the Module system that will be applied to the generated JavaScript code. You can select from the following options: none, commonjs (default), amd, system, umd, es2015, es2020, or ESNext. **outDir**: This is the directory where the compiled JavaScript code will be saved. **rootDir**: It is the location where the TypeScript files are stored. **strict**: This activates strict type-checking features (true by default).

esModuleInterop: It governs the compatibility between CommonJS and ES modules by generating namespace objects for all imported modules.

Compiling TypeScript files

To compile a TypeScript file (for example, **example.ts**) into JavaScript, run the following command in your terminal or command prompt: **tsc example.ts**

This command will generate a JavaScript file (for example, example.js) in the same directory as the TypeScript file. If you have a **tsconfig.json** file in your project, you can run tsc without any arguments to compile all TypeScript files according to the configuration: **Tsc**

Common compilation options

The TypeScript compiler offers many options that can be set in the **tsconfig.json** file or passed as command-line arguments. Some common options include:

--outDir: It specifies the output directory for the compiled JavaScript files.
--strict: It enables all strict type-checking options.
--watch: This watches for file changes and recompiles the project when changes are detected.
--esModuleInterop: This enables better compatibility with **CommonJS** and other non-ECMAScript module systems.

In summary, the TypeScript compiler is a powerful tool that transforms TypeScript code into JavaScript, allowing it to run in any JavaScript environment. By understanding how to configure and use the compiler, you can streamline your TypeScript development process and ensure that your code is ready for production.

Compiling TypeScript with popular frameworks

Using TypeScript with popular JavaScript frameworks like **React** or Node.js-based frameworks like **Express** is straightforward, as these frameworks have established patterns and tools for integrating TypeScript.

Usually there is no need for manually creating a **tsconfig.json** file, as these frameworks already have options to automate it. For example, to integrate TypeScript with React, Vue, or Express projects, whether new or existing, follow the given steps:

Integration with React

For a new project, use **Create React App** with the TypeScript template:

npx create-react-app my-app --template typescript

For an existing project, add TypeScript, type definitions for React, and the Babel preset for TypeScript: **npm install --save typescript @types/react @types/react-dom @babel/preset-typescript** Then, update your. babelrc or **babel.config.js** to include the TypeScript preset:

```
{
  "presets": ["@babel/preset-typescript"]
}
```

Integration with Vue

For a new project, use Vue CLI with the TypeScript plugin: **vue create my-app**
During the project creation process, select **TypeScript** from the features list.
For an existing project, add the TypeScript plugin to the Vue CLI: **vue add typescript**
Now that the compiler is set up, we are ready to use types in our code.

Conclusion: Harnessing the Power of TypeScript

As we have explored in this guide, TypeScript serves as a powerful extension to JavaScript, addressing its limitations while building on its strengths. From its foundational concepts to installation and setup, TypeScript is a tool designed for modern developers looking to write clean, maintainable, and robust codebases. Let's revisit its core benefits and broader significance.

The Value of TypeScript: A Recap

Static Typing: A Shield Against Errors

One of TypeScript's standout features is its ability to catch errors during the development process through static typing. This proactive approach to bug prevention saves developers significant time and effort, especially in larger projects. With TypeScript, the compiler acts as your first line of defence, ensuring that mismatched types, undefined variables, or improper function calls are identified before they cause runtime errors.

Example:

```
const calculateTotal = (price: number, quantity: number): number => {
    return price * quantity;
};
```

```
// Compile-time error if a string is passed instead of a number:
calculateTotal("50", 2); // Error: Argument of type 'string' is not assignable to parameter of type 'number'.
```

Enhanced Developer Experience

The integration of TypeScript with modern IDEs like Visual Studio Code elevates the developer experience. Features like autocompletion, intelligent code suggestions, and instant error detection create a smoother workflow, enabling developers to focus on problem-solving rather than debugging trivial issues.

Scalability and Maintainability

TypeScript introduces constructs like interfaces, classes, and generics, which facilitate building scalable applications. As teams grow and codebases expand, TypeScript ensures that code remains understandable and manageable. Explicit types act as a form of self-documentation, making it easier for developers to understand and extend existing code.

Compatibility with JavaScript Ecosystem

TypeScript compiles to plain JavaScript, ensuring compatibility with all environments where JavaScript runs. Whether you're developing for the browser, Node.js, or hybrid frameworks like React Native, TypeScript integrates seamlessly, giving you the best of both worlds.

Challenges and Solutions in Adopting TypeScript

While TypeScript offers numerous benefits, adopting it can come with challenges, especially for teams transitioning from pure JavaScript. Below are some common hurdles and strategies to overcome them:

Learning Curve

Developers accustomed to JavaScript might find the type system and strictness of TypeScript daunting at first. However, TypeScript allows incremental adoption, enabling developers to add type annotations gradually.

Solution: Begin by adding TypeScript to a small project or a module within a larger application. Use any for unknown types initially and refine them as your familiarity with the language grows.

Compilation Overhead

TypeScript requires an additional compilation step to convert TypeScript files into JavaScript. This might slow down the development process for teams unfamiliar with build tools.

Solution: Use tools like tsc --watch to compile files automatically as you save changes. For larger projects, integrate TypeScript into your build pipeline with tools like Webpack or Vite for optimized workflows.

Initial Setup

Setting up a TypeScript project may seem complex compared to starting a JavaScript project. However, tools like tsc --init and pre-configured templates simplify this process.

Solution: Use boilerplates or starter projects available in TypeScript's vibrant community to jumpstart your development process.

The Role of TypeScript in Modern Web Development

TypeScript is not just a tool but a movement toward better programming practices. In a world where applications are becoming increasingly complex, TypeScript equips developers to manage this complexity effectively. Its impact is evident in its adoption by major frameworks like Angular, which relies on TypeScript as its core language, and its growing popularity in libraries like React and Vue.

Case Studies in TypeScript Adoption:

Angular

Angular's reliance on TypeScript showcases its ability to build enterprise-grade, scalable applications. TypeScript's typing system complements Angular's dependency injection and modular architecture.

React

Although React is JavaScript-first, TypeScript's compatibility has made it a popular choice among React developers. Features like type-checking props and state management with tools like Redux are more robust when implemented in TypeScript.

Node.js

In server-side development, TypeScript enhances the reliability of APIs by enabling strict type definitions for request and response objects.

The Future of TypeScript

TypeScript's rise in popularity over the last decade shows no signs of slowing down. As JavaScript continues to evolve, TypeScript stays at the forefront by adopting and supporting new features even before they are widely available in JavaScript engines. For example, TypeScript has pioneered features like optional chaining and nullish coalescing before their inclusion in the ECMAScript standard.

Integration with Cutting-Edge Frameworks:

TypeScript is increasingly being used with emerging frameworks like SvelteKit, Next.js, and NestJS. Its role in facilitating seamless development in these ecosystems underlines its relevance.

Wider Community Adoption:

Open-source projects are increasingly adopting TypeScript, providing developers with type definitions (*.d.ts files) that enhance usability.

AI and Developer Tools:

As artificial intelligence tools like GitHub Copilot gain traction, TypeScript's type definitions and strong typing system make it easier for AI to suggest accurate and relevant code snippets.

Exploring Advanced TypeScript Features

For developers who have mastered the basics, TypeScript offers advanced features that elevate their programming capabilities:

Generics:

Generics allow functions and classes to operate on various types without sacrificing type safety.

```
function identity<T>(arg: T): T {
    return arg;
}

let output = identity<number>(42); // Works with any type
```

Type Guards:

Type guards enable developers to create more sophisticated type-checking logic.

```
function isString(value: any): value is string {
    return typeof value === "string";
}
```

Decorators:

Widely used in frameworks like Angular, decorators allow for meta-programming.

```
@Component({
    selector: 'app-root',
    templateUrl: './app.component.html',
})
export class AppComponent {}
```

Key Takeaways for Developers

Beginner-Friendly: TypeScript offers gradual adoption, making it accessible to developers new to static typing or coming from JavaScript.

Team Collaboration: TypeScript's type annotations act as documentation, improving communication among team members.

Industry Adoption: With its growing popularity, learning TypeScript is an investment in your career as a developer.

Call to Action: Getting Started with TypeScript

If you're considering adopting TypeScript, now is the time. Start by installing it in your current project or creating a new one. Leverage the tools and community resources available, including:

The official TypeScript documentation.

Tutorials and courses on platforms like Codecademy, Udemy, or freeCodeCamp.

Open-source projects that demonstrate TypeScript's capabilities in real-world applications.

Conclusion

TypeScript is more than just a tool for developers; it's a paradigm shift in how modern applications are built. By addressing JavaScript's shortcomings while embracing its strengths, TypeScript empowers developers to write code that is not only functional but also elegant, efficient, and robust.

Its adoption across frameworks, tools, and platforms signifies a larger trend toward sustainable and scalable coding practices. Whether you're working on a small project or an enterprise-grade application, TypeScript ensures that your code is future-proof.

So, take the first step, install TypeScript, and experience the transformation in your development workflow. TypeScript isn't just a language; it's your companion in building the future of web development.

2. Fundamentals and Declaration Files

Introduction

TypeScript is a superset of JavaScript that adds static typing, enabling developers to write more reliable and maintainable code. By enhancing JavaScript with type annotations, TypeScript helps catch errors early in the development process and facilitates better tooling support, such as autocompletion and refactoring. In this detailed introduction, we'll explore TypeScript fundamentals and delve into declaration files, focusing on their role in creating robust, scalable applications.

TypeScript Fundamentals

What is TypeScript?

TypeScript is developed by Microsoft and builds upon JavaScript by introducing:

Static typing: Allows developers to specify types for variables, parameters, and return values.
ESNext features: Supports modern JavaScript syntax and compiles down to older versions for compatibility.
Tooling: Provides better development experiences with IntelliSense, auto-completions, and error-checking.
TypeScript is particularly beneficial in large projects where code consistency and reliability are paramount.

Core TypeScript Features

1. Type Annotations

Type annotations enable you to define the expected type of variables, parameters, or return values:

```
let age: number = 25; // Explicit type annotation
let name: string = "Alice";
let isActive: boolean = true;
```
Using type annotations helps catch type-related errors during compilation.

2. Interfaces

Interfaces define the shape of an object, ensuring consistency across implementations:

```
interface User {
  id: number;
  name: string;
  isAdmin: boolean;
}

const user: User = {
  id: 1,
  name: "Alice",
  isAdmin: true,
};
```

3. Classes and Inheritance

TypeScript extends JavaScript's class syntax with additional features such as access modifiers (public, private, protected) and strict typing:

```
class Person {
  constructor(public name: string, private age: number) {}

  getAge(): number {
    return this.age;
  }
}

const person = new Person("Alice", 30);
console.log(person.name); // Accessible
console.log(person.getAge()); // Accessible
```

4. Enums

Enums define a set of named constants:

```
enum Status {
  Active,
  Inactive,
  Suspended,
}

let currentStatus: Status = Status.Active;
```

5. Generics

Generics enable the creation of reusable and type-safe components:

```
function identity<T>(value: T): T {
  return value;
}
const num = identity<number>(42);
const str = identity<string>("Hello");
```

6. Union and Intersection Types

Union types allow variables to hold multiple types:

```
let value: string | number;
value = "Hello";
value = 42;
```

Intersection types combine multiple types into one:

```
interface A { x: number; }
interface B { y: string; }
type AB = A & B;
```

```
const obj: AB = { x: 1, y: "hello" };
```

7. Type Aliases

Type aliases assign names to types for reuse and clarity:

```
type Point = {
  x: number;
  y: number;
};

const point: Point = { x: 10, y: 20 };
```

TypeScript Compilation

TypeScript compiles into plain JavaScript using the TypeScript compiler (tsc). Developers can configure the behavior of the compiler using the tsconfig.json file:

```
{
  "compilerOptions": {
    "target": "ES5",
    "module": "CommonJS",
    "strict": true,
    "outDir": "./dist"
  }
}
```

Key options include:

target: Specifies the ECMAScript version.
module: Defines the module system (e.g., CommonJS, ESNext).
strict: Enables strict type checking.
outDir: Specifies the output directory.

Declaration Files

What Are Declaration Files?

Declaration files (.d.ts) are used to define the shape of existing JavaScript libraries or codebases, enabling TypeScript to understand their types. These files contain type declarations but no implementations, providing type safety without altering the original JavaScript code.

Example Declaration File

```
declare module "example-lib" {
  export function greet(name: string): string;
}
```

Why Use Declaration Files?

Interoperability: Integrate JavaScript libraries into TypeScript projects.
Tooling Support: Enable autocompletion, error-checking, and IntelliSense.
Documentation: Serve as a source of documentation for third-party libraries.

Creating Declaration Files

1. Manual Creation

When a library lacks built-in TypeScript support, you can manually create a declaration file:

```
// greet.d.ts
declare module "greet" {
  export function sayHello(name: string): string;
}
```

2. Using declare Keyword

The declare keyword introduces ambient declarations:

```
declare let globalVar: string;
declare function logMessage(message: string): void;
declare class Animal {
  name: string;
  constructor(name: string);
}
```

3. Type Declaration for Variables

```
declare const VERSION: string;
declare var isDebugMode: boolean;
```

Using Third-Party Declaration Files

1. @types Package

Many libraries provide type definitions through the @types scope on npm:

```
npm install --save-dev @types/lodash
```

Example usage:

```
import _ from "lodash";
const array = [1, 2, 3];
console.log( .shuffle(array));
```

2. Custom Definitions

For libraries without existing types, create a custom .d.ts file and include it in your project:

```
declare module "custom-lib" {
  export function customFunction(): void;
}
```

Best Practices for Declaration Files

Follow Naming Conventions: Use .d.ts extensions.
Avoid Implementation: Focus solely on type definitions.
Test Thoroughly: Use the declaration file in a TypeScript project to ensure accuracy.

Advanced Features of Declaration Files

1. Namespaces

Namespaces group related declarations:

```
declare namespace MyLibrary {
  function greet(name: string): string;
}
```

2. Global Declarations

Declare types available globally across the application:

```
declare global {
  interface Window {
    customProperty: string;
  }
}
```

3. Module Augmentation

Extend existing module types:

```
declare module "lodash" {
  interface LoDashStatic {
    customMethod(): void;
  }
}
```

4. Conditional Types

TypeScript supports conditional and mapped types in declaration files:

```
type IsString<T> = T extends string ? true : false;
type Test = IsString<"Hello">; // true
```

The world of online applications has grown tremendously in the past few decades.

With it, web-based applications have grown not only in size but also in complexity. JavaScript, a language that was originally thought of and used as a go-between between the core application logic and the user interface, is being seen in a different light. It is the de facto language with which web apps are being developed. However, it just was not designed for the building of large applications with lots of moving parts.

Along came TypeScript

TypeScript is a superset of JavaScript that provides lots of enterprise-level features that JavaScript lacks, such as modules, types, interfaces, generics, managed asynchrony, and so on. They make our code easier to write, debug, and manage. In this chapter, you will first learn how the TypeScript compiler works, how transpilation occurs, and how you can set up the compiler options to suit your needs. Then, you will dive straight into TypeScript types, functions, and objects. You will also learn how you can make your own types in TypeScript. Finally, you can test your skills by attempting to create your own library to work with strings. This chapter serves as a launchpad with which you can jump-start your TypeScript journey.

The Evolution of TypeScript

TypeScript was designed by Microsoft as a special-purpose language with a single goal – to enable people to write better JavaScript. But why was that an issue at all? To understand the problem, we have to go back to the roots of the scripting languages for the web.
In the beginning, JavaScript was designed to enable only a basic level of interactivity on the web.

It was specifically not designed to be the main language that runs within a web page, but to be a kind of glue between the browser and the plugins, such as Java applets that run on the site. The heavy lifting was supposed to be done by the plugin code, with JavaScript providing a simple layer of interoperability. JavaScript did not even have any methods that would enable it to access the server. Another design goal for JavaScript was that it had to be easy to use for non-professional developers. That meant that the language had to be extremely forgiving of errors, and quite lax with its syntax.

For a few years, that was the task that JavaScript (or, more properly, ECMAScript, as it was standardized) was actually doing. But more and more web pages came into existence, and more and more of them needed dynamic content. Suddenly, people needed to use a lot of JavaScript. Web pages started getting more and more complex, and they were now being referred to as web applications. JavaScript got the ability (via AJAX) to access servers and even other sites, and a whole ecosystem of libraries appeared that helped us write better web applications.

However, the language itself was still lacking lots of features that are present in most languages – primarily features that are targeted toward professional developers.

Since it was designed for small-scale usage, it was very troublesome to build, and especially to maintain, large applications built with JavaScript. On the other hand, once it was standardized, JavaScript became the only way to actually run code inside the browser. So, one solution that was popular in the 2000s was to make an emulation layer – a kind of a tool that enabled developers to use their favourite language to develop an application that will take the original source code as input and output equivalent JavaScript code. Such tools became known as transpilers – a portmanteau of the word's "translator" and "compiler." While traditional compilers take source code as input and output machine code that can execute directly on the target machine, transpilers basically translated the source code from one language to another, specifically to JavaScript. The resulting code is then executed on the browser.

There were two significant groups of transpilers present – ones that transpiled from an existing language (C#, Java, Ruby, and so on) and ones that transpiled from a language specifically designed to make web development easier (CoffeeScript, Dart, Elm, and so on).

The major problem with most transpilers was that they were not native to the web and JavaScript. The JavaScript that was generated was confusing and non-idiomatic – it looked like it was written by a machine and not a human. That would have been fine, except that generated mess was the code that was actually executing. So, using a transpiler meant that we had to forgo the debugging experience, as we could not understand what was actually being run. Additionally, the file size of the generated code was usually large, and more often than not, it included a huge base library that needed to load before we would be able to run our transpiled code.

Basically, by 2012 there were two options in sight – write a large web application using plain JavaScript, with all the drawbacks that it had, or write large web applications using a transpiler, writing better and more maintainable code, but being removed from the platform where our code actually runs.
Then, TypeScript was introduced.

Design Goals of TypeScript

The core idea behind it was one that, in hindsight, seems quite obvious. Instead of replacing JavaScript with another language, why not just add the things that are missing? And why not add them in such a way that they can be very reasonably removed at the transpiling step, so that the generated code will not only look and be idiomatic but also be quite small and performant? What if we can add things such as static typing, but in an optional way, so that it can be used as much or as little as we want? What if all of that existed while we're developing and we can have nice tooling and use a nice environment, yet we're still able to debug and understand the generated code?

The design goals of TypeScript, as initially stated, were as follows:

Extend JavaScript to facilitate writing large applications.
Create a strict superset of JavaScript (that is, any valid JavaScript is valid TypeScript).
Enhance the development tooling support.
Generate JavaScript that runs on any JavaScript execution environment.
Easy transfer between TypeScript and JavaScript code.
Generate clean, idiomatic JavaScript.
Align with future JavaScript standards.

Sounds like a pie-in-the-sky promise, and the initial response was a bit lukewarm. But, as time progressed, and as people actually tried it and started using it in real applications, the benefits became obvious.

Two areas where TypeScript became a power player were JavaScript libraries and server-side JavaScript, where the added strictness of type checking and formal modules enabled higher-quality code. Currently, all of the most popular web development frameworks are either natively written in TypeScript (such as Angular, Vue, and Deno) or have tight integrations with TypeScript (such as React and Node).

Getting Started with TypeScript

Consider the following TypeScript program – a simple function that adds two numbers:

Example 01.ts

```
function add (x, y) {
return x + y;
}
```

Link to the example on GitHub:

No, that's not a joke – that's real-life TypeScript. We just did not use any TypeScript specific features. We can save this file as **add.ts** and can compile it to JavaScript using the following command:

```
tsc add.ts
```

This will generate our output file, **add.js**. If we open it and look inside, we can see that the generated JavaScript is as follows:

Example 01.js

```
function add(x, y) {
return x + y;
}
```

Link to the example on GitHub:

Yes, aside from some spacing, the code is identical, and we have our first successful transpilation.

The TypeScript Compiler

We will add to the example, of course, but let's take a moment to analyze what happened. First of all, we gave our file the **.ts** file extension. All TypeScript files have this extension, and they contain the TypeScript source code of our application. But, even if our code is valid JavaScript (as in this case), we cannot just load the **.ts** files inside a browser and run them. We need to compile/transpile them using the tool called the "TypeScript compiler," or **tsc** for short. What this tool does is takes TypeScript files as arguments and generates JavaScript files as outputs. In our case, our input was **add.ts** and our output was **add.js**. The **tsc** compiler is an extremely powerful tool, and it has a lot of options that we're able to set. We can get a full list of the options using this command:

tsc –all

The most common and important ones are as follows:

–outFile: With this option, we can specify the name of the output file we want to be generated. If it's not specified, it defaults to the same name as the input file, but with the **.js** extension.

–outDir: With this option, we can specify the location of the output file(s). By default, the generated files will be in the same location as the source files.

–types: With this option, we can specify additional types that will be allowed in our source code.

–lib: With this option, we specify which library files need to be loaded. As there are different execution environments for JavaScript, with different default libraries (for example, browser JavaScript has a **window** object, and Node.js has a **process** object), we can specify which one we want to target. We can also use this option to allow or disallow specific JavaScript functionality. For example, the **array.include** method was added in the **es2016** JavaScript version. If we want to assume that the method will be available, then we need to add the **es2016.array.include** library.

–target: With this option, we specify which version of the ECMAScript (that is, JavaScript) language we're targeting. That is, if we need to support older browsers, we can use the **ES3** or **ES5** values, which will compile our code to JavaScript code that will execute in any environment that supports, correspondingly, versions 3 and 5 of the JavaScript language. If, on the other hand, we know that we'll run in an ultra-modern environment, as the latest Node.js runtime, we can use the **ES2020** target, or even **ESNEXT**, which is always the next available version of the ECMAScript language.

There are several more options; however, we have only discussed a few here.

Setting Up a TypeScript Project

Since the TypeScript compiler has lots of options, and we'll need to use quite a few of them, specifying all of them each and every time we transpile a file will get tedious very fast. In order to avoid that, we can save our default options in a special file that will be accessed by the **tsc** command. The best way to generate this special file called **tsconfig.json** is to use **tsc** itself with the **--init** option. So, navigate to the folder where you want to store your TypeScript project and execute the following command:

tsc –init

This will generate a **tsconfig.json** file with the most commonly used option. The rest of the options are commented out, so if we want to use some other set of options, we can simply uncomment what we need. If we ignore the comments (which include a link to the documentation about the options), we get the following content:

```
{
  "compilerOptions": {
    "target": "es5",
    "module": "commonjs",
    "strict": true,
    "esModuleInterop": true,
    "skipLibCheck": true,
    "forceConsistentCasingInFileNames": true
  }
}
```

You can see that each and every option in the **tsconfig.json** file has a corresponding command-line switch, for example, **module**, **target**, and so on. If a command-line switch is specified, it takes precedence. However, if a command-line switch is not defined, then **tsc** looks for the nearest **tsconfig.json** file up the directory hierarchy and takes the value specified there.

Exercise: Using tsconfig.json and Getting Started with TypeScript

In this exercise, we'll see how to command TypeScript using the **tsconfig.json** file. We'll see how to create TypeScript files and transpile them to JavaScript, based on the options we specify:

Create a new folder and execute the following command in a new terminal within it:
tsc –init

Verify that a new **tsconfig.json** file is created within the folder and that its target value is **es5**.
Create a new file called **squares.ts** inside it.

In **squares.ts**, create a function called **squares**:
function squares(array: number[]) {

Create a new array from the input argument, using the JavaScript **map** function with an arrow function argument:

const result = array.map(x => x * x);

Return the new array from the function:

```
    return result;
}
```

Save the file and run the following command in the folder:

tsc squares.ts

Verify that there is a new file in the folder called **squares.js** with the following content:

```
function squares(array) {
var result = array.map(function (x) { return x * x; });
return result;
}
```

Here, we can see that the transpilation step did several things:

It removed the type annotation from the **array: number[]** parameter, transpiling it to **array**.
It changed the **const result** variable declaration to a **var result** declaration.
It changed the arrow function, **x=>x*x**, to a regular function, **function (x) { return x * x; }**.

While the first is TypeScript-specific code, the second and third are examples of TypeScript's backward compatibility – both the arrow functions and the **const** declarations are JavaScript features that were introduced in the ES6 version of the language.

Run the following command in the folder:

tsc --target es6 squares.ts

This will override the setting from the **tsconfig.json** file and it will transpile the TypeScript code to **ES6-compatible** JavaScript.

Verify that the contents of the **squares.js** file are now as follows:

```
function squares(array) {
const result = array.map(x => x * x);
return result;
}
```

You can note that, in contrast to the results in step 8, now the **const** keyword and the arrow functions are intact, because the target we specified supports them natively. This is an extremely important feature of TypeScript. With this feature, even if we don't use the rich type system that TypeScript provides, we can still write code in the most modern version of JavaScript available, and TypeScript will seamlessly transpile our code to a version that can actually be consumed by our customers.

Types and Their Uses

We've mentioned that TypeScript's type system is its distinguishing feature, so let's take a better look at it. JavaScript is what's called a loosely typed language. That means that it does not enforce any rules on the defined variables and their values. Consider, for example, that we define a variable called **count** and set it to the value of **3**:

let count = 3;

There is nothing that prevents us from setting that variable to a value that is a string, a date, an array, or basically any object. All of the following assignments are valid:

```
count = "string";
count = new Date();
count = false;
count = [1, 2, 3];
count = { key: "value" };
```

In almost all scenarios, this is not a behaviour we actually want. Moreover, since JavaScript does not know when we are writing the code whether a variable contains a string or a number, it cannot stop us from trying to, for example, convert it to lowercase. We cannot know whether that operation will succeed or fail until the moment we actually try it, when running the code.

Let's take the following example:

```
let variable;
if (Math.random()>0.5)
{variable = 3;}
else { variable = "String"; }
console.log(variable.toLowerCase());
```

This code will either output **"String"** or throw a **variable.toLowerCase is not a function** error. The only way to determine whether this code will break is to actually run it. In a nutshell, in a loosely typed language, while values themselves have types, variables, on the other hand, don't. They just take the type of the value they are currently holding. So, any checks whether a method is possible on a variable, such as **variable.toLowerCase()**, can only be done when we have the actual value, that is, when we run the code.

Once more, this is quite fine for small-sized applications, but it can become tedious for large-scale applications. In contrast, strongly typed languages enforce the type rules for both the values and the variables they live in. This means that the language itself can detect the error as you are typing the code, as it has more information about what is going on in your code.

So, in a large software product, (in most cases) we don't want variables that have values of different types. So, we want to be able to somehow say "this variable has to be a number, and if someone tries to put something that is not a number inside it, issue an error."

This is where TypeScript, as a strongly typed language, comes in. We have two ways that we can use to bind a variable to a type. The simpler one is to simply annotate the variable with the type we want it to be, like this:

```
let variable: number;
```

The: **number** part of the code is called a type annotation, and we're doing just that – saying "this variable has to be a number, and if someone tries to put something that is not a number inside it, issue an error."
Now, if we try to assign a number to that variable, everything is fine. But the minute we try to assign a string to the variable, we'll get an error message:

```
let variable: number;
```

```
Type 'string' is not assignable to type 'number'. ts(2322)
let variable: number
View Problem (Alt+F8)    No quick fixes available
variable = "string"
```

Figure: Error message from assigning an incorrect type

This type of annotation is explicit and specific to TypeScript. Another way is simply to assign a value to a variable and let TypeScript work its magic. The magic is called type inference, and that means that TypeScript will try to guess the type of the variable based on the value provided.

Let's define a variable and initialize it with a value, like this:

let variable = 3;

Now, if we try to assign a string to that variable, TypeScript will issue an error:

```
let variable = 3;
```

```
Type 'string' is not assignable to type 'number'. ts(2322)
let variable: number
View Problem (Alt+F8)    No quick fixes available
variable = "string"
```

Figure: Error message from assigning an incorrect type

From the error message, we can see the type that TypeScript correctly inferred for the variable – **number**. Actually, in most cases, we won't even need to add type annotations, as TypeScript's powerful type inference engine will correctly infer the type of the variable.

TypeScript and Functions

Another huge benefit of TypeScript is automatic function invocation checking. Let's say that we have the function we used for our first TypeScript file:

function add (x, y) { return x + y; }

Even without any type annotations, TypeScript still has some information about this function – namely, that it takes two, and exactly two, parameters.

In contrast, JavaScript does not enforce that the number of actual arguments has to conform to the number of parameters defined, so all of the following invocations are valid calls in JavaScript:

add(1, 2); // two arguments add(1, 2, 3); // three arguments add(1); // one argument add(); // no arguments
In JavaScript, we can call a function with more arguments than parameters, fewer arguments, or even without any arguments at all. If we have more arguments than needed, the extra arguments are simply

ignored (and stored in the magical **arguments** variable), and if we have fewer arguments than needed, the extra parameters are given the value **undefined**. So, in essence, the preceding calls will be correspondingly transformed into the following:

add(1, 2); // no changes, as the number of arguments match the number of parameters. add(1, 2); // the third argument is ignored add(1, undefined); // the second parameter is given a value of undefined add(undefined, undefined); // both parameters are given a value of undefined

In the third and fourth cases, the return value of the function will be the special numeric value **NaN**.

TypeScript has a radically different approach to this issue. A function can only be called using valid arguments – both in number and in type. So, if we write the same code, but this time in a TypeScript file, we'll get appropriate error messages. For a case where we have extra arguments, we'll get an error message on the extra arguments:

```
function add (x, y) {
    return x + y;
}
```

> Expected 2 arguments, but got 3. ts(2554)

```
add(1, 2); View Problem (Alt+F8)    No quick fixes available
add(1, 2, 3); // three arguments
add(1); // one argument
add(); // no arguments
```

Figure: Error message from using an incorrect number of arguments – too many in this case

For cases with too few arguments, we get the error message on the method itself:

```
function add (x, y) {
    return x + y;
}
```

> Expected 2 arguments, but got 1. ts(2554)
>
> images.ts(1, 18): An argument for 'y' was not provided.
>
> View Problem (Alt+F8)   No quick fixes available

```
add(1); // one argument
add(); // no arguments
```

Figure: Error message from using an incorrect number of arguments – too few in this case

In this case, we're notified that a required parameter is missing, as well as what the name and the type of that parameter should be. Note that it's a common JavaScript technique to have methods that accept a variable number of parameters, accept optional parameters, or provide some defaults if a parameter is not specified. All those cases (and many more) are correctly handled by TypeScript.

Of course, parameter checking works not only on the number but also on the type of the parameters as well. We would want the **add** function to work only with numbers – it does not make sense to add a Boolean and an object, for example. In TypeScript, we can annotate our function like this:

```
function add (x: number, y: number) {
return x + y;
}
```

This will cause the compiler not only to check that the number of arguments matches the number of parameters but also to verify that the types used for the arguments are actually valid. Since JavaScript can't check for that, adding a Boolean and an object is actually a valid call to the JavaScript equivalent of our **add** method. Furthermore, since JavaScript tries to be as forgiving as possible, we won't even get a runtime error the call will be successful, as JavaScript will coerce both the object and Boolean to a common string representation, and then try (and succeed) to add those two values together.

Let's interpret the following call to our function as both JavaScript and TypeScript:

```
const first = {property: 'value'};
const second = false;
const result = add(first, second);
```

This is valid, albeit nonsensical, JavaScript code. If run, it will yield the result **[object Object]false**, which would not be useful in any context.

The same code, interpreted as TypeScript, will yield the following compile type error:

```
function add (x: number, y: number) {
    return x + y;
}
```

Argument of type '{ property: string; }' is not assignable to parameter of type 'number'. ts(2345)

const first: {
    property: string;
}

```
const first = { pro
const second = fals
```

View Problem (Alt+F8)   No quick fixes available

```
const result = add(first, second);
```

Figure: Error message on VS Code

We can also annotate the return type of the function, adding a type annotation after the parameter list:

```
function add (x: number, y: number):
number
{
return x + y;
}
```

That is usually not necessary, as TypeScript can actually infer the return type from the return statements given. In our case, since **x** and **y** are numbers, **x+y** will be a number as well, which means that our function will return a number. However, if we do annotate the return type, TypeScript will enforce that contract as well:

```
function add (x: number, y: number): number  {

    Type 'string' is not assignable to type 'number'. ts(2322)

    View Problem (Alt+F8)   No quick fixes available
    return "not a number";

}
```

Figure: TypeScript enforcing the correct type

In either case, whether we explicitly annotate the return type or it's inferred, the type of the function will be applied to any values that are produced by calling the function. So, if we assign the return value to some variable, that variable will have the type of **number** as well:

```
function add (x: number, y: number): number  {

    return x + y;


}
                const result: number

const result = add(10,15)
```

Figure: VS Code showing the type of the variable

Also, if we try to assign the return value to a variable that is already known to be something else other than a number, we'll get an appropriate error:

```
function add (x: number, y: number): number  {
    return x + y;


}
        Type 'number' is not assignable to type 'string'. ts(2322)

        const result: string

        View Problem (Alt+F8)   No quick fixes available
const result: string  = add(10,15)
```

Figure: Error message on VS Code

Let's make another great point about TypeScript and its type system. As can be seen, the screenshots in this chapter don't show actual compiler error messages – they are taken from inside a code editor (VS Code, an editor that is itself written in TypeScript).

We did not even have to actually compile the code. Instead, we got the error messages while we typed the code – an experience that is familiar to developers in other strongly typed languages, such as C# or Java.

This happens because of the design of the TypeScript compiler, specifically its Language Service API. This enables the editor to easily use the compiler to check the code as it's written so that we can get a nice and intuitive GUI. Additionally, since all the editors will use the same compiler, the development experience will be similar across different editors. This is a dramatic change from the situation that we started with – fully writing, loading, and actually executing the JavaScript code in order to know whether it even makes sense.

In a nutshell, using TypeScript changes one of the most prevalent pain points for JavaScript development – inconsistent and sometimes even impossible tooling support – into a much easier and more convenient experience. In our case, we need only to open a parenthesis when calling the **add** function, and we'll see the following:

```
add(x: number, y: number): number
add()
```

Figure: List of parameters that the function can take

We are shown a list of parameters that shows that the function – which can be defined in another file, by another developer – takes two numbers and also returns a number.

Exercise: Working with Functions in TypeScript

In this exercise, we'll define a simple function and see how we can and can't invoke it. The function we will be developing will be a string utility function that shortens a string to a snippet. We'll basically cut off the text after a given length, but take care that we don't chop a word in half. If the string is larger than the maximum length, we'll add an ellipsis (**…**) to the end:

Create a new file called **snippet.ts**.
In **snippet.ts**, define a simple function called **snippet**:

```
function snippet (text: string, length: number): string {
```

Check whether the text is smaller than the specified length, and if it is, return it unchanged:

```
if (text.length < length) { return text;
}
```

If the text is larger than the maximum length, we'll need to add an ellipsis. The maximum number of characters that we'll be able to show is the specified length minus the length of our ellipsis (as it takes up space too). We'll use the **slice** string method to extract that many characters from the text:

```
const ellipsis = "...";
let result = text.slice(0, length - ellipsis.length);
```

We'll find the last word boundary before the cutoff, using **lastIndexOf**, and then combine the text up to that point with the ellipsis:

```
const lastSpace = result.lastIndexOf(" ");
result = `${result.slice(0, lastSpace)}${ellipsis}`;
```

Return the result from the function:

```
    return result;
}
```

After the function, create a few calls to the function with different parameter types:

```
// correct call and usage
const resultOne = snippet("TypeScript is a programming language that is a strict syntactical superset of JavaScript and adds optional static typing to the language.", 40);

console.log(resultOne); // missing second parameter
const resultTwo = snippet("Lorem ipsum dolor sit amet");
console.log(resultTwo);

// The first parameter is of incorrect type
const resultThree = snippet(false, 40); console.log(resultThree); // The second parameter is of incorrect
type const resultFour = snippet("Lorem ipsum dolor sit amet", false);
console.log(resultFour); // The result is assigned to a variable of incorrect type
var resultFive: number = snippet("Lorem ipsum dolor sit amet", 20);
console.log(resultFive);
```

Save the file and run the following command in the folder:

tsc snippet.ts

Verify that the file did not compile correctly. You will get specifics from the compiler about the errors found, and the compilation will end with the following message:

Found 3 errors.

Comment out or delete all invocations except the first one:

```
// correct call and usage

var resultOne = snippet ("TypeScript is a programming language that is a strict syntactical superset of JavaScript and adds optional static typing to the language.", 40);
console.log(resultOne);
```

Save the file and compile it again:

tsc snippet.ts

Verify that the compilation ended successfully and that there is a **snippet.js** file generated in the same folder. Execute it in the **node** environment with the following command:

node snippet.js

You will see an output that looks as follows:

TypeScript is a programming language...

In this exercise, we developed a simple string utility function, using TypeScript. We saw the two main strengths of TypeScript. For one, we can see that the code is idiomatic JavaScript – we could leverage our existing JavaScript knowledge to write the function. Steps 3 through 6, the actual body of the function, are exactly the same in JavaScript and TypeScript.

Next, we saw that TypeScript takes care that we invoke the function correctly. In step 7, we tried five different invocations of the function. The last four invocations are incorrect ones – they would have been errors either in JavaScript or TypeScript. The important difference is that with TypeScript, we immediately got feedback that the usage is invalid. With JavaScript, the errors would have only been visible when we, or a client, actually executed the code.

TypeScript and Objects

One great thing about JavaScript is its object literal syntax. While in some languages, to create an object we have to do a lot of groundwork, such as creating classes and defining constructors, in JavaScript, and by extension in TypeScript, we can just create the object as a literal. So, if we want to create a **person** object, with **firstName** and **lastName** properties, we only need to write the following:

```
const person = {firstName: "Ada", lastName: "Lovelace"}
```

JavaScript makes it easy to create and use the object, just like any other value. We can access its properties, pass it as an argument into **methods**, receive it as a **return** value from functions, and so on. And because of JavaScript's dynamic nature, it's very easy to add properties to our object. If we wanted to add an **age** property to our object, we could just write the following:

```
person.age = 36;
```

However, because of the loose typing, JavaScript has no knowledge of our object. It does not know what the possible properties of our object are, and what methods can and cannot use it as an argument or a return value. So, say we make a typo, for example, writing out something like this:

```
console.log("Hi, " + person.fristName);
```

JavaScript will happily execute this code and write out **Hi undefined**. That is not what we intended, and will only be visible and detectible when the code is actually run in the browser. Using TypeScript, we have a few options to remedy that. So, let's rewrite our **person** object using TypeScript:

```
const person = {    firstName: "Ada",    lastName: "Lovelace" }
console.log(`Hi, ${person.fristName}`);
```

This code will immediately be marked as invalid by the compiler, even when we haven't added any type information:

```
const person = {
    firstName: "Ada",
    lastName: "Lovelace"
}



console.log(`Hi, ${person.fristName}`);
```

Property 'fristName' does not exist on type '{ firstName: string; lastName: string; }'. Did you mean 'firstName'? ts(2551)

images.ts(2, 5): 'firstName' is declared here.

any

View Problem (Alt+F8)   Quick Fix... (Ctrl+.)

Figure: TypeScript compiler inferring the type of the object

From the error message, we can see what the TypeScript compiler inferred for the type of our object – it thinks that its type consists of two properties, **firstName** of type **string** and **lastName** of type **string**. And according to that definition, there is no place for another property called **fristName**, so we are issued an error.

So, once more, we have detected a bug in our code just by using TypeScript, with no additional code written. TypeScript does this by analyzing the definition of the object and extracts the data from there. It will allow us to write code such as the following:

person.lastName = "Byron";

But it will not allow us to write code where we set **lastName** to a number:

```
const person = {
    firstName: "Ada",



person.lastName = 7
```

Type 'number' is not assignable to type 'string'. ts(2322)

(property) lastName: string

View Problem (Alt+F8)   No quick fixes available

Figure: Error message by assigning an incorrect type to lastName

Sometimes, we know more about the shape of our objects than TypeScript does. For example, TypeScript inferred that our type has only the **firstName** and **lastName** properties. So, if we set the age in TypeScript, with **person.age = 36;**, we will get an error. In this case, we can explicitly define the type of our object, using a TypeScript interface.

The syntax that we can use looks as follows:

interface Person { firstName: string;   lastName: string;   age? : number; }

With this piece of code, we're defining an abstract – a structure that some object will need to satisfy in order to be allowed to be treated as a **Person** object. Notice the question mark (**?**) next to the **age** variable name. That denotes that that property is in fact optional. An object does not have to have an **age** property in order to be a **Person** object. However, if it does have an **age** property, that property has to be a number. The two other properties (**firstName** and **lastName**) are mandatory.

Using this definition, we can define and use our object using the following:

```
const person: Person = { firstName: "Ada", lastName: "Lovelace" }
person.age = 36;
```

We can use interfaces as type annotations for function arguments and return types as well. For example, we can define a function called **showFullName** that will take a person object and display the full name to the console:

```
function showFullName (person: Person) {console.log(`${person.firstName} ${person.lastName}`) }
```

If we invoke this function with **showFullName(person)**, we'll see that it will display **Ada Lovelace** on the console. We can also define a function that will take two strings, and return a new object that fits the **Person** interface:

```
function makePerson (name: string, surname: string): Person { const result = {firstName: name,
lastName: surname     }     return result; }
```

```
const babbage = makePerson("Charles", "Babbage");
showFullName(babbage);
```

One important thing that we need to point out is that, unlike in other languages, the interfaces in TypeScript are structural and not nominal. What that means is that if we have a certain object that fulfills the "rules" of the interface, that object can be considered to be a value of that interface. In our **makePerson** function, we did not specify that the **result** variable is of the **Person** type – we just used an object literal with **firstName** and **lastName** properties, which were strings. Since that is enough to be considered a person, the code compiles and runs just fine. This is a huge boon to the type inference system, as we can have lots of type checks without having to explicitly define them. In fact, it's quite common to omit the return type of functions.

Exercise: Working with Objects

In this exercise, we'll define a simple object that encapsulates a book with a few properties. We'll try to access and modify the object's data and verify that TypeScript constrains us according to inferred or explicit rules. We will also create a function that takes a book object and prints out the book's details:

Create a new file called **book.ts**.

In **book.ts**, define a simple interface called **Book**. We will have properties for the author and the title of the book, optional properties for the number of pages of the book, and a Boolean that denotes whether we have read the book:

```
interface Book {
author: string;
title: string;
pages?: number;
isRead?: boolean;
}
```

Add a function called **showBook** that will display the book's author and title to the console. It should also display whether the book has been read or not, that is, whether the **isRead** property is present:

```
function showBook(book: Book) { console.log(`${book.author} wrote ${book.title}`);
if (book.isRead !== undefined) {
console.log(` I have ${book.isRead ? "read": "not read"} this book`);
}
}
```

Add a function called **setPages** that will take a book and a number of pages as parameters, and set the **pages** property of the book to the provided value:

```
function setPages (book: Book, pages: number) {
book.pages = pages;
}
```

Add a function called **readBook** that will take a book and mark it as having been read:

```
function readBook(book: Book) { book.isRead = true; }
```

Create several objects that fulfill the interface. You can, but don't have to, annotate them with the interface we have created:

```
const warAndPeace = {author: "Leo Tolstoy", title: "War and Peace", isRead: false} const mobyDick:
Book = {author: "Herman Melville", title: "Moby Dick"}
```

Add code that will call methods on the books:

```
setPages(warAndPeace, 1225);
showBook(warAndPeace);
showBook(mobyDick);
readBook(mobyDick);
showBook(mobyDick);
```

Save the file and run the following command in the folder:

tsc book.ts

Verify that the compilation ended successfully and that there is a **book.js** file generated in the same folder. Execute it in the **node** environment with the following command:

node book.js

You will see an output that looks as follows:

Leo Tolstoy wrote War and Peace
I have not read this book
Herman Melville wrote Moby Dick
Herman Melville wrote Moby Dick
I have read this book

In this exercise, we created and used an interface, a purely TypeScript construct. We used it to describe the shape of the objects we will use. Without actually creating any specific objects of that shape, we were able to use the full power of TypeScript's tooling and type inference to create a couple of functions that operate on the objects of the given shape.

After that, we were able to actually create some objects that had the required shape (with and without making the declaration explicit). We were able to use both kinds of objects as parameters to our functions, and the results were in line with the interface we declared.

This demonstrated how a simple addition of an interface made our code much safer to write and execute.

Basic Types

Even though JavaScript is a loosely typed language, that does not mean that values do not have types. There are several primitive types that are available to the JavaScript developer. We can get the type of the value using the **typeof** operator, available both in JavaScript and TypeScript. Let's inspect some values and see what the results will be:

```
const value = 1234;
console.log(typeof value);
```

The execution of the preceding code will write the string **"number"** to the console. Now, consider another snippet:

```
const value = "textual value";
console.log(typeof value);
```

The preceding expression will write the string **"string"** to the console. Consider the following snippet:

```
const value = false;
console.log(typeof value);
```

This will write out **"boolean"** to the console.

All of the preceding types are what are called "primitives." They are baked directly into the execution environment, whether that is a browser or a server-side application. We can always use them as needed. There is an additional primitive type that has only a single value, and that's the undefined type, whose only value is undefined. If we try to call **typeof** undefined, we will receive the string **"undefined"**. Other than the primitives, JavaScript and by extension TypeScript have two so-called "structural" types.

Those are, respectively, objects, that is, custom-created pieces of code that contain data, and functions, that is, custom-created pieces of code that contain logic. This distinction between data and logic is not a clear-cut border, but it can be a useful approximation.

For example, we can define an object with some properties using the object literal syntax:

```
const days = {
    "Monday": 1,
    "Tuesday": 2,
    "Wednesday": 3,
    "Thursday": 4,
```

```
    "Friday": 5,
    "Saturday": 6,
    "Sunday": 7,
}
```

Calling the **typeof** operator on the **days** object will return the string **"object"**. We can also use the **typeof** operator if we have an **add** function as we defined before:

```
function add (x, y) {    return x + y; }
console.log(typeof add);
```

This will display the string **"function"**.

Exercise: Examining typeof

In this exercise, we'll see how to use the **typeof** operator to determine the type of a value, and we will investigate the responses:

Create a new file called **type-test.ts**.

In **type-test.ts**, define several variables with differing values:

```
const daysInWeek = 7;
const name = "Ada Lovelace";
const isRaining = false;
const today = new Date();
const months = ["January", "February", "March"];
const notDefined = undefined;
const nothing = null;
const add = (x:number, y: number) => x + y;
const calculator = { add }
```

Add all the variables into a containing array, using the array literal syntax:

```
const everything = [daysInWeek, name, isRaining, today, months, notDefined, nothing, add, calculator];
```

Loop all the variables using a **for..of** loop, and for each value, call the **typeof** operator. Show the result on the console, along with the value itself:

```
for (const something of everything)
{
const type = typeof something;
console.log(something, type);
}
```

Save the file and run the following command in the folder:

tsc type-test.ts

After the compilation is done, you will have a **type-test.js** file. Execute it in the **node** environment with the following command:

node type-test.js

You will see that the output is as follows:

7 number Ada Lovelace string false boolean 2021-04-05T09:14:56.259Z object ['January', 'February', 'March'] object undefined undefined null object [Function: add] function{ add: [Function: add] } object Note specifically the output from the **months** and **nothing. typeof** variables will return the string **"object"** both for arrays and the **null** value. Also note that the **calculator** variable is an object whose only property is actually a function; that is, we have an object whose piece of data is actually a piece of logic. This is possible because functions are first-class values in JavaScript and TypeScript, which means that we can manipulate them just like we would regular values.

Strings

Words and text are part of any application, just as they are part of everyday life. In JavaScript, they are represented by the **string** type. Unlike in other languages, such as C++ or Java, strings in Java Scripts are not treated as an array-like object that consists of smaller parts (characters). Instead, strings are a first-order citizen of JavaScript. In addition, JavaScript strings natively support Unicode, so we won't get any problems with characters with, for example, Cyrillic or Arabic script. Just like in JavaScript to define a string in TypeScript, we can use single quotes (') or double quotes (").

Of course, if we start the string with a single quote, we have to end it with a single quote, and vice versa. We can also use a special type of string definition, called template strings. These strings are delimited with the backtick character (`) and support two very important things for web development – newlines and embedded expressions. They are supported in all environments that support ES2015, but TypeScript is able to compile to any JavaScript target environment.

Using embedded expressions and newlines inside a string enables us to generate nice HTML, because instead of string concatenation, we're able to use embedded expressions to have a much clearer view of the generated output. For example, if we had a **person** object with **firstName** and **lastName** properties, and we wanted to display a simple greeting inside a **<div>** tag, we would have to write code as follows:

```
const html = "<div class=\"greeting\">\nHello, " + firstName + " " + lastName + "\n</div>";
```

From this code (which can get much more complex), it's difficult to see what will actually be written and where. Using template strings transforms this into the following:

```
const html = "<div class="greeting">
   Hello, ${firstName} ${lastName}
</div>";
```

In order to output the **firstName** and **lastName** values, we have to surround them with brackets ({}), preceded by a dollar sign ($). We are not limited to variable names, but can have whole expressions, including the conditional operator (?:).

Numbers

Numbers are an important aspect of the world. We use them to quantify everything around us. And, it's worth noting, that there are two quite different kinds of numbers that you encounter in your daily life – integers and real numbers. One distinguishing difference between the two kinds of numbers is that integers are numbers without any fractional part. These often result from counting things; for example, the number of people in town. On the other hand, real numbers can have a fractional component to them. For example, the weight or height of a person is often a real number.

In most programming languages, these two types of numbers are represented with (at least) two different primitive types; for example, in C#, we have a type called **int** for integers and a type called **float** for real numbers.

In JavaScript, and consequently in TypeScript, they are indeed the same primitive type. That primitive type is simply called **number**. Under the hood, it's a 64-bit floating-point number, fully implementing the IEEE 754 standard. This standard is specified for real numbers, and this leads to some weirdness that is specific to JavaScript. For example, in most environments, dividing by zero results in an error. In JavaScript and TypeScript, division by zero results in some special numbers such as **Infinity** or **NaN**. Additionally, there is no concept of integer division in JavaScript, as division is always done using real numbers.

However, even if everything is stored as floating-point real numbers, JavaScript guarantees that all operations that can be done using only integer arithmetic will be done exactly. One famous example of this behavior is adding **0.1** to **0.2**. In all compliant JavaScript engines, we get the result **0.30000000000000004** because of the finite precision of the underlying type. What we are guaranteed is that we can never get a decimal result if we are adding integers.

The engine makes sure that **1+1=2** with no decimal remainder. All integer operations are completely safe, but only if the results are within a specified range. JavaScript has a special constant defined (**Number.MAX_SAFE_INTEGER**) with a value of **9007199254740991** (with digit grouping, this is represented as **9.007.199.254.740.991**) over which we might get precision and rounding errors.

Booleans

Booleans are one of the simplest, and also one of the most used and useful, primitive types. This datatype has exactly two values, **true** and **false**. The useful thing is that if a variable of this type does not have a certain value, well, then it automatically has the other, as that is the only other possible option. In theory, this is sound, but in JavaScript, there are a lot of possibilities for things to go wrong. Since it has no type information, it cannot guarantee that a certain variable actually holds a Boolean value, which means that we always have to be careful of our Boolean checks.

TypeScript completely defines away this problem. Say we define a variable as a Boolean, using either a type annotation or type inference, as follows:

let isRead = false;

We can be absolutely sure that the variable will always have exactly one of the two possible values.

Arrays

One of the reasons computers are popular, aside from accessing social networking sites and playing video games, is that they are able to run the same processing algorithm on a whole collection of values, as many times as needed, without getting bored or making any errors. In order to be able to do that, we need to somehow organize the data into a collection of similar values that we can access one at a time. In JavaScript, the primary mechanism for such processing is the array. JavaScript has an extremely simple interface for creating arrays using the array literal syntax. We just list the elements, surrounded by brackets (**[ ]**), and we have an array:

const numbers = [1, 2, 3, 4, 5];

We can access that array using an index:

console.log(numbers[3]) // writes out 4, as arrays in JavaScript are //…0-based numbers[1] = 200; // the second element becomes 200

That makes it easy to use a **for** loop to go through the elements and process them all with a single piece of code:

```
for (let index = 0; index < numbers.length; index += 1) {
const element = numbers[index];
console.log(`The element at index ${index} has a value of ${element}`);
}
```

We can also use a **for..of** loop to iterate through the values, and the following snippet will calculate the sum of all the numbers in the array:

```
let sum = 0;
for (const element of numbers) {
sum += element;
}
```

As with anything in JavaScript, it has no mechanism to enforce that all the items in an array satisfy the "similarity" requirement we mentioned previously. So, there's nothing stopping us from adding a string, a Boolean, an object, or even a function to the array of numbers we have defined. All of these are valid JavaScript commands that will execute successfully:

```
numbers[1] = false;
numbers[2] = new Date();
numbers[3] = "three";
numbers[4] = function ()
{
console.log("I'm really not a number");
};
```

In almost all cases, it is not to our benefit to have an array with vastly different types as elements. The main benefit of arrays is that we can group similar items together and work with all of them with the same code. If we have different types, we lose that advantage, so we might as well not use an array at all.

With TypeScript, we can restrict the type so that an array will only allow a single type of value for its elements. Arrays have something that is referred to as a composite or generic type. That means that when we are specifying the type of the array, we're specifying it indirectly, via another type.

In this case, we define the type of the array through the type of the array's elements, for example, we can have an array whose elements will be numbers or an array whose elements will be strings. In TypeScript, we denote that by writing the type of the element and then appending brackets to the type name. So, if we needed our **numbers** array to only accept values whose type is **number**, we will denote that as follows:

let numbers: number[];

Even better, if we are initializing our array, we can omit the type annotation and let TypeScript infer the value:

```
const numbers = [1, 2, 3, 4, 5];

  Type 'string' is not assignable to type 'number'. ts(2322)

  const numbers: number[]

  View Problem (Alt+F8)   No quick fixes available
numbers[3] = "six";


numbers.push("six")
```

Figure: TypeScript inferring the type of the elements in the array

As shown previously, TypeScript will not let us use the **push** method with a value whose type does not match the type of the elements, nor will it allow elements to be set to invalid values.

Another, equivalent way to denote the type of the array is to use generic type syntax. In that case, we can use the **Array** type, with the type of the actual elements in angle brackets:

let numbers: Array<number>;

Generic classes and methods will be covered in detail, Generics and Conditional Types.

The benefit here is that we can be certain that if an array claims to have elements of a certain type, it will indeed have that kind of element, and we can process them without worrying that a bug introduced an incompatible element.

Tuples

Another common usage of arrays in JavaScript is to group data – just like objects, but without the hassle (and benefit) of property names. We could, for example, instead of creating a **person** object create a **person** array where, by convention, we'll use the first element to hold the first name, the second element to hold the last name, and the third element to hold the age.

We could define such an array using the following:

```
const person = ["Ada", "Lovelace", 36];
console.log(`First Name is: ${person[0]}`);
console.log(`Last Name is: ${person[1]}`);
console.log(`Age is: ${person[2]}`);
```

In this case, even as we are using the same structure – an array – we're not using it to group an unknown number of unrelated data of the same type, we're using it to group a known number of related data that can be of separate types. This kind of array is called a tuple. Once more, JavaScript has no mechanism to enforce the structure of a tuple, so in our code we can do lots of things that are syntactically valid, but nonsensical semantically. We could add a fourth element in the array, we can set the first element to be a number, the third to be a function, and so on.

With TypeScript, we can formally define the number and types of the data elements that we need inside a tuple, using syntax such as the following:

const person: [string, string, number] = ["Ada", "Lovelace", 36];

The **[string, string, number]** declaration tells TypeScript that we intend to use a tuple of three elements, that the first two elements will be a string, and the third will be a number. TypeScript now has enough information to enforce the structure. So, if we write code that will call the **toLowerCase** method on the first element of the tuple and multiply the third element by 10, that will work, as the first operation is valid on a string and the second is valid on a number:

console.log(person[0].toLowerCase());
console.log(person[2] * 10);

But if we try the operations the other way around, we'll get errors on both calls:

```
const person: [string, string, number] = ["Ada", "Lovelace", 36];

console.log(person[0].   Property 'toLowerCase' does not exist on type
console.log(person[2]    'number'. ts(2339)

                         any

                         View Problem (Alt+F8)   No quick fixes available
console.log(person[2].toLowerCase());
console.log(person[0] * 10);
```

Figure: TypeScript error when performing incorrect operations

Additionally, if we try to access an element that is outside of the defined range, we'll get an error as well:

```
const person: [string, string, number] = ["Ada", "Lovelace", 36];

                    Tuple type '[string, string, number]' of length '3' has no
                    element at index '3'. ts(2493)

                    View Problem (Alt+F8)   No quick fixes available
console.log(person[3]);
```

Figure: TypeScript when accessing elements outside the defined range

Schwartzian transform

Arrays have a helpful sort function, which we can use to sort the objects contained in the array. However, during the sorting process, multiple comparisons will be done on the same objects. For example, if we sort an array of 100 numbers, the method that compares two numbers will be called more than 500 times, on average. Let's say that we have a **Person** interface, defined with the following:

```
interface Person {
firstName: string;
lastName: string;
}
```

If we want to get the full name of the person, we might use a function such as this:

```
function getFullName (person: Person) {
return `${person.firstName} ${person.lastName}`;
}
```

If we have an array of **Person** objects, called **persons**, and want to sort it according to full name, we might use the following code:

```
persons.sort((first, second) => { const firstFullName = getFullName(first);
const secondFullName = getFullName(second);
return firstFullName.localeCompare(secondFullName);
})
```

This will sort the **persons** array, albeit in an inefficient manner. If we have 100 **Person** objects, this means that we have 100 different targets for the **getFullName** functions. But if we have more than 500 calls to the comparison function, that would mean that we have more than 1,000 calls to the **getFullName** function, so at least 900 calls are redundant.

Our method is fast and trivial, but if some expensive calculations were needed, simple sorting could slow down our application.

Fortunately, there's a simple technique called a Schwartzian transform that can help us with that. The technique has three parts:

We will transform each element in the array into a tuple of two elements. The first element of the tuple will be the original value, and the second will be the result of the ordering function (colloquially, the Schwartz).
We will sort the array on the second element of the tuple.
We will transform each tuple, discarding the ordering element and taking the original value.
We will employ this technique in the following exercise.

Exercise: Using Arrays and Tuples to Create an Efficient Sort of Objects

In this exercise, we are going to employ the Schwartzian transform to sort and print a predefined array of programmers. Each programmer object will be an instance of the **Person** interface, defined in the previous section.

We'll want to sort the programmers based on their full name, which can be calculated using the **getFullName** function, also from the previous section.

In order to implement a Schwartzian transform, we'll take the following steps:

We'll use the **map** method of the array in order to transform our programmers into a tuple of the

[Person, string] type, where the first element is the actual programmer and the second element is the full name string.

We'll use the **sort** method of the array to sort the tuples, using the second element of each tuple.

We'll use the **map** method once more to transform the tuples back to an array of programmers by just taking the first element and discarding the second element.

Let's start:

Create a new file called **person-sort.ts**.
Inside the file, create the interface for the **Person** objects:

```
interface Person {
firstName: string;
lastName: string;
}
```

Create the function that will get the full name of a given person:

```
let count = 0;
function getFullName (person: Person) {
count += 1;
return `${person.firstName} ${person.lastName}`;
}
```

We will use the **count** variable to detect the total number of calls of the function.

Define an array of persons and add a few objects with **firstName** and **lastName** properties:

```
const programmers: Person[] = [
    {
firstName: 'Donald', lastName: 'Knuth'},
    { firstName: 'Barbara', lastName: 'Liskow'},
    { firstName: 'Lars', lastName: 'Bak'},
    { firstName: 'Guido', lastName: 'Van Rossum'},
    { firstName: 'Anders', lastName: 'Hejslberg'},
    { firstName: 'Edsger', lastName: 'Dijkstra'},
    { firstName: 'Brandon', lastName: 'Eich'},
    // feel free to add as many as you want
];
```

Define a naïve and straight forward sorting function:

```
// a naive and straightforward sorting function
function naiveSortPersons (persons: Person[]): Person[] {
return persons.slice().sort((first, second) => {
const firstFullName = getFullName(first);
const secondFullName = getFullName(second);
return firstFullName.localeCompare(secondFullName);
    })
}
```

Use a Schwartzian transform and define a function that will take an array of persons and return (a sorted) array of persons:

```
function schwartzSortPersons (persons: Person[]): Person[] {
```

Use the array's **map** function to transform each element into a tuple:

```
const tuples: [Person, string][] = persons.map(person => [person, getFullName(person)]);
```

Sort the **tuples** array of tuples, using the standard **sort** method:

```
tuples.sort((first, second) => first[1].localeCompare(second[1]));
```

We should note that the **sort** function takes two objects, in our case, two tuples, and we sort the tuples according to their second element – the result of the **getFullName** call.

Transform the sorted array of tuples into the format we want – just an array of **person** objects – by taking the first element of each tuple, discarding the Schwartz:

```
const result = tuples.map(tuple => tuple[0]);
```

The last three steps are the three parts of the Schwartzian transform.
Return the new array from the function:

```
return result;
}
```

Add a line that will call the **naiveSortPersons** function on our defined array:

```
count = 0;
const sortedNaive = naiveSortPersons(programmers);
```

Output both the sorted array, and the count variable.
```
console.log(sortedNaive);
console.log(`When called using the naive approach, the function was called ${count} times`);
```

Add a line that will call the **schwartzSortPersons** function on our defined array:

```
count = 0;
const sortedSchwartz = schwartzSortPersons(programmers);
```

Output both the **sorted** array and the **count** variable. The **count** variable should be identical to the number of items in the array, which is 7 in our example. Without the optimization, the method would have been called 28 times:

```
console.log(sortedSchwartz); console.log(`When called using the Schwartzian transform approach, the function was called ${count} times`);
```

Save and compile the file:

```
tsc person-sort.ts
```

Verify that the compilation ended successfully and that there is a **personsort.js** file generated in the same folder. Execute it in the **node** environment with the following command:

node person-sort.js

You will see an output that looks as follows:

```
[
  { firstName: 'Anders', lastName: 'Hejslberg' },
  { firstName: 'Barbara', lastName: 'Liskow' },
  { firstName: 'Brandon', lastName: 'Eich' },
  { firstName: 'Donald', lastName: 'Knuth' },
  { firstName: 'Edsger', lastName: 'Dijkstra' },
  { firstName: 'Guido', lastName: 'Van Rossum' },
  { firstName: 'Lars', lastName: 'Bak' }
]
When called using the naive approach, the function was called 28 times [
  { firstName: 'Anders', lastName: 'Hejslberg' },
  { firstName: 'Barbara', lastName: 'Liskow' },
  { firstName: 'Brandon', lastName: 'Eich' },
  { firstName: 'Donald', lastName: 'Knuth' },
  { firstName: 'Edsger', lastName: 'Dijkstra' },
  { firstName: 'Guido', lastName: 'Van Rossum' },
  { firstName: 'Lars', lastName: 'Bak' }
]
When called using the Schwartzian transform approach, the function was
called 7 times
```

We can easily check that the values that are outputted are sorted according to their full names. We can also notice a 7 at the end of output – that's the total number of calls of the **getFullName** function. Since we have 7 items in the programmer's array, we can conclude that the function was called just once for each object.

We could have instead sorted the programmer's array directly, using code such as the following:

```
programmers.sort((first, second) => {
const firstFullName = getFullName(first);
const secondFullName = getFullName(second);
return firstFullName.localeCompare(secondFullName);
});
console.log(count);
```

In this case, for this array, the count of execution of the **getFullName** function would have been 28, which is four times as high as our optimized version.

Enums

Often, we have some types that have a predefined set of values, and no other value is valid. For example, there are four and only four cardinal directions (East, West, North, and South). There are four and only four different suits in a deck of cards. So, how do we define a variable that should have such a value?

In TypeScript, we can use an **enum** type to do that. The simplest way to define an enum would be as follows:

```
enum Suit {
    Hearts,
    Diamonds,
    Clubs,
    Spades
}
```

We can then define and use a variable of such type, and TypeScript will help us use it:

let trumpSuit = Suit.Hears;

TypeScript will infer that the type of the **trumpSuit** variable is **Suit** and will only allow us to access those four values. Any attempt to assign something else to the variable will result in an error:

```
let trumpSuit = Suit.Hearts;
```

```
Type '"invalid-value"' is not assignable to type
'Suit'. ts(2322)

let trumpSuit: Suit

View Problem (Alt+F8)   No quick fixes available
trumpSuit = "invalid-value"
```

Figure: TypeScript inferring the type of trumpSuit

So far, all the types we've encountered were JavaScript types that were augmented with TypeScript. Unlike that, enums are specific to TypeScript. Under the hood, the **Suit** class actually compiles into an object with values like this:

```
{
 '0': 'Hearts',
 '1': 'Diamonds',
 '2': 'Clubs',
 '3': 'Spades',
 Hearts: 0,
 Diamonds: 1,
 Clubs: 2,
 Spades: 3
}
```

TypeScript will automatically assign numbers starting with zero to the options provided and add a reverse mapping as well, so if we have the option, we can get the value, but if we have the value, we can map to the option as well. We can also explicitly set the provided numbers as well:

```
enum Suit {Hearts = 10,
    Diamonds = 20,
    Clubs = 30,
    Spades = 40
}
```

We can also use strings instead of numbers, with syntax like this:

```
enum Suit {    Hearts = "hearts",
    Diamonds = "diamonds",
    Clubs = "clubs",
    Spades = "spades"
}
```

These enums are called string-based enums, and they compile to an object like this:

```
{
  Hearts: 'hearts',
  Diamonds: 'diamonds',
  Clubs: 'clubs',
  Spades: 'spades'
}
```

Any and Unknown

So far, we have explained how TypeScript inference works, and how powerful it is. But sometimes we actually want to have JavaScript's "anything goes" behavior. For example, what if we genuinely need a variable that will sometimes hold a string and sometimes hold a number? The following code will issue an error because we're trying to assign a string to a variable that TypeScript inferred to be a number:

```
let variable = 3;
if (Math.random()>0.5) {
variable = "not-a-number";
}
```

This is how the code will appear on VS Code with the error message:

```
let variable = 3;
    Type 'string' is not assignable to type 'number'. ts(2322)

    let variable: number

if (  View Problem (Alt+F8)    No quick fixes available

    variable = "not-a-number";
}
```

Figure: TypeScript inferring the type of variable

What we need to do is somehow suspend the type inference for that specific variable. To be able to do that, TypeScript provides us with the **any** type:

```
let variable: any = 3;
if (Math.random()>0.5) {
variable = "not-a-number";
}
```

This type annotation reverts the **variable** variable to the default JavaScript behaviour, so none of the calls involving that variable will be checked by the compiler. Additionally, most calls that include a variable of the **any** type will infer a result of the same type. This means that the **any** type is highly contagious, and even if we define it in a single place in our application, it can propagate to lots of places.

Since using **any** effectively negates most of TypeScript's benefits, it's best used as seldom as possible, and only when absolutely necessary. It's a powerful tool to use the opt-in/opt-out design of TypeScript so that we can gradually upgrade existing JavaScript code into TypeScript.

One scenario that is sometimes used is a combination of the dynamic nature of **any** and the static nature of TypeScript – we can have an array where the elements can be anything:

```
const everything: any[] = [ 1, false, "string"];
```

Starting from version 3.0, TypeScript also offers another type with dynamic semantics – the **unknown** type. While still dynamic, it's much more constricted in what can be done with it. For example, the following code will compile using **any**:

```
const variable: any = getSomeResult(); // a hypothetical function //with some return value we know
nothing about
const str: string = variable; // this works, as any might be a //string, and "anything goes";
variable.toLowerCase();        // we are allowed to call a method, //and we'll determine at runtime whether
that's possible
```

On the other hand, the same code with an **unknown** type annotation result in the following:

```
const variable: unknown = 7; // a hypothetical function //with some

    Type 'unknown' is not assignable to type 'string'. ts(2322)

    const str: string

    View Problem (Alt+F8)    No quick fixes available
const str: string = variable;    // this works, as any might be a //s
variable.toLowerCase();          // we are allowed to call a method,
```

Figure: TypeScript compiler error message

The **unknown** type basically flips the assertion and the burden of proof. With **any**, the flow is that, since we don't know that it's not a string, we can treat it as a string. With **unknown**, we don't know whether it's a string, so we can't treat it as a string. In order to do anything useful with an **unknown**, we need to explicitly test its value and determine our actions based on that:

```
const variable: unknown = getSomeResult(); // a hypothetical function with some return value we know
nothing about
if (typeof variable === "string") {
const str: string = variable; // valid, because we tested if the value inside `variable` actually has a type of
```

```
string
variable.toLowerCase();
}
```

Null and Undefined

One of the specifics of JavaScript is that it has two separate values that signify that there isn't a value: **null** and **undefined**. The difference between the two is that **null** has to be specified explicitly – so if something is **null**, that is because someone set it to **null**. Meanwhile, if something has the value **undefined** usually it means that the value is not set at all. For example, let's look at a **person** object defined with the following:

```
const person = {firstName: "Ada", lastName: null
}
```

The value of the **lastName** property has been set to **null** explicitly. On the other hand, the **age** property is not set at all. So, if we print them out, we'll see that the **lastName** property has a value of **null**, while the **age** property has a value of **undefined**:

```
console.log(person.lastName);
console.log(person.age);
```

We should note that if we have some optional properties in an object, their default value will be **undefined**. Similarly, if we have optional parameters in a function, the default value of the argument will be **undefined** as well.

Never

There is another "not a value" type that's specific to TypeScript, and that is the special **never** type. This type represents a value that never occurs. For example, if we have a function where the end of the function is not reachable and has no return statements, its return type will be **never**. An example of such a function will be as follows:

```
function notReturning(): never
{
throw new Error("point of no return");
}
const value = notReturning();
```

The type of the **value** variable will be inferred as **never**. Another situation where **never** is useful is if we have a logical condition that cannot be **true**. As a simple example, let's look at this code:

```
const x = true;
if (x) {console.log (`x is true: ${x.toString()}`);
}
```

The conditional statement will always be **true**, so we will always see the text in the console. But if we add an **else** branch to this code, the value of **x** inside the branch cannot be **true** because we're in the **else** branch, but cannot be anything else because it was defined as **true**. So, the actual type is inferred to be **never**. Since **never** does not have any properties or methods, this branch will throw a compile error:

```
const x = true;                Property 'toString' does not exist on type
if (x) {                       'never'. ts(2339)
console.log(`x is true
} else {                       any

                               View Problem (Alt+F8)    No quick fixes available
    console.log(`x is false: ${x.toString()}`);

}
```

Figure: Compiler error from using the never type

Function Types

The last built-in type in JavaScript that we'll take a look at is not really a piece of data – it's a piece of code. Since functions are first-order objects in JavaScript, they remain so in TypeScript as well. And just like the others, functions get types as well. The type of a function is a bit more complicated than the other types. In order to identify it, we need all the parameters and their types, as well as the return values and their types.

Let's take a look at an **add** function defined with the following:

```
const add = function (x: number, y: number) {
return x + y;
}
```

To fully describe the type of the function, we need to know that it is a function that takes a number as the first parameter and a number as the second parameter and returns a number. In TypeScript, we'll write this as **(x: number, y: number) => number**.

Making Your Own Types

Of course, aside from using the types that are already available in JavaScript, we can define our own types. We have several options for that. We can use the JavaScript **class** specification to declare our own classes, with properties and methods. A simple class can be defined with the following:

```
class Person {    constructor(public firstName: string, public lastName: string,
public age?: number) {    }
   getFullName() {       return `${this.firstName} ${this.lastName}`;
   }
}
```

We can create objects of this class and use methods on them:

```
const person = new Person("Ada", "Lovelace");
console.log(person.getFullName());
```

Another way to formalize our complex structures is to use an interface:

```
interface Person {
firstName: string;
lastName: string;
age?: string;
}
```

Unlike classes, which compile to JavaScript classes or constructor functions (depending on the compilation target), interfaces are a TypeScript-only construct. When compiling, they are checked statically, and then removed from the compiled code.

Both classes and interfaces are useful if implementing a class hierarchy, as both constructs are suitable for extension and inheritance.

Yet another way is to use type aliases, with the **type** keyword. We can basically put a name that we will use as a type alias to just about anything available in TypeScript. For example, if we want to have another name for the primitive **number** type, for example, **integer**, we can always do the following:

```
type integer = number;
```

If we want to give a name to a tuple, **[string, string, number?]**, that we use to store a person, we can alias that with the following:

```
type Person = [string, string, number?];
```

We can also use objects and functions in the definition of a type alias:

```
type Person = {   firstName: string;   lastName: string;   age?: number; }
type FilterFunction = (person: Person) => boolean;
```

Exercise: Making a Calculator Function

In this exercise, we'll define a calculator function that will take the operands and the operation as parameters. We will design it so it is easy to extend it with additional operations and use that behaviour to extend it:

Create a new file called **calculator.ts**.
In **calculator.ts**, define an enum with all the operators that we want to support inside our code:

```
enum Operator {   Add = "add",
    Subtract = "subtract",
    Multiply = "multiply",
    Divide = "divide",
}
```

Define an empty (for now) **calculator** function that will be our main interface. The function should take three parameters: the two numbers that we want to operate on, as well as an operator:

```
const calculator = function (first: number, second: number, op: Operator) {
}
```

Create a type alias for a function that does a calculation on two numbers. Such a function will take two numbers as parameters and return a single number:

```
type Operation = (x: number, y: number) => number;
```

Create an empty array that can hold multiple tuples of the **[Operator, Operation]** type. This will be our dictionary, where we store all our methods:

```
const operations: [Operator, Operation][] = [];
```

Create an **add** method that satisfies the **Operation** type (you don't need to explicitly reference it):

```
const add = function (first: number, second: number) {return first + second;
};
```

Create a tuple of the **Operator.Add** value and the **add** function and add it to the **operations** array:

```
operations.push([Operator.Add, add]);
```

Repeat steps 6 and 7 for the subtraction, multiplication, and division functions:

```
const subtract = function (first: number, second: number) {    return first -
second;
}; operations.push([Operator.Subtract, subtract]);
const multiply = function (first: number, second: number) {    return first
* second;
}; operations.push([Operator.Multiply, multiply]);
const divide = function (first: number, second: number) {    return first /
second;
}; operations.push([Operator.Divide, divide]);
```

Implement the **calculator** function, using the **operations** array to find the correct tuple by the **Operator** provided, and then using the corresponding **Operation** value to do the calculation:

```
const calculator = function (first: number, second: number, op: Operator)
{
    const tuple = operations.find(tpl => tpl[0] === op);    const operation =
tuple[1];    const result = operation(first, second);    return result;
}
```

Note that, as long as a function has the required type, that is, it takes two numbers and outputs a number, we can use it as an operation.

Let's take the calculator for a test run. Write some code that will call the **calculator** function with different arguments:

```
console.log(calculator(4, 6, Operator.Add));
console.log(calculator(13, 3, Operator.Subtract));
console.log(calculator(2, 5, Operator.Multiply));
console.log(calculator(70, 7, Operator.Divide));
```

Save the file and run the following command in the folder:

tsc calculator.ts

Verify that the compilation ended successfully and that there is a **calculator. js** file generated in the same folder. Execute it in the **node** environment with the following command:

node calculator.js

You will see the output looks as follows:

10
10
10
10

Now, let's try to extend our calculator by adding a modulo operation. First, we need to add that option to the **Operator** enum:

```
enum Operator {    Add = "add",
    Subtract = "subtract",
    Multiply = "multiply",
    Divide = "divide",
    Modulo = "modulo"
}
```

Add a function called **modulo** of the **Operation** type, and add a corresponding tuple to the **operations** array:

```
const modulo = function (first: number, second: number) {    return first
% second;
}; operations.push([Operator.Modulo, modulo]);
```

At the end of the file, add a call to the **calculator** function that uses the **Modulo** operator:

console.log(calculator(14, 3, Operator.Modulo));

Save and compile the file and run the resulting JavaScript with the following command:

node calculator.js

You will see an output that looks as follows:

10
10
10
10
2

Note that when we extended our calculator with the modulo function, we did not change the **calculator** function at all. In this exercise, we saw how we can use the tuples, arrays, and function types to effectively design an extensible system.

Activity: Creating a Library for Working with Strings

Your task is to create a series of simple functions that will help you do some common operations on strings. Some of the operations are already supported in the standard JavaScript library, but you will use them as a convenient learning exercise, both of JavaScript internals and TypeScript as a language. Our library will have the following functions:

toTitleCase: This will process a string and will capitalize the first letter of each word but will make all the other letters lowercase.

Test cases for this function are as follows:

"war AND peace" => "War And Peace"
"Catcher in the Rye" => "Catcher In The Rye"
"tO kILL A mOCKINGBIRD" => "To Kill A MockingBird"

countWords: This will count the number of separate words within a string. Words are delimited by spaces, dashes (-), or underscores (_).

Test cases for this function are as follows:

"War and Peace" => 3
"catcher-in-the-rye" => 4
"for_whom the-bell-tolls" => 5

toWords: This will return all the words that are within a string. Words are delimited by spaces, dashes (-), or underscores (_).

Test cases for this function are as follows:
"War and Peace" => [War, and, peace]
"catcher-in-the-rye" => [catcher, in, the, rye]
"for_whom the-bell-tolls"=> [for, whom, the, bell, tolls]

repeat: This will take a string and a number and return that same string repeated that number of times.
Test cases for this function are as follows:

"War", 3 => "WarWarWar"
"rye", 1 => "rye"
"bell", 0 => ""

isAlpha: This will return **true** if the string only has alpha characters (that is, letters). Test cases for this function are as follows:

"War and Peace" => false
"Atonement" => true
"1Q84" => false

isBlank: This will return **true** if the string is blank, that is, consists only of whitespace characters.
Test cases for this function are as follows:

"War and Peace" => false
"   " => true
"" => true

When writing the functions, make sure to think of the types of the parameters and the types of the return values.
Here are some steps to help you create the preceding functions (note that there are multiple ways to implement each of the functions, so treat these steps as suggestions):

Creating the **toTitleCase** function: In order to change each word, we'll need first to get all the words. You can use the **split** function to make a single string into an array of words. Next, we'll need to **slice** off the first letter from the rest of the word. We can use the **toLowerCase** and **toUpperCase** methods to make something lower- and uppercase, respectively. After we get all the words properly cased, we can use the **join** array method to make an array of strings into a single large string.

Creating the **countWords** function: In order to get the words, we can split the original string on any occurrence of any of the three delimiters (**" "**, **"_"**, and **"-"**). Fortunately, the **split** function can take a regular expression as a parameter, which we can use to our benefit. Once we have the words in an array, we just need to count the elements.

Creating the **towards** function: This method can use the same approach as the preceding one. Instead of counting the words, we'll just need to return them. Take note of the return type of this method.

Creating the **repeat** function: Create an array with the required length (using the **Array** constructor), and set each element to the input value (using the array's **fill** method). After that, you can use the **join** method of the array to join the values into a single long string.

Creating the **isAlpha** function: We can design a regular expression that will test this, but we can also split the string into single characters, using the string **split** method. Once we have the character array, we can use the map function to transform all the characters to lowercase. We can then use the filter method to return only those characters that are not between "a" and "z". If we don't have such characters, then the input only has letters, so we should return true. Otherwise, we should return false.

Creating the **isBlank** function: One way to create such a function is to repeatedly test whether the first character is empty, and if it is, to remove it (a **while** loop works best for this). That loop will break either on the first non-blank characters or when it runs out of the first elements, that is, when the input is empty. In the first case, the string is not blank, so we should return **false**; otherwise, we should return **true**.

Declaration Files

Introduction

In this chapter, you will learn about TypeScript declaration files. Declaration files give you the ability to give TypeScript more information about how a function or class is structured.

Why is it important to understand how declaration files work? Technically, declaration files speak directly to the core motivations for why TypeScript is becoming so popular. One of the common rationales for using TypeScript is because it guides developers through the application process. Let's walk through a real-world example as a case study.

In pure JavaScript, if we start working with a code library that we've never used before that formats dates, such as **Moment JS**, we would have to start by looking through the documentation in order to know what type of data we can pass to the Moment JS functions. When working with a new library, it is tedious work to figure out requirements, such as how many function arguments are required for each function and what data type each argument needs to be.

With the declaration files, however, TypeScript informs the text editor of the requirements for every function that a library has. So, instead of having to rely solely on documentation and Google searches, the text editor itself informs the developer how to work with each function. For example, the text editor, with the help of TypeScript, would inform us that the Moment JS format function takes in zero to one argument, and the optional argument needs to be a string. And declaration files make all of this possible.

Declaration Files

Anytime we're asked to write additional boilerplate code, our first question is: why is it important to do this? With that in mind, before we walk through creating and managing declaration files, let's first analyze the role of declaration files in the development process.

The entire reason why we use TypeScript in the first place is to give our applications a specified structure based on types. Declaration files extend this functionality by allowing us to define the shape of our programs.

In this section, we will walk through two ways to work with declaration files. The first approach will be to create our own declaration files from scratch. This is a great place to start since it provides insight into how the declaration process works. In the second part, we will see how we can integrate types into third-party NPM libraries.

Before we get into this chapter's example project, let's look at the core elements that comprise a declaration file in TypeScript. Consider the following code, which assigns a string value to a variable:

```
firstName = "Kristine";
```

The preceding code in TypeScript will generate a compiler warning that says **Cannot find name 'firstName'**, which can be seen in the following screenshot:

```
TS hello.ts

1    firstName ="Kristine";

2    Cannot find name 'firstName'. ts(2304)

     any

     View Problem (Alt+F8)    Quick Fix... (Ctrl+.)
```

Figure: Compiler error when TypeScript cannot find a variable declaration

This error is shown because whenever we attempt to assign a value to a variable, TypeScript looks for where a variable name is defined. We can fix this by utilizing the **declare** keyword. The following code will correct the error that we encountered in the previous case:

```
declare let firstName: string;
firstName = "Kristine";
```

As you can see in the following screenshot, the compiler warning disappeared with the use of the **declare** keyword:

```
TS hello.ts > ...

1    declare let firstName: string;

2    firstName = "Kristine";

3
```

Figure: Example of a variable being defined in TypeScript

Now, that may not seem like a big deal, because we could accomplish the same goal by simply defining a **let** variable, such as the following:

```
let firstName: string;
firstName = "Kristine"
```

The preceding code would not generate an error when viewed in the Visual Studio Code editor.

So, what is the point of using **declare**? As we build out complex modules, the declare process allows us to describe the complete shape of our modules in a way that cannot be done by simply defining a variable. Now that you know the role of declaration files along with the basic syntax, let's walk through the full workflow of creating a declaration file from scratch in the following exercise.

Exercise: Creating a Declaration File from Scratch

In this exercise, we'll create a declaration file from scratch. We'll declare file conventions, import, and then use declared files. Consider that you are developing a web app that requires users to register themselves with credentials such as email, user roles, and passwords. The data types of these credentials will be stated in the declaration file that we'll be creating. A user won't be allowed to log in if they fail to enter the correct credentials.

Perform the following steps to implement this exercise:

Open the Visual Studio Code editor.
Create a new directory and then create a file named **user.ts**.

Start the TypeScript compiler and have it watch for changes to the file with the following terminal compile command:

tsc user.ts —watch

The following screenshot shows how the command appears inside the terminal:

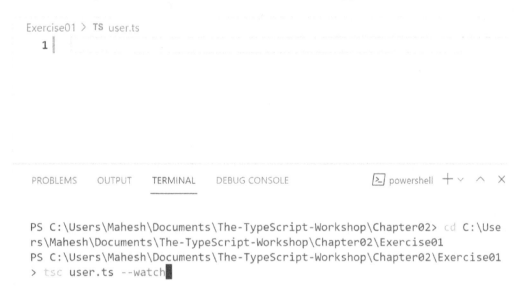

Figure: Running the TypeScript compiler with the watch flag

It's fine to leave this file empty for now. We'll start building out our implementation shortly. Now let's create our declaration file.

Create a directory called **types/** at the root of our program and then create a file inside it called **AuthTypes.d.ts**.

Our project's directory should now look like this:

Figure: AuthTypes file structure

Within the new declaration file, define the shape of our **AuthTypes** module. Use the **declare** keyword at the top of the file. This tells TypeScript that we are about to describe how the **AuthTypes** module should be structured:

```
declare module "AuthTypes" {export interface User {email: string; roles: Array<string>;}
}
```

In the preceding code, another bit of syntax that might be different than what you're used to writing is that we wrap the module name in quotation marks. When we implement the program, you'll see that if we remove the quotation marks, we won't be able to import the module. Inside the module, we can place any number of exports that we want the module to have. One of the most important concepts to keep in mind is that declaration files do not have any implementation code; they simply describe the types and structure for the elements used in the module. The following screenshot gives a visual representation of the code:

```
Exercise01 > types > TS AuthTypes.d.ts > {} "AuthTypes"
1    declare module "AuthTypes" {
2        export interface User {
3            email: string;
4            roles: Array<string>;
5            source?: string;
6        }
7    }
```

Figure: AuthTypes interface

The compiler messages suggest that the import should happen successfully as there have not been any errors up to this point.

In this step, we're exporting a user interface that defines two data points: email and roles. As far as the data types are concerned, the **email** attribute needs to be a string, and **roles** needs to be an array filled with strings. Such type definitions will ensure that anyone using this module will be informed immediately if they attempt to use the incorrect data structure.

Now that we have defined the **AuthTypes** module, we need to import it into our TypeScript file so that we can use it. We're going to use the reference import process to bring the file into our program.

Go to the **user.ts** file and add the following two lines of code:

/// <reference path = "./types/AuthTypes.d.ts" /> import auth = require("AuthTypes");

The code in the editor will look something like this:

```
TS hello.ts  U        TS user.ts  M  ×      TS AuthTypes.d.ts

Exercise01 > TS user.ts
   1    /// <reference path = "./types/AuthTypes.d.ts" />
   2    import auth = require("AuthTypes");
   3
```

```
PROBLEMS    OUTPUT    TERMINAL    DEBUG CONSOLE              >_ PowerShell

[12:12:58 pm] File change detected. Starting incremental compilation...

[12:12:58 pm] Found 0 errors. Watching for file changes.
```

Figure: Importing a declaration file

The first line in the preceding code will make **AuthTypes.d.ts** available to our program, and the second line imports the module itself. Obviously, you can use any variable name for the import statement that you prefer. In this code, we're importing the **AuthTypes** module and storing it in the **auth** keyword.

With our module imported, we can now start building the implementation for our program. We'll start out by defining a variable and assigning it to our user interface type that we defined in the declaration files.

Add the following code to the **user.ts** file:

let jon: auth.User;

The updated code of **user.ts** file will look something like this:

/// <reference path = "./types/AuthTypes.d.ts" /> import auth = require("AuthTypes");
let jon: auth.User;

What we've done here is quite impressive. We've essentially created our own type/interface in a separate file, imported it, and told the TypeScript compiler that our new variable is going to be of the **User** type.

Add the actual values of **email** and **roles** for the **jon** variable with the help of the following code:

jon = { email: "jon@snow.com", roles: ["admin"] };

With the required shape in place, the program compiles properly, and you can perform any tasks that you need to do.

Create another **User** and see how we can work with optional attributes. Add the following code to add details of the user **alice**:

let alice: auth.User;
alice = {email: "alice@snow.com", roles: ["super_admin"] };

Now, let's imagine that we sometimes keep track of how a user found our application. Not all users will have this attribute though, so we'll need to make it optional without breaking the other user accounts. You can mark an attribute as optional by adding a question mark before the colon.

Add a **source** attribute to the declaration file:

```
declare module "AuthTypes" {
export interface User {
email: string;
roles: Array<string>;
source?: string;}
}
```

Update our **alice** user with a **source** value of **facebook**:

```
/// <reference path = "./types/AuthTypes.d.ts" /> import auth =
require("AuthTypes"); let jon: auth.User; jon = {    email:
"jon@snow.com",    roles: ["admin"] }; let alice: auth.User;
alice = {    email: "alice@snow.com",    roles: ["super_admin"],
source: "facebook"
}
```

Notice that the **jon** variable still works perfectly fine, even without the **source** value. This helps us to build flexible interfaces for our programs that define both optional and required data points.

Open the terminal and run the following command to generate a JavaScript file:

tsc user.ts

Let's now look at the generated **user.js** file, which can be seen in the following screenshot:

```
Exercise01 > JS user.js > ...
  1    "use strict";
  2    exports.__esModule = true;
  3    var jon;
  4    jon = {
  5        email: "jon@snow.com",
  6        roles: ["admin"]
  7    };
  8    var alice;
  9    alice = {
 10        email: "alice@snow.com",
 11        roles: ["super_admin"],
 12        source: "facebook"
 13    };
 14
```

Figure: Declaration file rules not added to the generated JavaScript code

Well, that's interesting. There is literally not a single mention of the declaration file in the generated JavaScript code. This brings up a very important piece of knowledge to know when it comes to declaration files and TypeScript in general: declaration files are used solely for the benefit of the developer and are only utilized by the IDE.

Declaration files are completely bypassed when it comes to what is rendered in the program. And with this in mind, hopefully the goal of declaration files is becoming clearer. The better your declaration files are, the easier it will be for the IDE to understand your program and for yourself and other developers to work with your code.

Exceptions

Let's see what happens when we don't follow the rules of our interface. Remember in the previous exercise that our interface required two data elements (**email** and **roles**) and that they need to be of the **string** and **Array<string>** types. So, watch what happens when we don't implement the proper data type with the following code:

jon = {email: 123}

This will generate the following compiler error, as shown in the following screenshot:

```
TS hello.ts  U     Type 'number' is not assignable to type 'string'. ts(2322)

Exercise01 > T     AuthTypes.d.ts(3, 9): The expected type comes from property
  1    ///         'email' which is declared here on type 'User'
  2  , impo
  3 ▸ let          (property) auth.User.email: string
  4 ▸ jon    View Problem (Alt+F8)    No quick fixes available
  5 |         email: 123,
  6 |
  7 ▸ };
  8
  9 |
```

Figure: TypeScript showing the required data types for an object

That is incredibly helpful. Imagine that you are working with a library that you've never used before. If you were using vanilla JavaScript, this implementation would silently fail and would force you to dig through the library's source code to see what structure it required.

This compiler error makes sense, and in a real-life application, such as a **React** or an **Angular** app, the application wouldn't even load until the issue was fixed. If we update the data structure to match the declaration file for **AuthTypes** with the following code:

jon = {email: "jon@snow.com"}

We can see that the compiler will move the error message up to the **jon** variable name. If you hover over it, or look at the terminal output, you'll see the error shown in the following screenshot:

```
  1    /// <reference path = "./types/AuthTypes.d.ts" />
  2  , import auth = require("AuthTypes");
  3 ▸ let jon: auth.User;
  4 ▸ jon = {
  5 |
  6 |     Property 'roles' is missing in type '{ email: string; }' but
  7       required in type 'User'. ts(2741)
  8 ▸
  9     AuthTypes.d.ts(4, 9): 'roles' is declared here.

        let jon: auth.User

    View Problem (Alt+F8)    No quick fixes available
```

Figure: TypeScript showing the required attributes for an object

This is an incredibly useful functionality. If you're new to development, this may not seem like a very big deal. However, this type of information is the exact reason why TypeScript continues to grow in popularity. Error messages such as this instantly provide the information that we need in order to fix the bug and work with the program. In the preceding screenshot, the message is telling us that the program won't compile as we are missing a required value, namely, **roles**.

Now that we have built out our own declaration file from scratch, it's time to move on and see how declaration files are utilized by other libraries.

Third-Party Code Libraries
Depending on the types of applications that you build, you may never need to build your own

declaration files. However, if you're using TypeScript and working with third-party modules, you will need to understand how declaration files work because you will then be able to work seamlessly with external libraries.

DefinitelyTyped

Let's jump back in time for a moment. When TypeScript was originally developed, there was quite a bit of excitement around the idea of integrating types into JavaScript applications. However, developers began to get frustrated, because even though they were building their programs with types, every time that they imported an external library, such as lodash, they were forced to write code with no type signatures and little to no IDE guidance.

Essentially, this meant that each time we were to call a function from an external library, we didn't have a high level of assurance that we were working with it properly.

Thankfully, the open-source community had the answer, and the Definitely Typed library was created. Definitely Typed is a very large repository that contains literally thousands of declaration files for JavaScript code libraries. This means that libraries such as **react**, **lodash**, and pretty much every other popular library has a full set of declaration files that we can use in our TypeScript programs.

Analyzing an External Declaration File

Before we learn how to import and use types with external libraries, let's peek into what they look like:

Figure: Example of how DefinitelyTyped uses declaration files

In the preceding screenshot, if you look at the **lodash** declaration file for the array data structure, you'll see that a single declaration file is over 2,000 lines long. That can be a little intimidating to look at, so let's try to simplify it.

You'll be pleased to know that the elements in the preceding declaration file are exactly what we built out in Exercise: Creating a Declaration File from Scratch. It starts by declaring a **module** instance, and from that point, it lists out interfaces for each of the elements that utilize the array data structure. In fact, if you dissect the code, you'll see that **lodash** provides three interfaces for each of the functions in the library. You don't have to know what these do; however, it is helpful to realize that you can provide as many interfaces as needed when you're building your own code libraries.

Let's now look at the interface for the **last** function:

```
836    interface LoDashStatic {
837        /**
838         * Gets the last element of array.
839         *
840         * @param array The array to query.
841         * @return Returns the last element of array.
842         */
843        last<T>(array: List<T> | null | undefined): T | undefined;
844    }
```

Figure: How lodash implements interfaces

This is a good function to look at, because we'll use it when we get to the example for this section. You can see that the majority of the interface is actually a comment. If you've never seen this syntax before, it is using JSDoc syntax. This is very helpful, because IDEs such as Visual Studio Code will pull the comment, parameters, and return type directly into the IntelliSense interface. This means that when we start typing the **last** function when working with **lodash**, the IDE will automatically pull in the comment data so we can easily read how to use the function.

After that, the declaration is pretty basic. It simply describes the shape of the last function, specifically, that it takes a list of values as the argument and then returns either **T** or **undefined**. Don't worry about all the references to **T**; you'll learn about what this represents in Chapter 8, Generics. For now, just know that it means that it is returning a value.

Following the same pattern from when we created the declaration file from scratch, in the next section, let's create a new TypeScript project and walk through a practical example of why types are needed.

Exercise: Creating Types with External Libraries

In this exercise, we'll install types and integrate our types with external libraries. We will also be exploring a scenario wherein we'll check how the function behaves when the wrong type of parameter is passed to it. You'll need to start with an empty directory for this exercise.

Perform the following steps to implement this exercise:

Open the Visual Studio Code editor.

Create an empty directory on your computer and run the following command to create a new NPM project:

npm init -y

The preceding code will generate a **package.json** file.

To install the Lodash library, open the terminal and type the following command:

npm i lodash

The preceding command installs the Lodash library. The **package.json** file should now look something like this, with **lodash** installed in the dependencies list:

```
> {} package.json > ...
{
  "name": "Example",
  "version": "1.0.0",
  "description": "",
  "main": "index.js",
  ▷ Debug
  "scripts": {
    "test": "echo \"Error: no test specified\" && exit 1"
  },
  "keywords": [],
  "author": "",
  "license": "ISC",
  "dependencies": {
    "loadash": "^1.0.0"
  }
}
```

Figure: The generated package.json file

Create a file in that directory named **lodash_examples.ts**, start the TypeScript compiler, and have it watch for changes. Inside of the new **.ts** file, add the following code:

```
import _ = require("lodash"); const nums = [1, 2, 3];
console.log(_.last(nums));
```

Run the preceding program in the terminal by writing the following commands:

tsc lodash_examples.ts node lodash_examples.js

The console generates an output of **3**, as you can see in the following screenshot:

```
PS C:\Users\Mahesh\Documents\TypeScript_code\Chapter02_demo> tsc lodash_examples.ts

PS C:\Users\Mahesh\Documents\TypeScript_code\Chapter02_demo> node lodash_examples.js

3
```

Figure: Running the generated lodash_example.js program

Create another variable named **number** and assign it the value **10**. We'll then pass this number as an argument to the Lodash library's **_.last()** function. Write the following code to do this:

```
import _ = require("lodash"); //
const nums = [1, 2, 3]; //
console.log(_.last(nums));
const number = 10;
console.log(_.last(number));
```

Since we've looked at the declaration file, we know that the last function expects an array or some type of list. However, for now, let's pretend that we don't have that information, and this is the first time that we're working with the Lodash library.

Run the preceding program in the terminal by writing the following commands:
tsc lodash_examples.ts node lodash_examples.js

The following output is generated when the preceding commands are executed:

```
PS C:\Users\Mahesh\Documents\TypeScript_code\Chapter02_demo> node lodash_examples.js

undefined
PS C:\Users\Mahesh\Documents\TypeScript_code\Chapter02_demo> []
```

Figure: What happens when the wrong argument is passed to the last function

In such a small program, this may seem like a trivial issue. However, in a large system, getting an undefined value while expecting an actual value can be time-consuming, as we have to spend more time on debugging.
In order to fix this issue, let's leverage the Definitely Typed repository and bring in the **lodash** types. If you hover over the **import** statement at the top of the file, you'll even see the following warning and recommendation, as shown in the following screenshot:

```
import _ = require("lodash");
//const nums = [1,    Could not find a declaration file for module 'lodash'.
//console.log(_.las   'c:/Users/Mahesh/Documents/TypeScript_code/chapter02_example/node_modules/lc
const number = 10;   implicitly has an 'any' type.
console.log(_.last(    Try `npm i --save-dev @types/lodash` if it exists or add a new
|                      declaration (.d.ts) file containing `declare module 'lodash';` ts(7016)
                     Quick Fix... (Ctrl+.)
```

Figure: TypeScript recommending to install Lodash types from DefinitelyTyped

That's quite helpful. The warning itself is showing us how we can install the types for the library.

Follow the recommendation and run the following command in the terminal to install **lodash** types:

npm install @types/lodash

If you run that command, the warning in the **import** statement should go away automatically. But even more importantly, you should now see that the IDE is now complaining about the line of code where we're trying to pass a number to the **last** function. If you hover over the word **number**, you should see the error shown in the following screenshot:

```
import _ = require("lodash");
//const nums = [1, 2, 3];
//console.log(_.last(nums));
const number = 10;   Argument of type 'number' is not assignable to parameter of
                     type 'List<any>'. ts(2345)

                     const number: 10

                     View Problem (Alt+F8)   No quick fixes available
console.log(_.last(number));
```

Figure: IntelliSense revealing the correct type to use with the last function

From the preceding screenshot, it is clear that the **last** function won't take any argument of the **number** type. It accepts either an array or a list as an argument. So, let's imagine that we're building a real-world application, and we try to use the **last** function. If we were using vanilla JavaScript, we wouldn't realize our error until we, or even a user, encountered the error while running the program. However, by leveraging TypeScript and DefinitelyTyped, the program won't even compile if we attempt to use a function in the incorrect manner.

Development Workflow with DefinitelyTyped

Now that you've seen how to install and work with types, we will walk through a full development workflow so that you can observe the benefits of working with types. Without the integration of types into external libraries, we are forced to either have prior knowledge of the library or dig through the documentation to discover the proper usage.

However, with types, we're going to see how much more streamlined the process is when it comes to working with libraries such as **lodash**. Let's solve an exercise in the next section to get a proper understanding of this.

Exercise: Creating a Baseball Lineup Card Application

In this exercise, we'll create a baseball lineup application, wherein we have an array of player names that we'll be retrieving from an API, and then we have a constant variable in the application called **lineupOrder**. Our lineup card application needs to pair the names from the API with **lineupOrder**:

Open the Visual Studio Code editor.

Create a file named **lodash_newexamples.ts** and add the following code, wherein we have an array variable, **playerNames**, and a list, **lineupOrder**:

```
import _ = require("lodash");
const playerNames = [    "Springer",
    "Bregman",
    "Altuve",
    "Correa",
    "Brantley",
    "White",
    "Gonzalez",
    "Kemp",
    "Reddick" ];
const lineupOrder = [1, 2, 3, 4, 5, 6, 7, 8, 9];
```

This is a perfect situation for using the **zip** function from the Lodash library. Let's imagine that we've heard about the **zip** function, but aren't quite aware of how to use it yet. Start by writing the following code in the same file:

_.zip()

Once you've typed the preceding code, place the cursor in between the parentheses. You'll get some guidance on how to use the function straight from DefinitelyTyped, as shown in the following screenshot:

```
(method) _.LoDashStatic.zip<T1, T2>(arrays1: _.List<T1>,
arrays2: _.List<T2>): [T1, T2][] (+4 overloads)

Creates an array of grouped elements, the first of which contains the first
elements of the given arrays, the second of which contains the second
elements of the given arrays, and so on.

@param arrays — The arrays to process.

@return — Returns the new array of grouped elements.
_.zip
```

Figure: IntelliSense guidance on how to use the zip function in lodash

Let's now test it out. We know that the **zip** function takes in two arrays. So, let's provide it with the **playerNames** and **lineupOrder** arrays.

Add the following code to provide the **zip** function with two arrays, **playerNames** and **lineupOrder**:

console.log(_.zip(lineupOrder, playerNames));

If you run the preceding code, you'll see that the **zip** function does exactly what it said it would do. It groups the elements and returns the exact data structure that we needed. The rendered lineup card would look something like that shown in the following screenshot:

```
PS C:\Users\Mahesh\Documents\TypeScript_code\Chapter02_demo>
js

[
  [ 1, 'Springer' ],
  [ 2, 'Bregman' ],
  [ 3, 'Altuve' ],
  [ 4, 'Correa' ],
  [ 5, 'Brantley' ],
  [ 6, 'White' ],
  [ 7, 'Gonzalez' ],
  [ 8, 'Kemp' ],
  [ 9, 'Reddick' ]
]
```

Figure: Running the zip function properly from lodash

In completing this process, you can see how DefinitelyTyped allows you to extend types directly into third-party libraries so that you can get type guidance in your programs.

Activity: Building a Heat Map Declaration File

In this activity, you will build a TypeScript application named **heat map log system** for tracking baseball pitch data and ensuring data integrity. You will utilize a TypeScript declaration file to build the type system for the program. From that point, you will import the Lodash library and will add type checking to the program by implementing type definitions from DefinitelyTyped.

The steps are as follows:

Visit the following GitHub repository and download the activity project containing the specs and configuration elements:

Create a file called **heat_map_data.ts**.

Run the TypeScript compiler on the file and watch for changes.

Create a declaration file and define a module called **HeatMapTypes** and export the interface named **Pitcher**.

Define three attributes for the **Pitcher** module: **batterHotZones**, **pitcherHotZones**, and **coordinateMap**.

The data structures should be the same for all three attributes, **Array<Array<number>>**, but **coordinateMap** should be optional.

Then, import the declaration files into the **heat_map_data.ts** file. Then, create and export a **let** variable called **data** and assign it to the **Pitcher** type.

Add values that adhere to the declaration rules, ensuring that one of the nested arrays is identical in the **batterHotZones** and **pitcherHotZones** attributes.

Create a new function called **findMatch** that takes in both the **batterHotZones** and **pitcherHotZones** arrays and utilize the **lodash** function, **intersectionWith**, to return the identical nested array. You will need to import the Lodash library, which was installed when you initially ran **npm install**. Finally, store the value of **findMatch** in the **coordinateMap** attribute that was defined in the declaration file.

The expected output of this activity will be a nested array that looks similar to this:

[[10.2, -5], [3, 2]]

Conclusion: Mastering TypeScript Fundamentals and Declaration Files

TypeScript has emerged as a game-changing tool for modern web and application development, empowering developers to build reliable, scalable, and maintainable systems. It achieves this by introducing strong static typing, advanced features like interfaces and generics, and enhanced tooling that elevates the developer experience. The importance of TypeScript is magnified when working with large codebases, team projects, or integrating complex third-party libraries.

Declaration files, in particular, serve as a cornerstone for enabling TypeScript to seamlessly interface with JavaScript libraries and frameworks, thereby unifying the diverse world of JavaScript under a type-safe umbrella.

In this conclusion, we'll recap the foundational concepts of TypeScript, highlight the practical significance of declaration files, and explore how their combined use can transform your approach to software development.

The TypeScript Advantage: Enhancing JavaScript Development

1. Static Typing for Enhanced Reliability

JavaScript's dynamic nature, while flexible, is prone to runtime errors that can derail an application. TypeScript mitigates this by introducing static typing, allowing developers to:

Detect errors at compile time, preventing them from reaching production.

Write self-documenting code, as type annotations make the code more descriptive and easier to understand.
Enable better collaboration by clearly defining data structures, function signatures, and return types.

For instance, consider the simple example of a function:

```
function add(a: number, b: number): number {
  return a + b;
}
```

Here, TypeScript ensures that both parameters and the return value conform to their expected types, reducing ambiguity and runtime risks.

2. Scalability Through Structured Design

TypeScript's advanced features, such as interfaces, classes, and inheritance, empower developers to design complex, scalable systems. Interfaces define object shapes, ensuring uniformity across different parts of the application, while classes and inheritance provide a structured way to model real-world problems.

For example:

```
interface Vehicle {
  make: string;
  model: string;
  start(): void;
}

class Car implements Vehicle {
  constructor(public make: string, public model: string) {}
  start() {
    console.log(`Starting ${this.make} ${this.model}`);
  }
}

const myCar = new Car("Tesla", "Model 3");
myCar.start(); // Output: Starting Tesla Model 3
```

This structured approach enhances code readability and promotes reuse, making TypeScript a valuable tool for large-scale projects.

3. Generics for Code Reusability

Generics play a crucial role in enabling reusable, type-safe components, particularly in libraries and frameworks. They allow developers to define components that can work with any type, while still maintaining strict type-checking.

```
function identity<T>(value: T): T {
  return value;
}
console.log(identity<string>("TypeScript")); // Works with strings
console.log(identity<number>(42)); // Works with numbers
```

This flexibility is invaluable in scenarios where applications need to operate on various types without sacrificing safety or clarity.

4. Ecosystem and Tooling Support

TypeScript's ecosystem integrates seamlessly with popular editors like Visual Studio Code, offering features such as:

Autocompletion: Suggesting functions, variables, and type definitions.

Real-time error-checking: Highlighting errors as you code.

Refactoring tools: Simplifying complex operations, like renaming variables or functions across an entire project.

The tsconfig.json file provides developers with extensive configuration options, enabling fine-tuned control over how TypeScript compiles code. This ensures compatibility with various JavaScript environments, whether for frontend, backend, or hybrid applications.

Declaration Files: Bridging the Type Gap

Declaration files (.d.ts) are essential for extending TypeScript's benefits to JavaScript libraries and frameworks. They act as a contract, specifying the shape of modules, variables, and functions while leaving the actual implementation untouched.

This separation ensures that developers can:

Use JavaScript Libraries: By defining types for libraries lacking built-in TypeScript support.
Enable Tooling: Providing autocompletion and type-checking for third-party modules.
Improve Collaboration: Offering clear, type-safe documentation for shared code.

1. Writing Effective Declaration Files

When a library lacks type definitions, you can manually create a declaration file. This requires familiarity with the library's functionality and TypeScript's syntax. A simple example:

```
declare module "my-library" {
  export function greet(name: string): string;
}
```

These files ensure that developers can use greet with confidence, as the expected parameters and return types are explicitly defined.

2. Using @types Packages

Many popular JavaScript libraries offer prewritten type definitions through the @types scope on npm. These packages simplify integration and save development time:

```
npm install --save-dev @types/react
```
With this, TypeScript developers can leverage React's type definitions without manually writing them, enabling a smoother workflow.

3. Handling Global Declarations

In some cases, you may need to define types globally, especially when working with custom browser APIs or non-modular code. Declaration files allow you to extend global objects:

```
declare global {
  interface Window {
    myCustomProperty: string;
  }
}
```

This feature ensures that even non-standard extensions are type-safe, reducing the risk of integration errors.

The Synergy Between TypeScript and Declaration Files

By combining TypeScript fundamentals with declaration files, developers can create powerful, type-safe applications while leveraging the rich JavaScript ecosystem. Consider the following benefits:

Interoperability: Use any JavaScript library within TypeScript projects without losing type safety.

Maintainability: Clearly defined types make it easier to onboard new team members or revisit old code.

Tooling and Documentation: Declaration files provide an additional layer of clarity, serving as both a development aid and documentation.

For example, integrating a JavaScript analytics library into a TypeScript project becomes seamless with declaration files:

```
declare module "analytics-lib" {
  export function trackEvent(eventName: string, properties: Record<string, unknown>): void;
}
```

This ensures that all interactions with the library conform to expected types, reducing errors and improving code quality.

Best Practices for TypeScript and Declaration Files

Leverage Strict Mode: Always enable the strict compiler option in tsconfig.json for maximum type safety.

Use Declaration Files Wisely: Prefer official @types packages when available. For custom declarations, thoroughly test the files in your project.

Keep Types Up-to-Date: Regularly update declaration files as libraries evolve to avoid mismatches.

Document Your Code: Use JSDoc comments in conjunction with type annotations for clearer documentation.

Embrace Modern Features: Utilize advanced TypeScript features like conditional types and mapped types to enhance type safety.

Future of TypeScript and Declaration Files

The adoption of TypeScript continues to grow, with major frameworks like Angular, React, and Vue embracing it as a first-class citizen. As the JavaScript ecosystem evolves, TypeScript will remain a key player in ensuring that applications are robust, scalable, and maintainable. Declaration files will continue to bridge the gap between JavaScript and TypeScript, enabling seamless integration of legacy code and third-party libraries.

Emerging trends, such as improved type inference, enhanced tooling, and community-driven innovations, will further strengthen TypeScript's position as a cornerstone of modern software development.

Final Thoughts

TypeScript represents a significant step forward for developers, combining the flexibility of JavaScript with the rigor of static typing. Declaration files enhance this experience by extending TypeScript's capabilities to encompass the entire JavaScript ecosystem. Together, they empower developers to build high-quality applications with fewer errors, better documentation, and improved scalability.

Mastering TypeScript fundamentals and declaration files is an investment in writing cleaner, safer, and more efficient code. Whether you're a frontend developer integrating a JavaScript library, a backend engineer scaling a Node.js application, or a full-stack developer building cross-platform solutions, TypeScript and declaration files will remain invaluable tools in your arsenal. As the technology landscape evolves, adopting and leveraging these tools will keep you at the forefront of modern software development.

3. Type System and Type Annotations

Introduction

TypeScript, developed by Microsoft, is a strongly-typed superset of JavaScript that enhances developer productivity by introducing a robust **type system**. It allows developers to catch errors at compile time, ensures code predictability, and makes large-scale applications easier to maintain. Central to TypeScript's capabilities are its **type system** and **type annotations**, which form the foundation of its type-checking mechanism.

This comprehensive introduction explores TypeScript's type system, its benefits, and the role of type annotations, diving into their features, syntax, use cases, and best practices.

1. Understanding TypeScript's Type System

The type system in TypeScript provides a layer of abstraction over JavaScript, offering **static typing**. Unlike JavaScript, which is dynamically typed, TypeScript lets developers define types explicitly or rely on its type inference mechanism.

1.1 Static vs. Dynamic Typing

Static Typing: Types are checked at compile time. Errors such as passing incorrect argument types are caught before runtime.

Dynamic Typing: Types are determined at runtime, which can lead to runtime errors that are harder to debug.

1.2 Benefits of TypeScript's Type System

Error Prevention: Compile-time checks reduce the likelihood of runtime errors.

Enhanced Developer Experience: Integrated development environments (IDEs) with TypeScript support offer code completion, refactoring tools, and error diagnostics.

Improved Code Documentation: Explicit types serve as self-documenting code, making it easier for teams to understand and maintain codebases.

Scalability: In large projects, a robust type system prevents type-related bugs and ensures consistency.

1.3 TypeScript's Typing Model

TypeScript employs a **structural type system**, sometimes referred to as **duck typing**:

Objects are compatible if they have the same structure, regardless of explicit type definitions. This approach contrasts with **nominal typing**, where compatibility is determined by explicit declarations.

2. Type Annotations: The Core of TypeScript's Type System

Type annotations are the mechanism by which developers explicitly specify types for variables, functions, and objects in TypeScript. They make the codebase more predictable and easier to debug.

2.1 Syntax of Type Annotations

Type annotations use a colon (:) followed by the type. For example:

```
let age: number = 25;
let name: string = "John";
```

2.2 Key Areas for Type Annotations

2.2.1 Variables

You can annotate variables to specify their types:

```
let isActive: boolean = true;
let score: number = 95.5;
```

2.2.2 Function Parameters and Return Types

Functions can have annotated parameters and explicitly defined return types:

```
function add(a: number, b: number): number {
    return a + b;
}
```

2.2.3 Objects

Type annotations for objects define the shape and types of their properties:

```
let person: {
name: string;
age: number
} = {
name: "Alice", age: 30
};
```

2.2.4 Arrays

Arrays can be annotated to specify their element types:

```
let numbers: number[] = [1, 2, 3];
let strings: Array<string> = ["one", "two", "three"];
```

2.2.5 Tuples

Tuples are fixed-length arrays with specified types for each element:

```
let tuple: [string, number] = ["hello", 42];
```

2.2.6 Enums

Enums provide a way to define a set of named constants:

```
enum Status {
    Active,
    Inactive,
    Pending
}
let currentStatus: Status = Status.Active;
```

2.2.7 Type Aliases

Aliases allow reusability and readability in type definitions:

```
type User = { name: string;
age: number };
let user: User = { name: "Bob", age: 25 };
```

3. Advanced Features of TypeScript's Type System

3.1 Union and Intersection Types

Union Types: Variables can hold multiple types:

```
let id: number | string = 123; // can be a number or string
```

Intersection Types: Combines multiple types into one:

```
type Admin = { privileges: string[] };
type Employee = { name: string };
type AdminEmployee = Admin & Employee;
let admin: AdminEmployee = { name: "Eve", privileges: ["create-server"] };
```

3.2 Literal Types

Literal types restrict variables to specific values:

```
let status: "success" | "failure" | "pending";
status = "success";
```

3.3 Type Inference

TypeScript infers types when explicit annotations are absent:

```
let inferredString = "Hello"; // TypeScript infers `string`
```
While inference simplifies code, annotations are recommended for clarity and self-documentation.

3.4 Optional and Default Parameters

Optional parameters use ?, and default values are provided after =:

```
function greet(name?: string): string {
   return name ? `Hello, ${name}`: "Hello, world!";
}
```

3.5 Null and Undefined

By default, null and undefined are part of every type unless strict null checks are enabled:

```
let nullable: string | null = null;
```

3.6 Generics

Generics enable reusable components that work with multiple types:

```
function identity<T>(arg: T): T {
   return arg;
}
let output = identity<number>(42);
```

3.7 Interfaces

Interfaces define the structure of an object:

```
interface User {
   name: string;
   age: number;
}
let user: User = {name: "Sam", age: 32};
```

Interfaces can also describe functions, arrays, and classes.

4. Best Practices for Type Annotations

Leverage Type Inference When Appropriate: Avoid redundant annotations:

```
let count = 5; // No need to write `let count: number = 5;`
```
Use Readable and Reusable Types: Use type aliases or interfaces for complex structures.
Enable Strict Mode: Use strict: true in tsconfig.json to enforce strict typing rules.
Document APIs with Types: Provide clear type annotations for public APIs.
Avoid any Type: The any type disables type checking. Use it sparingly:
```
let data: any; // Avoid this when possible
```
Embrace Union and Intersection Types: Use them to represent flexible and combined types.

5. TypeScript 2024: What's New in the Type System?

With TypeScript 2024, several enhancements in type system capabilities have been introduced:

Enhanced Type Narrowing: Improved ability to infer and narrow down types in complex conditions.
Variadic Tuple Types: Simplify operations on tuples with varying lengths.
Template Literal Types: Expanded use cases for dynamic string type generation.

Example of variadic tuples:

```
type Tuple = [string, ...number[]];
let example: Tuple = ["age", 25, 30, 35];
```

6. Comparison with Other Type Systems

TypeScript's type system stands out due to its flexibility and compatibility with JavaScript. Compared to other languages:

Flow: TypeScript has better IDE integration and community support.
Java: TypeScript's structural typing contrasts with Java's nominal typing.

The Type System
What's in a Type?

A "type" is a description of what a JavaScript value shape might be. By shape I mean how a value looks and feels: its properties and methods, and what the built-in typeof operator would describe it as. The most basic types in TypeScript correspond to the seven basic primitives in JavaScript:

bigint: 0n, 2n, -4n, … **boolean**: true or false **null**

number: 0, 2, -4, … **string**: "", "Hi!", `"□롽, …

symbol: Symbol(), Symbol("hi"), … **undefined**
For example, when you create a variable: **let** singer = "Aretha";
TypeScript can figure out, or infer, that the singer variable is of type string.

For each of these values, TypeScript understands the type of the value to be one of the seven basic primitives:

```
1337n; // bigint
true; // Boolean
 null; // null
1337; // number
"Louise"; // string
Symbol("Franklin"); // Symbol
undefined; // undefined
```

TypeScript is also smart enough to figure out the type of a variable whose starting value is computed. In this example, TypeScript knows that the ternary expression always results in a string, so the bestSong value is a string:

```
let bestSong = Math.random() > 0.5 ? "Chain of Fools": "Respect";
```

Type Inferences in Detail

At its core, TypeScript's type system works by:

Reading in your code and understanding all the types and values in existence
For each object, seeing what type its initial declaration indicates it may contain

For each object, seeing all ways it's used later on
Complaining to the user if an object's usage doesn't match with its type
Let's walk through that type inference system in detail.

Take the following snippet, in which TypeScript is emitting a type error about a member variable being erroneously called as a function:

```
let firstName = "Cleopatra";
firstName.length(); // ~~~~~ // This expression is not callable.
//   Type 'Number' has no call signatures
```

TypeScript came to that complaint by, in order:

Reading in the code and understanding there to be one object: firstName
Concluding that firstName is of type string its initial value is a string, "Cleopatra"
Seeing that the code is trying to access a .length member of firstName and call it like a function
Complaining that the .length member of a string is a number, not a function (it can't be called like a function)

Understanding TypeScript's type inference is an important skill for understanding TypeScript code. Code snippets in this chapter and through the rest of this book will display more and more complex types that TypeScript will be able to infer from code.

Kinds of Errors

While writing TypeScript, the two kinds of "errors" you'll come across most frequently are:

- **Syntax**: blocking TypeScript from being converted to JavaScript.
- **Type**: something mismatched has been detected by the type checker.

It's useful to be able to understand the differences between the two.

Syntax Errors

Syntax errors are when TypeScript detects incorrect syntax that it cannot understand as code. These block TypeScript from being able to properly generate output JavaScript from your file. Depending on the tooling and settings you're using to convert your TypeScript code to JavaScript, you might to still get some kind of JavaScript output. If you do, it likely won't look like what you expect.

This input TypeScript has a syntax error for an unexpected let: **let let** wat;

Its compiled output in TypeScript, depending on the language version, may look something like:

let let, wat;

Type Errors

Type errors occur when your syntax is valid but the TypeScript type checker has detected an error with the program's types. These do not block TypeScript syntax from being converted to JavaScript. They do, however, often indicate something will crash or behave unexpectedly if your code is allowed to run.

You saw this earlier with the console.blub example, where it is syntactically valid code but TypeScript can detect it will likely crash when run:
console.blub("Hello world!");

Some projects are configured to block running code during development until all TypeScript type errors -not just syntax- are fixed. Many developers, myself included, generally find this to be annoying and unnecessary. Most projects have a way to disable it, such as with the tsconfig.json file covered.

Assignability

TypeScript reads variables' initial values to determine what type those variables are allowed to be. If it later sees an assignment of a new value to that variable, it will check if that assignment value's type is the same as the variable's.

TypeScript would be fine with later assigning a different value of the same type to a variable. If a variable is, say, initially a string value, later assigning it another string would be fine:

let firstName = "Carole";
firstName = "Louise";

When a variable is declared with an initial value, it's considered to be of that initial value's type — and must always be assigned values of that type. If TypeScript sees an assignment of a different type, it will give us type error. We couldn't, say, initially declare a variable with a string value and then later on put in a number:

let firstName = "King";
firstName = 1337; // Error: Type 'number' is not assignable to type 'string'.

TypeScript's checking of whether a value is allowed to be provided to a function call or variable is called
"assignability": whether that value is assignable to the location it's passed to. This will be an important term in later chapters as we compare more complex objects.

Type Annotations

Sometimes a variable doesn't have an initial value for TypeScript to read. TypeScript won't attempt to figure out what value those variables are from later usage. It'll consider them to be implicitly the any type: a type indicating that it could be anything in the world.

let rocker;
rocker = "Joan Jett";

Allowing variables to be of type any defeats the purpose of TypeScript's type checking! TypeScript works best when it knows what types your values are meant to be. Most of TypeScript's type checking can't be applied to any typed values because they don't have known types to be checked.

Although TypeScript can still emit JavaScript code despite an implicit any, it will yell at you about them in the form of type errors. Chapter ?? will cover how to configure TypeScript's implicit any complaints. Instead, TypeScript provides a syntax for declaring the type of a variable, using what's called a type annotation. A type annotation is placed after the name of a variable and includes a colon followed by the name of a type.

```
let rocker: string;
rocker = "Joan Jett";
```

These type annotations are unique to TypeScript. If you run tsc to compile TypeScript source code to JavaScript, they'll be erased.

```
For example:
// output .js file
let rocker;
rocker = "Joan Jett";
```

TypeScript contains an assortment of new pieces of syntax such as these type annotations that exist only in the type system. Nothing that exists only in the type system gets copied over into emitted JavaScript.

Unnecessary Type Annotations

Type annotations allow us to provide information to TypeScript that it wouldn't have been able to glean on its own. You could use them on variables that have immediately inferable types, but you wouldn't be telling TypeScript anything it doesn't already know:

```
let firstName: string = "Tina"; // ~~~~~~~ Does not change the type system...
```

If you do add a type annotation to a variable with an initial value, TypeScript will check that it matches the type of the variable's value.

The following firstName is declared to be of type string but its initializer is the number 42, which is TypeScript sees as an incompatibility:

```
let firstName: string = 42; // ~~~~~~~~~ // Error: Type 'number' is not assignable to type 'string'.
```

Most developers -myself included- generally prefer not to add type annotations in places where they don't change anything. Having to manually write out type annotations can be cumbersome — especially when they change, and for the complex types I'll show you later in this book.

Type Shapes

TypeScript doesn't only check that the values assigned to variables match their original types: it also knows what member properties should exist on objects. If you attempt to access a property of a variable, TypeScript will make sure that property is known to exist on that variable's type.

Suppose we declare a rapper variable of type string. Later on, when we use that string variable, operations that TypeScript knows work on strings are allowed:

```
let rapper = "Queen Latifah";
rapper.length; // ok
```

Operations that TypeScript doesn't know to work on strings will not be allowed:

rapper.asdfqwerty; // ~~~~~~~~~~ // Property 'asdfqwerty' does not exist on type 'string'.

Types can also be more advanced shapes, most notably complex objects. In the following snippet, TypeScript knows the birthNames object doesn't have a rihanna key and complains:

```
let cher = { firstName: "Cherilyn",   lastName: "Sarkisian", };
cher.middleName; //   ~~~~~~~~~~
//   Property 'middleName' does not exist on type //   '{ firstName: string; lastName: string; }'.
```

Basic Type Annotations

In this chapter, we are going to dive straight in and start looking at the basic types that TypeScript supports. We looked at some basic JavaScript examples in the last chapter, but from this point on, we'll be working solely with TypeScript files.

The aim of this chapter is to give a thorough introduction to the use of some of the most fundamental aspects of TypeScript. This will give you a solid foundation for moving forward in your learning and which subsequent chapters will build upon.

All the code examples in this chapter have corresponding TypeScript files in the downloadable companion content for this book. For example, any example code shown in the BigInt section can be found in a folder called at the root of the project, in a file called **bigint.ts**, while examples in the Union Types section will be found in the folder in a file called **union.ts**.

These files are provided as a reference aid, and I would encourage you to actively try out all of the examples in an editor in order to get a good feel for TypeScript development.

Primitive types

TypeScript supports all of the same primitives that JavaScript itself supports, so variables, function parameters, and class members can be described as being of one of these fundamental types:

bigint boolean number null string symbol • undefined

Unlike JavaScript, TypeScript has primitive types as well as primitive values. Primitive values behave the same way in TypeScript as they do in JavaScript, but for each primitive value in TypeScript, there is a corresponding primitive type.

Let's take a quick look at each of these different types in turn.

BigInt

The **bigint** type is used to create and work with very large or very small numbers that are considered unsafe to use as regular integers in JavaScript due to the limitations of JavaScript's numerical support. To specify that a variable is of the type **bigint**, we add a colon after the variable's identifier on the left-hand side of the declaration followed by the type **bigint**:

```
let bignum: bigint = BigInt(0);
```

The variable **bignum** will now have the type **bigint** associated with it. Note that we use the lowercase type **bigint** as opposed to the Camel Cased **BigInt**. We should always ensure that we use the lowercase versions of all of the primitive types when adding type annotations because the Camel Cased versions are the constructors.

Note that the **bigint** type is only available in environments supporting ECMAScript 2020 or later and will produce errors in TypeScript files when the target option in the **tsconfig.json** file is set to a lower version than es2020.

If we now try to do something illegal with the **bignum** variable, something prohibited by JavaScript itself, like multiplying it with a number, we'll see an error for it right there in the editor, before we even try to compile the file:
const result = bignum * 1;

If we hover the mouse pointer over the left-hand part of the above expression, we'll see a warning that:

Operator * cannot be applied to types 'bigint' and 'number'.

If we do try to compile the file, we'll see the same errors in the terminal output, but note that the compiler will still compile the file into JavaScript and emit it to the output directory by default.
It's very common for projects to disable this default behavior of still compiling invalid TypeScript into JavaScript failing the compilation when the TypeScript is invalid is one of the best tools, we have for creating bug-free applications. So, for production applications, it is almost always recommended to configure this behaviour.

To fail the compiler when the TypeScript contains errors, we can enable the **noEmitOnError** option in the **tsconfig.json** file. Once this option has been enabled, output files will no longer be emitted if any TypeScript file inside the project contains errors, although we can still compile individual files that do not contain errors.

We'll be looking at the compiler and how to use it in much more detail later in the book; so, don't worry too much about it at this point.

Boolean

As in JavaScript, the **boolean** type in TypeScript is a primitive that may have only one of the two values **true** or **false**. We use the same colon followed by type syntax when declaring any of the primitive types including Booleans:

let isEnabled: boolean = true;

In this format, we are free to change the value to **false** at some point later in our program, and even back again to **true** later on if we choose. Note that as well as supplying the type **boolean**, we can also specify that the type should be one of the literal values **true** or **false**:

let legacySupport: false = false;

The variable **legacySupport** now has the immutable value of **false**, and this value cannot be changed to **true** later on in the application, even though we declared the variable using let as opposed to **const**. Aside from the explicit literal **true** and **false** types described above, Booleans in TypeScript work exactly the same way as they do in regular JavaScript, and there should be no surprises for anyone with anything but the most basic of JavaScript experience.

Number

In TypeScript - exactly as in JavaScript - numbers may be either integer or floating-point values and have a "safe" range of -253 to +235 – anything outside of this range needs to be used with **bigint** instead. Although in fairness, it does represent quite a wide range of values and bigint is a relatively recent addition to the ECMAScipt specification.

To specify a value of the type **number**, we use the same format as with other primitive types – a colon, followed by the type in lowercase: let num: number;

In this case, the variable **num** is declared but not initialized with the type **number**. The usual JavaScript variable declaration rules apply when using TypeScript, so only **const** values must be initialized with a value at declaration time. This is true for all variable declarations in TypeScript.

One common problem in JavaScript is the misuse of **NaN** in comparisons. **NaN** is a special numerical value that can be the result of performing impossible numerical operations, like dividing by zero, or trying to multiply a string.

Because nothing is equal to **NaN**, not even **NaN** itself, comparing a value to **NaN** directly will always return **false**. As this is such a common mistake, TypeScript will automatically warn against direct comparisons to **NaN** with an error and advise to use the **Number.isNaN** method instead:

```
This condition will always return 'false'. ts(2845)

number.ts(6, 5): Did you mean 'Number.isNaN(num)'?

if (num === NaN) {
    // ...
}
```

Figure: Condition will always return false error in Visual Studio Code

Null

In JavaScript, everything is either a primitive, or an object, and just like in JavaScript, in TypeScript the value **null** is used to signify that an object explicitly does not exist, or intentionally has no value.
For example, imagine that a user logged into our application is represented using an object. If the user logs out, we can set their user object to **null** to signify that it intentionally no longer exists.

How **null** is treated in TypeScript depends on the configuration in use, although by default the strictest level of type-checking for **null** (and **undefined**) is enabled when creating a new project using the TypeScript compiler; so, both **null** (and **undefined**) are fully type-checked by default when generating a **tsconfig.json** file with the compiler.

Syntactically, we can specify that a value has the type **null** in exactly the same format as we have with other primitives:

let nothing: null = null;

This is perfectly valid TypeScript, however, doing this is incredibly unhelpful in almost all situations because, with the **strictNullChecks** configuration enabled, we will not be able to change the value of the variable to anything else later on, so the value is effectively locked to **null** forever.

For example:

```
let nothing: null = null;
// later…
nothing = 1; // Type '1' is not assignable to type 'null'
```

We will see an error in our editor here that '1' cannot be assigned to 'null'. Due to this, we will almost never see the **null** type used in this way in a variable declaration.

Similarly, if we specify a variable is of one particular type, say a **string**, we cannot then set this value to **null** later on – in that case, we will see a similar message that null cannot be assigned to a string.

In light of these facts, the **null** type is much more commonly used as part of a union type to say that a value may be, for example, a number or the value **null**. We'll be looking at union types in much more detail later in this chapter.

String

Strings in TypeScript have no special meaning or functionality beyond that found in JavaScript. We can denote that a value is of the type **string** in the same way as we can with other primitive types:

```
let greeting: string = 'Hello';
```

The same guideline of avoiding such overly-verbose declarations apply also to strings; commonly we would denote the types of class members or parameters using this format, but rarely simple variable declarations like this.

It is common in ESLint to have a lint rule that forbids unnecessary type declarations such as in the above example.

Symbol

The symbol primitive was added to JavaScript in the ES2015/ES6 release, and as such, must be used with the target option of the **tsconfig.json** file set to es2015 or above.

TypeScript gives us both a primitive type of **symbol**, and a sub-type of this type called **unique symbol**. Both can be used in an expected way:

```
let aSym: symbol = Symbol();
const otherSym: unique symbol = Symbol();
```

The difference between them is that **unique symbol** may only be used with **const** declarations as opposed to **var** or **let**, while **symbol** can be used with **const**, **var** or **let** declarations.

A symbol is a globally unique primitive value, so strict comparisons between them will always return **false**, and if we try to compare two values annotated with **unique symbol**, then we will see an error that there is no overlap between the two values.

Symbols are often used to create unique keys for objects, like this:

```
const unique = Symbol();
const obj = { [unique]: 'unique value' };
```

This offers a form of weak information hiding, as the **unique value** string is only accessible using the reference to the symbol, stored in the **unique** variable. Symbol-keyed properties are not revealed in for loops so without a reference to the symbol, the value of the property cannot be read.

Undefined

Similar to **null**, **undefined** is a special primitive in JavaScript for a variable that exists but has not been assigned a value, or for the value of an object property that has not been defined. Of course, **undefined** is also a value itself and can be directly set as the value of a variable, object property, or class member.

TypeScript has a corresponding **undefined** type that technically could be used as a type annotation for a variable declaration:
```
let notYet: undefined = undefined;
```

Although legal code, we would probably not want to do this for the simple fact that now the **notYet** variable can only ever contain the value **undefined**. Like the **null** type, this is a primitive type that we will rarely use ourselves directly outside of union types.

Also like the **null** type, how **undefined** is treated in TypeScript is also determined by whether either the **strict** or **strictNullChecks** configuration options are enabled, these are often handled in the same way by TypeScript.

With either of these configuration options enabled, TypeScript will strictly require us to check whether something is **undefined** before we attempt to access any of its properties or methods.

We'll look at this topic in more detail later in this chapter when we discuss type assertions.

The any type

TypeScript adds a special type, that is not a part of JavaScript at all, called **any**; this type means that the value in question could literally be of any supported type, with the implication that the value may be called like a function, or have its properties read like an object, or treated like any primitive.

Values of this type may be used in TypeScript in any way that is legal in JavaScript.

We can set values to this type ourselves manually, just like any of the primitive types we have already looked at:
```
let anything: any = 'still any';
```

Our type annotation will override TypeScript's inference mechanism. So, in this case, the variable **anything** will be of type **any**, and we will have no restrictions on the types of values that may be assigned to the variable at any future point, or how the value is used later in the code.

When we use the **any** type, we basically tell the compiler not to do any further type-checking on this value at all. We will use the **any** type in our applications from time to time. There are some valid use cases for it, including simply wishing to disable type-checking on a particularly complex object in order to avoid having to write an overly descriptive type for it.

The **any** type is also used by TypeScript itself, and values may be marked as **any** when TypeScript is unable to infer what their type should be.
Consider the following code:

```
function len(a) {
return a.length;
}
let test = 'a'; len(test);
```

We declare a simple function called **len**, which accepts a single argument called **a** and returns the **length** property of this argument. Immediately we should see some error underlining in the editor, and when we hover the mouse pointer over it, we should see the following error description:

Parameter 'a' implicitly has an 'any' type.

This is an error because there is no way for TypeScript to correctly infer what the parameter's type is and so it can't check that the value is being used correctly – the value may not even have a **length** property. When we use **any** explicitly, we should know exactly which type a value is and are hopefully using it in a limited and controlled way, the implications of which we fully understand.

But when TypeScript implicitly treats a value as **any**, it needs to warn us that no type-checking will occur on this value at all from this point on because we haven't explicitly told it not to check this value's type by intentionally setting it to the **any** type. We may therefore use the value incorrectly and TypeScript wouldn't be able to warn us, which is sort of the whole point of TypeScript.

Even though we call the function with a string immediately after declaring it, TypeScript still cannot infer that the parameter's type will always be **string**, even though we pass it a string on the next line, so we may not be able to return its **length** property. As the function may not be able to return the object's **length** property, it will also have its return type set to **any**.

We'll be looking at functions in much more detail later in the book, including how to annotate them to let TypeScript know what types the function should accept as arguments and return.

NOTE: We are able to switch off the error for the implicit any in our code if we wish to use the tsconfig.json configuration file by disabling either the strict or noImplicitAny options, depending on which of them is enabled.

You should also note that if we declare a variable without initializing it, TypeScript will infer the type **any** for that variable too, which effectively turns off type-checking in the editor for the variable anywhere:

```
let later;
```

Even if we set the value of the **later** variable to, say, a string value, the editor will continue to see the variable as having the type **any**:

```
let later;

┌──────────────────────┐
│ let later: any       │
└──────────────────────┘

later = 'test';
```

Figure: Inferred any type

In this case, we should specifically add the type of the **later** variable with a type annotation, as a **string** in this example, to avoid this.

The **any** type can be useful if we are converting JavaScript to TypeScript and can't, or don't want to, specify all of the type information immediately – setting types to **any** can be a useful interim measure in this case, but usages of it should be temporary and be replaced with proper types as soon as possible to gain the maximum benefit from using TypeScript.

The unknown type

Another special TypeScript type that is not familiar to us already from JavaScript is the **unknown** type. This can be thought of as a kind of polar opposite to **any**; whereas the **any** type allows us to do anything at all with a value, such as assign to it, invoke methods on it, or read its properties, the **unknown** type restricts the operations we can do on it.

We can specify a value that has an **unknown** type using a colon as expected:
let notKnown: unknown;

At this point, the only thing we can do is assign a primitive value to the **notKnown** variable. Even if we assign an object to the variable and give it a property and corresponding value, like this:
notKnown = { test: 'test' };

Typescript still won't let us access the **test** property due to it being of the type **unknown**. Similarly, if we assign a function as the value of the **notKnown** variable, like this:
notKnown = () => 'test';

Then, TypeScript will not let us invoke the variable as a function. Additionally, we may assign an array to a variable with the type **unknown**:
notKnown = [1, 2, 3];

But in this case, we won't be able to access any of the elements inside it.

We are able to assign any type of primitive value to it, however, and simple equality comparisons will work as expected:

notKnown = 'test'; if (notKnown === 'test') {
console.log('we will see this log message'); }

The **unknown** type is considered safer to use than the **any** type because it prevents us from using values in ways that were not intended for them to be used. Conversely, the **any** type does nothing to prevent us from using a value entirely incorrectly, which could cause our application to fail.

The never type

One more TypeScript type without a corresponding JavaScript equivalent is the **never** type. This type represents a state that should never exist and may be inferred by TypeScript in certain situations, such as for the return value of a function that never stops executing, in the case that the function throws an error, for example.

It is also commonly used with **switch** statements to ensure that the case checking carried out by the switch is exhaustive. A switch statement is exhaustive if it covers all possible cases.

We can use the **never** type to make sure that a **switch** expression handles all of the types in a union type with case statements, and it is commonly used as the **return** type of a function invoked in the **switch** statement's default clause. We'll see a full example of this later in the book once we have finished covering the basics of TypeScript.

The as operator

So far, we have added all of our type information using a colon followed by the type that we want to use, like this:
let myVar: string;

This is the most common way of specifying type information when using TypeScript, but it's not the only way; we can also use the **as** operator as a form of type-casting to specify that a value is of a particular type:

let anotherVar = 'another' as string;

This time, the annotation appears on the right-hand side of the expression, following the value rather than the variable declaration. We use the **as** keyword followed by the type that we want to cast the value to. This is known as a **type-assertion** – we are specifically asserting to TypeScript what the type of this value is.

Although valid, the previous example is something we would almost never see in actual day-to-day TypeScript. Instead, we would most likely use the **as** operator to down-cast from a less-specific to a more-specific type, or as a compound cast where we cast a value from one type immediately to another type. Let's see what both of these techniques look like in real code.

Down-casting

Down-casting is a useful technique where we have an object of a general type, and we want to cast it down to a more specific type in order to use a property that only specific sub-classes of that object have.

A good example is when working with an event object inside a handler method attached to a DOM element.

Consider the following code:

```
function clickHandler(event: Event) {
const childElement = event.target.querySelector('#child');
}
```

The event parameter of the **clickHandler** function above will be of the built-in type **Event**.

The **Event** object passed to handler functions by browsers will have a **target** property, and this property will be a reference to the HTML element that the handler is attached to, and as it is an element, it will have a **querySelector** method.

However, the **event.target** has its own special type, which is **EventTarget**, and the declaration of this type does not include a **querySelector** method - this method is found on the **HTMLElement** type instead. The preceding code will produce the following TypeScript error:

Property 'querySelector' does not exist on type 'EventTarget'.

To tell TypeScript that the **event.target** will actually be a HTML element, and therefore will have a **querySelector** method, we can down-cast the property to the desired sub-type:

const childElement = (event.target as HTMLElement).querySelector('#child');

This is allowed because in JavaScript **HTMLElement** is a subclass of **EventTarget**, and correspondingly, in TypeScript the **HTMLElement** type is a sub-type of the **EventTarget** type.

In this case, we also need to wrap the part of the expression where we use the **as** operator in parentheses. Now, the TypeScript compiler will know our intentions and the error will disappear.

As well as down-casting, the opposite of this is up-casting, where a type is broadened from a more specific type to a less specific type. Up-casting is less commonly used than down-casting, but may still be required occasionally.

Compound casting

Another type-casting technique using the **as** operator is called compound casting, or double assertion; this is where we use multiple **as** operators in a single statement and is usually used in conjunction with the **unknown** type to create objects that have some but not all of the required properties of another type. As an example, imagine that we want to use a fake **Event** object in a unit test to test the **clickHandler** function from the previous example. We will have to pass this function a parameter of the type **Event** when we call it. Let's try to create one with a **target** property, (otherwise, the function will simply return immediately, and we won't be able to test it):

```
const testEvent: Event = { target: document.createElement('div') };
```

Immediately, we should see an error in the editor, with TypeScript complaining that the **testEvent** object is missing many properties that belong to objects of the type **Event**.

There are 21 properties in total missing from our fake event object, it would be extremely arduous to create them all manually, especially when we are really only interested in testing the **target** property anyway.

To fix this situation, we can use a compound cast that first casts our object to the special **unknown** type, and then to the desired type, **Event** in this case:

```
const testEvent = { target: document.createElement('div') } as unknown as Event;
```

Now, the error should be gone. In this case, TypeScript will treat the **testEvent** object as if it really were an object of the **Event** type and simply ignores the missing properties.

This is safer than simply casting our **testEvent** object to the **any** type, which would also solve our problem, but would leave us open to, for example, trying to invoke methods that real **Event** objects don't have. In our case, if we try to call a method that **Event** objects don't have, TypeScript will produce an error:

```
testEvent.banana(); // Property 'banana' does not exist on 'Event'
```

If we had used the **any** type instead, that error would not appear and TypeScript would allow the code to run and crash our application.

Note that TypeScript will prevent us from making an impossible assertion: let boolean = 1 as boolean; In this case, TypeScript will show the following error message in the editor:

```
Conversion of type 'number' to type 'boolean'
may be a mistake because neither type
sufficiently overlaps with the other. If this
was intentional, convert the expression to
'unknown' first. ts(2352)
let boolean = 1 as boolean;
```

Figure: Type conversion error on Visual Studio Code

Helpfully, TypeScript hints at the end of the error message to use compound casting to first cast the value to the **unknown** type, before casting it to the desired type.

Older type-casting syntax

There is also an older form of type-casting in TypeScript which uses a different syntax entirely from the **as** operator. This form uses angle brackets to surround the type, and like the **as** operator, appears on the right-hand side of assignment expressions, although in this format, it precedes the value being cast:

```
let myNum = <number>1;
```

This expression will set the type of the **myNum** variable to the type **number** in exactly the same way that using the **as** operator would. This syntax is now deprecated since TypeScript added support for TSX files. TSX is TypeScript for JSX, and JSX is an embeddable XML syntax that compiles to JavaScript, and which is commonly used with the popular React framework. JSX syntax looks like a combination of

JavaScript and HTML and this is the reason that the older angle-bracket syntax for type-casting cannot be used – TSX would interpret it as an HTML element instead of a type assertion.

This older type-casting could be used in plain TypeScript files, or when using frameworks that don't use JSX, such as Angular, but as this syntax is now deprecated, it is recommended to use the **as** operator always instead, regardless of whether JSX/TSX is actually in use.

Union types

A union type in TypeScript is where a value may be one of a predefined set of distinct types – we use it to tell the compiler that a value might be this type or it might be that type. The syntax is straight-forward – we separate each of the types in our union with the pipe character:

let either: string | number = 1;
Here, we're saying that the **either** variable may be of the type **string** or the type **number**, and then initializing it with the numerical value 1.

Note that we could also initialize it with a string, but if we try to set it to any other type, either now during initialization, or later in our application, TypeScript will show us an error, like this:

```
either = true;
Type 'boolean' is not assignable to type
'string | number'. ts(2322)

let either: string | number
```

Figure: Type not assignable to type error in Visual Studio Code

When working with the **either** variable, or any other union type, we will only be able to call methods or access properties that are available to all members of the union – so strings or numbers in this case. There is very little overlap between these two types, so we will need to know more about which type it actually is in order to do something useful with it.

Using the example above, we could have a value that might be of the type **string** if it's coming from the value of an HTML input element, or it could be of the type **number** if it's coming from somewhere else in our application.

Let's say we have a function that is passed a value as either a **string** or a **number**:

```
function getRefNumber(refNumber: string | number) {
if (typeof refNumber === 'string') {
refNumber = parseInt(refNumber, 10);
}
return refNumber;
}
```

We declare a function called **getRefNumber** that is passed a parameter called **refNumber**, and this parameter is a union of the types **string** and **number**. Inside the function, we need to check what the **typeof** operator reports the type of the parameter to be, so we check to see if it's **string**. If it is, we can safely work with it as if the parameter had been defined with only the **string** type. This is known as a type guard – we'll be looking at these in more detail later in the book.

In this example, we just convert the value to a number using the **parseInt** method, and from this point on inside the function, we know that **refNumber** will always be of the type **number**. Here, we just return the number, but we could do any other numerical operations on that value that we wanted to in a real-world application.

This process of determining the actual type from a union of types is known as **narrowing**, and this is another topic we'll be looking at in much greater detail later in the book.
There are no restrictions on the number of types that we can include in a union type, we just need to separate each type in the union with the pipe symbol.

Union types are flexible and allow us to work with values that could logically be one of several different types, possibly depending on the context in which the value is used. But using them also means that we ourselves need to be sure of exactly which type it actually is when we want to work with it.

Literal types

A literal type is a primitive sub-type that takes a specific value; we saw this briefly earlier when we looked at the Boolean type, and in that case, the literal sub-type of a Boolean type is when the specific values **true** or **false** are specified as the type.

Just like Booleans, the primitive types of **number**, **bigint**, and **string** also support literal sub-types, in these cases to specifically set a value to a particular number or string respectively.

When we looked at the literal Boolean sub-type earlier, we told the compiler that we were using a literal type by specifically supplying the value in the type position (after the colon), like this:

let isEnabled: true = true;

Strictly speaking, we can do the same with numbers and strings, like:

let literalNum: 1 = 1;
Or: let literalString: 'literal';
Or: **let literalBigInt: 1n = 1n;**

The variable **literalNum** is locked to the literal sub-type and value **1**, **literalBigInt** is locked to the literal subtype **1n**, and **literalString** is locked to the literal sub-type **'literal'**.

As well as explicitly typed variable declaration/initialization, TypeScript can also infer literal sub-types if we use **const** to declare a variable as opposed to **let** or **var**. For example, with the following code:

const inferredLiteral = 1;

In this case, because we specifically used **const** to declare the variable, TypeScript will set the type of **inferredLiteral** to the literal numerical sub-type **1**. The same behaviour is seen with strings as well, as long as we use **const** in the declaration.

Literal union types

Literal types are most commonly seen when working with type unions. As we've seen, using literal types alone do not provide much value, and are rarely seen in day-to-day code.
But using them in union types is a great way of restricting values to one of a predefined range of different literals. Let's see how with a quick example.

Imagine that we have a function for moving an element on a web page in one dimension:

```
function move1D(direction: 'left' | 'right') { // move the element }
```

This function takes a single parameter called **direction**, which we have specified is a union type of the literal string values **left** or **right**. The benefit of this is that when we come to invoke this function at a later time, we will get code completion for all of the different types in the union, making it clear exactly which values the function expects to be passed when it is invoked:

Figure: Literal union function signature tooltip and type code-completion in Visual Studio Code

This makes it almost impossible to use the function incorrectly and inadvertently introduce bugs into our application and is especially useful when working in larger teams of developers where the person invoking or using the function may not be the person who wrote it originally. It becomes a form of living inline documentation for using the function correctly.

We also get feedback in the editor or terminal when compiling if we supply a value that isn't one of the types in the union. For example, if we pass the string **up**, we'll see the error message:

Argument of the type 'up' is not assignable to parameter of type '"left" | "right"'.
Literal union types therefore represent an excellent way of leveraging TypeScript to guide others on how to use specific bits of code, for example, to ensure that a function is called with the correct arguments.

Type aliases

Type aliases are a way of declaring types in a reusable way using an identifier – like a variable declaration but for types. So far, we've added all of our example types as annotations directly after the thing they are used to describe. In the previous section, for example, we had a function that accepted a parameter with a union type:

```
function move1D(direction: 'left' | 'right') { // move the element }
```

Here, the type annotation appears in line with the parameter declaration. Instead, we could add a type alias for it, like this:

type directions = 'left' | 'right';

To declare a type alias, we use the **type** keyword followed by a name for the alias, and its type as a value, very similar to a regular variable declaration but using **type** instead of **var**, **let** or **const**.

Now, we can use this type alias anywhere that we want to make use of this literal union type, like in the **move1D** function, for example:

function move1D(direction: directions) { // move the element }

In this case, we get exactly the same code completion in the editor, exactly as if we had used an inline type annotation instead of the alias. We can of course reuse this type in other places too now that we have an identifier for it.

Note however that once the type is declared, we cannot modify it later on. If we try to extend it by adding some more types to the union for example: directions = 'left' | 'right' | 'up' | 'down'; Then, we will see an error:

```
'directions' only refers to a type, but is being
used as a value here. ts(2693)

any

    directions = 'left' | 'right' | 'up' | 'down';
```

Figure: Type used as a value error in Visual Studio Code

If we want to extend a type alias, we basically need to create a new one with a different identifier, and then include the type that we want to extend, like this:

type directions2D = directions | 'up' | 'down';
The new type, **directions2D**, will include all of the members from both the **directions** union and the new union members explicitly specified in the expression, the literal strings **up** and **down** in this case.

We could then set it as the type for a parameter in a **move2D** function, for example:

function move2D(direction: directions2D) { // move the element }

Type aliases are a simple way to reuse a type declaration in multiple places, but they have no other special behavior; they are merely a way to refer to a type using an identifier. They also don't have to be union types – any type can be used with an alias.

Type assertion

We've looked briefly at the **null** and **undefined** primitive types, as well as union types, and we've also seen how to use the **as** operator to make type assertions. Let's take a moment to look at these topics together.

Consider the following function:

```
function splitString(str: string | null) {
return str.split('');
}
```

We have a function called **splitString** which accepts a single parameter called **str** and this parameter is the union type **string | null**. The function simply returns the result of calling the **split** method on the **str** parameter.

The editor will immediately highlight an error on the line where we call the **split** method on **str** inside the function:

```
function splitString(str: string | null) {
  return str.split('');
}
    'str' is possibly 'null'. ts(18047)

    (parameter) str: string | null
```

Figure: Object is possibly 'null' warning in Visual Studio Code

The correct way to fix this issue is to check that **str** is actually of the type **string** before trying to call string methods on it, for example, we could return earlier from the function if we detect that **str** is **null**:

```
function splitString(str: string | null) {
if (str == null) return; return str.split('');
}
```

We can use a simple **if** statement to check **str** isn't equal to **null** and returns from the function if it is. Note that we can use the non-strict equality operator as a short hand to check for both **null** and **undefined** at the same time. This will remove the error in the editor.

We can also use a type assertion to fix the error in a different way:

```
function splitString(str: string | null) {
return (str as string).split('');
}
```

This time instead of explicitly checking if **str** is **null**, we can use the **as** operator to assert that **str** definitely is a string. However, we should use this only where we are sure that the argument being passed when this function is invoked is definitely the expected type – if it is actually **null**, the code will happily compile without errors, but we definitely would see an error in the actual browser.

For example, this code will not produce any warnings in the editor or in the terminal when compiling the TypeScript into JavaScript:

```
splitString(null);
```

But it will cause an error in the browser when the JavaScript is executed. It is safer to avoid using type assertion in this way for this reason. With the explicit check that **str** is not **null**, if we do for some reason invoke the **splitString** method with a null value, the resulting compiled JavaScript will not cause our program to crash in the browser.

We'll be looking at compiling TypeScript using a terminal application or Visual Studio Code, in much more detail in the next chapter.

Non-null assertion operator

The non-null assertion operator is another way to specify that a value definitely isn't **null**. This will disable both **null** and **undefined** checks made by TypeScript for the value it is used on and prevent the editor displaying errors.

For example, instead of specifically casting the **str** parameter to a string using the **as** operator, we could instead use the non-null assertion operator to achieve the same outcome:

```
function splitString(str: string | null) {
return str!.split('');
}
```

The non-null assertion operator is a postfix exclamation point – we use it directly after the value that we want to assert is not **null**.

This will disable any further **null** or **undefined** checking carried out by TypeScript. With the use of the **as** operator that we saw previously, if the value that we are asserting is not **null** does happen to actually be **null**, we will end up with errors in the compiled JavaScript, so take care when using it.

Conclusion: The Power and Promise of TypeScript's Type System and Type Annotations

TypeScript's type system and its feature-rich annotations have revolutionized JavaScript development by introducing static typing to an otherwise dynamically typed language. They provide developers with a powerful toolset to write error-free, maintainable, and scalable code. From small-scale applications to enterprise-level software, the advantages of TypeScript are evident in every stage of the development lifecycle, transforming the way modern applications are built.

1. Strengthening Code Robustness

One of the most significant benefits of TypeScript's type system is its ability to prevent errors at compile time. The early detection of type-related issues ensures that developers can fix bugs before they reach production. This proactive approach to error management reduces downtime, enhances application stability, and minimizes debugging efforts.

Type annotations, in particular, are invaluable for defining clear expectations in code. When every variable, function parameter, return type, or object property has an explicitly declared type, ambiguity is eliminated. Developers can focus on building features without worrying about unforeseen runtime errors caused by type mismatches.

2. Enhancing Code Readability and Maintainability

Codebases evolve as teams grow and projects scale. One of the common challenges in larger projects is maintaining code written by multiple developers, often over extended periods. Type annotations act as a form of self-documentation, making codebases easier to understand. They describe the intent of variables, functions, and APIs, reducing the need for external documentation.

For instance, consider a function without type annotations:

```
function process(data) {
    return data.name.toUpperCase();
}
```

In JavaScript, it's unclear what type data is expected to be. However, in TypeScript:

```
function process(data: { name: string }): string {
    return data.name.toUpperCase();
}
```

The explicit type declaration clarifies the function's contract, helping other developers (and the TypeScript compiler) understand its requirements.

3. Streamlining Collaboration and Onboarding

TypeScript fosters collaboration by providing a common language of types. New team members can quickly understand the structure and purpose of a codebase by reviewing type annotations. Tools like Visual Studio Code Leverage TypeScript's type information to offer intelligent code suggestions, making it easier for developers to adhere to established conventions.

In addition, type-safe codebases reduce miscommunication between developers, designers, and product managers. For example, a backend API that uses TypeScript can define type contracts shared across frontend and backend teams, ensuring consistency in data structures and reducing integration issues.

4. Enabling Advanced Development Patterns

TypeScript's advanced type system encourages developers to adopt sophisticated design patterns that might be cumbersome or error-prone in plain JavaScript. Features like generics, union and intersection types, and conditional types allow developers to write highly reusable and flexible code.

4.1 Generics for Flexibility

Generics empower developers to create reusable components without sacrificing type safety. For instance, a generic function like identity can work with any type while maintaining strict type checks:

```
function identity<T>(value: T): T {
    return value;
}
```

This flexibility extends to data structures, libraries, and frameworks, enabling teams to build robust, type-safe abstractions.

4.2 Conditional and Mapped Types

Conditional and mapped types further expand TypeScript's ability to handle complex scenarios, such as transforming types based on conditions. These capabilities are particularly useful in libraries and APIs, where the types of inputs and outputs need to be dynamically adjusted while ensuring correctness.

5. Bridging the Gap Between Development and Production

TypeScript's type system bridges the gap between development and production environments. With features like strict null checks, type narrowing, and discriminated unions, developers can write code that explicitly handles edge cases. This reduces the likelihood of errors arising from unhandled scenarios.

For instance, discriminated unions allow developers to safely handle different states in applications, such as managing API response statuses:

```
type ApiResponse =
  | { status: "success"; data: string }
  | { status: "error"; error: string };

function handleResponse(response: ApiResponse) {
  if (response.status === "success") {
    console.log(response.data);
  } else {
    console.error(response.error);
  }
}
```

By enforcing exhaustive checks, TypeScript ensures that no state is left unhandled, improving application resilience.

6. Facilitating Tooling and Ecosystem Growth

TypeScript's type system enhances the developer experience by powering sophisticated tooling and integrations. IDEs like Visual Studio Code Leverage TypeScript for features such as:

Code Completion: Predictive suggestions based on type information.
Refactoring Tools: Safe renaming and restructuring of code without breaking functionality.
Static Analysis: Real-time error checking and code quality insights.

Moreover, the TypeScript ecosystem has grown exponentially, with libraries and frameworks adopting TypeScript to improve developer experience. Popular projects like Angular, NestJS, and Deno use TypeScript as their primary language, showcasing its impact on modern development.

7. Addressing Challenges and Misconceptions

While TypeScript's type system is powerful, it does come with a learning curve, especially for developers transitioning from dynamically typed languages like JavaScript. However, this initial investment pays off in the long term as developers become more productive and confident in managing larger, more complex codebases.

Another common misconception is that TypeScript slows down development due to its strict type checks. On the contrary, TypeScript speeds up development by reducing debugging time and providing immediate feedback during coding.

8. Looking to the Future: TypeScript in 2024 and beyond

The future of TypeScript's type system is bright. With TypeScript 2024, Microsoft continues to push the boundaries of static typing in JavaScript. Enhancements like variadic tuple types, improved type inference, and better support for template literal types showcase TypeScript's commitment to staying at the forefront of modern development practices.

The adoption of TypeScript by major tech companies and its integration into popular frameworks signal its long-term relevance. As web and software development trends evolve, TypeScript's type system is expected to play a central role in shaping the future of strongly-typed JavaScript development.

Conclusion: The Final Word

The journey into TypeScript's type system and type annotations reveals a toolset designed to empower developers at every level. By offering static typing, intelligent tooling, and robust error-checking capabilities, TypeScript elevates JavaScript development to new heights. Its type annotations, though simple in syntax, are profound in impact, serving as the cornerstone of its type-checking mechanisms.

In 2024, TypeScript remains an essential language for developers seeking to build reliable, maintainable, and scalable applications. Whether you are crafting a small web application, architecting a large-scale enterprise system, or exploring cutting-edge frameworks, TypeScript's type system will continue to be a trusted ally in the quest for high-quality software development.

With its promise of safety, scalability, and clarity, TypeScript is not just a language—it's a philosophy of better coding, one type annotation at a time.

4. Basic Types and Generics

Introduction

TypeScript, a superset of JavaScript, introduces a type system that enables developers to write safer, more maintainable, and scalable code. One of TypeScript's core strengths is its support for both **basic types** and **generics**, which together enable developers to work with diverse data structures and create reusable, type-safe components. This article provides a comprehensive guide to understanding these fundamental features of TypeScript.

1. Basic Types in TypeScript

TypeScript extends JavaScript's existing data types with a powerful type system, ensuring code clarity and reducing runtime errors. Below are the basic types supported by TypeScript:

1.1. Primitive Types

These are the most fundamental data types in TypeScript:

number: Represents both integer and floating-point numbers.

Example:

```
let age: number = 25;
let pi: number = 3.1415;
```

string: Represents textual data, enclosed in single, double, or backticks.

Example:

```
let name: string = "TypeScript";
let greeting: string = `Hello, ${name}`;
```
boolean: Represents a logical value: true or false.

Example:

```
let isPublished: boolean = true;
```
null and undefined: Represent absence of value.

Example:

```
let emptyValue: null = null;
let uninitialized: undefined = undefined;
```
bigint: Represents large integers beyond the number type's safe range.

Example:

```
let largeNumber: bigint = 12345678901234567890n;
```

symbol: Used to create unique values.

Example:
const uniqueId: symbol = Symbol("id");

1.2. Complex Types

any: A dynamic type that allows any value.

Example:
let dynamicValue: any = 42;
dynamicValue = "TypeScript";

Use sparingly, as it bypasses TypeScript's type-checking.
unknown: A safer alternative to any, requiring explicit type assertion before use.

Example:

```
let data: unknown = "Hello, TypeScript!";
if (typeof data === "string") {
    console.log(data.toUpperCase());
}
```

void: Used for functions that do not return a value.

Example:

```
function logMessage(message: string): void {
    console.log(message);
}
```

never: Represents values that never occur, often used in functions that throw errors or infinite loops.

Example:

```
function error(message: string): never {
    throw new Error(message);
}
```

array: Represents a collection of values of the same type.

Example:

let numbers: number[] = [1, 2, 3];

tuple: Represents a fixed-length array with specific types for each element.

Example:

let user: [string, number] = ["Alice", 25];

enum: Enumerates named constants, improving code readability.

Example:

```
enum Color {
    Red,
    Green,
    Blue,
}
let favoriteColor: Color = Color.Green;
```

2. Generics in TypeScript

Generics are a powerful feature in TypeScript that allow you to create reusable and type-safe components, functions, and classes. By introducing type parameters, generics enable developers to work with a wide range of data types without sacrificing type safety.

2.1. Why Use Generics?

Reusability: Write code that works with any data type.
Type Safety: Avoid type mismatches by explicitly defining expected types.
Flexibility: Build components that can handle a variety of data types.

2.2. Basic Syntax of Generics

Generics are defined using angle brackets (<>) with a type parameter, typically represented by T.

Example:

```
function identity<T>(value: T): T {
    return value;
}

let numberValue = identity<number>(42);  // T is number
let stringValue = identity<string>("Hello!");  // T is string
```
Here, T is a placeholder for the actual type, inferred or specified when the function is called.

3. Working with Generics

3.1. Generic Functions

Generic functions allow you to define reusable logic.

Example:

```
function reverseArray<T>(items: T[]): T[] {
    return items.reverse();
}

let numbers = reverseArray([1, 2, 3]);  // Inferred as number[]
let strings = reverseArray(["a", "b", "c"]);  // Inferred as string[]
```

3.2. Generic Classes

Generic classes enable you to define classes that operate on various types.

Example:

```
class DataStore<T> {
  private items: T[] = [];

  add(item: T): void {
    this.items.push(item);
  }

  getAll(): T[] {
    return this.items;
  }
}

let numberStore = new DataStore<number>();
numberStore.add(42);

let stringStore = new DataStore<string>();
stringStore.add("TypeScript");
```

3.3. Generic Interfaces

Generic interfaces define contracts that can be applied to various types.

Example:

```
interface Pair<T, U> {
  first: T;
  second: U;
}

let pair: Pair<string, number> = {
  first: "Age",
  second: 25,
};
```

3.4. Constraints on Generics

You can constrain generic types to ensure they meet certain criteria.

Example:

```
function printLength<T extends { length: number }>(item: T): void {
  console.log(item.length);
}
```

```
printLength("Hello");  // Works
printLength([1, 2, 3]);  // Works
// printLength(42);  // Error: number does not have length
```

3.5. Default Type Parameters

Generics can have default values.

Example:

```
function fetchData<T = string>(url: string): T {
    // Implementation
    return {} as T;
}
let data = fetchData();  // Defaults to string
```

4. Advanced Topics in Generics

4.1. Using Multiple Type Parameters

You can use multiple type parameters for complex relationships.

Example:

```
function merge<T, U>(obj1: T, obj2: U): T & U {
    return { ...obj1, ...obj2 };
}
```

```
let merged = merge({ name: "Alice" }, { age: 25 });
```

4.2. Generic Utility Types

TypeScript includes built-in utility types, many of which use generics:

Partial<T>: Makes all properties in T optional.

Readonly<T>: Makes all properties in T read-only.

Record<K, T>: Creates an object type with keys of type K and values of type T.

Example:

```
type User = {
    name: string;
    age: number;
};
```

```
let partialUser: Partial<User> = { name: "Bob" };
let readonlyUser: Readonly<User> = { name: "Alice", age: 30 };
// readonlyUser.age = 31;  // Error: Cannot assign to 'age'
```

4.3. Generic Type Aliases

You can create reusable type aliases using generics.

Example:

```
type ApiResponse<T> = {
    data: T;
    error: string | null;
};

let response: ApiResponse<string> = {
    data: "Success",
    error: null,
};
```

Now that you are all set up, it's time to write some TypeScript! Starting out should be easy, but you will very soon run into situations where you're unsure if you're doing the right thing. Should you use interfaces or type aliases? Should you annotate or let type inference do its magic? What about any and unknown, are they safe to use? Some people on the internet said you should never use them, so why are they part of TypeScript anyways?

All these questions will be answered in this chapter. We look at the basic types that make TypeScript and learn how an experienced TypeScript developer will make use of them. Use this as a foundation for the upcoming chapters, so you get a feeling of how the TypeScript compiler gets to its types, and how it interprets your annotations.

This is a lot about the interaction between your code, the editor, and the compiler. And about going up and down the type hierarchy. If you are an experienced TypeScript developer, this chapter will give you the missing foundation. If you're just starting out, you will learn the most important techniques to go really far!

Annotating Effectively

A type annotation is a way to explicitly tell which types to expect. You know, the stuff that was very prominent in other programming languages, where the verbosity of StringBuilder stringBuilder = new StringBuilder() makes sure that you're really, really dealing with a StringBuilder . The opposite is type inference, where TypeScript tries to figure out the type for you.

```
// Type inference let aNumber = 2; // aNumber: number
// Type annotation
let anotherNumber: number = 3;
// anotherNumber: number
```

Type annotations are also the most obvious and visible syntax difference between TypeScript and JavaScript.

When you start learning TypeScript, you might want to annotate everything to express the types you'd expect. This might feel like the obvious choice but you can also use annotations sparingly and let TypeScript figure out types for you.

A type annotation is a way for you to express where contracts have to be checked. If you add a type annotation to a variable declaration, you tell the compiler to check if types match during the assignment.

```
type Person = {name: string;
age: number;
};
const me: Person = createPerson();
```

If createPerson returns something that isn't compatible with Person, TypeScript will throw an error. Do this is if you really want to be sure that you're dealing with the right type here.
Also, from that moment on, me is of type Person, and TypeScript will treat it as a Person. If there are more properties in me, e.g. a profession, TypeScript won't allow you to access them. It's not defined in Person.
If you add a type annotation to a function signature's return value, you tell the compiler to check if types match the moment, you return that value.

```
function createPerson(): Person {   return { name: "Stefan", age: 39 };
}
```

If I return something that doesn't match Person, TypeScript will throw an error. Do this if you want to be completely sure that you return the correct type. This especially comes in handy if you are working with functions that construct big objects from various sources.

If you add a type annotation to a function signature's parameters, you tell the compiler to check if types match the moment you pass along arguments.

```
function printPerson(person: Person) {
console.log(person.name, person.age);
}
printPerson(me);
```

This is in my opinion the most important, and unavoidable type annotation. Everything else can be inferred.

```
type Person = {
 name: string;
age: number;
};
// Inferred!
// return type is { name: string, age: number }
function createPerson() {
return { name: "Stefan", age: 39 };
}
// Inferred!
// me: { name: string, age: number}
const me = createPerson(); // Annotated! You have to check if types are compatible function

printPerson(person: Person) {
console.log(person.name, person.age);
}// All works
```

printPerson(me);

You can use inferred object types at places where you expect an annotation because TypeScript has a structural type system. In a structural type system, the compiler will only take into account the members (properties) of a type, not the actual name.

Types are compatible if all members of the type to check against are available in the type of the value. We also say that the shape or structure of a type has to match.

```
type Person = {
  name: string;
  age: number;
};
type User = {
name: string;
age: number;
id: number;
};
function printPerson(person: Person) {console.log(person.name, person.age);
}
const user: User = {
name: "Stefan", age: 40, id: 815,
};
printPerson(user); // works!
```

Person
printPerson

User has more properties than Person, but all properties that are in   are also in User, and they have the same type. This is why it's possible to pass User objects to, even though the types don't have any explicit connection.
However, if you pass a literal, TypeScript will complain that there are excess properties that should not be there.
```
printPerson({  name: "Stefan",  age: 40,  id: 1000, // ^- Argument of type
'{name: string;
age: number;
id: number;
}'  //is not assignable to parameter of type 'Person'.
 // Object literal may only specify known properties, and 'id' does not exist in
type 'Person'.(2345)
});
```

This is to make sure that you didn't expect properties to be present in this type, and wonder yourself why changing them has no effect.

With a structural type system, you can create interesting patterns where you have carrier variables with the type inferred, and reuse the same variable in different parts of your software, with no similar connection to each other.

```
type Person = {
name: string;
```

```
age: number;
};
type Studying = {
semester: number;
};
type Student = {
id: string;
age: number;
semester: number;
};
function createPerson() {
return {
name: "Stefan", age: 39, semester: 25, id: "XPA"
};
}
function printPerson(person: Person) {
console.log(person.name, person.age);
}
function studyForAnotherSemester(student: Studying) {
student.semester++;
}
function isLongTimeStudent(student: Student) {
return student.age - student.semester / 2 > 30 && student.semester > 20;
}
const me = createPerson();
// All work!
printPerson(me);
studyForAnotherSemester(me);
isLongTimeStudent(me);
```

Student, Person, and Studying have some overlap, but are unrelated to each other. createPerson returns something that is compatible with all three types. If you have annotated too much, you would need to create a lot more types and a lot more checks than necessary, without any benefit.

Both any and unknown are top types, which means that every value is compatible with any or unknown.
```
const name: any = "Stefan";
const person: any = { name: "Stefan", age: 40 };
const notAvailable: any = undefined;
```

Since any is a type, every value is compatible with, you can access any property without restriction.

```
const name: any = "Stefan"; // This is ok for TypeScript, but will crash in JavaScript
```

```
console.log(name.profession.experience[0].level);
```
any is also compatible with every sub-type, except never. This means you can narrow the set of possible values by assigning a new type.
```
const me: any = "Stefan"; // Good!
const name: string = me; // Bad, but ok for the type system.
const age: number = me;
```

With any being so permissive, any can be a constant source of potential errors and pitfalls since you effectively deactivate type checking.

While everybody seems to agree that you shouldn't use any in your codebases, there are some situations where any is really useful:

Migration. When you go from JavaScript to TypeScript, chances are that you already have a large codebase with a lot of implicit information on how your data structures and objects work. It might be a chore to get everything spelled out in one go. any can help you migrate to a safer codebase incrementally.

Untyped Third-party dependencies. You might have one or the other JavaScript dependency that still refuses to use TypeScript (or something similar). Or even worse: There are no up-to-date types for it. Definitely Typed is a great resource, but it's also maintained by volunteers. It's a formalization of something that exists in JavaScript but is not directly derived from it. There might be errors (even in such popular type definitions like React's), or they just might not be up to date!

This is where any can help you greatly. When you know how the library works, if the documentation is good enough to get you going, and if you use it sparingly, any can be a relief instead of fighting types.

JavaScript prototyping. TypeScript works a bit differently from JavaScript and needs to make a lot of trade-offs to make sure that you don't run into edge cases. This also means that if you write certain things that would work in JavaScript, you'd get errors in TypeScript.

```
type Person = {
name: string;
age: number;
};
function printPerson(person: Person) {
for (let key in person) {
console.log(`${key}: ${person[key]}`); // Element implicitly has an 'any' --^ type because expression of
type 'string' can't be used to index type 'Person'. No index signature with a parameter of type 'string'
// was found on type 'Person'.(7053)
  }
}
```

Find out why this is an error. In cases like this, any can help you to switch off type checking for a moment because you know what you're doing. And since you can go from every type to any, but also back to every other type, you have little, explicit unsafe blocks throughout your code where you are in charge of what's happening.

```
function printPerson(person: any) {
for (let key in person) {
console.log(`${key}: ${person[key]}`);
  }
}
```

Once you know that this part of your code works, you can start adding the right types, work around TypeScript's restrictions, and type assertions.

```
function printPerson(person: Person) {
for (let key in person) {
console.log(`${key}: ${person[key as keyof Person]}`);
  }
}
```

Whenever you use; it is any, make sure you activate the noImplicitAny flag in your tsconfig.json strict mode. With that, TypeScript needs you to explicitly annotate any activated by default in when you don't have a type through inference or annotation. This helps find potentially problematic situations later on. An alternative to is unknown. It allows for the same values, but the things you can do with it are very different. Where allows you to do everything, unknown allows you to do nothing. The only thing you can do is pass values around, the moment you want to call a function or make the type more specific, you need to do type checks first.

```
const me: unknown = "Stefan";
const name: string = me; //   ^- Type 'unknown' is not assignable to type 'string'.(2322)
const age: number = me; //   ^- Type 'unknown' is not assignable to type 'number'.(2322)
Type checks and control flow analysis help to do more with unknown:
function doSomething(value: unknown) {
if (typeof value === "string") { // value: string
console.log("It's a string", value.toUpperCase());
  }
else if (typeof value === "number") {
   // value: number
console.log("it's a number", value * 2);
  }
}
```

If your apps should work with a lot of different types, unknown is great to make sure that you can carry values throughout your code, but don't run into any safety problems because of any 's permissiveness.

Choosing the Right Object Type

TypeScript divides its types into two branches. The first branch, primitive types, include number, Boolean, string, symbol, bigint, and some sub-types. The second branch is called compound types and includes everything that is a sub-type of an object and is ultimately composed of other compound types or primitive types.

There are situations where you want to target values that are compound types. Either because you want to modify certain properties, or just want to be safe that we don't pass any primitive values. For example, Object.create creates a new object and takes its prototype as the first argument. This can only be a compound type, otherwise, your runtime JavaScript code would crash.

```
Object.create(2);
// Uncaught TypeError: Object prototype may only be an Object or null: 2
//   at Function.create (<anonymous>)
```

In TypeScript, there are three types that seem to do the same thing: The empty object type {}, the uppercase O Object interface, and the lowercase O object type. Which one do you use for compound types? {} and Object allow for roughly the same values, which is everything but null or undefined (given that strict mode or strictNullChecks is activated).

```
let obj: {}; // Similar to Object
obj = 32;
obj = "Hello";
obj = true; obj = () => {
console.log("Hello")
};
obj = undefined; // Error
obj = null; // Error
obj = { name: "Stefan", age: 40 };
obj = []; obj = /.*/;
```

The Object interface is compatible with all values that have the Object prototype, which is every value from every primitive and compound type.

However, Object is a defined interface in TypeScript, and has some requirements for certain functions. For example, the toString method which is toString() => string and part of any non-nullish value, is part of
the Object prototype. If you assign a value with a different tostring method, TypeScript will error.

```
let okObj: {} = { toString() {
return false;
  }
}; // OK
let obj: Object = { toString() {
return false;
  }
// ^- Type 'boolean' is not assignable to type 'string'.ts(2322)
}
```

Object can cause some confusion due to this behaviour, so in most cases, you're good with {}.

TypeScript also has a lowercase object type. This is more the type you're looking for, as it allows for any compound type, but no primitive types.

```
let obj: object;
obj = 32; // Error
obj = "Hello"; // Error
obj = true; // Error
obj = () => { console.log("Hello") };
obj = undefined; // Error
obj = null; // Error
obj = { name: "Stefan", age: 40 };
obj = [];
obj = /.*/;
```

If you want a type that excludes functions, regexes, arrays, and the likes, where we create one on our own.

Working with Tuple Types

Next to objects, JavaScript arrays are a popular way to organize data in a complex object. Instead of writing a typical Person object as we did in other recipes, you can store entries element by element:

const person = ["Stefan", 40]; // name and age

The benefit of using arrays over objects is that array elements don't have property names. When you assign each element to variables using destructuring, it gets really easy to assign custom names:

```
// objects.js // Using objects
const person = {
name: "Stefan",   age: 40,
};
const { name, age } = person;
console.log(name); // Stefan
console.log(age); // 40
const {
anotherName = name, anotherAge = age
} = person;
console.log(anotherName); // Stefan
console.log(anotherAge); // 40
// arrays.js // Using arrays
const person = ["Stefan", 40]; // name and age
const [name, age] = person;
console.log(name); // Stefan
console.log(age); // 40
const [anotherName, anotherAge] = person;
console.log(anotherName); // Stefan
console.log(anotherAge); // 40
```

When using TypeScript and relying on type inference, this pattern can cause some issues. By default, TypeScript infers the array type from an assignment like that. Arrays are open-ended collections with the same element in each position.

const person = ["Stefan", 40]; // person: (string | number)[]

So, TypeScript thinks that person is an array, where each element can be either a string or a number, and it allows for plenty of elements after the original two. This means when you're destructuring, each element is also of type string or number.

const [name, age] = person; // name: string | number
// age: string | number

That makes a comfortable pattern in JavaScript really cumbersome in Typescript. You would need to do control flow checks to narrow down the type to the actual one, where it should be clear from the assignment that this is not necessary.

Whenever you think you need to do extra work in JavaScript just to satisfy TypeScript, there's usually a better way. In that case, you can use tuple types to be more specific on how your array should be interpreted.

Tuple types are a sibling to array types that work on a different semantic. While arrays can be potentially endless in size and each element is of the same type (no matter how broad), tuple types have a fixed size and each element has a distinct type.

The only thing that you need to do to get tuple types is to explicitly annotate.

```
const person: [string, number] = ["Stefan", 40];
const [name, age] = person;
// name: string
// age: number
```

Fantastic! Tuple types have a fixed length, this means that the length is also encoded in the type. So, assignments that go out of bounds are not possible, and TypeScript will throw an error.

```
person[1] = 41; // OK!
person[2] = false; // Error
//^- Type 'false' is not assignable to type 'undefined'. (2322)
```

TypeScript also allows you to add labels to tuple types. This is just meta information for editors and compiler feedback but allows you to be clearer about what to expect from each element.

```
type Person = [name: string, age: number];
```

This will help you and your colleagues to easier understand what to expect, just like object types. Tuple types can also be used to annotate function arguments. This function

```
function hello(name: string, msg: string): void {   // ...
}
```

Can also be written with tuple types.
```
function hello(...args: [name: string, msg: string]): {   // ...
}
```

And you can be very flexible in defining it:

```
function h(a: string, b: string, c: string): void {   //...
}
// equal to function h(a: string, b: string, ...r: [string]): void {   //...
}
// equal to function h(a: string, ...r: [string, string]): void {   //...
}
// equal to function h(...r: [string, string, string]): void {   //...
}
```

This is also known as rest elements, something that we have in JavaScript and that allows you to define functions with an almost limitless argument list, where the last element, the rest element sucks all excess arguments in.

When you need to collect arguments in your code, you can use a tuple before you apply them to your function.

```
const person: [string, number] = ["Stefan", 40];
function hello(...args: [name: string, msg: string]): {  // ... } hello(...person);
```

Tuple types are really useful for many scenarios.

Understanding Interfaces vs Type Aliases

Both approaches to defining object types have been subject to lots of blog articles over the years. And all of them became outdated as time progressed. Right now, there is little difference between type aliases and interfaces. And everything that was different has been gradually aligned.

Syntactically, the difference between interfaces and type aliases is nuanced.

```
type PersonAsType = {
name: string;
age: number;
address: string[];
greet(): string;
};
interface PersonAsInterface {
name: string;
age: number;
address: string[];
greet(): string;
}
```

You can use interfaces and type aliases for the same things, in the same scenarios:

In an implements declaration for classes
As a type annotation for object literals
For recursive type structures

There is however one important difference that can have side affects you usually don't want to deal with: Interfaces allow for declaration merging, but type aliases don't. Declaration merging allows for adding properties to an interface even after it has been declared.

```
interface Person {
name: string;
}
interface Person {
age: number;
}// Person is now
{
name: string;
age: number;
}
```

TypeScript itself uses this technique a lot in lib.d.ts files, making it possible to just add deltas of new JavaScript APIs based on ECMAScript versions. This is a great feature if you want to extend e.g. Window, but it can fire back in other scenarios. Take this as an example:

```
// Some data we collect in a web form interface
FormData {
name: string;
age: number;
address: string[];
} // A function that sends this data to a back-end function
send(data: FormData) {
console.log(data.entries()) // this compiles! but crashes horrendously in runtime
}
```

So, where does the entries() method come from? It's a DOM API! FormData is one of the interfaces provided by browser APIs, and there are a lot of them. They are globally available, and nothing keeps you from extending those interfaces. And you get no notification if you do.

You can of course argue about proper naming, but the problem persists for all interfaces that you make available globally, maybe from some dependency where you don't even know they add an interface like that to the global space.

Changing this interface to a type alias immediately makes you aware of this problem:
```
type FormData = { //   ^-- Duplicate identifier 'FormData'.(2300)
name: string;
age: number;
address: string[];
};
```

Declaration merging is a fantastic feature if you are creating a library that is consumed by other parts in your project, maybe even other projects entirely written by other teams. It allows you to define an interface that describes your application but allows your users to adapt it to reality if needed. Think of a plug-in system, where loading new modules enhances functionality. Here, declaration merging is a feature you don't want to miss.

Within your module's boundaries, however, using type aliases prevents you from accidentally re-using or extending already declared types. Use type aliases when you don't expect others to consume them.

Performance

Using type aliases over interfaces has sparked some discussion in the past, as interfaces have been considered much more performant in their evaluation than type aliases, even resulting in a performance recommendation on the official TypeScript wiki. This recommendation is meant to be taken with a grain of salt, though, and is as everything much more nuanced.

On creation, simple type aliases may perform faster than interfaces because interfaces are never closed and might be merged with other declarations. But interfaces may perform faster in other places because they're known ahead of time to be object types. Ryan Canavaugh from the TypeScript team expects performance differences to be really measurable with an extraordinary number of interfaces or type aliases to be declared (around 5000 according to this tweet).

If your TypeScript code base doesn't perform well, it's not because you declared too many type aliases instead of interfaces, or vice versa

Defining Function Overloads

JavaScript is very flexible when it comes to function arguments. You can pass basically any parameters, of any length. As long as the function body treats the input right, you're good. This allows for very ergonomic APIs, but it's also very tough to type.

Think of a conceptual task runner. With a task function you define new tasks by name, and either passes a callback or pass a list of other tasks to be executed. Or both: a list of tasks that needs to be executed before the callback runs.

```
task("default", ["scripts", "styles"]);
task("scripts", ["lint"], () => {    // ... });
task("styles", () => {    // ...
});
```

If you think "this looks a lot like Gulp 6 years ago", you're right. Its flexible API where you couldn't do much wrong was also one of the reasons Gulp was so popular.

Typing functions like this can be a nightmare. Optional arguments, different types at the same position, this is tough to do even if you use union types1.

This catches all variations from the example above, but it's also wrong, as it allows for combinations that don't make any sense.

```
task(  "what",  () => { console.log("Two callbacks?");
  }, () => {
console.log("That's not supported, but the types say yes!");
  }
);
```

Thankfully, TypeScript has a way to solve problems like this: Function overloads. Its name hints at similar concepts from other programming languages: Defining the same, but with different behaviour. The biggest difference in TypeScript, as opposed to other programming languages, is that function overloads only work on a type system level and have no effect on the actual implementation.

The idea is that you define every possible scenario as its own function signature. The last function signature is the actual implementation.

```
// Types for the type system function
task(name: string, dependencies: string[]): void;
function task(name: string, callback: CallbackFn): void function task(name: string, dependencies: string[], callback: CallbackFn): void
// The actual implementation function task(name: string, param2: string[] | CallbackFn, param3?: CallbackFn): void
```

There are a couple of things that are important to note:

First, TypeScript only picks up the declarations before the actual implementation as possible types. If the actual implementation signature is also relevant, duplicate it.

Also, the actual implementation function signature can't be anything. TypeScript checks if the overloads can be implemented with the implementation signature.

If you have different return types, it is your responsibility to make sure that inputs and outputs match.

```
function fn(input: number): number function fn(input: string): string function fn(input: number | string):
number | string {   if(typeof input === "number") {
return "this also works";
  } else {
return 1337;
  }
}
```

```
const typeSaysNumberButItsAString = fn(12);
const typeSaysStringButItsANumber = fn("Hello world");
```

The implementation signature usually works with a very broad type, which means you have to do a lot of checks that you would need to do in JavaScript anyways. This is good as it urges you to be extra careful.

If you need overloaded functions as their own type, to use them in annotations and assign multiple implementations, you can always create a type alias:

```
type TaskFn = {
  (name: string, dependencies: string[]): void;
  (name: string, callback: CallbackFn): void;
  (name: string, dependencies: string[], callback: CallbackFn): void;
}
```

As you can see, you only need the type system overloads, not the actual implementation definition.

Defining this Parameter Types

If there has been one source of confusion for aspiring JavaScript developers it has to be the ever-changing nature of this object pointer.

Sometimes when writing JavaScript, I want to shout "This is ridiculous!". But then I never know what this refers to.

Unknown JavaScript developer

Especially if your background is a class-based object-oriented programming language, where this always refers to an instance of a class. this in JavaScript is entirely different, but not necessarily harder to understand. What's, even more, is that TypeScript can greatly help us get more closure about this in usage.

this lives within the scope of a function, and that points to an object or value that is bound to that function. In regular objects, this is pretty straightforward.

```
const author = { name: "Stefan",   // function shorthand
hi() {
console.log(this.name);
  },
};
```

author.hi(); // prints 'Stefan'

But functions are values in JavaScript, and can be bound to a different context, effectively changing the value of this.

```
const author = {
name: "Stefan",
};
function hi() {
console.log(this.name);
}
const pet = {
name: "Finni",  kind: "Cat",
};
hi.apply(pet); // prints "Finni"
hi.call(author); // prints "Stefan"
const boundHi = hi.bind(author);
boundHi(); // prints "Stefan"
```

It doesn't help that the semantics of this change again if you use arrow functions instead of regular functions.

```
class Person {
constructor(name) {
this.name = name;
  }
  hi() {
console.log(this.name);
  }
  hi_timeout() {
setTimeout(function() {
console.log(this.name);
 }, 0);
}
  hi_timeout_arrow() {
setTimeout(() => {
    console.log(this.name);
   }, 0);
  }
}
```

```
const person = new Person("Stefan") person.hi(); // prints "Stefan"
person.hi_timeout(); // prints "undefined"
person.hi_timeout_arrow(); // prints "Stefan"
```

With TypeScript, we can get more information on what this is and, more importantly, what it's supposed to be through this parameter types.

Take a look at the following example. We access a button element via DOM APIs and bind an event listener to it.

Within the callback function, this is of type HTMLButtonElement, which means you can access properties like classList.

```
const button = document.querySelector("button");
button?.addEventListener("click", function() {
this.classList.toggle("clicked");
});
```

The information on this is provided by the addEventListener function. If you extract your function in a refactoring step, you retain the functionality, but TypeScript will error, as it loses context to this.

```
const button = document.querySelector("button");
button.addEventListener("click", handleToggle);
function handleToggle() {
this.classList.toggle("clicked"); // ^- 'this' implicitly has type 'any'
// because it does not have a type annotation
}
```
The trick is to tell TypeScript that this is supposed to be of a specific type. You can do this by adding a parameter at the very first position in your function signature that is named this.

```
const button = document.querySelector("button");
button?.addEventListener("click", handleToggle);
function handleToggle(this: HTMLButtonElement) {
this.classList.toggle("clicked");
}
```

This handleToggle

This argument gets removed once compiled. TypeScript now has all the information it needs to make sure you needs to be of type HTMLButtonElement , which also means that you get errors once we use in a different context.

```
handleToggle(); // ^- The 'this' context of type 'void' is not assignable to method's 'this' of type
'HTMLButtonElement'.
```

You can make handleToggle even more useful if you define this to be HTMLElement a super-type of HTMLButtonElement.

```
const button = document.querySelector("button");
button?.addEventListener("click", handleToggle);
const input = document.querySelector("input");
input?.addEventListener("click", handleToggle);
function handleToggle(this: HTMLElement) {
this.classList.toggle("clicked");
}
```
When working with this parameter types, you might want to make use of two helper types that can either extract or remove this parameter from your function type.

```
function handleToggle(this: HTMLElement) {
this.classList.toggle("clicked");
```

```
}
```

```
type ToggleFn = typeof handleToggle; // (this: HTMLElement) => void
type WithoutThis = OmitThisParameter<ToggleFn>
// () = > void
type ToggleFnThis = ThisParameterType<ToggleFn>
// HTMLElement
```

There are more helper types when it comes to this in classes and objects.

Working with Symbols

Symbol is a primitive data type in JavaScript and TypeScript, which, amongst other things, can be used for object properties. Compared to number and string, symbols have some unique features that make them stand out.

Symbols can be created using the Symbol() factory function:

```
const TITLE = Symbol('title')
```
Symbol has no constructor function. The parameter is an optional description. By calling the factory function, TITLE is assigned the unique value of this freshly created symbol. This symbol is now unique, distinguishable from all other symbols, and doesn't clash with any other symbols that have the same description.

```
const ACADEMIC_TITLE = Symbol('title') const ARTICLE_TITLE = Symbol('title')
if(ACADEMIC_TITLE === ARTICLE_TITLE) {
  // This is never true
}
```

The description helps you to get info on the Symbol during development time:

```
console.log(ACADEMIC_TITLE.description) // title console.log(ACADEMIC_TITLE.toString()) //
Symbol(title)
```

Symbols are great if you want to have comparable values that are exclusive and unique. For runtime switches or mode comparisons:

```
// A really bad logging framework const LEVEL_INFO = Symbol('INFO') const LEVEL_DEBUG =
Symbol('DEBUG') const LEVEL_WARN = Symbol('WARN') const LEVEL_ERROR =
Symbol('ERROR')
function log(msg, level) {
switch(level) {
case LEVEL_WARN:
    console.warn(msg);
break
case LEVEL_ERROR:
    console.error(msg);
break;
case LEVEL_DEBUG:
    console.log(msg);
debugger; break;
```

```
case LEVEL_INFO:
console.log(msg);
  }
}
```

Symbols also work as property keys but are not iterable, which is great for serialization
```
const print = Symbol('print')
const user = {
name: 'Stefan',   age: 40,
  [print]: function() { console.log(`${this.name} is ${this.age} years old`)
  }
}
```

```
JSON.stringify(user) // { name: 'Stefan', age: 40 } user[print]() // Stefan is 40 years old
```

There's a global symbols registry that allows you to access tokens across your whole application.
```
Symbol.for('print') // creates a global symbol
const user = {
name: 'Stefan', age: 37, // uses the global symbol
  [Symbol.for('print')]: function() {
 console.log(`${this.name} is ${this.age} years old`)
  }
}
```

The first call to Symbol.for creates a symbol, the second call uses the same symbol. If you store the symbol value in a variable and want to know the key, you can use Symbol.keyFor()
```
const usedSymbolKeys = []
function extendObject(obj, symbol, value) {   //Oh, what symbol is this?
  const key = Symbol.keyFor(symbol) //Alright, let's better store this
if(!usedSymbolKeys.includes(key)) {
usedSymbolKeys.push(key)
}
obj[symbol] = value
}
// now it's time to retreive them all function printAllValues(obj) {   usedSymbolKeys.forEach(key => {
console.log(obj[Symbol.for(key)])
  })
}
```

TypeScript has full support for symbols, and they are prime citizens in the type system. symbol itself is a data type annotation for all possible symbols. See the extendObject function from earlier on. To allow for all symbols to extend our object, we can use the symbol type:
```
const sym = Symbol('foo')
```

```
function extendObject(obj: any, sym: symbol, value: any) {   obj[sym] = value
}
extendObject({}, sym, 42) // Works with all symbols
```

There's also the sub-type unique symbol. A unique symbol is closely tied to the declaration, only allowed in const declarations and references this exact symbol, and nothing else.

You can think of a nominal type in TypeScript for a very nominal value in JavaScript.
To get to the type of `unique symbol`s, you need to use the typeof operator.

```
const PROD: unique symbol = Symbol('Production mode') const DEV: unique symbol =
Symbol('Development mode')
function showWarning(msg: string, mode: typeof DEV | typeof PROD) {  // ...
}
```

At the time of writing, the only possible nominal type is TypeScript's structural type system.
Symbols stand at the intersection between nominal and opaque types in TypeScript and JavaScript. And
are the closest things we get to nominal type checks at runtime.

Understanding Value and Type Namespaces

TypeScript is a superset of JavaScript, which means it adds more things to an already existing and
defined language.

Over time you learn to spot which parts are JavaScript, and which parts are TypeScript.

It really helps to see TypeScript as this additional layer of types upon regular JavaScript. A thin layer of
metainformation, which will be peeled off before your JavaScript code runs in one of the available
runtimes.

Some people even speak about TypeScript code "erasing to JavaScript" once compiled.

TypeScript being this layer on top of JavaScript also means that different syntax contributes to different
layers. While a function or const creates a name in the JavaScript part, a type declaration or an interface
contributes a name in the TypeScript layer.

```
// Collection is in TypeScript land! --> type type Collection = Person[]
// printCollection is in JavaScript land! --> value function printCollection(coll: Collection) {
console.log(...coll.entries)
}
```

We also say that declarations contribute either a name to the type namespace or to the value namespace.
Since the type layer is on top of the value layer, it's possible to consume values in the type layer, but not
vice versa. We also have explicit keywords for that.

```
// a value
const person = {   name: "Stefan", };
// a type
type Person = typeof person;
```

typeof creates a name available in the type layer from the value layer below.

It gets irritating when there are declaration types that create both types and values. Classes for instance
can be used in the TypeScript layer as a type, as well as in JavaScript as a value.

```
// declaration class Person {
name: string;
```

```
constructor(n: string) {
this.name = n;
  }
}// used as a value
const person = new Person("Stefan");
// used as a type
type Collection = Person[];
function printPersons(coll: Collection) {   //...
}
```

And naming conventions trick you. Usually, we define classes, types, interfaces, enums, etc. with a capital first letter. And even if they may contribute values, they for sure contribute types. Well, until you write uppercase functions for your React app, as the convention dictates.

If you're used to using names as types and values, you're going to scratch your head if you suddenly get a good old TS2749: YourType refers to a value, but is being used as a type error.

```
type PersonProps = {
name: string;
};
function Person({ name }: PersonProps) {   // ... }
type PrintComponentProps = {
collection: Person[];
  //       ^- 'Person' refers to a value,
  //          but is being used as a type
}
```

This is where TypeScript can get really confusing. What is a type, what is a value, why do we need to separate this, and why doesn't this work like in other programming languages? Suddenly, you see yourself confronted with typeof calls or even the InstanceType helper type, because you realize that classes actually contribute two types.

Classes contribute a name to the type namespace, and since TypeScript is a structural type system, they allow values that have the same shape as an instance of a certain class. So this is allowed.

```
class Person {
name: string;
  constructor(n: string) {
this.name = n;
  } }
function printPerson(person: Person) {
console.log(person.name);
}
printPerson(new Person("Stefan")); // ok
printPerson({ name: "Stefan" }); // also ok
```

However, instanceof checks, which are working entirely in the value namespace and just have implications on the type namespace, would fail, as objects with the same shape may have the same properties, but are not an actual instance of a class.

```
function checkPerson(person: Person) {
return person instanceof Person;
}
checkPerson(new Person("Stefan")); // true
checkPerson({ name: "Stefan" }); // false
```

So, it's good to understand what contributes types, and what contributes value. This table, adapted from the TypeScript docs, sums it up nicely:

Table. Type and value namespaces

Declaration type	Type	Value
Class	X	X
Enum	X	X
Interface	X	
Type Alias	X	
Function	X	
Variable	X	

If you stick with functions, interfaces (or type aliases), and variables at the beginning, you will get a feeling of what you can use where. If you work with classes, think about the implications a bit longer.

Generics

Up until now, our main goal was to take the inherent flexibility of JavaScript and find a way to formalize it through the type system. We added static types for a dynamically typed language, to communicate intent, get tooling, and catch bugs before they happen.

Some parts in JavaScript don't really care about static types, though. E.g. an isKeyAvailableInObject function should only check if a key is available in an object, it doesn't need to know about the concrete types. To properly formalize a function like this we can either use TypeScript's structural type system and describe a very wide type for the price of information, or a very strict type for the price of flexibility.

But we don't want to pay any price. We want both flexibility and information. Generics in TypeScript are just the silver bullet we need. We can describe complex relationships, formalize structure for data that has not been defined yet.

Generics, along with its gang of mapped types, type maps, type modifiers, and helper types, open us the door to meta typing, where we can create new types based on old ones, keep relationships between types intact while the newly generated types challenge our original code for possible bugs.

This is the entrance to advanced TypeScript concepts. But fear not, there shan't be dragons, unless we define them.

Generalizing Function Signatures

You are writing an application that stores several language files (for e.g. subtitles) in an object. The keys are the language codes, the values are URLs. You load language files by selecting them via a language code, which comes from some API or user interface as string. To make sure the language code is correct and valid, you add an isLanguageAvailable function, that does an in check and sets the correct type using a type predicate.

```
type Languages = {
de: URL;
en: URL;
pt: URL;
es: URL;
fr: URL;
ja: URL;
};
function isLanguageAvailable(
collection: Languages,  lang: string
): lang is keyof Languages {
return lang in collection;
}
function loadLanguage(collection: Languages, lang: string) {
if (isLanguageAvailable(collection, lang)) {
   // lang is keyof Languages
collection[lang]; // access ok!
  }
}
```

Same application, different scenario, entirely different file. You load media data into an HTML element. Either audio, video, or a combination with certain animations in a canvas element. All elements exist in the application already, but you need to select the right one based on some input from an API. Again, the selection comes as string AllowedElements, and you write an isElementAllowed function to ensure that the input is actually a valid key of your collection.

```
type AllowedElements = {
video: HTMLVideoElement;
audio: HTMLAudioElement;
canvas: HTMLCanvasElement;
};
function isElementAllowed(
collection: AllowedElements,  elem: string
): elem is keyof AllowedElements {
return elem in collection;
}
function selectElement(collection: AllowedElements, elem: string) {
if (isElementAllowed(collection, elem)) {     // elem is keyof AllowedElements
collection[elem]; // access ok
  }
}
```

You don't need to look too closely to see that both scenarios are very similar. Especially the type guard functions catch our eye. If we strip away all the type information and align the names, they are identical!
```
function isAvailable(obj, key) {
return key in obj;
}
```

The only thing two of them exist is because of the type information we get. Not because of the input parameters, but because of the type predicates. In both scenarios we can talk more about the input parameters by asserting a specific keyof type.

The problem is that both input types for the collection are entirely different and have no overlap. Except for the empty object, which we don't get that many valuable information out of if we create a keyof type. keyof {} is actually never.

But there is some type information here that we can generalize. We know that the first input parameter is an object. And the second one is a property key. If this check evaluates to true, we know that the first parameter is a key of the second parameter.

To generalize this function, we can add a generic type parameter to isAvailable called Obj, put in angle brackets. This is a placeholder for an actual type, that will be substituted once isAvailable is used. We can use this generic type parameter like we would use AllowedElements or Languages, and can add a type predicate. Since Obj can be substituted for every type, key needs to include all possible property keys: string, symbol, and number.

```
function isAvailable<Obj>(   obj: Obj,   key: string | number | symbol
): key is keyof Obj {
return key in obj;
}
function loadLanguage(collection: Languages, lang: string) {
if (isAvailable(collection, lang)) {
   // lang is keyof Languages
collection[lang]; // access ok!
 } }
function selectElement(collection: AllowedElements, elem: string) {
if (isAvailable(collection, elem)) {     // elem is keyof AllowedElements
collection[elem]; // access ok
 }
}
```

And there we have it: One function that works in both scenarios, no matter which types we substitute Obj for. Just like JavaScript works! We still get the same functionality, and we get the right type information. Index access becomes safe, without sacrificing flexibility.

The best part? We can use isAvailable just like we would use an untyped JavaScript equivalent. This is because TypeScript infers types for generic type parameters through usage. And this comes with some neat side effects.

Creating Related Function Arguments

Similar, our application stores a list of subtitles in an object of type Languages. Languages has a set of keys describing the language code, and a URL as value.

```
type Languages = {
de: URL;
en: URL;
pt: URL;
es: URL;
```

```
fr: URL;
ja: URL;
};
const languages: Languages = { /* ... */ };
```

There are several lists like this in our application, and we can abstract them in a type called URLList , whose index signatures allows for any string key.

```
type URLList = {   [x: string]: URL;
};
```

URLList

URLList is a super-type of Languages: Every value of type Languages is a is Languages. Still, we can use URLList to write a function called URLList fetchFile, but not every, where we load a specific entry from thist list.

```
function fetchFile(urls: URLList, key: string) {
return fetch(urls[key]).then((res) => res.json());
}
const de = fetchFile(languages, "de");
const it = fetchFile(languages, "it");
```

The problem is that type string for key allows for way too many entries. There are e.g. no Italian subtitles defined, but fetchFile doesn't keep us from loading "it" as language code anyway. When we load items from a specific URLList , it would be great to also know which keys we can access.

We can solve this by substituting the broader type for a generic, and setting a generic constraint to make sure we pass a sub-type of URLList. This way the function signature behaves very similar to before, but we can work with the substituted types much better. We define a generic type parameter List which is a sub-type of URLList , and set key to keyof List .

```
function fetchFile<List extends URLList>(urls: List, key: keyof List) {
return fetch(urls[key]).then((res) => res.json());
}
const de = fetchFile(languages, "de");
const it = fetchFile(languages, "it"); // Argument of type '"it"' is not assignable to
// parameter of type 'keyof Languages'.(2345)
```

The moment we call fetchFile, List will be substituted for an actual type, and we know that "it" is not part of the keys of Languages. TypeScript will show us when we made a typo, or selected elements which aren't part of our data-types.

This also works if we aren't only loading one key, but many. The same constraints, the same effect.

```
function fetchFiles<List extends URLList>(urls: List, keys: (keyof List)[]) {
const els = keys.map((el) =>    fetch(urls[el])
    .then((res) => res.json())
    .then((data) => [el, data])
  );
return els;
```

}

```
const de_and_fr = fetchFiles(languages, ["de", "fr"]); // Promise<any[]>≥[] const de_and_it =
fetchFiles(languages, ["de", "it"]); //                                        ^
//  Type '"it"' is not assignable to type 'keyof Languages'.(2322)
```

We store the results in a tuple with the language key as first element, and the data as the second element. However, when we get the result, it's an array of promises that resolve to an any[] . This is understandable, as fetch does not tell us anything about the data loaded, and with data being of type any and thus having the broadest type, it just swallows el which is keyof List.

But we know more at this stage. We know for example that [el, data] is not an array, but a tuple. There is a subtle, but important difference, as shown. If we annotate the result with a tuple type, we get more information out of our return values.

```
function fetchFiles<List extends URLList>(urls: List, keys: (keyof List)[]) {
const els = keys.map((el) =>     fetch(urls[el])
    .then((res) => res.json())
    .then((data) => {
const entry: [keyof List, any] = [el, data];
return entry;
    }));
return els;
} const de_and_fr = fetchFiles(languages, ["de", "fr"]);
```

fetchFiles now returns an array of Promises of [keyof List, any]. So, the moment we substitute List for Languages, we know that the only possible keys can be language codes.

Great, however there's still one caveat. We know that we fetch only German and French language codes, why can we do checks for English?
```
for (const result of de_and_fr) {
if (result[0] === "en") {     // English?
  }
}
```

The problem is that we are dealing again with a type that is way too broad. Yes, keyof List is already a lot narrower than string, but we can substitute all keys for a smaller set as well.

We repeat the same process:

1.   Create a new generic type parameter.
2.   Set the broader type as constraint of the newly created generic type parameter.
3.   Use the parameter in your function signature to be substituted for an actual type.

And just like that, we can also substitute keyof List with a sub-type: "de" | "fr".
```
function fetchFiles<List extends URLList, Keys extends keyof List>(  urls: List,  keys: Keys[]
) {  const els = keys.map((el) =>     fetch(urls[el])
    .then((res) => res.json())
    .then((data) => {
const entry: [Keys, any] = [el, data];
return entry;
```

```
    })
  );
  return els;
} const de_and_fr = fetchFiles(languages, ["de", "fr"]);
```

What's nice about this is that we can set relationships between generic type parameters. The second type parameter can be constrained by something from the first generic type parameter. This allows us to narrow down very specifically, until we substitute with real values. The effect? We know about possible values of our types anywhere in our code. So, we won't check for the English language if we can already say that we never requested to load English.

```
for (const entry of de_and_fr) {
const result = await entry;
if (result[0] === "en") { //  This condition will always return 'false' since the types. '"de" | "fr"' and '"en"'
have no overlap. (2367)
  }
}
```

One check that we didn't get rid of is to see which language is at position 0 at all.

One thing that we didn't take into account is generic instantiation. We let type parameters be substituted for real values through usage, just like type inference. But we also could substitute them explicitly through annotations.

```
const de_and_ja = fetchFiles<Languages, "ja" | "de">(languages, ["de"]);
```

Here we see that the types tell us that there might be Japanese subtitles as well, even though we can see from usage that we only load German ones.

Getting Rid of any and unknown

When using generics, it might first seem like a substitute for any and unknown. Take an identity function. Its only job is to return the value passed as input parameter.

```
function identity(value: any): any {
return value;
}
let a = identity("Hello!");
let b = identity(false);
let c = identity(2);
```

It takes values of every type, and the return type of it can also be anything. We can write the same function using unknown if we want to safely access properties.

```
function identity(value: unknown): unknown {
return value;
}
let a = identity("Hello!");
let b = identity(false);
let c = identity(2);
```

We can even mix and match any and unknown, but the result is always the same: Type information is lost. The type of the return value is what we define it to be.

Now let's write the same function with generics instead of any or unknown. It's type annotations say that the
generic type is also the return type.

```
function identity<T>(t: T): T {
  return t;
}
```

We can use this function to pass in any value and see which type TypeScript infers.

```
let a = identity("Hello!"); // a is string
let b = identity(2000);     // b is number
let c = identity({ a: 2 }); // c is { a: number }
```

Assigning to a binding with const instead of let , gives slightly different results.

```
const a = identity("Hello!"); // a is "Hello!"
const b = identity(2000);     // b is 2000
const c = identity({ a: 2 }); // c is { a: number }
```

For primitive types, TypeScript substitutes the generic type parameter with the actual type. This is a fact that we can make great use of in more advanced scenarios.

With TypeScript's generics, there is also the possibility to annotate the generic type parameter.

```
const a = identity<string>("Hello!"); // a is string
const b = identity<number>(2000);     // b is number
const c = identity<{ a: 2 }>({ a: 2 }); // c is { a: 2 }
```

If this behaviour reminds you of annotation and inference you are absolutely right. It's very similar, but with generic type parameters in functions.

When using generics without constraints, we can write functions that work with values of any type. Inside, they behave like unknown, which means we can do type guards to narrow down the type. The biggest difference is that once we use the function, we substitute our generics with real types, not losing any information on typing at all.

This allows us to be a bit clearer with our types than just allowing everything. This pair's function takes two arguments and creates a tuple.
```
function pairs(a: unknown, b: unknown): [unknown, unknown] {
return [a, b];
} const a = pairs(1, "1"); // [unknown, unknown]
```

With generic type parameters, we get a nice tuple type.

```
function pairs<T, U>(a: T, b: U): [T, U] {   return [a, b];
} const b = pairs(1, "1"); // [number, string]
```

Using the same generic type parameter, we can make sure we only get tuples where each element is of the same type.

So, should you use generics everywhere? Not necessarily. In this chapter you find many solutions which rely on getting the right type information at the right time. When you are happy enough with a wider set of values and can rely on sub-types being compatible, you don't need to use any generic at all. If you have any and unknown in your code, think if you need to the actual type at some point in time. Adding a generic type parameter instead might help you greatly.

Understanding Generic Instantiation

You create a filter logic for your application. You have different filter rules, that you can combine using "and" | "or" combinators. You can also chain regular filter rules with the outcome of combinatorial filters. You create your types based on this behaviour.

```
type FilterRule = {
field: string;
operator: string;
value: any;
};
type CombinatorialFilter = {
combinator: "and" | "or";
rules: FilterRule[];
};
type ChainedFilter = {
rules: (CombinatorialFilter | FilterRule)[];
};
type Filter = CombinatorialFilter | ChainedFilter;
```

Now you want to write a reset function that — based on an already provided filter — resets all rules. You use type guards to distinguish between CombinatorialFilter and ChainedFilter.

```
function reset(filter: Filter): Filter {
if ("combinator" in filter) {     // filter is CombinatorialFilter
return { combinator: "and", rules: [] };
  }
  // filter is ChainedFilter
return { rules: [] };
}
const filter: CombinatorialFilter = { rules: [], combinator: "or" };
const resetFilter = reset(filter); // resetFilter is Filter
```

The behaviour is what you are after, but the return type of reset is too wide. When we pass a CombinatorialFilter, we already should be sure that the reset filter is also a CombinatorialFilter. Here it's the union type, just like our function signature indicates. But you want to make sure that if you pass a filter of a certain type, you also get the same return type. So you replace the broad union type with a generic type parameter that is constrained to Filter. The return type works as intended, but the implementation of your function throws errors.

```
function reset<F extends Filter>(filter: F): F {
if ("combinator" in filter) {
return { combinator: "and", rules: [] }; // ^
```

'{combinator: "and"; rules: never[]; }' is assignable to the constraint of type 'F', but 'F' could be instantiated with a different subtype of constraint 'Filter'.
```
  }
return { rules: [] }; //^
```
'{ rules: never[]; }' is assignable to the constraint of type 'F', //   but 'F' could be instantiated with a different subtype of constraint 'Filter'.
```
}
const resetFilter = reset(filter); // resetFilter is CombinatorialFilter
```

While you want to differentiate between two parts of a union, TypeScript thinks broader. It knows that you might pass in an object which is structurally compatible to Filter, but has more properties, and is therefore a sub-type. Which means that you can call reset with F instantiated to a sub-type, and your program would happily override all excess properties. This is wrong, and TypeScript tells you that.

```
const onDemandFilter = reset({ combinator: "and",   rules: [],   evaluated: true,   result: false,
});
/* filter is { combinator: "and";   rules: never[];   evaluated: boolean;   result: boolean;
}; */
```

Overcome this by writing sub-type friendly code. Clone the input object (still type F), set the properties that need to be changed accordingly, and return something that is still of type F.

```
function reset<F extends Filter>(filter: F): F {
const result = { ...filter }; // result is F
result.rules = [];
if ("combinator" in result) {
result.combinator = "and";
  }
return result;
} const resetFilter = reset(filter); // resetFilter is CombinatorialFilter
```

Generic types can be one of many in a union, but they can also be much, much more. TypeScript's structural type system allows you to work on a variety of sub-types, and your code needs to reflect that.

A different scenario, but with a similar outcome. You want to create a tree data structure, and write a recursive type that stores all tree items. This type can be sub-typed, so you write a createRootItem function with generic type parameter since you want to instantiate it with the correct sub-type.

```
type TreeItem = {
id: string;
children: TreeItem[];
 collapsed?: boolean;
};
function createRootItem<T extends TreeItem>(): T {   return {    id: "root",    children: [],
  };
// '{ id: string; children: never[]; }' is assignable to the constraint
//   of type 'T', but 'T' could be instantiated with a different subtype
//   of constraint 'TreeItem'.(2322)
}
const root = createRootItem(); // root is TreeItem
```

We get a similar error as before, as we can't possibly say that the return value will be compatible with all the subtypes. To solve this problem, get rid of the generic! We know how the return type will look like, it's a TreeItem!

```
function createRootItem(): TreeItem {
  return {id: "root", children: [],
  };
}
```

The simplest solutions are often the better ones. But now you want to extend your software, by being able to attach children of type or sub-type TreeItem to a newly created root. We don't add any generics yet, and are somewhat dissatisfied.

```
function attachToRoot(children: TreeItem[]): TreeItem {
return { id: "root", children,
  };
} const root = attachToRoot([]); // TreeItem
```

root is of type TreeItem , but we lose any information regarding the sub-typed children. Even if we add a generic type parameter just for the children, constrained to TreeItem , we don't retain this information on the go.

```
function attachToRoot<T extends TreeItem>(children: T[]): TreeItem {   return {  id: "root", children,
  }; }
const root = attachToRoot([
  {id: "child", children: [],    collapsed: false,    marked: true,
  },
]); // root is TreeItem
```

When we start adding a generic type as return type, we run into the same problems as before. To solve this issue, we need to split the root item type from the children item type, by opening up TreeItem to be a generic, where we can set Children to be a sub-type of TreeItem.

Since we want to avoid any circular references, we need to set Children to a default BaseTreeItem , so we can use TreeItem both as constraint for Children and for attachToRoot.

```
type BaseTreeItem = {
id: string;
children: BaseTreeItem[];
};
type TreeItem<Children extends TreeItem = BaseTreeItem> = {
id: string;
children: Children[];
collapsed?: boolean;
};
function attachToRoot<T extends TreeItem>(children: T[]): TreeItem<T> { return { id: "root",
children,
  }; }
const root = attachToRoot([
  {
id: "child", children: [], collapsed: false, marked: true,
  },
```

```
]);
/* root is TreeItem<{ id: string;
children: never[];
collapsed: false;
marked: boolean;
}>
*/
```

Again, we write sub-type friendly and treat our input parameters as their own, instead of making assumptions.

Generating New Object Types

Let's go back to the toy shop. Thanks to union types, intersection types, and discriminated union types, we were able to model our data quite nicely.

```
type ToyBase = {
name: string;
description: string;
minimumAge: number;
};
type BoardGame = ToyBase & {
kind: "boardgame";
players: number;
};
type Puzzle = ToyBase & {
kind: "puzzle";
pieces: number;
};
type Doll = ToyBase & {
kind: "doll";
material: "plush" | "plastic";
};
type Toy = Doll | Puzzle | BoardGame;
```

Somewhere in our code, we need to group all toys from our model in a data structure that can be described by a type called GroupedToys . GroupedToys has a property for each category (or "kind"), and a Toy array as value. A groupToys function takes an unsorted list of toys, and groups them by kind.

```
type GroupedToys = {
boardgame: Toy[];
puzzle: Toy[];
doll: Toy[];
};
function groupToys(toys: Toy[]): GroupedToys {
const groups: GroupedToys = {
boardgame: [], puzzle: [], doll: [],
};
for (let toy of toys) {
groups[toy.kind].push(toy);
}
return groups;
```

```
}
```

There are already some niceties in this code. First, we use an explicit type annotation when declaring groups. This ensures that we are not forgetting any category. Also, since the keys of GroupedToys are the same as the union of "kind" types in Toy, we can easily index access groups by toy.kind .

Months and sprints pass, and we need to touch our model again. The toy shop is now selling original or maybe alternate vendors of interlocking toy bricks. We wire the new type Bricks up to our Toy model.

```
type Bricks = ToyBase & {
kind: "bricks", pieces: number;
brand: string;
}
type Toy = Doll | Puzzle | BoardGame | Bricks;
```

And since groupToys needs to deal with Bricks, too. We get a nice error since GroupedToys has no clue about a "bricks" kind.

```
function groupToys(toys: Toy[]): GroupedToys {
const groups: GroupedToys = {
boardgame: [], puzzle: [], doll: [],
 };
for (let toy of toys) {
groups[toy.kind].push(toy);
// ^- Element implicitly has an 'any' type because expression
//    of type '"boardgame" | "puzzle" | "doll" | "bricks"' can't be used to index type 'GroupedToys'.
//    Property 'bricks' does not exist on type 'GroupedToys'.(7053)
}
return groups;
}
```

This is desired behaviour in TypeScript: Knowing when types don't match anymore. This should draw our attention.

Let's give GroupedToys and groupToys an update.
```
type GroupedToys = {
boardgame: Toy[];
puzzle: Toy[];
doll: Toy[];
bricks: Toy[];
};
function groupToys(toys: Toy[]): GroupedToys {
const groups: GroupedToys = {
boardgame: [], puzzle: [], doll: [], bricks: [],
 };
for (let toy of toys) {
groups[toy.kind].push(toy);
 }
return groups;
}
```

There is one big thing that is bothersome: The task of grouping toys is always the same. No matter how much our model changes, we will always select by kind, and push into an array. We would need to maintain groups with every change, but if we change how we think about groups, we can optimize for change. First, we change the type GroupedToys to feature optional properties. Second, we initialize each group with an empty array if there hasn't been any initialization, yet.

```
type GroupedToys = {
boardgame?: Toy[];
puzzle?: Toy[];
doll?: Toy[];
bricks?: Toy[];
};
function groupToys(toys: Toy[]): GroupedToys {
const groups: GroupedToys = {};
for (let toy of toys) {
   // Initialize when not available
groups[toy.kind] = groups[toy.kind] ?? [];
groups[toy.kind]?.push(toy);
  }
return groups;
}
```

Now we don't need to maintain groupToys anymore. The only thing that needs maintenance is the type GroupedToys. If we look closely at GroupedToys, we see that there is an implicit relation to Toy. Each property key is part of Toy["kind"]. Let's make this relation explicit. With a mapped type, we create a new object type based on each type in Toy["kind"].

Toy["kind"] is a union of string literals: "boardgame" | "puzzle" | "doll" | "bricks". Since we have a very reduced set of strings, each element of this union will be used as its own property key. Let that sink in for a moment: We can use a type to be a property key of a newly generated type. Each property has an optional type modifier and points to a Toy[].

```
type GroupedToys = {
[k in Toy["kind"]]?: Toy[];
};
```

Fantastic! Every time we change Toy, we immediately change Toy[] . Our code needs no change at all, we can still group by kind as we did before.

This is a pattern that where we have a potential to generalize. Let's create a Group type, that takes a collection and groups it by a specific selector. We want to create a generic type with two type parameters:

The, can be anything.
Collection
Selector

The, a key of Collection, so it can create the respective properties.
Our first attempt would be to take what we had in GroupedToys and replace the concrete types with type parameters. This creates what we need, but also causes an error.

```
// How to use it type
GroupedToys = Group<Toy, "kind">;
```

```
type Group<Collection, Selector extends keyof Collection> = {[x in Collection[Selector]]?:
Collection[]; //    ^ Type 'Collection[Selector]' is not assignable // to type 'string | number | symbol'.
//      Type 'Collection[keyof Collection]' is not //      assignable to type 'string | number | symbol'.
//      Type 'Collection[string] | Collection[number]
//      | Collection[symbol]' is not assignable to //      type 'string | number | symbol'.
//      Type 'Collection[string]' is not assignable to
//      type 'string | number | symbol'.(2322)
};
```

TypeScript warns us that Collection[string] | Collection[number] | Collection[symbol] could
result in anything, not just things that can be used as a key. That's true, and we need to prepare for that.
We have two options.

First, use a type constraint on Collection that points to Record<string, any> . Record is a utility type
that generates a new object where the first parameter gives you all keys, the second parameter gives you
the types.

```
// This type is built-in! type Record<K extends string | number | symbol, T> = { [P in K]: T; };
```
This elevates Collection to be a wildcard object, effectively disabling the type check from Groups. This
is ok as if something would be an unusable type for a property key, TypeScript will throw it away
anyway. So, the final Group has two constrained type parameters.

```
type Group<Collection extends Record<string, any>, <Selector extends keyof Collection> = {
  [x in Collection[Selector]]: Collection[];
};
```

The second option that we have is to do a check for each key to see if it is a valid string key. We can use
a conditional type to see if Collection[Selector] is in fact a valid type for a key. Otherwise, we would
remove this type by choosing never. Conditional types are their own beast, and we tackle this
extensively.

```
type Group<Collection, Selector extends keyof Collection> = {
  [k in Collection[Selector] extends string
    ? Collection[Selector]
    : never]?: Collection[];
};
```

Note that we did remove the optional type modifier as well. We do this because making keys optional is
not the task of grouping. We have another type for that: Partial<T>. Again, a mapped type that makes
every property in an object type optional.

```
// This type is built-in! type Partial<T> = { [P in keyof T]?: T[P] };
```
Group helper you create, we can now create a (changing everything to optional properties) of a
GroupedToys Partial Group of No matter which object by telling TypeScript that we want a Toys by
"kind".
```
type GroupedToys = Partial<Group<Toy, "kind">>;
```
Now that reads nicely.

Modifying Objects with Assertion Signatures

JavaScript is a very flexible language. Its dynamic typing features allow you to change objects at runtime, adding new properties on the fly. And developers use this. There are situations where you e.g. run over a collection of elements and need to assert certain properties. You then store a checked property and set it to true, just so you know that you passed a certain mark.

```
function check(person: any) {
person.checked = true;
}
const person = {
name: "Stefan", age: 27,
};
check(person); // person now has the checked property
person.checked; // this is true!
```

You want to mirror this behaviour in the type system, otherwise you would need to constantly do extra checks if certain properties are in an object, even though you can be sure that they exist.

One way to assert that certain properties exist are, well, type assertions. We say that at a certain point in time, this property has a different type.

```
(person as typeof person & { checked: boolean }).checked = true;
```

Good, but you would need to do this type assertion over and over again, as they don't change the original type of person. Another way to assert that certain properties are available is to create type predicates,

```
function check<T>(obj: T): obj is T & { checked: true } {   (obj as T & { checked: boolean }).checked =
true;
return true;
}
const person = {
name: "Stefan", age: 27,
};
if (check(person)) {
person.checked; // checked is true!
}
```

The situation is a bit different though, which makes the check function feel clumsy: You need to do an extra condition, and return true in the predicate function. This doesn't feel right.

Thankfully, TypeScript has another technique we can leverage in situations like this: assertion signatures. Assertion signatures can change the type of a value in control flow, without the need for conditionals. They have been modelled for the Node.js assert function, which takes a condition, and if throws an error if it isn't true. Which means that after calling assert, you might have more information than before. For example, if you call assert and check if a value has a type of string, you should know that after this assert function the value should be string.

```
function assert(condition: any, msg?: string): asserts condition {
if (!condition) {
throw new Error(msg);
  } }
```

```
function yell(str: any) {
assert(typeof str === "string"); // str is string
return str.toUpperCase();
}
```

Please note that the function short circuits if the condition is false. It throws an error, the never case. If this function passes, you can really assert the condition.

While assertion signatures have been modelled for the Node.js assert function, you can assert any type you like. For example, you can have a function that takes any value for an addition, but you assert that the values need to be number to continue.

```
function assertNumber(val: any): asserts val is number {
if (typeof val !== "number") {
   throw Error("value is not a number");
 }
}
function add(x: unknown, y: unknown): number {   assertNumber(x); // x is number
assertNumber(y); // y is number
return x + y;
}
```

All the examples you find on assertion signatures are based after assertions and short-circuit with errors. We can take the same technique though to tell TypeScript that more properties are available. We write a function that is very similar to check in the predicate function before, but this time, we don't need to return true. We set the property, and since objects are passed by value in JavaScript, we can assert that after calling this function whatever we pass has a property checked, which is true.

```
function check<T>(obj: T): asserts obj is T & { checked: true } {
  (obj as T & { checked: boolean }).checked = true;
}
const person = {
name: "Stefan", age: 27,
};
check(person);
```
And with that we can modify a value's type on the fly. A little-known technique that can greatly help you.

Mapping Types with Type Maps
Factory functions are great if you want to create variants of complex objects based on just some basic information.
One scenario that you might know from browser JavaScript is the creation of elements. The document.createElement function accepts an element's tag name, and you get an object where you can modify all necessary properties.

You want to spice this creation up with a neat factory function you call createElement. Not only does it take the element's tag name, but it also a list of properties so you don't need to set each property individually.

```
// Using create Element
// a is HTMLAnchorElement const a = createElement("a", { href: "https://fettblog.eu" });
```

```
// b is HTMLVideoElement const b = createElement("video", { src: "/movie.mp4", autoplay: true });
// c is HTMLElement const c = createElement("my-element");
```

You want to create good types for this. There are two things you need to take care of:

Making sure you only create valid HTML elements.
Providing a type that accepts a sub-set of an HTML element's properties.

Let's take care of the valid HTML elements first. There are around 140 possible HTML elements, which is a lot.

Each of those elements has a tag name, which can be represented as string, and a respective prototype object in the DOM. Using the dom lib in your tsconfig.json , TypeScript has information on those prototype objects in form of types. And you can figure out all 140 element names.

A good way to provide a mapping between element tag names and prototype objects is to use a type map. A type map is a technique where you take a type alias or interface, and let keys point to the respective type variants. You can then get the correct type variant using index access of a string literal type.

```
type AllElements = {
a: HTMLAnchorElement;
div: HTMLDivElement;
video: HTMLVideoElement;   //... and ~140 more!
};
// HTMLAnchorElement
type A = AllElements["a"];
```

It really looks like accessing a JavaScript object's properties using index access, but remember that we're still working on a type level. Which means that index access can be broad if we intend to:

```
type AllElements = {
a: HTMLAnchorElement;
div: HTMLDivElement;
video: HTMLVideoElement;   //... and ~140 more!
};
// HTMLAnchorElement | HTMLDivELement
type AandDiv = AllElements["a" | "div"];
```

Let's use this map to type the createElement function. We use a generic type parameter constrained to all keys of AllElements, which allows us to only pass valid HTML elements.

```
function createElement<T extends keyof AllElements>(tag: T): AllElements[T] {
return document.createElement(tag as string) as AllElements[T];
}// a is HTMLAnchorElement
const a = createElement("a");
```

Using generics here is really great to pin a string literal to a literal type, which we can use to index the right HTML element variant from the type map. Also note that using document.createElement requires two type assertions.

One to make the set wider (T to string), one to make the set narrower (HTMLElement to AllElements[T]). Both assertions indicate that we have to deal with an API outside our control. We deal with the assertions later on.

Step 2. Now we want to provide the option to pass extra properties for said HTML elements, to set an href to an HTMLAnchorElement , etc. All properties are already in the respective HTMLElement variants, but they're required, not optional. We can make all properties optional with the built-in type Partial<T>. It's a mapped type that takes all properties of a certain type and adds a type modifier.

type Partial<T> = { [P in keyof T]?: T[P] };

We extend our function with an optional argument prop that is a Partial of the indexed element from AllElements HTMLAnchorElement. This way we know that if we pass an "a", we can only set properties that are available in.

```
function createElement<T extends keyof AllElements>( tag: T,   props?: Partial<AllElements[T]>
): AllElements[T] {
const elem = document.createElement(tag as string) as AllElements[T];
return Object.assign(elem, props);
}
const a = createElement("a", { href: "https://fettblog.eu" });
const x = createElement("a", { src: "https://fettblog.eu" });
//                       ^--
// Argument of type '{ src: string; }' is not assignable to parameter // of type
'Partial<HTMLAnchorElement>'.
// Object literal may only specify known properties, and 'src' does not
// exist in type 'Partial<HTMLAnchorElement>'.(2345)
```

Fantastic! Now it's up to you to figure out all 140 HTML elements. Or not. Somebody already did the work and put HTMLElementTagNameMap into lib.dom.ts. So, let's use this instead.

```
function createElement<T extends keyof HTMLElementTagNameMap>(tag: T, props?:
Partial<HTMLElementTagNameMap[T]>): HTMLElementTagNameMap[T] {
const elem = document.createElement(tag);
return Object.assign(elem, props);
}
```

This is also the interface used by document.createElement , so there is no friction between your factory function and the built-in one. No extra assertions necessary.

There is only one caveat. You are restricted to the 140 elements provided by HTMLElementTagNameMap . What if you want to create SVG elements as well, or web components where you don't know yet if they exist. Your factory function suddenly is too constrained for its own good.

To allow for more — as document.createElement does — we would need to add all possible strings to the mix again. HTMLElementTagNameMap is an interface. So, we can use declaration merging to extend the interface with an indexed signature, where we map all remaining strings to HTMLUnknownElement.

```
interface HTMLElementTagNameMap {
```

```
  [x: string]: HTMLUnknownElement;
};
function createElement<T extends keyof HTMLElementTagNameMap>( tag: T,  props?:
Partial<HTMLElementTagNameMap[T]>): HTMLElementTagNameMap[T] {
const elem = document.createElement(tag);
return Object.assign(elem, props); }
// a is HTMLAnchorElement
const a = createElement("a", { href: "https://fettblog.eu" });
// b is HTMLUnknownElement
const b = createElement("my-element");
```

Now we have everything we want: 1. A great factory function to create typed HTML elements. 2. The possibility to set an elements property with just one configuration object. 3. The flexibility to create more elements than defined.

The last is great, but what if you only want to allow for web components? Web components have a convention, they need to have a dash in their tag name. We can model this using a mapped type on a string template literal type. For now, the only thing you need to know is that we create a set of strings where the pattern is any string followed by a dash followed by any string. This is enough to ensure we only pass correct element names.

Mapped types only work with type aliases, not interface declarations, so we need to define an AllElements type again.

```
type AllElements = HTMLElementTagNameMap &
  {
   [x in `${string}-${string}`]: HTMLElement;
  };
function createElement<T extends keyof AllElements>( tag: T,  props?: Partial<AllElements[T]>
): AllElements[T] {
const elem = document.createElement(tag as string) as AllElements[T];
return Object.assign(elem, props);
}
const a = createElement("a", { href: "https://fettblog.eu" }); // OK
const b = createElement("my-element"); // OK
const c = createElement("thisWillError");
//                     ^
// Argument of type '"thisWillError"' is not
// assignable to parameter of type '`${string}-${string}`
// | keyof HTMLElementTagNameMap'.(2345)
```

Fantastic. With the AllElements type we also get type assertions back, which we don't like that much. In that case, instead of asserting, we can also use a function overload, defining two declarations: One for our users, and one for us to implement the function.

```
function createElement<T extends keyof AllElements>(tag: T,  props?: Partial<AllElements[T]>
): AllElements[T];
function createElement(tag: string, props?: Partial<HTMLElement>): HTMLElement {
const elem = document.createElement(tag);
return Object.assign(elem, props);
}
```

Now we are all set and done. We defined a type map with mapped types and index signatures, using generic type parameters to be very explicit about our intentions. A great combination of multiple tools in our TypeScript tool belt.

Using ThisType to Define this in Objects

Frameworks like VueJS rely a lot on factory functions, where you pass a comprehensive configuration object to define initial data, computed properties, and methods for each instance. You want to create a similar behaviour for components of your app. The idea is to provide a configuration object with three properties:

1.   A data function. The return value is the initial data for the instance. You should not have access to any other properties from the configuration object in this function.
2.   A computed property. This is for, well, computed properties; properties, which are based on the initial data.
Computed properties are declared using functions. They can access initial data just like normal properties.
3.   A methods property. Methods that can be called, and that can access computed properties as well as the initial data. When methods access computed properties, they access it like they would access normal properties, no need to call the function.

Looking at the configuration object in use, there are three different ways how to interpret this. In data, this doesn't have any properties at all. In computed, each function can access the return value of data via this just like it would be part of their object. In methods, each method can access computed properties and data via this just in the same way.

```
const instance = create({   data() {    return {
firstName: "Stefan", lastName: "Baumgartner",
    };
},
computed: {
fullName() {  // has access to the return object of data
return this.firstName + " " + this.lastName;
    },
},
methods: {
hi() {   // use computed properties just like normal properties
alert(this.fullName.toLowerCase());
    },
}, });
```

This behaviour is special, but not uncommon. And with a behaviour like that, we definitely want to rely on good types.

Let's create types for each property. We define a type Options, which we are going to refine step by step. First is the data function. data can be user-defined, so we want to specify data using a generic type parameter. The data we are looking for is specified by the return type of the data function.

```
type Options<Data> = {
data(this: {})?: Data;
```

```
};
```

So, once we specify an actual return value in the data function, the Data placeholder gets substituted with the real object's type. Note that we also define this to point to the empty object. Which means that we don't get access to any other property from the configuration object.

Next, we define computed. computed is an object of functions. We add another generic type parameter called, and let the value of Computed be typed through usage. Here, this changes to all the properties of Computed Data. Since we can't set this like we do in the data function, we can use the built-in helper type ThisType and set it to the generic type parameter Data.

```
type Options<Data, Computed> = {
data(this: {})?: Data;
computed?: Computed & ThisType<Data>;
};
```

This allows us to access e.g this.firstName like in the example before. Last, but not least we want to specify methods. methods are again special as you are not only getting access to Data via this, but also to all methods, and to all computed properties as properties.

Computed holds all computed properties as functions. We would need their value, though. More specific, their return value. If we access fullName via property access, we expect it to be a string.

For that, we create a little helper type called MapFnToProp. It takes a type that is an object of functions, and maps it to their return values' types. The built-in ReturnType helper type is perfect for this scenario.

```
// An object of functions ... type
FnObj = Record<string, () => any>;
// ... to an object of return types
type MapFnToProp<FunctionObj extends FnObj> = {
[K in keyof FunctionObj]: ReturnType<FunctionObj[K]>;
};
```

MapFnToProp to set ThisType for a newly added generic type parameter called Methods and Methods itself to the mix. To pass the Computed generic type parameter to MapFnToProp FnObj, the same constraint of the first parameter FunctionObj in MapFnToProp We can use. We also add Data, it needs to be constrained to type Options<Data,

```
Computed extends FnObj, Methods> = {
data(this: {})?: Data;
computed?: Computed & ThisType<Data>;
methods?: Methods & ThisType<Data & MapFnToProp<Computed> & Methods>;
};
```

And that's the type! We take all generic type properties and add them to the create factory function.

```
declare function create<Data, Computed extends FnObj, Methods>( options: Options<Data, Computed, Methods> ): any;
```

Through usage, all generic type parameters will be substituted. And the way Options is typed, we get all the autocomplete necessary to make sure we don't run into troubles.

The methods configuration in the factory function having all the access to the correct properties. This example shows wonderfully how TypeScript can be used to type elaborate APIs where a lot of object manipulation is happening underneath:footnote[Special thanks to the creators of Type Challenges for this beautiful example.].

Adding const Context to Generic Type Parameters

Single-Page Application frameworks tend to reimplement a lot of browser functionality in JavaScript. For example, features like the History API made it possible to override the regular navigation behavior, which SPA frameworks use to switch between pages without a real page reload, just by swapping the content of the page and changing the URL in the browser.

Imagine working on a minimalistic SPA framework that uses a so-called router to navigate between pages. Pages are defined as components, and a ComponentConstructor interface knows how to instantiate and render new elements on your website.

```
interface ComponentConstructor {
new(): Component;
}
interface Component {
render(): HTMLElement;
}
```

The router should take a list of components and associated paths, stored as string. When creating a router through the router function, it should return an object that lets you navigate the desired path.

```
type Route = {
path: string;
component: ComponentConstructor;
};
function router(routes: Route[]) {
return {
navigate(path: string) {      // ...
   },
 };
}
```

How the actual navigation is implemented is of no concern to us right now, we want to focus on the typings of the function interface.

The router works as intended, it takes an array of Route objects, and returns an object with a navigate function, which allows us to trigger the navigation from one URL to the other, and renders the new component.

```
const rtr = router([
  {   path: "/",
   component: Main,
  },
  {
path: "/about", component: About,
  }, ])
```

```
rtr.navigate("/faq");
```

What you immediately see though is that the types are way too broad. If we allow navigating to every string available, nothing keeps us from using bogus routes that lead to nowhere. We would need to implement some sort of error handling for information that is already ready and available. So why not use it?

Our first idea would be to replace the concrete type with a generic type parameter. The way TypeScript deals with generic substitution is that if we have a literal type, TypeScript will sub-type accordingly. Introducing T for Route and using T["path"] instead of string comes close to what we want to achieve.

```
function router<T extends Route>(routes: T[]) {   return {    navigate(path: T["path"]) {      // ...
    },
  };
}
```

In theory, this should work. If we remind ourselves what TypeScript does with literal, primitives' types in that case, we would expect the value to be narrowed down to the literal type.

```
function getPath<T extends string>(route: T): T {
return route;
}
const path = getPath("/"); // "/"
```

One important detail is that path in the previous example is in a const context, due to the fact the returned value is immutable.

The only problem is that we are working with objects and arrays, and TypeScript tends to widen types in objects and arrays to something more general to allow for the mutability of values. If we look at a similar example, but with a nested object, we see that TypeScript takes the broader type instead.

```
type Routes = {
paths: string[];
};
function getPaths<T extends Routes>(routes: T): T["paths"] {
return routes.paths;
}
const paths = getPaths({ paths: ["/", "/about"] }); // string[]
```

For objects, the const context for paths is only for the binding of the variable, not for its contents. This eventually leads us to lose some of the information we need to correctly type navigate.

A way to work around this limitation is to manually apply const context, which needs us to re-define the input parameter to be read only.

```
function router<T extends Route>(routes: readonly T[]) {
return {
navigate(path: T["path"]) {
history.pushState({}, "", path);
    },
  };
}
const rtr = router([
```

```
{    path: "/",    component: Main,
  },  {
path: "/about",
 component: About,
  },
] as const); rtr.navigate("/about");
```

This works, but also requires us to not forget a very important detail when coding. And actively remembering workarounds is always a recipe for disaster.

Thankfully, TypeScript allows us to request const context from generic type parameters. Instead of applying it to the value, we substitute the generic type parameter for a concrete value but in const context by adding the const modifier to the generic type parameter.

```
function router<const T extends Route>(routes: T[]) {   return {
navigate(path: T["path"]) {
    // tbd
  },
 };
}
```

With that, we can use our router just as we are used to, and even get autocomplete for possible paths.
```
const rtr = router([
  { path: "/",    component: Main,
  },
{
path: "/about", component: About,
  },
]) rtr.navigate("/about");
```

Even better, we get proper errors when we pass in something bogus.

```
const rtr = router([
  {
path: "/", component: Main,
  },
{
path: "/about", component: About,
  },
])
rtr.navigate("/faq");
//          ^
// Argument of type '"/faq"' is not assignable to
// parameter of type '"/" | "/about"'.
```

The beautiful thing is that all is hidden in the function's API. What we expect becomes clearer, the interface tells us the constraints, and we don't have to do anything extra when using router to ensure type safety.

Detailed Conclusion: Understanding Basic Types and Generics in TypeScript

TypeScript is a game-changer for JavaScript developers, offering features that enhance productivity and robustness in large-scale application development. Among its many powerful features, **basic types** and **generics** form the cornerstone of its type system, providing both structure and flexibility to developers. This detailed conclusion examines the significance of these concepts, their practical applications, and their impact on modern programming practices. By understanding and mastering basic types and generics, developers can write scalable, maintainable, and error-resistant code.

1. Significance of Basic Types in TypeScript

TypeScript's basic types form the foundation of its type system. These types ensure that developers can enforce consistency and clarity in their code, significantly reducing runtime errors that are common in vanilla JavaScript.

1.1. Enhanced Type Safety

With basic types like number, string, and Boolean, developers can explicitly define what kind of data is expected, catching potential errors at compile time rather than at runtime. This leads to more predictable and stable applications. For example:

```
let username: string = "Alice"; // TypeScript ensures this is always a string.
```

Without such type safety, JavaScript developers often rely on runtime checks, which can be error-prone and cumbersome. By enforcing types, TypeScript eliminates entire classes of bugs.

1.2. Improved Code Readability and Maintainability

Code with explicitly defined types is easier to read and maintain. A developer can understand the intended use of variables, functions, and classes without guessing or referring to documentation. This is especially valuable in collaborative environments or in projects with long lifespans.

For instance:

```
function calculateTotal(price: number, tax: number): number {
    return price + tax;
}
```
This code snippet immediately conveys what the function does and what arguments it expects, making it intuitive for other developers.

1.3. Advanced Features Like Tuples and Enums

Beyond the primitive types, TypeScript introduces advanced types like tuple and enum, which bring additional structure to data management. For example, tuple allows for fixed-length arrays with specific types:

```
let user: [string, number] = ["Alice", 30];
```
Enums improve code clarity by replacing magic numbers or strings with meaningful names:

```
enum Role {
    Admin,
    User,
    Guest,
```

```
}
let currentRole: Role = Role.Admin;
```
These features enable developers to model real-world data more accurately.

1.4. Control Over Null and Undefined

In JavaScript, null and undefined often cause unexpected behavior. TypeScript provides tools like strict null checks to enforce discipline when dealing with these values, minimizing runtime surprises:

```
let optionalValue: string | null = null; // Explicitly allows null.
```

2. Importance of Generics in TypeScript

Generics take the type system to the next level, enabling developers to create reusable, type-safe abstractions. They offer a powerful way to handle different types while maintaining type safety and flexibility.

2.1. Reusability Without Sacrificing Type Safety

Generics allow developers to write components, functions, or classes that work with various types without duplicating code for each type. For example:

```
function getFirstElement<T>(array: T[]): T {
   return array[0];
}
```

This function can handle arrays of any type (number[], string[], etc.) while ensuring type safety.

2.2. Flexibility in Application

Unlike basic types, which are predefined, generics allow developers to define their own type parameters, offering unmatched flexibility. For instance:

```
class Stack<T> {
   private items: T[] = [];
   push(item: T): void {
      this.items.push(item);
   }
   pop(): T | undefined {
      return this.items.pop();
   }
}
```
This Stack class works seamlessly with any data type while retaining type safety.

2.3. Constraints for Specific Use Cases

Generics can be constrained to ensure they meet certain criteria. For example:

```
function printObject<T extends { id: number }>(obj: T): void {
   console.log(obj.id);
}
```

Here, T must have an id property, ensuring that the function is only called with objects that meet this requirement.

2.4. Building Type-Safe Data Structures

Generics shine in scenarios involving custom data structures. For example, a generic linked list or tree structure can be implemented once and reused across various data types:

```
class Node<T> {
  value: T;
  next: Node<T> | null = null;

  constructor(value: T) {
    this.value = value;
  }
}
```

Such implementations demonstrate how generics bring type safety and flexibility to advanced programming tasks.

2.5. Simplifying API and Library Design

Modern libraries like React and Angular heavily rely on generics to provide reusable, type-safe APIs. For example, React's useState hook uses generics to infer the state type:

```
const [count, setCount] = useState<number>(0);
```

This pattern allows developers to write cleaner and more intuitive code.

3. Bridging Basic Types and Generics

While basic types offer a strong foundation for individual data elements, generics provide the tools to scale and generalize type safety across complex systems. Together, they ensure that every aspect of a TypeScript application is both robust and reusable.

3.1. Combining Basic Types and Generics

Generics can incorporate basic types to create versatile constructs. For example:

```
function mapArray<T, U>(array: T[], transform: (item: T) => U): U[] {
  return array.map(transform);
}

let numbers = [1, 2, 3];
let strings = mapArray(numbers, num => num.toString());
```

Here, the function works with any input-output combination of types, blending flexibility with explicit type safety.

3.2. Advanced Techniques Using Basic Types and Generics

TypeScript's utility types, such as Partial<T>, Readonly<T>, and Record<K, T>, rely on generics while building upon basic types. For example:

```
type ReadonlyUser = Readonly<{ name: string; age: number }>;
```

```
let user: ReadonlyUser = { name: "Alice", age: 30 };
// user.age = 31; // Error: Cannot assign to 'age' because it is a read-only property.
```

4. Real-World Applications

The real power of TypeScript's type system becomes evident in real-world scenarios, where basic types and generics work together to simplify complex requirements:

4.1. API Design

When working with APIs, developers often deal with diverse data structures. Using basic types and generics ensures that requests and responses are type-safe:

```
type ApiResponse<T> = {
    data: T;
    error: string | null;
};
```

```
let userResponse: ApiResponse<{ name: string; age: number }> = {
    data: { name: "Alice", age: 30 },
    error: null,
};
```

4.2. UI Component Libraries

Libraries like React rely heavily on generics to create flexible and reusable components:

```
type ButtonProps<T> = {
    label: string;
    onClick: (event: T) => void;
};
```

```
function Button<T>(props: ButtonProps<T>) {
    // Component implementation
}
```

4.3. Data Validation and Parsing

Generics combined with basic types help validate and parse dynamic data structures:

```
function parseJSON<T>(json: string): T {
    return JSON.parse(json);
}
```

5. Challenges and Best Practices

5.1. Challenges

Overuse of Generics: Using generics when not necessary can lead to overly complex code.

Learning Curve: Understanding advanced generic patterns may take time.

Balancing Flexibility and Constraints: Striking the right balance between flexibility and strictness can be tricky.

5.2. Best Practices

Use Generics Judiciously: Only introduce generics when they add value.

Combine Basic Types and Generics: Leverage the strengths of both for optimal results.

Follow TypeScript Guidelines: Stick to idiomatic TypeScript patterns for readability and maintainability.

Conclusion

The combination of basic types and generics makes TypeScript an incredibly versatile language. Basic types provide the foundation for type safety, clarity, and maintainability, while generics unlock the potential for reusable and scalable code. Together, they allow developers to write robust applications, enhance collaboration in teams, and minimize bugs.

In modern development, where projects grow in size and complexity, mastering these concepts is essential. Basic types ensure the correctness of individual data elements, while generics enable flexibility in handling complex data structures and logic. By learning to wield both effectively, developers can harness the full power of TypeScript, creating applications that are not only functional but also elegant and maintainable.

This mastery ultimately leads to a significant boost in productivity and code quality, making TypeScript a must-have tool in any developer's toolkit.

5. Metaprogramming in JavaScript

Introduction

Metaprogramming is the art of writing programs that manipulate themselves or other programs. In JavaScript and TypeScript, this is achieved through techniques like reflection, proxies, decorators, and dynamic typing. Combining these capabilities with TypeScript's strong type system opens the door to creating more robust, maintainable, and expressive applications.

This guide provides a comprehensive overview of metaprogramming in JavaScript with TypeScript, covering fundamental concepts, tools, and real-world applications.

1. Understanding Metaprogramming

1.1. What is Metaprogramming?

Metaprogramming involves writing code that can:

Inspect itself or other code at runtime.

Modify its structure or behaviour dynamically.

1.2. Why Use Metaprogramming?

Metaprogramming offers several advantages:

Dynamic Behavior: Add or modify features at runtime.
Code Abstraction: Reduce boilerplate and enhance maintainability.
Enhanced Reflection: Implement more sophisticated debugging or testing utilities.

1.3. Challenges

Complexity: Metaprogramming can make code harder to understand.
Performance Overhead: Dynamic features may introduce runtime costs.
Type Safety: Ensuring correctness in TypeScript requires careful design.

2. Core Metaprogramming Tools

2.1. Reflection and Introspection

Reflection allows programs to examine their own structure.

In JavaScript:

```
const obj = { name: "Alice", age: 25 };
console.log(Object.keys(obj)); // ['name', 'age']
console.log(typeof obj.name);  // 'string'
```

In TypeScript:

TypeScript's type system is erased at runtime, but you can use utilities like typeof or decorators for static type checks.

```
type Person = { name: string; age: number };
function printKeys<T>(obj: T): void {
  console.log(Object.keys(obj));
}
```

2.2. Proxies

Proxies intercept and redefine fundamental operations on objects.

Example: Logging Access

```
const user = { name: "Alice", age: 25 };
const userProxy = new Proxy(user, {
  get(target, prop) {
    console.log(`Accessing ${String(prop)}`);
    return target[prop];
  },
});
console.log(userProxy.name); // Logs: Accessing name
```

Proxies are particularly powerful for:

Data Validation
Lazy Initialization
Access Control

2.3. Decorators

Decorators modify class behavior and are widely used in TypeScript.

Example: Logging a Method Call

```
function Log(target: any, propertyKey: string, descriptor: PropertyDescriptor) {
  const originalMethod = descriptor.value;
  descriptor.value = function (...args: any[]) {
    console.log(`Calling ${propertyKey} with args:`, args);
    return originalMethod.apply(this, args);
  };
}

class User {
  @Log
  greet(name: string): string {
    return `Hello, ${name}`;
  }
}
const user = new User();
```

```
console.log(user.greet("Alice")); // Logs: Calling greet with args: ["Alice"]
```

2.4. Dynamic Code Evaluation

eval and the Function constructor allow execution of code strings, but these should be used sparingly due to security risks.

```
const code = "console.log('Hello, World!')";
eval(code); // Prints: Hello, World!
```

2.5. Symbols

Symbols provide unique keys for object properties.

```
const sym = Symbol("unique");
const obj = { [sym]: "value" };
console.log(obj[sym]); // 'value'
```

Symbols are invaluable for creating hidden properties and ensuring no key collisions.

3. TypeScript-Specific Features

3.1. Type Reflection with Conditional Types

TypeScript's conditional types allow you to create dynamic types.

Example: Extracting Read-Only Keys

```
type ReadonlyKeys<T> = {
  [K in keyof T]: T[K] extends Readonly<T[K]> ? K : never;
}[keyof T];
type Example = ReadonlyKeys<{ readonly id: number; name: string }>;
// Result: 'id'
```

3.2. Mapped Types

Modify types dynamically using mapped types.

Example: Making All Properties Optional

```
type Optional<T> = { [K in keyof T]?: T[K] };
type User = { name: string; age: number };
type OptionalUser = Optional<User>;
```

3.3. Utility Types

TypeScript provides a set of utility types like Partial, Required, Pick, and Omit.

Example: Using Pick

```
type User = { id: number; name: string; age: number };
```

```typescript
type UserPreview = Pick<User, "id" | "name">;
```

4. Applications of Metaprogramming

4.1. Frameworks and Libraries

Angular: Uses decorators for dependency injection and metadata.
Express Middleware: Proxies and decorators for route handling.
GraphQL Resolvers: Dynamic introspection and validation.

4.2. Code Generation

Generate boilerplate code dynamically at build time or runtime.

Example: REST API Client

```typescript
function createApiClient<T>(baseUrl: string): T {
  return new Proxy({} as T, {
    get(_, endpoint: string) {
      return async (params: any) => {
        const response = await fetch(`${baseUrl}/${endpoint}`, {
          method: "POST",
          body: JSON.stringify(params),
        });
        return response.json();
      };
    },
  });
}
```

```typescript
const api = createApiClient<{ getUser: (id: number) => Promise<any> }>("https://api.example.com");
api.getUser(1).then(console.log);
```

4.3. Validation

Simplify validation rules using proxies or decorators.

Example: Proxy-Based Validation

```typescript
const validator = {
  set(obj: any, prop: string, value: any) {
    if (prop === "age" && value < 0) {
      throw new Error("Age must be positive");
    }
    obj[prop] = value;
    return true;
  },
};
const user = new Proxy({}, validator);
user.age = -5; // Throws error
```

4.4. Testing and Mocking

Enhance testing by dynamically replacing methods or objects.

Example: Mocking API Calls

```
const fetchMock = new Proxy(global.fetch, {
  apply(target, thisArg, args) {
    console.log(`Intercepting fetch call to: ${args[0]}`);
    return Promise.resolve({ json: () => ({ data: "mocked data" }) });
  },
});
global.fetch = fetchMock;
```

4.5. Dynamic UI Components

Create dynamic React or Vue components with metaprogramming.

Example: React Higher-Order Component

```
function withLogger(WrappedComponent: React.ComponentType) {
  return function (props: any) {
    console.log("Rendering with props:", props);
    return <WrappedComponent {...props} />;
  };
}
```

5. Best Practices

5.1. Type Safety

Ensure strong typings when metaprogramming in TypeScript.

5.2. Minimal Overhead

Use proxies and decorators judiciously to avoid performance hits.

5.3. Security

Avoid unsafe constructs like eval.

5.4. Documentation

Thoroughly document dynamic behaviours for better maintainability.

Metaprogramming represents an approach in coding where a software can alter or adapt its own composition, functionality, or characteristics of supplementary programs during execution. In JavaScript and TypeScript, numerous methodologies facilitate metaprogramming, including:

Reflection: Investigating and adjusting an entity's attributes and techniques at runtime. The Reflect object in JavaScript offers an array of introspection methods, such as Reflect.get(), Reflect.set(), and

Reflect.apply().

Proxy: In JavaScript, the Proxy object enables the delineation of bespoke conduct for core operations on entities, encompassing property searches, assignments, and function executions. A surrogate can intercept and transform these actions on the intended object. As an illustration, one can establish tailored getter and setter actions for an object utilizing a surrogate.

```
const target = {x: 1};
const handler = {get (obj, prop) {console.log (`Getting ${prop}`);
return obj[prop];
},
set(obj, prop, value) {console.log(`Setting ${prop} to ${value}`);
obj[prop] = value;
return true;
}
};
const proxy = new Proxy(target, handler);
console.log(proxy.x); // "Getting x" and 1 proxy.x = 2; // "Setting x to 2"
```

Function creation: JavaScript facilitates generating new functions during runtime via the Function constructor or the eval() function. Nonetheless, this method is not recommended due to security and performance issues.

Decorators: This syntactic characteristic, introduced in TypeScript and now compatible with JavaScript, enables the attachment of metadata or behaviour to classes, methods, or properties.

Code alteration: In TypeScript, transformers can be utilized to adjust the Abstract Syntax Tree (AST) throughout the compilation phase. This enables manipulation of the produced code before execution. Although TypeScript is a strict syntactical extension of JavaScript, it does not introduce new metaprogramming features. However, TypeScript's static typing aspect can enhance metaprogramming safety and predictability through type information and improved tooling support.

Consider the following TypeScript-specific elements when using metaprogramming techniques: Type Guards:

TypeScript enables the creation of custom type guards, which are functions capable of narrowing a variable's type at runtime. Type guards are beneficial in metaprogramming situations where confirming an object's type or structure is necessary before executing reflective operations on it.

```
interface Animal {speak: () => string;
}

interface Dog extends Animal {   bark: () => string;
}

function isDog(animal: Animal): animal is Dog {   return "bark" in animal;
}

const myAnimal: Animal = {speak: () => "Hello", bark: () => "Woof"};
```

```typescript
if (isDog(myAnimal)) {console.log(myAnimal.bark()); // TypeScript knows that myAnimal is of type
Dog here
}
```

Mapped Types: TypeScript provides a powerful type-level programming feature called mapped types. Mapped types allow you to create new types by transforming the properties of existing types.

```typescript
type Readonly<T> = {readonly [K in keyof T]: T[K];
};
```

```typescript
interface User {name: string;
age: number;
}
```

```typescript
type ReadonlyUser = Readonly<User>;
```

In this example, ReadonlyUser is a new type that has the same properties as User, but all properties are marked as readonly.

Conditional Types: Conditional types enable you to create types that depend on other types. This can be useful for creating utility types or validating the types of metaprogramming code.

```typescript
type NonFunctionPropertyNames<T> = {
  [K in keyof T]: T[K] extends Function ? never : K;
}
[keyof T];
```

```typescript
type NonFunctionProperties<T> = {
  [P in NonFunctionPropertyNames<T>]: T[P];
};
```

```typescript
interface Person {name: string; age: number; greet: () => void;
}
```

```typescript
type DataProperties = NonFunctionProperties<Person>; //
{
name: string;
age: number;
}
```

In this example, the NonFunctionProperties type takes an input type T and removes any properties whose values are functions.

These TypeScript features can enhance metaprogramming by providing more control over types and ensuring type safety when performing operations like reflection or code generation. However, it's essential to be cautious when using metaprogramming, as it can lead to code that is harder to understand, maintain, and debug. Creating a typed event emitter

```typescript
interface EventMap {
[event: string]: (...args: any[]) => void;
}
```

```typescript
class TypedEventEmitter<T extends EventMap> {   private listeners: { [K in keyof T]?: Array<T[K]> }
= {};
on<K extends keyof T>(event: K, listener: T[K]): void {     if (!this.listeners[event]) {
this.listeners[event] = [];
   } this.listeners[event]!.push(listener);
  }
emit<K extends keyof T>(event: K, ...args: Parameters<T[K]>): void {
const listeners = this.listeners[event];
if (!listeners) return;
for (const listener of listeners) {listener(...args);
   }
  }
}

// Usage interface
MyEvents {
textReceived: (text: string) => void;
dataUpdated: (data: number[]) => void;
}

const eventEmitter = new TypedEventEmitter<MyEvents>();

eventEmitter.on("textReceived", (text) => {console.log("Text received:", text);
});

eventEmitter.on("dataUpdated", (data) => {console.log("Data updated:", data);
});

eventEmitter.emit("textReceived", "Hello, world!");
eventEmitter.emit("dataUpdated", [1, 2, 3]);
```

This example demonstrates the use of TypeScript generics and mapped types to create a type-safe event emitter. The TypedEventEmitter class takes an event map as a type parameter and enforces type safety for event names and listener functions.

Using decorators to measure function execution time function measureExecutionTime<T extends (...args: any[]) => any>(target: Object,   propertyKey: string | symbol,   descriptor: TypedPropertyDescriptor<T>): TypedPropertyDescriptor<T> {
const originalMethod = descriptor.value!;

```typescript
descriptor.value = function (...args: Parameters<T>) {
const start = performance.now();
const result = originalMethod.apply(this, args);
const end = performance.now();
console.log(`Execution time for ${String(propertyKey)}: ${end - start} ms`);
   return result;
  };
  return descriptor;
}
class MathOperations {@measureExecutionTime   add(a: number, b: number): number {
return a + b;
```

```
  }
  @measureExecutionTime   multiply(a: number, b: number): number {     return a * b;
  }
}
const math = new MathOperations();
console.log(math.add(1, 2));
console.log(math.multiply(3, 4));
```

In this example, we use TypeScript decorators to measure the execution time of class methods. The measureExecutionTime decorator wraps the original method with a function that calculates the time taken to execute the method and logs the result.

Note that decorators are an experimental feature in TypeScript, and you'll need to enable the experimentalDecorators option in your tsconfig.json file to use them.

Using Proxy to create an auto-save feature for objects

```
type AutoSaveHandler<T> = {autoSave: (updatedObject: T) => void;
};
function createAutoSaveProxy<T extends object>(target: T, handler: AutoSaveHandler<T>): T {
return new Proxy(target, {
set: (obj, prop, value) => {
(obj as any)[prop] = value;
handler.autoSave(obj);
return true;
  },
 });
}
// Usage interface
Person {name: string; age: number;
}
const person: Person = {name: "John", age: 30};
const autoSaveHandler: AutoSaveHandler<Person> = {autoSave: (updatedObject) =>
{console.log("Auto-saving updated object:", updatedObject);
  },
};
const autoSaveProxy = createAutoSaveProxy(person, autoSaveHandler);
autoSaveProxy.name = "Jane"; // Auto-saving updated
object: {name: 'Jane', age: 30}
autoSaveProxy.age = 35; // Auto-saving updated
object: {name: 'Jane', age: 35}
```

In this example, we create a createAutoSaveProxy function that returns a proxy object. The proxy object intercepts all property assignments and triggers an auto-save function, which in this case, logs the updated object to the console.

Using TypeScript decorators to apply validation

```
interface Validator {
  (value: any): boolean;
}
interface ValidationMap {
  [property: string]: Validator[];
```

```
}
function createValidatorDecorator(validator: Validator):

PropertyDecorator { return (target, propertyKey) => {const validationMap: ValidationMap =
Reflect.getMetadata("validation", target) || {};
validationMap[propertyKey as string] = validationMap[propertyKey as string] || [];
validationMap[propertyKey as string].push(validator);
Reflect.defineMetadata("validation", validationMap, target);
  };
}
function validate(target: any): boolean {
const validationMap: ValidationMap = Reflect.getMetadata("validation", target) || {};
return Object.keys(validationMap).every((property) => {
const validators = validationMap[property];
return validators.every((validator) => validator(target[property]));
  });
}
const isNotEmpty = createValidatorDecorator((value) => value && value.trim().length > 0);
class User {@isNotEmpty
  public name: string;
  constructor(name: string) {this.name = name;
  }
}
// Usage
const validUser = new User("John");
console.log("Valid user?", validate(validUser)); // Valid user? true
const invalidUser = new User("  ");
console.log("Valid user?", validate(invalidUser)); // Valid user? False
```

This example demonstrates the use of TypeScript decorators to create a simple validation system for class properties. The createValidatorDecorator function generates property decorators that apply a validation function to the class property. The validate function checks whether all class properties pass their respective validation functions.

To run this example, you'll need to have the reflect-metadata package installed and enable the experimentalDecorators and emitDecoratorMetadata options in your tsconfig.json file.

Remember that metaprogramming can make code more challenging to understand and maintain. It's essential to use these techniques judiciously and thoroughly document their purpose and usage.

Singleton pattern using decorators

```
function Singleton<T extends new (...args: any[]) => any>(constructor: T): T {
return new Proxy(constructor, {
instance: null, construct: (target, args) => {
if (!this.instance) {
    this.instance = new target(...args);
  }
return this.instance;
  },
  });
```

```
}
```

```typescript
@Singleton class Database {
private constructor() {
console.log("Database created.");
  }
  query(sql: string): any {
console.log(`Executing query: ${sql}`);
  }
}
const db1 = new Database(); const db2 = new Database();
db1.query("SELECT * FROM users");
console.log(db1 === db2); // true
```

In this example, we use a class decorator to implement the Singleton pattern. The Singleton decorator wraps the constructor with a Proxy that ensures only one instance of the class is created. When attempting to create multiple instances, it returns the same instance.
Creating a simple dependency injection container

```typescript
const dependencyContainer = new Map<string | symbol | object, object>();
function register<T>(token: string | symbol | object, constructor: new () => T): void {
if (dependencyContainer.has(token)) {
throw new Error(`Dependency with token '${token.toString()}' is already registered.`);
  }
dependencyContainer.set(token, new constructor());
}
function resolve<T>(token: string | symbol | object): T {
const dependency = dependencyContainer.get(token);
if (!dependency) {
throw new Error(`Dependency with token '${token.toString()}' is not registered.`);
  }
return dependency as T;
}
// Example services
class Logger {
log(message: string): void {
console.log(message);
  }
}
class UserService {
constructor(private logger: Logger) {}
  createUser(name: string): void {
this.logger.log(`User created: ${name}`);
}
}
// Register dependencies
register("logger", Logger);
register("userService", () => new UserService(resolve<Logger>("logger")));
// Resolve and use dependencies
const logger = resolve<Logger>("logger");
const userService = resolve<UserService>("userService");
```

```
logger.log("Hello, world!");
userService.createUser("John");
```

In the provided example, a basic dependency injection container is established using a TypeScript map. The register function serves to register dependencies, while the resolve function aids in resolving and obtaining dependencies. This approach contributes to better organization and management of dependencies and their lifecycles.

Memoization with TypeScript decorators

```
function Memoize<T extends (...args: any[]) => any>(  target: Object,  propertyKey: string | symbol,
descriptor: TypedPropertyDescriptor<T> ): TypedPropertyDescriptor<T> {
const originalMethod = descriptor.value!;
const cache = new Map<string, ReturnType<T>>();
  descriptor.value = function (...args: Parameters<T>) {
const cacheKey = JSON.stringify(args);
    if (!cache.has(cacheKey)) {
cache.set(cacheKey, originalMethod.apply(this, args));
    }
    return cache.get(cacheKey);
  };
  return descriptor;
}

class ExpensiveOperations {
  @Memoize
  public expensiveCalculation(a: number, b: number): number {
console.log("Performing expensive calculation...");
return a * b;
  }
}
const operations = new ExpensiveOperations();
console.log(operations.expensiveCalculation(2, 3)); // Performing expensive calculation... 6
console.log(operations.expensiveCalculation(2, 3)); // 6 (cached result, no calculation performed)
```

In this example, we create a Memorize decorator that caches the result of a function based on its input arguments. If the function is called again with the same arguments, the cached result is returned instead of recalculating. This can improve the performance of functions with expensive computations.

Type-safe action creators for Redux using mapped types

```
interface Action<T extends string> {
type: T;
}
interface PayloadAction<T extends string, P> extends Action<T> {
payload: P;
}
type ActionCreator<T extends string, P> = (...args: any[]) => PayloadAction<T, P>;
type ActionsMap = {
  [actionType: string]: ActionCreator<any, any>;
};
```

```typescript
type ActionTypes<T extends ActionsMap> = {
  [K in keyof T]: ReturnType<T[K]>;
}
[keyof T];
function createAction<T extends string, P>( type: T,   payloadCreator: (...args: any[]) => P ):
ActionCreator<T, P> {   return (...args: any[]): PayloadAction<T, P> => ({   type,   payload:
payloadCreator(...args),
  });
}
// Usage
const increment = createAction("INCREMENT", (value: number) => value);
const setName = createAction("SET_NAME", (name: string) => name);
type MyActions = ActionTypes<typeof increment | typeof setName>;
function reducer(state: any, action: MyActions) {
switch (action.type) {
case "INCREMENT":
    return { ...state, counter: state.counter + action.payload };
  case "SET_NAME":
    return { ...state, name: action.payload };    default:
    return state;
  }
}
```

In this example, we create a type-safe action creator function for Redux. The createAction function generates action creators with the given type and payload creator function. The ActionTypes mapped type is used to create a union type of all possible actions, which can be used in the reducer function for type-safe action handling.

Metaprogramming techniques are used in the example of Type-safe action creators for Redux using mapped types to automatically generate type-safe action creators. The use of mapped types in this example is a form of metaprogramming, where the code is generating code automatically at compile time.

In the example, mapped types are used to transform an interface of action types into a set of type-safe action creators. The mapped type creates a set of functions that take a payload as an argument and return an action object with the correct type and payload. By using mapped types, the action creators are generated automatically, reducing the potential for human error and improving type safety.

This is an example of metaprogramming because the code is generating code automatically at compile time. Instead of manually creating each action creator function, the code is generating them automatically based on the interface of action types. This approach reduces the amount of manual work needed to create type-safe action creators, and also reduces the potential for errors in the creation of action objects.

Using a decorator to automatically unsubscribe from Observables (Angular Framework example)
```typescript
import {Component, OnDestroy} from '@angular/core';
import {Observable, Subject} from 'rxjs';
import {takeUntil} from 'rxjs/operators';
function AutoUnsubscribe(destroy$: string = 'ngOnDestroy'): ClassDecorator {
return (constructor) => {
const original = constructor.prototype[destroy$];
```

```typescript
if (typeof original !== 'function') {console.warn(`AutoUnsubscribe: ${constructor.name} does not
implement OnDestroy`);
}
    constructor.prototype[destroy$] = function ()
{
if (this[destroy$])
{
this[destroy$].next();
this[destroy$].complete();
}if (original)
{
original.apply(this, arguments);
    }
  };
 };
}
@Component({
  selector: 'app-example', template: `...`,
})
@AutoUnsubscribe() export class ExampleComponent implements OnDestroy {
private readonly destroy$ = new Subject<void>();
public someObservable$: Observable<any>;
  constructor() {    this.someObservable$ = new Observable().pipe(takeUntil(this.destroy$))
    .subscribe((data) => console.log(data));
  }
  ngOnDestroy() {    console.log('Component destroyed');
  }
}
```

In this example, we create an AutoUnsubscribe decorator that enhances the component's ngOnDestroy
lifecycle hook. This decorator ensures that any subscriptions using the destroy$ subject are
automatically unsubscribed when the component is destroyed, preventing potential memory leaks.

TypeScript Decorator for memoizing component methods, and how can be used in a React.js class

```typescript
// Memoize decorator function
Memoize(target: any, key: string, descriptor: PropertyDescriptor): PropertyDescriptor {
const originalMethod = descriptor.value;
const memoizedKey = Symbol(`${key}_memoized`);
descriptor.value = function (...args: any[]) {
if (!this[memoizedKey]) {
this[memoizedKey] = new Map();
}
const key = JSON.stringify(args);
if (!this[memoizedKey].has(key)) {
this[memoizedKey].set(key, originalMethod.apply(this, args));
}
return this[memoizedKey].get(key);
};
return descriptor;
}
```

```typescript
// Usage
import React, {Component} from 'react';
interface MyComponentProps {
  items: string[];
}
class MyComponent extends Component<MyComponentProps> {
  @Memoize
  processItems(items: string[]): string[] {
console.log('Expensive operation performed');
return items.map(item => item.toUpperCase());
  }
  render() {
const { items } = this.props;
const processedItems = this.processItems(items);
    return (
      <ul>
        {processedItems.map((item, index) => (
          <li key={index}>{item}</li>
        ))}
      </ul>
    );
  }
}
export default MyComponent;
```

In this example, we create a Memoize decorator that can be applied to component methods to cache their return values based on input arguments. The process Items method is decorated with @Memoize, so the expensive operation will only be performed once for a given set of input arguments.

Creating a TypeScript-Decorated Redux Store

We'll create a Redux store that uses TypeScript decorators to manage state updates. We'll create decorators for actions and reducers, making it easier to manage the store's behaviour.

```typescript
// decorators.ts export function
reducer<T, K extends keyof T>(stateKey: K, initialState: T[K]) {
return (target: any, key: string, descriptor: PropertyDescriptor) => {
const originalMethod = descriptor.value;
descriptor.value = function (...args: any[]) {
const state = this.getState();
const newState = { ...state };
newState[stateKey] = originalMethod.apply(this, [state[stateKey], ...args]);
this.setState(newState);
    };
    return descriptor;
  };
}
export function action(target: any, key: string, descriptor: PropertyDescriptor) {
const originalMethod = descriptor.value;
descriptor.value = function (...args: any[]) {
this.dispatch({ type: key, payload: originalMethod.apply(this, args) });
```

```typescript
  };
  return descriptor;
}// store.ts
interface Action {
type: string;
payload?: any;
}
export abstract class Store<T> {
private state: T;
private listeners: Function[] = [];
constructor(private reducer: (state: T, action: Action) => T, initialState: T) {
this.state = initialState;
  }
  getState(): T {
return this.state;
  }
  dispatch(action: Action): void {
this.state = this.reducer(this.state, action);
this.listeners.forEach((listener) => listener());
  }
  subscribe(listener: Function): void {
this.listeners.push(listener);
  }
  setState(newState: T): void {
this.state = newState;
this.listeners.forEach((listener) => listener());
  }
}
// counter.store.ts
import { Store } from './store';
import { reducer, action } from './decorators';
interface State {
counter: number;
}
const initialState: State = {
counter: 0,
};
class CounterStore extends Store<State> {
constructor() {
super(counterReducer, initialState);
  }
  @reducer<State, 'counter'>('counter', 0)
  @action   increment(): number {
   return 1;
  }
  @reducer<State, 'counter'>('counter', 0)
  @action   decrement(): number {
   return -1;
  }
}
```

```
function counterReducer(state: State, action: Action): State {
switch (action.type) {
case 'increment':
    return { ...state, counter: state.counter + action.payload };
case 'decrement':
    return { ...state, counter: state.counter + action.payload };
default:
return state;
  }
}
const counterStore = new CounterStore();
counterStore.subscribe(() => {
console.log('Counter:', counterStore.getState().counter);
});
counterStore.increment(); // Counter: 1
counterStore.increment(); // Counter: 2
counterStore.decrement(); // Counter: 1
```

In this example, we use TypeScript decorators to manage the store's behaviour. The @reducer decorator creates a reducer function that updates a specific state property. The @action decorator creates an action that dispatches a specific action type to the store.

We also use the Store class, which contains the generic methods for dispatching actions, getting the state, and subscribing to state updates. The CounterStore class extends the Store class and manages a single counter state property.

This solution demonstrates how TypeScript decorators can be used to create a Redux store with clean and maintainable code.

In this demonstration, we exhibit the application of metaprogramming techniques via TypeScript decorators. Decorators facilitate the modification of class and class member declarations during runtime, leading to simplified and more readable code.

The @reducer decorator within the decorators.ts file exemplifies metaprogramming. It produces a reducer function responsible for updating a specific state property based on the action dispatched to the store. The @action decorator generates an action that dispatches a distinct action type to the store. Both decorators alter class member declarations and modify their behaviour at runtime.

Using decorators in this instance allows for the abstraction of Redux complexity by eliminating the boilerplate code typically necessary for defining and managing reducers and actions. This results in more concise, comprehensible, and maintainable code.

Similar TypeScript-decorated Redux store in an Angular application, you can follow these steps:
First, create a new Angular service called counter.store.ts and move the CounterStore class implementation and the reducer and action decorators into this file:

```
// counter.store.ts
import { Injectable } from '@angular/core';
interface State {counter: number;
}
const initialState: State = {counter: 0,
```

```
};

function counterReducer(state: State, action: any): State {
switch (action.type) {
case 'increment':
    return { ...state, counter: state.counter + action.payload };
case 'decrement':
    return { ...state, counter: state.counter + action.payload };
default:
    return state;
  }
}

@Injectable({   providedIn: 'root',
}) class CounterStore extends Store<State> {
constructor() {
super(counterReducer, initialState);
  }

  @reducer<State, 'counter'>('counter', 0)
  @action   increment(): number {
   return 1;
  }

  @reducer<State, 'counter'>('counter', 0)
  @action   decrement(): number {
   return -1;
  }
}

const counterStore = new CounterStore();
Next, import and use the CounterStore in an Angular component:
// app.component.ts
import { Component } from '@angular/core';
import { CounterStore } from './counter.store';
@Component({
  selector: 'app-root',   template: `   <div>
    Counter: {{ counter }}
    <button (click)="counterStore.increment()">Increment</button>
    <button (click)="counterStore.decrement()">Decrement</button>   </div>
  `,
}) export class AppComponent {
constructor(public counterStore: CounterStore) {}
  get counter() {
return this.counterStore.getState().counter;
  }
}
```

In this example, we import the CounterStore and use it in the AppComponent. We access the counter state through the getState method and bind the increment and decrement actions to button click events. This example showcases the utilization of the TypeScript-decorated Redux store, as created in the previous demonstration, within an Angular component. The store implementation can be expanded and enhanced based on the specific requirements of your application.

To integrate the TypeScript-decorated Redux store within a React.js application, adhere to these steps Initially, generate a new file named counter.store.ts and relocate the CounterStore class implementation along with the reducer and action decorators into this file.

```typescript
// counter.store.ts interface State {   counter: number;
}
const initialState: State = {
  counter: 0,
};

function counterReducer(state: State, action: any): State {
switch (action.type) {
case 'increment':
    return { ...state, counter: state.counter + action.payload };
case 'decrement':
    return { ...state, counter: state.counter + action.payload };
default:      return state;
  }
}

class CounterStore extends Store<State> {
constructor() {
super(counterReducer, initialState);
  }

  @reducer<State, 'counter'>('counter', 0)
  @action   increment(): number {
   return 1;
  }

  @reducer<State, 'counter'>('counter', 0)
  @action   decrement(): number {
   return -1;
  }
}

const counterStore = new CounterStore();
```

Next, import and use the CounterStore in a React component:

```tsx
// Counter.tsx
import React from 'react';
import { CounterStore } from './counter.store';

export function Counter() {
const [counter, setCounter] = React.useState(0);
React.useEffect(() => {
const unsubscribe = counterStore.subscribe(() => {
```

```
setCounter(counterStore.getState().counter);
    });
    return unsubscribe;
  }, []);
  function handleIncrement() {
counterStore.increment();
  }
  function handleDecrement() {
counterStore.decrement();
  }
  return (
    <div>
      Counter: {counter}
      <button onClick={handleIncrement}>Increment</button>
      <button onClick={handleDecrement}>Decrement</button>
    </div>
  );
}
```

In this example, we import the CounterStore and use it in the Counter component. We access the counter state through the getState method and update the state using the increment and decrement actions.

We use the useEffect hook to subscribe to state updates, and the useState hook to store the counter state. We call the subscribe method of the CounterStore and update the counter state in the subscription callback.

This demonstrates how to use the TypeScript-decorated Redux store created in the previous example in a React component. The store implementation can be extended and improved as needed, depending on your application's requirements.

Does this store secure immutability

Yes, the store implementation in the previous examples enforces immutability by returning a new state object for each state update. The counterReducer function in the counter.store.ts file, for example, uses the spread operator to create a new state object with the updated counter property:

```
function counterReducer(state: State, action: any): State {
switch (action.type) {
case 'increment':
    return { ...state, counter: state.counter + action.payload };    case 'decrement':
    return { ...state, counter: state.counter + action.payload };    default:
    return state;
  }
}
```

This ensures that the state is always immutable, as the original state object is not modified. Instead, a new state object is created with the updated properties.

Additionally, the @reducer decorator in the decorators.ts file uses the spread operator to create a new state object with the updated property:

```
export function reducer<T, K extends keyof T>(stateKey: K, initialState: T[K]) {
```

```
return (target: any, key: string, descriptor: PropertyDescriptor) => {
const originalMethod = descriptor.value;
descriptor.value = function (...args: any[]) {
const state = this.getState();
const newState = { ...state };
newState[stateKey] = originalMethod.apply(this, [state[stateKey], ...args]);
this.setState(newState);
  };
  return descriptor;
 };
}
```

This ensures that only the state property specified by the stateKey argument is updated, while the other properties remain unchanged. Overall, the store implementation enforces immutability by always returning a new state object, ensuring that state updates are always safe and predictable.

Creating a Type-Safe Event Emitter with Metaprogramming

In this demonstration, we will construct a type-safe event emitter utilizing metaprogramming methods in TypeScript. We will use TypeScript decorators to define and manage events, simplifying the usage and maintenance of the event emitter.

```
type Listener<T> = (data: T) => void;

class EventEmitter<T extends Record<string, any>> {
private listeners: Record<keyof T, Listener<any>[]> = {} as Record<keyof T, Listener<any>[]>;
addEventListener<K extends keyof T>(event: K, listener: Listener<T[K]>): void {
if (!this.listeners[event]) {
this.listeners[event] = [];
  }
  this.listeners[event].push(listener);
 }
removeEventListener<K extends keyof T>(event: K, listener: Listener<T[K]>): void {
if (!this.listeners[event]) {
return;
  }
this.listeners[event] = this.listeners[event].filter((l) => l !== listener);
}
emit<K extends keyof T>(event: K, data: T[K]): void {
if (!this.listeners[event]) {
return;
  }
  this.listeners[event].forEach((listener) => listener(data));
 }
}
function event<K extends string>(name: K) {
return function <T extends Record<string, any>>(target: EventEmitter<T>, propertyKey: string) {
if (!target[propertyKey]) {
target[propertyKey] = new EventEmitter<T>();
  }
  const emitter = target[propertyKey] as EventEmitter<T>;
```

```
    if (!emitter.listeners[name]) {
emitter.listeners[name] = [];
    }
const originalMethod = target[propertyKey][name];
target[propertyKey][name] = function (this: EventEmitter<T>, data: T[K]) {
originalMethod.apply(this, [data]);
this.emit(name, data);
    };
  };
}

// usage class
MyComponent { @event('onButtonClick')   onClick(data: { buttonId: string }) {
console.log(`Button clicked: ${data.buttonId}`);   }
}
const myComponent = new MyComponent();
myComponent.onClick.addEventListener('onButtonClick', (data) => console.log(data.buttonId));
myComponent.onClick.emit('onButtonClick', { buttonId: 'myButton' });
```

In this example, we use TypeScript decorators to define and manage events in an event emitter. The event decorator creates a new event emitter instance for the decorated method and adds it to the target object. The decorator also modifies the decorated method to call the original method and emit the event with the specified name and data.

We also define a Listener type and a generic EventEmitter class that use the Record type to ensure type safety for event names and data payloads.

This example demonstrates the application of TypeScript decorators to construct a type-safe event emitter using metaprogramming techniques. By treating events as first-class citizens within the code, event management and usage become more maintainable and scalable.

The type-safe event emitter created in the prior example can be a valuable asset for any application necessitating event-driven architecture. Treating events as first-class citizens within the code simplifies event management and usage, promoting maintainability and scalability. Some advantages of using a type-safe event emitter include:

Type safety: Leveraging the Record and keyof types in TypeScript ensures correct event and event data definition and usage, preventing common errors at compile-time.

Maintainability: Utilizing decorators to define events enables easy event management and extension without modifying the original code, reducing code complexity and enhancing maintainability. Scalability: Implementing an event emitter pattern facilitates component and service decoupling, streamlining application scaling and modification.

Flexibility: Using an event emitter pattern creates a loosely-coupled architecture that allows greater flexibility in component and service interaction. In summary, the type-safe event emitter developed in the previous example can be a potent tool for managing events in TypeScript or Angular applications, offering type safety, maintainability, scalability, and flexibility.

To use the type-safe event emitter created in the previous example in an Angular application, you can follow these steps:

First, create a new Angular service called my-component-events.service.ts and define your component events using the @event decorator:

```
import { Injectable } from '@angular/core';
import { EventEmitter } from './event-emitter';
@Injectable({   providedIn: 'root',
}) export class MyComponentEvents {
@event('onButtonClick')   onClick: EventEmitter<{ buttonId: string }> = new EventEmitter();
}
```

In this example, we define the onClick event using the @event decorator and the EventEmitter class. We set the type of the event data to { buttonId: string }.

Next, import the MyComponentEvents service in your Angular component and use it to handle events:

```
import { Component } from '@angular/core';
import { MyComponentEvents } from './my-component-events.service';
@Component({
selector: 'app-my-component', template: `
   <button (click)="handleClick()">Click me</button> `,
})
export class MyComponent {
constructor(private events: MyComponentEvents) {}   handleClick() {
this.events.onClick.emit({ buttonId: 'myButton' });
  }
```

In this example, we import the MyComponentEvents service and utilize it to emit the onClick event with the specified data. This showcases the integration of the type-safe event emitter, created in the previous example, within an Angular component. The event emitter implementation can be expanded and enhanced based on your application's requirements.

To use the type-safe event emitter within a React.js application, adhere to these steps:

Initially, generate a new file named event-emitter.ts and copy the code from in your React component, import the EventEmitter class and instantiate it.

```
import { EventEmitter } from './event-emitter';
type MyComponentProps = {   onClick: EventEmitter<{ buttonId: string }>;
}
function MyComponent(props: MyComponentProps) {
const handleClick = () => {
props.onClick.emit('onButtonClick', { buttonId: 'myButton' });
  };
  return <button onClick={handleClick}>Click me</button>;
}
```

In this example, we establish a create React component named MyComponent that accepts a prop called onClick.

This prop represents an instance of the EventEmitter class, which emits events containing a buttonId property. In the parent component, generate a new instance of the EventEmitter class and pass it to the MyComponent component as a prop.

```
import React from 'react';
import { EventEmitter } from './event-emitter';
import MyComponent from './MyComponent';
function App() {
const onClick = new EventEmitter<{ buttonId: string }>();
onClick.addEventListener('onButtonClick', (data) => {
console.log(`Button clicked: ${data.buttonId}`);
  });
  return (
   <div>
    <MyComponent onClick={onClick} />
   </div>
  );
}
export default App;
```

In this example, we create a new instance of the EventEmitter class called onClick and add a listener to it to log the buttonId data to the console. We then pass this instance to the MyComponent component as a prop.

Finally, in the MyComponent component, emit the onButtonClick event with the specified data when the button is clicked.

This demonstrates how to use the type-safe event emitter created. By defining events as first-class citizens in the code, it becomes easier to manage and use events in a maintainable and scalable way.

Creating a Type-Safe JSON Serializer with Metaprogramming

In this example, we will develop a type-safe JSON serializer by leveraging metaprogramming techniques in TypeScript. We will employ TypeScript decorators to establish and control serialization rules for our data classes, streamlining object serialization and deserialization.s.

```
type Class<T> = new (...args: any[]) => T;

const serializerMetadataKey = Symbol('Serializer');
function serialize<T>(value: T): string {
const serializedValue: any = {};

  for (const key in value) {
if (value.hasOwnProperty(key)) {
const propertyMetadata = Reflect.getMetadata(serializerMetadataKey, value, key);
    if (propertyMetadata && propertyMetadata.serialize === false) {continue;
    }
    serializedValue[key] = value[key];
   }
  }
  return JSON.stringify(serializedValue);
}
```

```typescript
function deserialize<T>(json: string, clazz: Class<T>): T {
const deserializedValue = JSON.parse(json);
  const instance = new clazz();
  for (const key in instance) {
if (instance.hasOwnProperty(key)) {
const propertyMetadata = Reflect.getMetadata(serializerMetadataKey, instance, key);
    if (propertyMetadata && propertyMetadata.serialize === false) {
continue;
    }
    instance[key] = deserializedValue[key];
  }
 }
  return instance;
}
function serializer(options: { serialize?: boolean } = {}) {
return function (target: any, key: string) {
    Reflect.defineMetadata(serializerMetadataKey, options, target, key);
  };
}
class User {
@serializer()   id: number;
@serializer()   name: string;
@serializer({ serialize: false })
password: string;
constructor(id: number, name: string, password: string) {
this.id = id;
this.name = name;
this.password = password;
  }
}
const user = new User(1, 'John Doe', 'password');
const serializedUser = serialize(user); // {"id":1,"name":"John Doe"}
const deserializedUser = deserialize(serializedUser, User); // User { id: 1, name: 'John Doe', password:
'password' ----}
```

In this example, we define a serializer decorator that adds metadata to the class properties to control their serialization behaviour. We use the Reflect API to read and write metadata to class properties. We also define a serialize function that takes an object and returns a JSON string representing the object. We use the metadata added by the serializer decorator to exclude properties that should not be serialized. We also define a deserialize function that takes a JSON string and a class constructor and returns an instance of the class with the properties set to the deserialized values.

This solution demonstrates how TypeScript decorators can be used to create a type-safe JSON serializer with metaprogramming techniques. By defining serialization rules as first-class citizens in the code, it becomes easier to manage and use serialization in a maintainable and scalable way.

Creating a Type-Safe Validation Framework
In this example, we'll create a type-safe validation framework. We'll use TypeScript decorators to define validation rules for our data classes, making it easier to validate object.

In this example, we develop a serializer decorator that attaches metadata to class properties, managing their serialization behaviour. The Reflect API is used to read and write metadata for class properties. Moreover, we establish a serialize function that takes an object as input and returns a JSON string representing the object.

The metadata introduced by the serializer decorator is utilized to exclude properties that are not meant to be serialized.

Additionally, we develop a deserialize function that accepts a JSON string and a class constructor, resulting in a class instance with properties assigned to the deserialized values.

This solution illustrates the use of TypeScript decorators to create a type-safe JSON serializer with metaprogramming techniques. By treating serialization rules as first-class citizens within the code, serialization management and usage become more maintainable and scalable.

Creating a Type-Safe Validation Framework:

In this example, we will construct a type-safe validation framework. We will employ TypeScript decorators to define validation rules for our data classes, simplifying object validation.

```
type Class<T> = new (...args: any[]) => T;
const validatorMetadataKey = Symbol('Validator');
function validate<T>(value: T): string[] {
const errors: string[] = [];
  for (const key in value) {
if (value.hasOwnProperty(key)) {
const propertyMetadata = Reflect.getMetadata(validatorMetadataKey, value, key);
    if (propertyMetadata) {const validators = propertyMetadata.validators;
      for (const validator of validators) {
if (!validator.fn(value[key])) {errors.push(`${key}: ${validator.message}`);
      }
     }
    }
   }
  }
  return errors;
}
function validator(options: { message: string, fn: (value: any) => boolean }) {
return function (target: any, key: string) {
const validators = Reflect.getMetadata(validatorMetadataKey, target, key) ||
[];
validators.push(options);
   Reflect.defineMetadata(validatorMetadataKey, { validators }, target, key);
  };
}
class User {
@validator({ message: 'Invalid email', fn: (value) => /^[^\s@]+@[^\s@]+\.[^\s@]+$/.test(value) })
email: string;
@validator({ message: 'Password must be at least 8 characters long', fn: (value) => value.length >= 8 })
password: string;
  constructor(email: string, password: string) {
```

```
this.email = email;
this.password = password;
  }
}
const user = new User('johndoe@example.com', 'password');
const errors = validate(user); // []
```

In this example, we define a validator decorator that adds metadata to the class properties to define validation rules. We use the Reflect API to read and write metadata to class properties.

We also develop a validate function that accepts an object and returns an array of validation errors.

The metadata introduced by the validator decorator is employed to execute validation rules on each property.

This solution shows the use of TypeScript decorators to create a type-safe validation framework with metaprogramming techniques.

By treating validation rules as first-class citizens within the code, validation management and usage become more maintainable and scalable.

Creating a Type-Safe Routing Framework with Metaprogramming:

In this example, we will construct a type-safe routing framework utilizing metaprogramming techniques in TypeScript.

We will use TypeScript decorators to define routing rules for our application, simplifying page management and navigations.

```
type Class<T> = new (...args: any[]) => T;

const routerMetadataKey = Symbol('Router');
function route(path: string) {
return function (target: any) {
    Reflect.defineMetadata(routerMetadataKey, { path }, target);
  };
}
function getRoutes() {   const routes: { path: string, component: Class<any> }[] = [];
for (const key of Reflect.getMetadataKeys(routerMetadataKey)) {
const component = Reflect.get(key, Reflect.getMetadata(routerMetadataKey, key));
const path = Reflect.getMetadata(routerMetadataKey, component).path;
routes.push({ path, component });
  }
  return routes;
}
class HomeComponent {
  render() {    return <h1>Welcome to the home page</h1>;
  }
}
@route('/')
class AboutComponent {
```

```
render() {    return <h1>Welcome to the about page</h1>;
   }
}
const routes = getRoutes(); const activeRoute = routes.find(route => window.location.pathname ===
route.path);
if (activeRoute) {const component = new activeRoute.component();
document.body.appendChild(component.render());
}
```

In this example, we define a route decorator that adds metadata to a component to define a routing rule. We use the Reflect API to read and write metadata to the component.

We also define a getRoutes function that returns an array of route objects with the path and component class.
We then use these route objects to navigate between pages in the application based on the current URL path.
This solution showcases the application of TypeScript decorators to create a type-safe routing framework using metaprogramming techniques.

By treating routing rules as first-class citizens within the code, page management and navigation become more maintainable and scalable.

Creating a Type-Safe Property Decorator with TypedPropertyDescriptor:

In this demonstration, we will create a type-safe property decorator by using TypedPropertyDescriptor and metaprogramming methods in TypeScript.

We will use the TypedPropertyDescriptor interface to establish the property descriptor for the decorated property, streamlining the process of incorporating custom behaviour into class properties.s.

```
function log(target: any, key: string, descriptor: TypedPropertyDescriptor<any>) {
const originalMethod = descriptor.value;
descriptor.value = function (...args: any[]) {
console.log(`Calling ${key} with arguments: ${args}`);
const result = originalMethod.apply(this, args);
console.log(`Result: ${result}`);
return result;
  };
  return descriptor;
}
class Calculator {
@log   add(a: number, b: number) {
return a + b;
   }
}
const calculator = new Calculator();
const result = calculator.add(2, 3); // Calling add with arguments: 2,3
// Result: ---5
```

In this example, we create a log decorator that introduces logging behaviour to the add method of the Calculator class. The TypedPropertyDescriptor interface is utilized to specify the property descriptor for the decorated property, which permits us to adjust the behaviour of the original method.

We subsequently use the apply method to invoke the original method with the provided arguments and return its output. This enables us to modify the behaviour of the original method without altering its signature or implementation.

This solution shows how TypedPropertyDescriptor and metaprogramming techniques can be employed to produce a type-safe property decorator with custom behaviour for class properties. By treating property behaviour as first-class citizens within the code, property management and usage become more maintainable and scalable.

Creating a Type-Safe Memoization Decorator with TypedPropertyDescriptor

In this example, we will create a type-safe memoization decorator by utilizing TypedPropertyDescriptor and metaprogramming methods in TypeScript.

We will use the TypedPropertyDescriptor interface to specify the property descriptor for the decorated method, streamlining the process of memoizing function calls.

```
type MemoizationCache = { [key: string]: any };
function memoize(target: any, key: string, descriptor: TypedPropertyDescriptor<any>) {
const originalMethod = descriptor.value;
const cache: MemoizationCache = {};
descriptor.value = function (...args: any[]) {
const cacheKey = JSON.stringify(args);
if (cacheKey in cache) {console.log(`Cache hit for ${key} with arguments: ${args}`);
return cache[cacheKey];
}
console.log(`Cache miss for ${key} with arguments: ${args}`);
const result = originalMethod.apply(this, args);
cache[cacheKey] = result;
 return result;
  };
return descriptor;
}
class Calculator {
 @memoize
 add(a: number, b: number) {
return a + b;
 }
}
const calculator = new Calculator();
const result1 = calculator.add(2, 3); // Cache miss for add with arguments: 2,3
const result2 = calculator.add(2, 3); // Cache hit for add with arguments: 2,----3
```

The memoize decorator adds memoization behaviour to the add method of the Calculator class by utilizing the TypedPropertyDescriptor interface to define the property descriptor for the decorated method. The cache object is then used to store the results of function calls based on the provided arguments. By returning the cached result instead of recomputing it, we can improve the performance of function calls that are expensive to compute.

This solution explains how TypedPropertyDescriptor and metaprogramming techniques can be employed to generate a type-safe memoization decorator with custom behaviour for class methods. By treating method behaviour as firstclass citizens within the code, method management and usage become more maintainable and scalable.

Creating a Type-Safe Retry Decorator with TypedPropertyDescriptor

In this example, we'll create a type-safe retry decorator using TypedPropertyDescriptor and metaprogramming techniques in TypeScript. We'll use the TypedPropertyDescriptor interface to define the property descriptor for the decorated method, making it easier to retry function calls in case of errors.

```typescript
function retry(options: { retries: number }) {return function (target: any, key: string, descriptor:

TypedPropertyDescriptor<any>)
{
const originalMethod = descriptor.value;
descriptor.value = async function (...args: any[])
{
let retries = options.retries;
while (retries > 0) {
try {
const result = await originalMethod.apply(this, args);
return result;
} catch (error)
{
console.log(`Error while calling ${key}: ${error.message}`);
        retries--;
      }
    }
    throw new Error(`Failed to call ${key} after ${options.retries} retries`);
  };
  return descriptor;
 };
}
class ApiService {@retry({ retries: 3 })
async fetchData(url: string) {
const response = await fetch(url);
   if (!response.ok) {
throw new Error(`Failed to fetch data from ${url}: ${response.statusText}`);
   }
   const data = await response.json();
return data;
  }
}
const api = new ApiService();
const data = await api.fetchData('https://jsonplaceholder.typicode.com/todos/1')----;
```

In this example, we define a retry decorator that gives the fetchData method of the ApiService class retry functionality. We use the TypedPropertyDescriptor interface to define the property descriptor for the decorated method, allowing us to retry function calls if something goes wrong.

The function call is then retried as many times as necessary, up until it succeeds or the allotted number of times, in the while loop. In a nutshell, to put it in a phrase, synchronous operations.

In this example, we'll create a type-safe validation decorator using TypedPropertyDescriptor and metaprogramming techniques in TypeScript. We'll use the TypedPropertyDescriptor interface to define the property descriptor for the decorated method, making it easier to validate the inputs and outputs of function calls.

```
type Validator = (value: any) => boolean;
function validateInput(validator: Validator) {

return function (target: any, key: string, descriptor:

TypedPropertyDescriptor<any>) {
const originalMethod = descriptor.value;
descriptor.value = function (...args: any[])
{
const validatedArgs = args.map((arg, index) => {
if (!validator(arg)) {
throw new Error(`Invalid input at index ${index} for ${key}`);
}
return arg;
    });
    return originalMethod.apply(this, validatedArgs);
  };
  return descriptor;
 };
}
function validateOutput(validator: Validator) {
return function (target: any, key: string, descriptor: TypedPropertyDescriptor<any>) {
const originalMethod = descriptor.value;
descriptor.value = function (...args: any[]) {
const result = originalMethod.apply(this, args);
if (!validator(result)) {
throw new Error(`Invalid output for ${key}`);
    }
    return result;
  };
  return descriptor;
 };
}
class Calculator {
  @validateInput((value: number) => value > 0)  @validateOutput((value: number) => value > 0)
squareRoot(value: number) {    return Math.sqrt(value);
  }
}
const calculator = new Calculator();
const result = calculator.squareRoot(-1); // Throws "Invalid input at index 0 for squareRoot---"
```

In this example, we define two decorators validateInput and validateOutput that add input and output validation behaviour to the squareRoot method of the Calculator class. We use the TypedPropertyDescriptor interface to define the property descriptor for the decorated method, which allows us to validate the inputs and outputs of function calls.

We then use the map method to iterate over the arguments and validate each input using the provided validator function. If an input fails validation, we throw an error with a detailed message.

We also use the apply method to call the original method with the validated arguments and return its result. After we receive the result, we validate it using the provided validator function. If the result fails validation, we throw an error with a detailed messag—-

In this example, we define two decorators validateInput and validateOutput, which add input and output validation behavior to the Calculator class's squareRoot method. We define the property descriptor for the decorated method using the TypedPropertyDescriptor interface, which allows us to validate the inputs and outputs of function calls.

The map method is then used to iterate over the arguments and validate each input with the provided validator function. If an input fails validation, an error with a detailed message is thrown.

We also call the original method with the validated arguments and return the result using the apply method. After receiving the result, we validate it with the validator function provided. We throw an error if the result fails validation.

Creating a Type-Safe Property Mapper with TypedPropertyDescriptor

In this example, we'll create a type-safe property mapper using TypedPropertyDescriptor and metaprogramming techniques in TypeScript. We'll use the TypedPropertyDescriptor interface to define the property descriptor for the decorated class, making it easier to map properties between different classes.

```
type PropertyMapper<T, U> = (source: T) => U;
function mapProperties<T, U>(propertyMapper: PropertyMapper<T, U>) {
return function (target: any) {
const originalConstructor = target;
function newConstructor(this: any, ...args: any[]) {
const source = new originalConstructor(...args);
const mappedProperties = propertyMapper(source);
    Object.assign(this, mappedProperties);
  }
  newConstructor.prototype = originalConstructor.prototype;
return newConstructor;
 };
}
class Person {
constructor(public name: string, public age: number) {}
}
class Employee {
constructor(public name: string, public age: number, public salary: number) {}
}
const toEmployeeMapper: PropertyMapper<Person, Employee> = (person: Person) => {
```

```
return new Employee(person.name, person.age, 0);
};
@mapProperties(toEmployeeMapper) class EmployeeCreator {
constructor(public person: Person) {}
}
const employeeCreator = new EmployeeCreator(new Person('John', 30));
console.log(employeeCreator instanceof EmployeeCreator); // true
console.log(employeeCreator instanceof Employee); // true
```

In this example, we define a mapProperties decorator that adds property mapping behaviour to the EmployeeCreator class. We use the TypedPropertyDescriptor interface to define the property descriptor for the decorated class, which allows us to map properties between different classes.

We then define a PropertyMapper type that describes a function that maps properties from one class to another. We use this type to define the toEmployeeMapper function those maps properties from Person to Employee.

Additionally, a new constructor function is defined, which calls the propertyMapper function to translate properties from the source class to the new target class instance.

It is simpler to map properties between classes by using the Object. assign method to assign the mapped properties to the new instance of the target class.

This solution demonstrates how to create a type-safe property mapper with unique behaviour for class properties using the TypedPropertyDescriptor and metaprogramming techniques. It is simpler to manage and use properties in a scalable and maintainable way because property behaviour is defined in the code as first-class citizens, which also reduces code repetition.

Creating a Type-Safe Singleton with TypedPropertyDescriptor

```
function singleton(target: any) {
const originalConstructor = target;
let instance: any;
  function newConstructor(...args: any[]) {
if (!instance) {
instance = new originalConstructor(...args);
    }
    return instance;
  }
  newConstructor.prototype = originalConstructor.prototype;
return newConstructor;
}
@singleton class Database {
private constructor(public connectionString: string) {}
  public static getInstance(connectionString: string) {
return new Database(connectionString);
    }
}
const db1 = Database.getInstance('localhost');
const db2 = Database.getInstance('remote');
console.log(db1 === db2); // true
console.log(db1.connectionString); // "localhost"
```

console.log(db2.connectionString); // "localhost"

This time we will try TypeScript's TypedPropertyDescriptor create a type-safe singleton pattern First we should define the property descriptor using the TypedPropertyDescriptor interface to make it easier to create a singleton instance of the decorated class.

Singleton decorator will be used to provide singleton functionality to the Database class. The TypedPropertyDescriptor interface is used to define the decorated class's property descriptor and to allow the creation of a singleton instance of the class.

After that, if the target class doesn't already exist, a new constructor function is defined that creates a single instance of it. Creating a singleton instance of the class is made simpler by using the Object. assign method to assign the instance to the new constructor function.

The singleton instance of the class is then more easily accessible thanks to the static method getInstance, which we define later.

Creating a Type-Safe Memoization Decorator with PropertyDescriptor

In this example, we'll create a type-safe memoization decorator using PropertyDescriptor and metaprogramming techniques in TypeScript. We'll use the PropertyDescriptor interface to define the property descriptor for the decorated method, making it easier to memoize function calls.

```
function memoize(target: any, key: string, descriptor: PropertyDescriptor) {
const originalMethod = descriptor.value;
const cache = new Map();
  descriptor.value = function (...args: any[]) {
    const cacheKey = JSON.stringify(args);
    if (cache.has(cacheKey)) {
return cache.get(cacheKey);
    }
    const result = originalMethod.apply(this, args);
    cache.set(cacheKey, result);
return result;
  };
  return descriptor;
}
class Calculator {
  @memoize
  add(x: number, y: number) {
console.log('Performing add calculation...');
return x + y;
  }
}
const calculator = new Calculator();
console.log(calculator.add(1, 2)); // Performing add calculation... 3
console.log(calculator.add(1, 2)); // 3 (Cached)
console.log(calculator.add(2, 3)); // Performing add calculation... 5
console.log(calculator.add(2, 3)); // 5 (Cached----)
```

In this example, we define a memoize decorator that gives the add method of the Calculator class memoization functionality. We can memoize function calls because we define the property descriptor for the decorated method using the PropertyDescriptor interface.

The outcomes of earlier function calls are then put into a new cache object, which is defined next. To invoke the original method with the specified arguments and return the result, we use the apply method. We retrieve the cached result and return it if the arguments have already been called. If not, we return the outcome and cache it for upcoming calls.

In order to create a type-safe memoization decorator with unique behaviour for class methods, this solution demonstrates how PropertyDescriptor and metaprogramming techniques can be used. The definition of method behaviour as first-class code citizens makes it simpler to manage and use methods in a scalable and maintainable manner while reducing code repetition.

Creating a Type-Safe Builder Pattern with Metaprogramming

In this example, we'll create a type-safe builder pattern using metaprogramming techniques in TypeScript. We'll use the Proxy object to dynamically create a builder object that enforces type safety and makes it easier to construct complex objects.

```
type Partial<T> = {
  [P in keyof T]?: T[P];
};
function builder<T extends Record<string, any>>(options: T) {
return new Proxy({}, {
get(target: any, key: string) {
if (key === 'build') {
return () => options;
    }
    return (value: T[keyof T]) => builder({ ...options, [key]: value });
   }
  }) as Builder<T>;
}
interface Person {
name: string;
age: number;
address: string;
}
interface Builder<T> {
  [K in keyof T]: (value: T[K]) => Builder<T>;
build(): T;
}
const person = builder<Person>({ name: 'John' })
  .age(30)
  .address('123 Main St')
  .build();
console.log(person); // { name: 'John', age: 30, address: '123 Main St' }
```

In this example, we define a builder function that creates a builder object for constructing complex objects. We use the Proxy object to dynamically create a builder object that enforces type safety and makes it easier to construct complex objects.

We define a Partial type that allows us to make all properties of an object optional. We then use this type to define the options parameter for the builder function.

We define a builder interface that uses the keyof operator to ensure that all builder methods are type-safe and enforce the correct property type.

We then define a new Proxy object that intercepts all property access and method calls. If the build method is accessed, we return a function that returns the completed options object. Otherwise, we return a function that creates a new builder object with the updated property value.

Using Metaprogramming and Reflection to Generate Type Guards

In this example, we'll use metaprogramming and reflection to generate type guards for TypeScript classes. We'll use the Reflect object to extract the type information from class instances, making it easier to generate type guards dynamically.

```
function isInstanceOf<T>(object: any, constructor: new (...args: any[]) => T): object is T {
return object instanceof constructor;
}
function isObject(value: any): value is object {
return typeof value === 'object' && value !== null;
}
function isClass(value: any): value is Function {
return typeof value === 'function' && /^\s*class\s+/.test(value.toString());
}
function generateTypeGuard<T>(constructor: new (...args: any[]) => T) {
return function (object: any): object is T {
if (!isObject(object)) {
return false;
    }
    const target = Reflect.construct(constructor, []);
for (const key in target) {
if (object.hasOwnProperty(key) && typeof object[key] !== typeof target[key]) {
return false;
      }
    }
    return true;
  };
}
class Person {
constructor(public name: string, public age: number) {}
}
const isPerson = generateTypeGuard(Person);
console.log(isPerson({ name: 'John', age: 30 })); // true
console.log(isPerson({ name: 'John', age: '30' })); // false
console.log(isPerson('John')); // false
console.log(isPerson(new Person('John', 30))); // true
```

In this example, we define a generateTypeGuard function that generates a type guard for the specified class constructor. We use the Reflect object to extract the type information from class instances, making it easier to generate type guards dynamically.

It is possible to tell whether a value is an object or a class constructor by using two helper functions that we create, isObject and isClass.

Then we add a new function called isInstanceOf that checks to see if an object is an instance of the class whose constructor is specified.

The newly defined function generateTypeGuard is then used to extract the type information from a brand-new instance of the specified class constructor.

The following action is to iterate through the keys of the new instance and check to see if the type of each property matches that of the corresponding property on the object.

Finally, we define a Person class and generate a type guard for it using the generateTypeGuard function. We then use the generated type guard to check if various objects are instances of the Person class.

Using Metaprogramming and Reflection to Implement basic Dependency Injection

In this example, we'll use metaprogramming and reflection to implement dependency injection in TypeScript. We'll use the Reflect object to extract the type information from class constructors and dynamically instantiate dependencies, making it easier to manage and inject dependencies in a maintainable and scalable way.

```
interface InjectableOptions {
providedIn?: 'root' | Type<any>;
}
function Injectable(options?: InjectableOptions) {
return function (target: any) {
if (options && options.providedIn) {  // Register provider with root injector
   } else { // Register provider with local injector
   }
 };
}
function Inject(token: Type<any>) {
return function (target: any, key: string, index: number) {
const dependencies = Reflect.getMetadata('design:paramtypes', target) || [];
dependencies[index] = token;
   Reflect.defineMetadata('design:paramtypes', dependencies, target);
 };
}
class UserService {
getUsers() {
return ['John', 'Jane', 'Bob'];
 }
}
class AppComponent {
constructor(@Inject(UserService) private userService: UserService) {}
 render() {
```

```
const users = this.userService.getUsers();   // Render users
  }
}
const app = new AppComponent(new UserService());
app.render();
```

In this example, we define an Injectable decorator that registers a class as a provider with either the root injector or a local injector, depending on the provided In option. We also define an Inject decorator that injects a dependency into a constructor parameter and updates the constructor's metadata to reflect the dependency injection.

Then, using the Inject decorator, we define a UserService class and an AppComponent class that both inject instances of the UserService class.

A fresh instance of the UserService class is added as a parameter to the newly created AppComponent instance.

After that, we invoke the AppComponent instance's render method, which retrieves and renders users using the UserService instance that was just injected.

With the help of reflection and metaprogramming, dependency injection in TypeScript is demonstrated in this solution.

The ability to manage and inject dependencies in a maintainable and scalable manner while reducing code repetition is made possible by extracting type information from class constructors and dynamically instantiating dependencies.

Metaprogramming techniques in TypeScript to track the order of called methods in a Class, execution performance, classname, and how many time each method is getting called;

```
function logCalls<T extends {
new(...args: any[]): {} }>(constructor: T) {
const className = constructor.name;
const methodNames = Object.getOwnPropertyNames(constructor.prototype);

methodNames.forEach((methodName) => {
const descriptor = Object.getOwnPropertyDescriptor(constructor.prototype, methodName);
const isMethod = descriptor?.value instanceof Function;

if (methodName !== 'constructor' && isMethod) {
const originalMethod = descriptor?.value;

if (originalMethod) {
constructor.prototype[methodName] = function (this: InstanceType<T>, ...args: Parameters<typeof
originalMethod>) {
const start = Date.now();
const result = originalMethod.apply(this, args);
const end = Date.now();
const executionTime = end - start;
console.log(`Called method: ${className}.${methodName}, execution time: ${executionTime}ms`);
    return result;
  };
```

```
      }
    }
  });
  return constructor;
}
```

logCalls decorator makes use of metaprogramming techniques in TypeScript. Metaprogramming is the practice of writing code that operates on code itself, and this decorator modifies the behavior of class methods at runtime by replacing them with wrapped versions that include logging functionality.

Specifically, the logCalls decorator modifies the prototype of the class being decorated to replace each method with a new function that logs the method name and execution time before invoking the original method. This is accomplished by using the Object.getOwnPropertyNames method to obtain the list of method names for the class, and then iterating over each method to replace it with a wrapped version that includes logging functionality.

This use of reflection and runtime manipulation of class methods is a common metaprogramming technique, and is particularly powerful in TypeScript due to its support for strong typing and runtime introspection.

Conclusion

1. Recap of Core Concepts

Metaprogramming, as explored in this discussion, represents a transformative approach to writing software by allowing programs to manipulate their behaviour, structure, or execution flow dynamically. JavaScript, with its highly flexible nature, provides a fertile ground for metaprogramming through tools like **reflection**, **proxies**, **symbols**, and **dynamic evaluation**. TypeScript enhances this paradigm by introducing **type safety**, **introspection**, and **compile-time checks**, offering developers a robust toolkit for building dynamic yet reliable software systems.

Key Concepts Reviewed:

Reflection and its ability to inspect and modify objects at runtime.
Proxies for intercepting and redefining fundamental operations.
Decorators, which simplify metadata handling and augment class functionality.
TypeScript-specific utilities like conditional types, mapped types, and utility types, which enable type-level metaprogramming.

Each tool has unique strengths and use cases, ranging from creating dynamic API clients to enforcing validation and implementing framework-level features.

2. The Role of Metaprogramming in Modern Software Development

Metaprogramming has evolved from being a niche concept to a critical tool in modern programming. With the growing demand for frameworks, libraries, and systems that can adapt dynamically to various requirements, metaprogramming offers solutions that are:

Flexible: Code can adapt to varying scenarios, reducing boilerplate and increasing reusability.

Expressive: Metaprogramming allows developers to encode complex logic in concise, maintainable abstractions.

Future-Ready: By dynamically adapting behaviour based on input or environment, meta programmed solutions are inherently more resilient to changing requirements.

Frameworks like **Angular**, **Vue**, and **NestJS** extensively use metaprogramming constructs like decorators and reflection to simplify dependency injection, routing, and other advanced features. The trend underscores how indispensable metaprogramming has become for scalable and maintainable application development.

3. Challenges and Trade-offs

Despite its benefits, metaprogramming comes with inherent challenges that developers must navigate carefully:

Complexity: Writing and understanding meta programmed code can be daunting for teams unfamiliar with its principles. Misuse can lead to code that is difficult to debug or extend.

Performance: Dynamic features, such as proxies or reflection, can incur performance costs, making them unsuitable for performance-critical applications.

Type Safety: While TypeScript alleviates some concerns by providing compile-time guarantees, runtime behaviour can still introduce bugs if not handled carefully.

Security: Dynamic code evaluation (e.g., eval) remains a risky operation, susceptible to injection attacks.

Addressing these challenges requires adopting **best practices**:

Use metaprogramming sparingly and only when necessary.
Document dynamic behaviour thoroughly.
Leverage TypeScript to enforce safety wherever possible.

4. Advanced Use Cases and Future Potential

Metaprogramming isn't just a tool for reducing boilerplate or enhancing readability. Its applications extend to advanced domains such as artificial intelligence, compiler design, and dynamic UI systems.

4.1. Artificial Intelligence and Machine Learning

In AI, metaprogramming can:

Dynamically adjust algorithms based on real-time data.
Generate adaptive code for models that evolve during runtime.
Facilitate meta-learning frameworks where the learning process itself is optimized.

4.2. Compiler Design

Tools like Babel and TypeScript transpilers already leverage metaprogramming principles:

Syntax trees (ASTs) are inspected and manipulated to generate optimized code.

Dynamic plugins can adapt to project-specific requirements.

4.3. Dynamic User Interfaces

Modern UI frameworks increasingly demand flexibility in rendering components based on user interaction or data state. Metaprogramming simplifies this by:

Dynamically injecting component logic (e.g., with React's HOCs or Vue's directives). Optimizing rendering performance through memoization and lazy loading.

5. Philosophical Perspective on Metaprogramming

Metaprogramming bridges the gap between **human intention** and **machine execution**. It allows developers to encode higher-level abstractions that make code closer to the language of thought, not just machines. Philosophically, it embodies principles of:

Expressiveness: Programs describe **what** they do rather than **how**.

Self-awareness: A metaprogramming-enabled system "knows" its behavior and can adapt it dynamically.
However, the power of metaprogramming necessitates responsibility. Overuse or poor implementation can obscure the intent behind the code, turning elegant solutions into unmanageable technical debt.

6. Balancing Metaprogramming in Practical Development

To effectively integrate metaprogramming into day-to-day programming:

Start Small: Introduce proxies or decorators in isolated use cases before scaling.

Leverage Existing Libraries: Use frameworks and utilities that have already implemented common metaprogramming patterns (e.g., TypeORM for database modeling).

Collaborate and Review: Engage team members in code reviews to ensure clarity and maintainability of dynamic code.

Measure Impact: Profile your application to ensure that metaprogramming constructs don't introduce significant performance bottlenecks.

7. Future of Metaprogramming in JavaScript and TypeScript

The future of JavaScript and TypeScript is deeply intertwined with metaprogramming. With the increasing emphasis on **dynamic applications**, **scalable architecture**, and **developer productivity**, metaprogramming will play a pivotal role in shaping the programming paradigms of tomorrow.

7.1. Language Evolution

JavaScript and TypeScript will continue to expand their support for metaprogramming constructs. Features like **records and tuples** or improvements in **type inference** will further empower developers to write dynamic yet type-safe applications.

7.2. Integration with Web Standards

Web APIs may incorporate metaprogramming patterns directly into the DOM or WebAssembly, allowing for:

Dynamic optimizations in browser-based applications.
Enhanced reflection capabilities for web components.

7.3. Emerging Frameworks

New frameworks will likely emerge, designed entirely around metaprogramming concepts. These frameworks will focus on:

Reducing boilerplate to near-zero.
Automatically adapting to changing environments or user needs.

8. Final Thoughts

Metaprogramming represents a powerful paradigm that pushes the boundaries of what software can do. By combining JavaScript's dynamic features with TypeScript's type safety, developers can create applications that are not only functional but also adaptable, maintainable, and future-proof.

However, the true art of metaprogramming lies in **knowing when to use it**. Like any powerful tool, it is most effective in the hands of a skilled practitioner who understands its capabilities, limitations, and implications. As the software industry evolves, so too will the role of metaprogramming—continuing to challenge and redefine how we think about code.

Mastering metaprogramming in JavaScript with TypeScript is not just a technical achievement; it's an exploration of the creative potential of software engineering itself.

6. Unions, Narrowing, and Literals

1. Introduction

TypeScript is a strongly typed superset of JavaScript that introduces features like static typing, interfaces, and more. One of its primary strengths is the ability to define complex types, ensuring robust and predictable code. Among these features are **union types**, **type narrowing**, and **literal types**, which provide the flexibility to model data precisely and safely.

2. Union Types in TypeScript

2.1 Definition

A union type allows a variable to hold more than one type. It's defined using the pipe (|) operator.

```
let value: string | number;
value = "Hello"; // valid
value = 42;      // valid
value = true;    // Error: Type 'true' is not assignable to type 'string | number'.
```

2.2 Use Cases

Flexibility in APIs: Union types are useful when dealing with functions or APIs that can accept multiple types of input.

```
function format(value: string | number): string {
    return value.toString();
}
```

Handling Nullable Values: Union types help represent optional or nullable values.

```
let name: string | null;
name = "Alice";  // valid
name = null;     // valid
```

Event Handling: In frameworks like Angular or React, event handlers might deal with different event types.

```
type Event = MouseEvent | KeyboardEvent;
```

3. Type Narrowing

Type narrowing refers to refining the type of a variable within a certain scope based on runtime checks. TypeScript uses control flow analysis to achieve this.

3.1 How Narrowing Works

TypeScript can narrow types using:

Type guards (typeof, instanceof)
Equality checks
Discriminated unions

3.2 Examples

Using typeof

```
function process(value: string | number) {
   if (typeof value === "string") {
      console.log("String length:", value.length);
   } else {
      console.log("Number squared:", value * value);
   }
}
```

Using instanceof

```
class Dog {
   bark() {
      console.log("Woof!");
   }
}

class Cat {
   meow() {
      console.log("Meow!");
   }
}
function speak(animal: Dog | Cat) {
   if (animal instanceof Dog) {
      animal.bark();
   } else {
      animal.meow();
   }
}
```

Discriminated Unions Discriminated unions leverage a shared property to narrow down the type.

```
type Shape =
   | { kind: "circle"; radius: number }
   | { kind: "rectangle"; width: number; height: number };

function calculateArea(shape: Shape) {
   if (shape.kind === "circle") {
      return Math.PI * shape.radius ** 2;
   } else {
      return shape.width * shape.height;
   }
}
```

Equality Checks

```
function handleInput(value: string | null) {
    if (value === null) {
        console.log("No input provided");
    } else {
        console.log("Input:", value);
    }
}
```

3.3 Benefits of Narrowing

Improved Type Safety: Reduces runtime errors by ensuring type-specific operations.
Better Readability: Makes the code self-documenting.
Performance Optimization: Helps the compiler generate more efficient JavaScript.

4. Literal Types

4.1 Definition

Literal types restrict a variable to a specific set of values, such as a string, number, or boolean literal.

```
let direction: "north" | "south" | "east" | "west";
direction = "north"; // valid
direction = "up"; // Error: Type "'up'" is not assignable to type "'north'" | "'south'" | "'east'" | "'west'".
```

4.2 Use Cases

Enumerations: Literal types can act as lightweight enums.

```
type Color = "red" | "green" | "blue";
let color: Color = "red";
```

Configuration Parameters: Define acceptable values for function parameters.

```
function setLogLevel(level: "debug" | "info" | "warn" | "error") {
    console.log("Log level set to", level);
}
setLogLevel("info");  // valid
setLogLevel("verbose"); // Error
```

State Representation: Represent finite states in state machines or similar constructs.

```
type State = "loading" | "success" | "error";
```

5. Combining Union Types, Narrowing, and Literals

These three features often work together to create powerful type-safe constructs.

5.1 Example: Handling a State Machine

```typescript
type State =
  | { status: "loading" }
  | { status: "success"; data: string }
  | { status: "error"; error: string };

function handleState(state: State) {
  if (state.status === "loading") {
    console.log("Loading...");
  } else if (state.status === "success") {
    console.log("Data:", state.data);
  } else {
    console.log("Error:", state.error);
  }
}
```

5.2 Example: Complex Configurations

```typescript
type Config =
  | { mode: "simple"; value: number }
  | { mode: "advanced"; settings: { threshold: number; debug: boolean } };

function setup(config: Config) {
  if (config.mode === "simple") {
    console.log("Simple mode with value:", config.value);
  } else {
    console.log("Advanced mode with settings:", config.settings);
  }
}
```

6. Practical Scenarios

6.1 API Design

Unions and literals are instrumental in defining function signatures with clear intent.

```typescript
function fetchData(type: "user" | "admin", id: number) {
  if (type === "user") {
    // fetch user data
  } else {
    // fetch admin data
  }
}
```

6.2 Handling User Input

Validate user input against a set of permissible values.

```typescript
function handleCommand(command: "start" | "stop" | "pause") {
  switch (command) {
    case "start":
      console.log("Starting...");
      break;
```

```
    case "stop":
      console.log("Stopping...");
      break;
    case "pause":
      console.log("Pausing...");
      break;
  }
}
```

6.3 Finite State Management

Track and respond to application states in a predictable way.

```
type AppState = "init" | "running" | "stopped";

function handleAppState(state: AppState) {
  if (state === "init") {
    console.log("Initializing...");
  } else if (state === "running") {
    console.log("App is running");
  } else {
    console.log("App has stopped");
  }
}
```

7. Best Practices

Keep Unions Simple: Avoid overly complex union types that may confuse developers.

```
type SimpleUnion = string | number | boolean; // Simple
```

Use Discriminated Unions: When defining unions with shared properties, always include a discriminant.

```
type Animal =
  | {type: "dog"; barkVolume: number }
  | {type: "cat"; purrVolume: number };
```

Combine with Enums: Use enums alongside literals for added clarity.

```
enum Direction {
  North = "north",
  South = "south",
  East = "east",
  West = "west",
}
```

Avoid Exhaustiveness Issues: Ensure all possible cases in a union are handled, using exhaustive checks where applicable.

```
function handleShape(shape: Shape) {
```

```
    switch (shape.kind) {
      case "circle":
        console.log("Circle");
        break;
      case "rectangle":
        console.log("Rectangle");
        break;
      default:
        const _exhaustive: never = shape;
        throw new Error("Unhandled case: " + _exhaustive);
    }
}
```

This chapter covered the concept of the "type system" and how it can read values to understand the types of variables. Before I talk about all the various syntax features of TypeScript, I'd like to introduce two key concepts that TypeScript works with to make inferences on top of those values:

- **Unions**: When a value is known to be one of two or more possible types.
- **Narrowing**: Deducing that a value to not be one or more possible types.

Put together, unions and narrowing are a powerful concept that allow TypeScript to make informed inferences on your code many other mainstream languages cannot.

Union Types

Take this mathematician variable:

```
let mathematician = Math.random() > 0.5
    ? 9001
    : "Mark Goldberg";
```

What type is mathematician?

It's neither only number nor only string, even though those are both potential values. mathematician can be either number or string. This kind of "either or" type is called a "union". Union types are a wonderful concept that let us handle code cases where we don't know exactly which type a variable is, but do know it's one of a two or more options.

TypeScript represents union types to us using the | (pipe) operator between the possible values. The above mathematician type is thought of as number | string.

```
    let mathematician: string | number

let mathematician = Math.random() > 0.5
      ? 9001
      : "Mark Goldberg";
```

Figure. TypeScript reporting the mathematician variable as being type string | number.

Declaring Union Types

Union types are an example of a time when it might be useful to give an explicit type annotation for a variable even though it has an initial value. In this example, thinker starts off false but is known to potentially contain a string instead:

```
let thinker: boolean | string = false;
if (Math.random() > 0.5) {thinker = "Susanne Langer";}
```

Union Properties

When a value is known to be a union type, TypeScript will only allow you to access member properties that exist on all possible types in the union. It will give you a type checking error if you try to access a type that doesn't exist on all possible types.

In the following snippet, physicist is of type number | string, so while.toString() exists in both types and is allowed to be used, .toUpperCase() and .toFixed() each missing on one of the union types and therefore are not allowed:

```
let physicist = Math.random() > 0.5
    ? "Marie Curie"
    : 84; physicist.toString(); // Ok
physicist.toUpperCase();  // Error: Property 'toUpperCase' does not exist on type 'string | number'.
Property 'toUpperCase' does not exist on type 'number'.
physicist.toFixed();  // Error: Property 'toFixed' does not exist on type 'string | number. Property 'toFixed'
does not exist on type 'string'.
```

If you want to use a member of a union typed value that only exists on a subset of the potential types, your code will need to indicate to TypeScript that the value is one of those more specific types: a process called narrowing.
The order of a union type declaration does not matter.
You can write boolean | number or number | boolean and TypeScript will treat both the exact same.

Narrowing
Narrowing is when TypeScript deduces from your code that a value is of a more specific type than what it was defined, declared, or previously inferred as. Once TypeScript knows that a type is narrower than previously known, it will allow you to treat it like that more specific type.

I'll use the remainder of this chapter to show you the common ways TypeScript can deduce type narrowing from your code.
Assignment Narrowing
If you directly assign a value to a variable, TypeScript will understand the variable to have been narrowed to that value's type:

```
let biochemist: number | string; biochemist = "Katalin Kariko"; biochemist.toUpperCase(); // Ok: string
biochemist.toFixed();  // Error: Property 'toFixed' does not exist on type 'string'.
```

Assignment narrowing comes into play when a variable is given an explcit union type annotation and an initial value, too. TypeScript will understand that while the variable may later receive a value of any of the union typed values, it starts off as only the type of it's in itial value.

In the following snippet, inventor is declared as type number | string, but TypeScript knows it's immediately narrowed to a string from its initial value:

```
let inventor: number | string = "Hedy Lamarr"; inventor.toUpperCase(); // Ok: string
inventor.toFixed();   // Error: Property 'toFixed' does not exist on type 'string'.
```

Conditional Checks

One of the simplest ways to get TypeScript to narrow a variable's value without assigning the value yourself is to write an if statement checking the variable for being equal to a known value. TypeScript is smart enough to understand that inside the body of that if statement, the variable must be the same type as the known value.

```
let scientist = Math.random() > 0.5
    ? "Rosalind Franklin"
    : 51;
if (scientist === "Rosalind Franklin") {
scientist.toUpperCase(); // Ok: string
}
physicist.toUpperCase(); // Error: Property 'toUpperCase' does not exist on type 'string | number'.
Property 'toUpperCase' does not exist on type 'number'.
```

TypeScript also recognizes the typeof operator in narrowing down variable types:
```
if (typeof scientist === "string") {
scientist.toUpperCase(); // Ok: string
}
```
Logical negations from ! and else statements work as well:
```
if (!(typeof scientist === "string")) {
scientist.toFixed(); // Ok: number } else {
scientist.toUpperCase(); // Ok: string
}
```

The above can be rewritten with a ternary statement, which is also supported for type narrowing:

```
typeof scientist === "string"
    ? scientist.toUpperCase() // Ok: string
    : scientist.toFixed(); // Ok: number
```

Narrowing with conditional logic shows TypeScript's type checking logic mirroring good JavaScript coding patterns. If a variable might be one of several types, you'll generally want to check its type for being what you need. TypeScript is forcing us to play it safe with our code. Thanks, TypeScript!

Literals
I'll now go the opposite direction by introducing literal types: more specific versions of primitive types.

Literal Types

Take this philosopher variable: **const** philosopher = "Hypatia";

What type is `philosopher?

At first glance, you might say string — and you'd be correct. philosopher is indeed a string. But! philosopher is not just any old string. It's specifically the value "Hypatia". Therefore, the philosopher variable's type is technically "Hypatia" itself as well.

Such is the concept of a literal: a value that is known to be a distinct instance of a primitive.

If you declare a variable as const and directly give it a literal value, TypeScript will understand the variable to be that literal value as a type. This is why, when you hover a mouse over a const variable in an IDE such as VS Code, it will show you the variable's type as that literal (Figure 4-1) instead of the more general primitive.

```
const philosopher: "Hypatia"
const philosopher = "Hypatia";
```

Figure. TypeScript reporting a const variable as being specifically its literal type.

```
let philosopher: string
let philosopher = "Hypatia";
```

Figure. TypeScript reporting a let variable as being generally its primitive type.

You can think of each primitive type as a union of every possible matching literal value. Most primitive types have a theoretically infinite number of literal types, but not all. Out of some common ones you'll find in typical TypeScript code:

boolean: Just true | false
null and undefined: both just have one literal value, themselves
number: 0 | 1 | 2 | ... | 0.1 | 0.2 | ...
string: "" | "a" | "b" | "c" | ... | "aa" | "ab" | "ac" | ...

Union type annotations can mix and match between literals and primitives. A representation of a lifespan, for example, might be represented by any number or one of a couple known edge cases:

let lifespan: number | "ongoing" | "unknown";

```
lifespan = 89; // Ok
lifespan = "ongoing"; // Ok
lifespan = true;
// Error: Type 'true' is not assignable to
// type 'number | "ongoing" | "unknown"'
```

Literal Assignability

Literal types are subsets of their general primitive types. A value that is known to be a different literal, or only as a general primitive, may not be assigned to a variable that only allows a different literal.

In this example, specificallyAda is declared as being of the literal type "Ada", so the types "?!" and string are not assignable to it:

```
let specificallyAda: "Ada";
specificallyAda = "Ada"; // Ok
specificallyAda = "?!"; // Error: Type '"?!"' is not assignable to type '"Ada"'.
let someString = "";
specificallyAda = someString; // Error: Type 'string' is not assignable to type '"Ada"'.
```

Literal types are, however, allowed to be assigned to their corresponding primitive types. A specific literal string is still generally a string, after all.

In this code example, the value ":)", which is of type ":)", is being assigned to the someString variable previously inferred to be of type string. someString = ":)";

Who would have thought a simple variable assignment would be so theoretically intense?

Strict Null Checking

The power of narrowed unions with literals is particularly visible when working with potentially undefined valuables, an area of type systems known as strict null checking. TypeScript is part of a surge of modern programming languages that utilizes strict null checking to fix the dreaded "billion-dollar mistake".

The Billion Dollar Mistake

The "billion-dollar mistake" is a catchy industry term for many type systems allowing values such as null to be used in places that require a different type. In languages without strict null checking, code like example that assign null to a string is allowed:

```
const firstName: string = null;
```

If you've previously worked in a typed language such as C++ or Java that suffers from the billion-dollar mistake, it may be surprising to you that some languages don't allow such a thing. If you're never worked in a language with the billion-dollar mistake before, it may be surprising that some languages do allow such a thing in the first place!

In the words of the developer who coined the phrase:

I call it my billion-dollar mistake. It was the invention of the null reference in 1965… This has led to innumerable errors, vulnerabilities, and system crashes, which have probably caused a billion dollars of pain and damage in the last forty years.

The TypeScript compiler has an --strictNullChecks option to toggle whether strict null checking is enabled. With the option disabled, the following code is considered totally type safe:

```
let nameMaybe = Math.random()
  ? "Tony Hoare"
  : undefined; nameMaybe.toLowerCase();
```

Roughly speaking, disabling strict null checking adds | null | undefined to every type in your code, thereby allowing any variable to receive null or undefined.

TypeScript best practice is generally to enable strict null checking. Doing so helps prevent crashes and eliminates the billion-dollar mistake.

With strict null checking enabled, TypeScript sees the potential crash in the code snippet:

```
let nameMaybe = Math.random()
? "Tony Hoare": undefined;
nameMaybe.toLowerCase(); // Error: Object is possibly 'undefined'.
```

Truthiness Narrowing

TypeScript can also narrow a variable's type from a truthiness check if only some of its potential values may be truthy. In the following snippet, cytogeneticist is of type string | undefined, and because undefined is always falsy, TypeScript can deduce that it must be of type string within the if statement's body:

```
let cytogeneticist = Math.random() > 0.5 ? "Barbara McClintock": undefined;
if (cytogeneticist) {
cytogeneticist.toUpperCase(); // Ok: string }
cytogeneticist.toUpperCase(); // Error: Object is possibly 'undefined'.
```

Logical operators that perform truthiness checking work as well, namely?. and &&:

```
cytogeneticist.toUpperCase(); // Ok:
string cytogeneticist && cytogeneticist.toUpperCase(); // Ok: string
```

Unfortunately, truthiness checking doesn't go the other way for primitive values. If all we know about a string | undefined value is that it's falsy, that doesn't tell us whether it's "" or undefined.

Here, placeholder is of type false | string, and while it can be narrowed down to just string in the if statement body, the else statement body knows it can still be a string if it's "":

```
let biologist = Math.random() > 0.5 && "Rachel Carson";
if (!biologist) {
biologist.toUpperCase();
}
```

Implicit Union Type Truthiness

If you declare a variable with a type and no initial value, TypeScript is smart enough to understand that the variable is undefined until a value is assigned. It will even give you a specialized error message letting you know if you try to access a member before assigning a value:

```
let mathematician: string;
mathematician.length; // Error: Variable 'mathematician' is used before being assigned.
mathematician = "Mark Goldberg";
mathematician.length; // Ok
```

Conclusion

The journey through **Unions, Narrowing, and Literals in TypeScript** highlights their indispensable role in modern software development. These features form the cornerstone of TypeScript's typing system, allowing developers to write more expressive, flexible, and type-safe code. Let's revisit their core attributes and understand their broader implications in software design.

1. Revisiting the Foundations

TypeScript is more than just a superset of JavaScript; it's a language that bridges the gap between dynamic and static typing, offering the best of both worlds. Among its rich feature set, **Union Types**, **Type Narrowing**, and **Literal Types** stand out as tools for crafting precise type definitions that align closely with real-world problems.

1.1 Union Types

Union types bring a dynamic aspect to static typing. By allowing variables to represent multiple possible types, they introduce flexibility without sacrificing type safety. The inclusion of union types makes TypeScript particularly adept at handling diverse and complex data structures, where values might originate from multiple sources, APIs, or user inputs.

1.2 Type Narrowing

While union types provide flexibility, narrowing ensures that flexibility doesn't lead to chaos. Through type guards, control flow analysis, and discriminated unions, narrowing refines variable types during runtime. This refinement enhances clarity, reduces potential errors, and allows developers to perform operations confidently, knowing the type constraints are enforced.

1.3 Literal Types

Literal types, by constraining values to specific, immutable options, ensure predictable behaviour. They serve as a lightweight alternative to enums, facilitating the creation of clear, finite states or configurations. This precision, combined with their ease of use, makes literal types a favourite for defining constants, configuration parameters, and states in applications.

2. Practical Applications

The real power of these features becomes evident when applied to practical scenarios. Across various domains—whether it's API design, user input validation, state management, or event handling—unions, narrowing, and literals consistently deliver both versatility and reliability.

2.1 In API Design

APIs often need to accommodate multiple input types or respond with different data structures. Union types model this variability effectively, while narrowing ensures the logic remains type-safe when processing these inputs.

For example, a function accepting different request types can use union types to define its parameters and narrowing to handle each case distinctly:

```
type Request = { method: "GET"; url: string } | { method: "POST"; url: string; body: string };

function handleRequest(req: Request) {
  if (req.method === "GET") {
    console.log("Fetching:", req.url);
  } else {
    console.log("Posting to:", req.url, "with body:", req.body);
  }
}
```

2.2 In State Management

Modern applications often involve finite states that dictate their behaviour. Literal types, combined with discriminated unions, model these states elegantly. This approach is particularly valuable in frameworks like React, where state transitions are common.

```
type State =
  | { status: "idle" }
  | { status: "loading" }
  | { status: "success"; data: string }
  | { status: "error"; error: string };

function render(state: State) {
  switch (state.status) {
    case "idle":
      return "Ready to start.";
    case "loading":
      return "Loading...";
    case "success":
      return `Data: ${state.data}`;
    case "error":
      return `Error: ${state.error}`;
  }
}
```

2.3 Error Handling

Union types are invaluable when managing operations that can fail, such as API calls or file manipulations. By representing success and failure states explicitly, they promote clear and predictable error handling.

```
type Result<T> = { success: true; value: T } | { success: false; error: string };
```

```
function parseJSON(json: string): Result<object> {
  try {
    return { success: true, value: JSON.parse(json) };
  } catch (e) {
    return { success: false, error: "Invalid JSON" };
  }
}
```

3. Enhancing Code Readability and Maintenance

A critical benefit of TypeScript's type system, particularly with unions, narrowing, and literals, is improved code readability. By making type constraints explicit, developers can infer how variables should behave without extensive documentation or runtime debugging.

3.1 Self-Documenting Code

Type annotations act as inline documentation, reducing ambiguity and aiding collaboration in large teams. For instance, a parameter typed as string | number immediately communicates its acceptable values and hints at the kind of logic expected in the function body.

3.2 Refactoring with Confidence

Strong typing enables safer refactoring. When types are defined explicitly and used consistently, changing application logic or introducing new features becomes a more predictable process.

3.3 Error Prevention

TypeScript's compile-time checks catch errors early, long before the code reaches production. Union types and narrowing are especially effective at preventing type-related bugs, such as calling a method on an incompatible type.

4. Comparison with Alternatives

While JavaScript offers tremendous flexibility, it lacks the static type safety that TypeScript provides. This absence often results in runtime errors that could have been avoided with proper type definitions.

4.1 JavaScript

In pure JavaScript, managing multiple types often involves manual checks and error-prone logic:

```
function process(value) {
  if (typeof value === "string") {
    console.log(value.toUpperCase());
  } else if (typeof value === "number") {
    console.log(value * value);
  }
}
```

This approach lacks the guarantees TypeScript offers, where the compiler enforces type constraints and ensures completeness.

4.2 Enums vs. Literal Types

While Enums in TypeScript provide a way to define a set of named constants, literal types are more lightweight and often easier to use:

```
// Enum
enum Direction {
    North,
    South,
    East,
    West,
}
// Literal Type
type DirectionLiteral = "north" | "south" | "east" | "west";
```

Literal types avoid the boilerplate associated with enums and integrate seamlessly with union types and narrowing.

5. Limitations and Challenges

While these features are powerful, they are not without limitations:

Overly Complex Unions: Combining too many types in a union can make the code harder to read and maintain.

Narrowing Edge Cases: Certain narrowing scenarios might require manual type assertions, which can undermine type safety.

Literal Type Exhaustiveness: When the set of allowed values grows large, managing literals becomes cumbersome.

6. Encouraging Adoption

For developers transitioning from JavaScript or other dynamic languages, adopting TypeScript may seem daunting. However, the benefits of union types, narrowing, and literals far outweigh the learning curve. Here are some tips for integrating these features into your workflow:

Start Small: Gradually introduce TypeScript into existing JavaScript projects by typing critical functions and modules.

Use IDE Support: Tools like Visual Studio Code provide autocompletion and type-checking, making it easier to experiment with unions and literals.

Leverage the Community: The TypeScript community is vast and supportive, with ample resources, tutorials, and open-source libraries.

7. A Glimpse into the Future

The continuous evolution of TypeScript ensures that features like unions, narrowing, and literals will remain relevant and likely see enhancements. With growing adoption across industries, TypeScript's type system will continue to shape how modern JavaScript applications are built.

Emerging Trends

Tooling and Frameworks: Frameworks like Angular, React, and NestJS increasingly embrace TypeScript, making these features more accessible.

AI-Assisted Development: Tools powered by AI, such as GitHub Copilot, integrate TypeScript features like unions and narrowing to generate intelligent code suggestions.

Integration with Other Ecosystems: As TypeScript integrates with technologies like Deno and WebAssembly, its type system will adapt to even more diverse use cases.

8. Final Thoughts

Unions, narrowing, and literals are not just technical features—they embody the philosophy of TypeScript: enhancing JavaScript with static typing to make code more robust, readable, and maintainable. These tools empower developers to build reliable applications while retaining the dynamic nature that makes JavaScript so popular.

By mastering these features, you unlock the full potential of TypeScript, enabling you to tackle complex software challenges with confidence. Whether you're designing APIs, managing application states, or creating user interfaces, unions, narrowing, and literals will remain invaluable companions in your development journey.

7. Conditional and Recursive Types

Introduction

In the realm of modern programming, particularly in languages with robust type systems like TypeScript, advanced typing constructs such as conditional types and recursive types are essential for building complex, reusable, and type-safe code. These features allow developers to express sophisticated relationships between types, enforce constraints at compile time, and model intricate data structures and behaviours.

This detailed guide will explore the foundations, usage, and benefits of **Conditional and Recursive Types**, along with practical examples to demonstrate their utility in real-world scenarios.

1. Understanding Conditional Types

1.1 What Are Conditional Types?

Conditional types are a form of type inference in TypeScript (and other statically typed languages with advanced type systems) that allow the creation of types based on a condition. They are often compared to if-else statements in programming but are applied at the type level.

The syntax for a conditional type in TypeScript is:

T extends U ? X : Y
T: The type being tested.
U: The condition or constraint to check against.
X: The type returned if the condition is true.
Y: The type returned if the condition is false.

1.2 Key Use Cases of Conditional Types

Type Filtering

Select specific types from a union based on conditions.

```
type ExtractString<T> = T extends string ? T : never;
type Result = ExtractString<string | number | boolean>;
// Result: string
```

Type Transformation

Map or transform types based on their characteristics.

```
type Transform<T> = T extends string ? Uppercase<T> : T;

type Example = Transform<'hello' | 42>;
// Example: 'HELLO' | 42
```

Utility Type Implementation

Build complex utility types like Exclude, Extract, and NonNullable.

```
type Exclude<T, U> = T extends U ? never : T;
type WithoutString = Exclude<string | number | boolean, string>;
// WithoutString: number | Boolean
```

Deep Object Manipulation

Traverse and modify types recursively.

```
type DeepReadonly<T> = {
readonly [K in keyof T]: T[K] extends object ? DeepReadonly<T[K]> : T[K];
};
type ExampleObject = { a: { b: { c: number } } };
type ReadonlyExample = DeepReadonly<ExampleObject>;
// ReadonlyExample: { readonly a: { readonly b: { readonly c: number } } }
```

1.3 Characteristics of Conditional Types

Distributive Property

When applied to union types, conditional types distribute across each member of the union.

```
type Distributed<T> = T extends string ? 'string' : 'other';
type Result = Distributed<'hello' | 42>;
// Result: 'string' | 'other'
```

Short-Circuiting

Conditional types short-circuit when the condition can be resolved early.

Constraint Enforcement

Conditional types can enforce constraints at compile time, helping prevent runtime errors.

2. Recursive Types
2.1 What Are Recursive Types?

Recursive types are types that reference themselves directly or indirectly. They are particularly useful for modelling recursive data structures like trees, linked lists, and JSON objects.

2.2 Key Characteristics of Recursive Types

Self-Referential

Recursive types refer to themselves, often to describe hierarchical or nested data structures.

```
type Tree<T> = {
   value: T;
   children?: Tree<T>[];
```

```
};
```

Infinite Potential with Base Cases

Recursive types always include a base case to prevent infinite recursion.

```
type JSONValue = string | number | boolean | null | JSONValue[] | { [key: string]: JSONValue };
```

Type-Safe Traversal

Recursive types enable safe traversal of complex data structures by defining their shape upfront.

2.3 Real-World Applications

Hierarchical Data Structures

Recursive types excel at defining trees, graphs, and nested objects.

```
type TreeNode<T> = {
    value: T;
    left?: TreeNode<T>;
    right?: TreeNode<T>;
};
```

Dynamic Typing for JSON

Recursive types is ideal for modeling JSON objects.

```
type JSONObject = {
    [key: string]: string | number | boolean | JSONObject | JSONArray;
};
type JSONArray = JSONObject[];
```

Deeply Nested Arrays

Recursive types can represent arbitrarily deep nesting.

```
type NestedArray<T> = T | NestedArray<T>[];
```

Versioned Data Structures

Recursive types can define structures where versions or states are linked.

```
type VersionedNode<T> = {
    current: T;
    previous?: VersionedNode<T>;
};
```

3. Combining Conditional and Recursive Types

The true power of these types emerges when they are used together to model dynamic and recursive transformations at the type level.

3.1 Example: Deep Transformation of Objects

Transform an object type recursively, converting all string properties to uppercase.

```
type DeepTransform<T> = T extends string
    ? Uppercase<T>
    : T extends object
    ? { [K in keyof T]: DeepTransform<T[K]> }
    : T;
type Example = {
  name: string;
  details: {
    age: number;
    hobbies: string[];
  };
};
type TransformedExample = DeepTransform<Example>;
// TransformedExample:
// {
//   name: 'string';
//   details: {
//     age: number;
//     hobbies: string[];
//   };
// }
```

3.2 Example: Validating Recursive Structures

Create a type that ensures all keys in a nested object match a specific pattern.

```
type ValidateKeys<T, KeyPattern extends string> = T extends object
    ? { [K in keyof T & string as K extends KeyPattern ? K : never]: ValidateKeys<T[K], KeyPattern> }
    : T;
type Input = {
  valid_key1: {
    valid_key2: string;
    invalidKey: number;
  };
  anotherInvalidKey: boolean;
};
type Validated = ValidateKeys<Input, 'valid_*'>;
// Validated:
// {
//   valid_key1: {
//     valid_key2: string;
//   };
// }
```

4. Best Practices and Challenges

4.1 Best Practices

Use Constraints Wisely: Overuse of conditional types can lead to complicated and hard-to-read code.

Combine with Utility Types: Leverage built-in utility types for common patterns and extend them as needed.

Document Complex Types: Provide inline comments to explain intricate recursive and conditional logic.

Test Thoroughly: Validate types against diverse scenarios to ensure correctness.

4.2 Challenges

Complexity: Deeply nested recursive types can become difficult to comprehend and debug.

Performance: Type-checking performance can degrade with extremely complex or deeply recursive types.

Tooling Limitations: Some IDEs or compilers may struggle with rendering deeply recursive or conditional types.

From this point onward, things are going to get even more interesting. Let's look at another feature of JavaScript being a dynamic language. In the following example, what is the return type of the function?

```
function parseBoolean(s: string) /* What is the return type here? */ {
if (s === 'yes') {return true;
}
   if (s === 'no') {return false;
}
   throw new Error(`Unrecognized boolean value ${s}`);
}
```

What is the return type of a function containing conditions (e.g., if statements)?

What we want is a type that essentially represents the logic of the function in the example, like this:

1. If **s** is "yes", then the return value's type is **true**.
2. If **s** is "no", then the return value's type is **false**.
3. Otherwise, the return value's type is **never**.

The return type depends on the literal type of "s", so we need to make "s" into something we can interrogate as a type.

We can do this by making it a generic parameter:

```
function parseBoolean<S extends string>(s: S) /* now we can query 'S' */
{
}
```

Store the subject type of the condition so that we can use it to compute the return type.

Using the generic parameter, we can use TypeScript to encode the logic of the function as a type ternary, called a **conditional type**. And to make this, we need to use the **extends** keyword. **Extends Keyword**

Knowing the logic inside the **parseBoolean** function, we can write its return type as a type ternary, or "conditional type," like this:

```
type ParseBooleanResult<S> =     S extends 'yes' ? true
  : S extends 'no' ? false
  : never;

function parseBoolean<S extends string>(s: S): ParseBooleanResult<S> {
}
const a = parseBoolean('yes');
>    const a: true; const b = parseBoolean('no');
>    const b: false;
const c = parseBoolean('carrots and bananas');
>    const c: never;
```

A simple conditional type

This special **extends** keyword ternary is the normal way to write conditional types. There is an alternative stylistic approach that we'll cover in the "Conditional Types via Property Accessors" section, further down, but for now, let's concentrate on this standard (and more powerful) approach. The **extends** keyword allows you to check if a type covers at least the contract specified.

Here's another example:
```
interface Person {name: string email?: string  phone?: string    address?: {street: string postcode: string
  }
}// Here the extends keyword allows us to do pattern-matching against type T.
type PrimaryContactDetails<T extends Person> =
  T extends { email: string } ? T['email']
  : T extends { phone: string } ? T['phone']
  : T extends { address: string } ? T['address']
  : never;
function getPrimaryContact<T extends Person>(p: T): PrimaryContactDetails<T> {
}
```

TypeScript early-exits when evaluating conditional types.

Leveraging the "minimum contract" aspect of structural typing, we can see in the preceding example how the **extends** keyword allows us to effectively achieve pattern matching against the type. Notice how the ternary, like normal ternaries in JavaScript, is early-exiting, so we only match one result even if the type could match other options:

```
const x = getPrimaryContactDetails({    name: 'Dave',    email: 'dave@email.com',    phone: '012345678',
} as const)
```

> const x: "dave@email.com"; // The 'email' case has precedence in the type's ternary's ordering

Where the **extends** keyword allows us to use pattern matching to compute type shapes, the **infer** keyword takes the pattern matching even further to give you access to the parts of the pattern you didn't match on.

Let's take an example to illustrate. Let's make a type that will give us the "head" element of an array (the first item in the array). Using pattern matching, we could do it like this:

```
type HeadOf<T extends any[]> =  T extends string[] ? string
    : T extends number[] ? number
    : T extends boolean[] ? boolean
    : T extends Date[] ? Date : T extends ... // Oh no, how many of these cases do we need to write..??!
...etc...
    ...etc...
    ...etc...
```

But we can see in the preceding example that it would be hard to cover every case, and our pattern matching would end up unmanageably long. Instead, the **infer** keyword allows us to just pattern-match that **T** is an array and then infer the actual type of the array from the match:

```
type HeadOf<T extends any[]> =
    T extends (infer Head)[] ? Head
    : never;
```

Pattern matching in conditional types using the infer keyword to store the located type. Well, that was a lot simpler, wasn't it? The **infer** keyword allows us to infer and store the rest of a matched type into an inline type, which can then be used a bit like a generic parameter thereafter.

This ability to infer types is very powerful and can be used in a lot of handy ways. For example, you can infer the value of a generic parameter:

```
type HeadOf<T> =
    T extends Iterable<infer Head> ? Head: never; // Now our HeadOf<..> type works with non-arrays
too:
const a: HeadOf<NodeList> = // ...>
const a: Node;
const b: HeadOf<Set<string>> = //...
    > const b: string;
const c: HeadOf<Map<string, Person> = //...
    > const c: [string, Person];
```

You can also infer function parameters:

```
type ParametersOf<T> = T extends (...params: infer Params) => any ? Params: never;
// ...or even a function's
```

```
returned type: type ReturnOf<T> = T extends () => infer Returned ? Returned: never;
// (This is how TypeScript's inbuilt Parameters<T> and
// ReturnType<T> utility types work)
```

```
const params: ParametersOf<typeof console.log> = ❯
const params: [message?: any, ...optionalParams: any[]];
const interval: ReturnOf<typeof window.setInterval> = ❯
const interval: number;
```

And lastly you can pattern-match on tuples and infer their contents:

```
type MixItUp<T> =    T extends []
      ? []
   : T extends [infer First]
       ? [First]
   : T extends [infer First, infer Last]
       ? [Last, First]        //
   : T extends [infer First, ...infer Middle, inferLast]  ? [...Middle, First, Last]  // !
   : never;
const a: MixItUp<[1]> = // ...
 ❯    const a: [1];
const b: MixItUp<[1, 2]> = // ...
 ❯    const b: [2, 1];
const c: MixItUp<[1, 2, 3, 4, 5, 6, 7]> = // ...  ❯
const c: [2, 3, 4, 5, 6, 1, 7];
```

Extracting Inferred Types

There are cases where it is useful to use the infer keyword outside of a conditional type. You can use the following technique for this:

```
interface WrappedType<T> { id: number    name: string    description: string  value: T }
type Unwrapper<W extends WrappedType<any>> =
    W extends WrappedType<infer T>
      ? T       // Effectively return the inferred type
      : never;
type PackagedPerson = WrappedType<Person>;
type ExtractedPerson = Unwrapper<PackagedPerson>;
 ❯    type ExtractedPerson = Person; // the extracted
 // inferred type
```

Returning an inferred type allows us to assign it to a type alias and therefore reuse it.

In fact, this is actually how utility types like React's **ComponentProps<C>** type work:

```
type ButtonProps = React.ComponentProps<typeof Button>;
```

React's ComponentProps<C> utility function works by returning the inferred generic parameter.

If you need more than one type returned, you can return them as an inline type instead:

```
interface WrappedType<A, B, C> {
a: SomeComplexType<A>    b: SomeComplexType<B>    c: SomeComplexType<C>
}
```

```typescript
type Unwrapper<W extends WrappedType<any, any, any>> = W extends WrappedType<infer A, infer
B, infer C> ? { a: A        b: B        c: C
} : never;
type ReshapedType<W extends WrappedType<any, any, any>> =
    SomeNewType<
        Unwrapper<W>['a'], // Use the inferred types
        Unwrapper<W>['b']  // provided by the Unwrapper's    // inline return type.
```

Distributive and Non distributive Conditional Types

One quirk of conditional types is that if you assign a union type to any of the generic parameters, the conditional type is applied to each member of the union type. This is called a **distributed conditional type**, because the conditional is distributed across the union.

```typescript
type ArrayOf<T> =
    T extends any ? T[]
    : never;
// Given...
type A = ArrayOf<string | number>; // ...TS's conditional typing is 'distributed' onto each member
// of the union, therefore the above becomes equivalent to...
type A = ArrayOf<string> | ArrayOf<number>; // ...whose individual conditional types then evaluate
down to essentially:
type A = string[] | number[];
```

Each case of a union is matched against a conditional type, and the result re-unioned as a "distributed conditional type"

The reason TypeScript uses this "distributing" behaviour on unions is because the aforementioned is the outcome most usually needed. However, in some cases, this isn't helpful – take the following example:

```typescript
// We want
A = { items: (Cat | Dog)[] }
type CatsAndDogs = List<Cat | Dog>
// But distribution means that the above evaluates to...
type A = List<Cat> | List<Dog>
// ...which is essentially this:
type A = { items: Cat[] } | { items: Dog[] }
```

Example of when conditional unions' distributive behaviour isn't desired.
Not helpful if you want to store both, right? Well, there's a neat trick we can use to make unions non distributive, which is to wrap the generic in a tuple during comparison – which circumvents TypeScript's default behaviour:

```typescript
type List<T> =
    [T] extends any[] ? { items: T[] }
    : never;
type A = List<Cat | Dog> // equivalent to
A = { items: (Cat | Dog)[] }
```

Method for avoiding distributive unions in conditional types if necessary.

Conditional Types via Property Accessors

In some cases, where your conditional type is only comparing a type to literal type values, you may use a stylistic alternative as shown in the following code snippet:

```
// Longhand conditional type:
type HexOfColor<Color extends string> =
    Color extends 'Red' ? '#ff0000'
    : Color extends 'Green' ? '#00ff00'
    : Color extends 'Blue' ? '#0000ff'
    : Color extends 'White' ? '#ffffff'
    : Color extends 'Black' ? '#000000'
    : never;
// VS a conditional type alternative via property accessor: interface ColorNameToHexMap {
    Red: '#ff0000'
    Green: '#00ff00'
    Blue: '#0000ff'
    White: '#ffffff'
    Black: '#000000'
}
type HexOfColor<Color extends keyof ColorNameToHexMap> = ColorNameToHexMap[Color];
const green: HexOfColor<"Green"> = '#000000'; ✘ // Error
const green: HexOfColor<"Green"> = '#00ff00'; ✔ // Correct
```

Mapped Types

Conditional types, as we've just looked at, are a form of what are called computed types – types that compute a target type from a source type. In conditional types, we've seen how to perform a simple wholesale translation of source to result type. In **mapped types**, we can perform a more granular transformation by translating each individual field in the source type.

Changing the Type of Fields

To translate individual fields in a type, we need to use a tool we've looked at previously: type indexes. The following example is a quick refresher:

```
type StringStringDictionary = {
    [key: string]: string
}
const favouriteThings: StringStringDictionary = {};
>   const favouriteThings: {
        [key: string]: string;
    };
favouriteThings['color'] = 'Red';
```

If we couple this with Ok, fine – but we've covered indexed types. How do they help us transform? Well, let's refine the indexed type we have to take a generic parameter:

```
type OurType<T extends object> = {
    [Key in keyof T]: string
}
```

This is now a mapped type – it has exactly the same fields as the type specified in the generic parameter, but redefines (maps) the field values to new types, in this case strings. Let's see how this works in a more practical example:

```
interface Person { firstName: string  lastName: string }
type OurType<T extends object> = {
    [Key in keyof T]: boolean
}
const validatedPersonData: OurType<Person> = {} as any;
validatedPersonData['firstName'] = true;    ✓
validatedPersonData['lastName'] = false;    ✓
validatedPersonData['color'] = true;        ✗  // Invalid key
validatedPersonData['lastName'] = 'Foo';    ✗  // Invalid value
```

Great – now we've constrained the key to match the key of a generic type parameter. But we're still not exactly transforming the type – how do we do that?

Now that we have constrained the index key, we can use that index key as a field reference to reference each field, as follows:

```
type OurType<T extends object> = {
    [Key in keyof T]: T[Key]
}
```

The preceding simplistic example would match every field of the computed type the same type as the originating field – so firstName would be string, age would be number, etc.

Now, let's bring in other computational types to translate each field loosening the fields by unions to make them (for example) nullable or optional:

```
// Transforming (mapping) the type: Changing the type of each field
// in this case to also allow null.

type Nullable<T extends object> = {
    [Key in keyof T]: T[Key] | null
}
const doug: OurType<Person> = {firstName: 'Doug', ✓ // All fields now allow values per their
lastName: null, ✓ // originating type, OR null, to be // assigned.
age: 'Ten', ✗ // But we can't assign incorrect type values,
aage: 5, ✗ // nor make typos.
}
type Partial<T extends object> = {
    [Key in keyof T]?: T[Key] // Shorthand, equivalent to
                    // 'T[Key] | undefined'
}
const someOfDoug: Partial<Person> = {firstName: 'Doug', lastName: 'Smith',
    // Remaining fields are acceptable now to leave as 'undefined'
}
// The inverse of Partial uses an adjustment in the special
```

// syntax to remove the undefined as a valid value for the field.

```typescript
type Required<T extends object> = {
[Key in keyof T]-?: T[Key] } Shorthand to make non-optional (prohibiting undefined)
```

Extending the field values in our mapped type to also permit null...or extending the fields using generics:

```typescript
interface Person { name: string    age: number     dateOfBirth: Date }
interface HistoryEntry<T> { value: T
effectiveDate: Date }
type History<T> = {
[Key in keyof T]: HistoryEntry<T[Key]>[]
}
type Result = History<Person>;
> type Result = {
name: {
value: string
effectiveDate: Date
}[];
age: {
value: number
effectiveDate: Date
}[];
dateOfBirth: {
value: Date
effectiveDate: Date
}[];
}
```

Extending the field values in our mapped type to be history metadata...or using conditional types to translate the field values themselves:

```typescript
interface Person {
   name: string    age: number    dateOfBirth: Date }
type TypesOf<T extends object> = {
   [Key in keyof T]:
      T[Key] extends boolean ? 'I am a boolean'
      : T[Key] extends number ? 'I am a number'
      : T[Key] extends Date ? 'I am a date'
      : T[Key] extends string ? 'I am a string'
      : never;
}
type Result = TypesOf<Person>
> type Result = {name: "I am a string"; age: "I am a number";
dateOfBirth: "I am a date";}
```

Adding and Removing Fields

Adding fields to a mapped type is simple – we can add new fields by using an intersection:

```
// Add new fields by using an intersection:
type WithEmployeeData<T> = {employeeNumber: string  startedDate: Date } & T;
// Now TS requires the employee fields to be defined too:
const doug: WithEmployeeData<Person> = { firstName: 'Doug',    lastName: 'Smith',    age: 21,
employeeNumber: '12345',    startedDate: new Date(2000, 1, 1) }
```

But how can we remove fields? As seen before, we can use the **Exclude<T, U>** utility type to remove values from a union. **keyof T** is a union, so we can use **Exclude<T, U>** to remove keys from it:

```
type Remove<T, RemoveKey extends keyof T> = {
   [Key in Exclude<keyof T, RemoveKey>]: T[Key]
};
function remove<T, RemoveKey extends keyof T>(value: T, key: RemoveKey):
Remove<T, RemoveKey> {const result = { ...value };
delete result[key];
return result;
}
interface Employee {name: string employeeNumber: string    favoriteColor: string
}
const bob = {name: 'Bob Smith', employeeNumber: 'A01234', favoriteColor: 'Purple', } satisfies
Employee;
const redacted = remove(bob, 'name');
❯ const redacted: {employeeNumber: string; favoriteColor: string;
}
```

Renaming Fields

As well as adding and removing fields, you can also use mapped types to rename fields. To do this, you use the **as** keyword to cast the field key to a new type. The following code example shows the cleanest way of doing this, by casting to a generic type that can do the renaming for us. This example makes use of conditional types that we've already covered, as well as template literals that are covered later in this chapter:

```
interface Person {firstName: string    lastName: string    age: number}
type RenamedField<Key extends keyof any> = Key extends string ? `${Key}__renamed`: Key;
type Rename<T> = {[Key in keyof T as RenamedField<Key>]: T[Key]}
// Rename all fields type
Result = Rename<Person>;
❯   type Result = {
firstName__renamed: string;
lastName__renamed: string;
age__renamed: number;
}
```

Recursive Types

As well as mapping over the contents of a type, you can also map recursively into a type, using type recursion. We will explore two ways of doing this: recursion within an object type and recursion over a tuple type.

Recursion Within an Object Type

To recurse within an object type, we use the same index over the **keyof T** approach; but we also recursively call our own mapped type for field types as needed:

```
type SaveData<T> = {
id: number    value: T    dateSaved: Date
}
type Saved<T extends object> = SaveData<{
  [Key in keyof T]:
    T[Key] extends object
       ? Saved<T[Key]>      // Recursion into subfields as needed
 : T[Key]
}>
interface Person {firstName: string    lastName: string    address: {street: string
  }
}
type SavedPerson = Saved<Person>;
❯   type SavedPerson = {id: number; value: {firstName: string;
lastName: string;  address: {id: number; value: {
street: string;
        };
          dateSaved: Date;
      };
    };
    dateSaved: Date;
}
```

Recursion over a Tuple Type

To recurse over a tuple type, you use a conditional type to extract each value from the tuple and map it and then pass the remainder to a recursive call as follows:

```
type MapValue<T> =
T extends ...etc    // Fill this out with your own // mapping conditional // Then use it to map the
recursively evaluated item types from the tuple:

type MapTuple<T extends readonly any[]> =
  T extends readonly [infer Item]
    ? readonly [MapValue<Item>]
  : T extends readonly [infer Item, ...infer Rest]
    ? readonly [MapValue<Item>, ...MapTuple<Rest>]
  : never;
```

Using conditional types and the rest operator to recurse through a tuple type, why would we do this? When you are dealing only with an array, it's easy to change the type as shown in the following code:

```
type SaveData<T> = {id: number    value: T    dateSaved: Date}
// T[] goes in,
```

SaveData<T>[] comes out. But is this all
// we need? function
save<T>(values: T[]): SaveData<T>[] {
return values.map((value, id) => ({id, value, dateSaved: new Date() }));
}

Returning a simple array result, we lose any narrowness of the input value. However, using simple arrays gives a less safe developer experience when the number of items could otherwise be knowable:

const people = ['Kelly', 'Jim', 'Ash', 'Fiona'] as const;
const fiona = people[700]; ✘ // TypeScript knows there are only 4 items in this tuple, so helpfully flags this error.
const savedPeople = save(people); // Returning a simple array means
❯   const savedPeople: SaveData<string>[];   // TypeScript no longer knows the result is still 4 items long...
const savedFiona = savedPeople[700];   // ...and so where is should flag an
❯   const savedFiona: SaveData<string> // error, instead it assumes the value exists

Without the narrowness translated to the save method's return type, we lose some type safety. So instead, we can map the returned tuple type to preserve the const type data:

// Use of readonly array below supports the tuple 'as const' shorthand.

```
type Result<T extends readonly any[]> =
    T extends readonly [infer Item]
      ? readonly [SaveData<Item>]
    : T extends readonly [infer Item, ...infer Rest]
      ? readonly [SaveData<Item>, ...SaveResult<Rest>]
    : never;
function save<Values extends readonly any[]>(values: Values): Result<Values> {
return values.map(value => ({ value, dateSaved: new Date() })) as any;
}
const people = ['Kelly', 'Jim', 'Ash', 'Fiona'] as const;
// TypeScript now infers savedPeople to be a correctly-typed
// tuple with the right number of elements:
const savedPeople = save(people);
```
❯   const savedPeople: readonly [
        SaveData<"Kelly">,
        SaveData<"Jim">,
        SaveData<"Ash">,
        SaveData<"Fiona">
     ];
// And so it will correctly flag if we index erroneously:
const savedFiona = savedPeople[700]; ✘
// And will be able to correctly infer derived or subvalues:
const fiona = savedPeople[3].value;
❯   const fiona: "Fiona"; ✔
Without the narrowness translated to the save method's return type, we lose some type safety.

Template Literals

Template literals allow you to embed type expressions within string literals. To define a template literal, use backticks "`" rather than simple quotes around your string literal, as shown in the following example:

```
type Email = `${string}@${string}.com`;
const wrong1: Email = 'Porridge'; ✗
const wrong2: Email = 'steve@example'; ✗
const correct: Email = 'steve@example.com'; ✓
```

Defining a template literal type

As these template literals can include any type that can be evaluated to a string, you can include union types in them:

```
type DomainSuffix = 'com' | 'org' | 'net';
type Email = `${string}@${string}.${DomainSuffix}`;
const wrong: Email = 'steve@example.toast'; ✗
const correct: Email = 'steve@example.com'; ✓
```

Using a union type in a template literal

TypeScript also includes some special string-translation utility types for use with string types, which of course can be used with template literals:

Uppercase<StringType>   Changes the given string type to its uppercase equivalent

Lowercase<StringType>   Changes the given string type to its lowercase equivalent

Capitalize<StringType>   Changes only the first character in the given string type to its uppercase equivalent

Uncapitalize<StringType>   Changes only the first character in the given string type to its lowercase equivalent

Template literals can also be used in conditional types, and the embedded templated types inferred, as shown here:

```
type SystemCaseFullname<Name extends string> = Name extends `${infer FirstName} ${infer LastName}` ? `${Capitalize<FirstName>} ${Uppercase<LastName>}` : Capitalize<Name>;
function toSystemCase<Name extends string>(n: Name): SystemCaseFullname<Name>;
const name = toSystemCase('jane smith');
❯ const name: "Jane SMITH";
```

Conclusion: The Power and Potential of Conditional and Recursive Types

The journey through the intricacies of conditional and recursive types highlights their indispensable role in modern programming. These constructs represent the pinnacle of type system evolution, enabling developers to handle complex data structures, implement dynamic behaviors, and enforce compile-time constraints with unparalleled precision. Let's delve into the impact, benefits, challenges, and future prospects of these powerful features, providing a holistic closure to their discussion.

1. Restating Their Core Strengths

Conditional and recursive types are not mere theoretical constructs but practical tools that address real-world problems:

Conditional Types empower programmers to model dynamic decision-making at the type level, mirroring logical branching in runtime code. Whether filtering unions, mapping transformations, or crafting utility types like Exclude or Extract, they excel at fine-grained type manipulation.

Recursive Types extend this power by defining self-referential patterns, making them ideal for hierarchical structures, nested data formats, and algorithms that traverse layered entities.

Together, they create a framework that is expressive, reusable, and robust, bringing type systems closer to the real-world complexities they aim to model.

2. Real-World Applications and Impacts

The utility of conditional and recursive types extends across various domains, making them essential in professional software development:

a) Data Modeling

Recursive types shine in modeling data structures such as trees, graphs, or deeply nested objects. For example:

Tree Structures: Binary trees and hierarchical file systems can be represented succinctly, with recursive types allowing infinite depth while maintaining clarity.

JSON Validation: Recursive types elegantly handle the variability of JSON, ensuring correctness across diverse inputs.

Conditional types, on the other hand, facilitate:

Dynamic Properties: Modifying or transforming properties based on criteria (e.g., converting all string types in a nested object to Uppercase).

b) Utility Types in Libraries

TypeScript's built-in utility types (Partial, Pick, Exclude) are powered by conditional and recursive logic. Developers can extend these patterns to create domain-specific utilities, ensuring more expressive APIs and safer code.

c) Framework and Tooling Enhancements

In popular frameworks like React, conditional and recursive types provide type-safe utilities:

Enforcing type safety in complex state management libraries.
Ensuring component props validation based on generic constraints.

d) Enhanced Developer Productivity

By shifting error detection to compile time, these advanced types reduce runtime errors, leading to:

More reliable codebases.
Faster development cycles due to fewer debugging sessions.

3. Challenges in Adoption

While the advantages are compelling, mastering these constructs requires careful consideration of their challenges:

a) Complexity

Steep Learning Curve: Understanding nested recursive and conditional logic can be daunting, especially for developers new to advanced type systems.

Readability: Complex types, especially recursive ones, can make code harder to comprehend without proper documentation.

b) Type Performance

The TypeScript compiler may struggle with deeply nested or infinite recursion in types, leading to degraded performance or stack overflow errors during compilation.

c) Tooling and Ecosystem Support

Although most modern IDEs support TypeScript's advanced features, tooling might lag behind in providing intuitive feedback or rendering for extremely complex types.

d) Debugging Types

Unlike runtime errors, type-level errors often involve intricate logic and require a strong understanding of the type system to resolve effectively.

4. Future Possibilities and Evolving Type Systems

The evolution of conditional and recursive types paves the way for even more powerful abstractions in the future. Some promising directions include:

a) Improved Type Inference

As languages like TypeScript and others evolve, type inference will become more intuitive, allowing conditional and recursive types to integrate seamlessly with everyday programming patterns.

b) Advanced Recursive Algorithms

Recursive types can be extended to model algorithms at the type level, such as compile-time computations, memorization strategies, or optimization techniques.

c) Cross-Language Adoption

Other statically typed languages, like Rust, Swift, and Kotlin, are likely to adopt similar constructs, enriching their type systems to handle real-world complexities.

d) Enhanced Tooling

As IDEs and type-checkers mature, developers can expect:

Better Visualization: Tools for visualizing deeply nested types.

Simplified Debugging: Intelligent suggestions for resolving type-level errors.

5. Best Practices for Maximizing Their Benefits

To leverage conditional and recursive types effectively, developers should adhere to best practices:

a) Prioritize Simplicity

Avoid overengineering types for problems that can be solved more directly.
Break down complex conditional logic into smaller, modular types.

b) Document and Name Types Clearly

Readable and descriptive type names, combined with inline comments, can greatly enhance comprehension.

c) Test Types Thoroughly

Use extensive test cases to validate complex types, ensuring they behave as expected in diverse scenarios.

d) Leverage Community Resources

Engage with the rich TypeScript community, which provides libraries, utilities, and patterns to simplify type system complexities.

6. A Reflection on Their Philosophical Significance

Conditional and recursive types represent more than just technical tools; they embody the philosophy of modern programming:

Declarative Power: By abstracting logic into types, they align closely with the declarative programming paradigm.

Safety and Precision: By emphasizing compile-time guarantees, they reduce runtime errors, fostering robust software design.

Expressiveness: They empower developers to express intent clearly, ensuring code reflects the problem domain accurately.

These traits align with the broader shift in software development toward more type-safe, maintainable, and scalable codebases.

7. Conclusion: Looking Forward

Conditional and recursive types are a testament to the progress in type system design, bridging the gap between theoretical computer science and practical software engineering. Their application extends beyond TypeScript, influencing how developers think about type safety, modularity, and correctness across programming languages.

By mastering these constructs, developers gain the ability to model complex systems effectively, anticipate and prevent errors before they occur, and build codebases that are not just functional but resilient. As the programming landscape evolves, conditional and recursive types will continue to play a pivotal role, shaping the future of type-driven development.

This exploration serves as both an introduction and a call to action for developers to delve deeper into these constructs. By embracing their potential, we not only elevate our coding practices but also contribute to a future where software is safer, smarter, and more aligned with human ingenuity.

8. Structuring and Extending Types

Introduction

In this chapter, we will go deeper into TypeScript's type system, focusing on how to structure and extend types to write code that is maintainable and easier to understand, which leads to less bugs and a better development experience.

TypeScript, being a superset of JavaScript, introduces static typing and structural type systems that allow developers to create robust, scalable, and maintainable codebases. One of its most powerful features is the ability to structure and extend types, enabling greater code reuse, flexibility, and type safety. This document explores these concepts in detail.

1. Introduction to TypeScript Types

TypeScript's type system can be broadly categorized into two types:

Primitive Types: Number, string, boolean, bigint, symbol, null, undefined.

Custom Types: Interfaces, type aliases, classes, enums, tuples, and union/intersection types.

Structuring and extending types revolve around custom types, as they allow the creation of more meaningful and reusable abstractions in code.

2. Interfaces: The Foundation of Structuring Types

Interfaces in TypeScript define the structure of an object, specifying the properties and their types.

```
interface User {
  id: number;
  name: string;
  email?: string; // Optional property
}
```

Optional Properties: Properties marked with a ? are optional, allowing more flexible object structures.

Readonly Properties: Properties can be made immutable using the readonly modifier.

```
interface Config {
  readonly apiKey: string;
}
```

3. Type Aliases: Alternative to Interfaces

Type aliases provide another way to define types. They are particularly useful when dealing with: Union or intersection types.

Complex types that cannot be expressed as interfaces.

```
type Point = {
  x: number;
  y: number;
};
```

```
type Response = string | number | boolean;
```

4. Extending Types: Reusing and Composing Types

4.1 Extending Interfaces

Interfaces can extend one or more interfaces, combining their properties.

```
interface Person {
  name: string;
}
```

```
interface Employee extends Person {
  employeeId: number;
}
```

This allows Employee to inherit all properties of Person while adding its own.

4.2 Extending Type Aliases

Type aliases can be composed using intersection types.

```
type Person = {
  name: string;
};
```

```
type Employee = Person & {
  employeeId: number;
};
```

Intersection types allow combining multiple types into one, with all the properties of the involved types.

5. Advanced Structuring Techniques

5.1 Index Signatures

Index signatures allow defining types for objects with dynamic keys.

```
interface Dictionary {
  [key: string]: string;
}
```

5.2 Mapped Types

Mapped types enable transformations of existing types.

```
type ReadOnly<T> = {
  readonly [K in keyof T]: T[K];
};
type UserReadOnly = ReadOnly<User>;
```

5.3 Conditional Types

Conditional types provide type inference based on conditions.

```
type IsString<T> = T extends string ? true : false;
type Test = IsString<'hello'>; // true
```

6. Utility Types

TypeScript provides built-in utility types that simplify common type transformations:

Partial<T>: Makes all properties optional.
Required<T>: Makes all properties required.
Readonly<T>: Makes all properties readonly.
Pick<T, K>: Extracts a subset of properties.
Omit<T, K>: Excludes specified properties.

7. Structuring Types in Large Codebases

7.1 Modularizing Types

Break down types into separate files and modules for better organization.

```
// models/User.ts
export interface User {
  id: number;
  name: string;
}
// services/UserService.ts
import { User } from '../models/User';
function getUser(id: number): User { ... }
```

7.2 Namespace Usage

Namespaces can group related types.

```
namespace Geometry {
  export interface Point {
    x: number;
    y: number;
  }
  export interface Circle {
    center: Point;
    radius: number;
  }
}
```

8. Extending Classes with Interfaces

Classes can implement interfaces, enforcing a specific structure.

```
interface Logger {
  log(message: string): void;
}
class ConsoleLogger implements Logger {
  log(message: string) {
    console.log(message);
  }
}
```

9. Extending and Structuring Types in Generic Code

Generics make types reusable and flexible.

```
interface ApiResponse<T> {
  data: T;
  error?: string;
}
const response: ApiResponse<string> = {
  data: 'Success',
};
```

Generics can also extend types.

```
function merge<T extends object, U extends object>(a: T, b: U): T & U {
  return { ...a, ...b };
}
```

10. Practical Use Cases

10.1 Dynamic Data Models

Dynamic API responses often require conditional and mapped types.

```
type ApiResponse<T> = T extends { success: boolean } ? T & { timestamp: number } : T;
```

10.2 Framework Development

Frameworks often rely on extending base interfaces or types.

```
interface ComponentProps {
  id: string;
  children?: React.ReactNode;
}

interface ButtonProps extends ComponentProps {
  onClick: () => void;
}
```

11. Best Practices

Prefer Interfaces Over Type Aliases: Use interfaces for objects and classes, and type aliases for unions and intersections.

Use Utility Types: Leverage built-in utility types for common transformations.

Modularize Types: Separate types into logical files and modules.

Document Types: Use comments or JSDoc to explain complex types.

Avoid Overengineering: Keep type structures simple and easy to understand.

12. Future Enhancements in TypeScript

TypeScript's type system continues to evolve. Some anticipated features include:

Enhanced support for variadic tuple types.
Better type inference for template literals.
Improvements in conditional and mapped types.

Role of type system in structuring and extending types

TypeScript's type system can be extended to represent richer data models, helping to organize and scale your software's architecture. It provides a suite of tools for creating and managing types that enables you to write cleaner, easier to understand, and more maintainable code. By creating custom types you can ensure that objects in your program adhere to a specific structure, this is especially useful when working with complex data structures.

The type system allows you to create interfaces and classes, which provides a blueprint for creating objects and organizing related data and functions. They allow you to extend existing types with new properties and methods. You can also create abstract classes, which provide a base for creating more specific data structures.

Additionally, TypeScript's type system introduces utility types, such as Read-only and Partial, which allows you to transform existing types into new ones. These utility types are powerful tools for modifying type behavior and provide greater flexibility when working with types.

It also comes with advanced features like mapped and conditional types, enabling developers to create more complex and dynamic types. These advanced type manipulation features open up a world of possibilities for type design, making TypeScript's type system incredibly versatile and adaptable.

The type system is rich and expressive, but also has its complexities and limitations. Understanding these trade-offs is crucial. It is also important to consider performance when working with types, as certain type patterns can lead to slower compile times.

We have discussed in the lack of a static type system in JavaScript can sometimes lead to confusion and potential runtime errors. This is because variables can hold values of any type, and those values can be freely reassigned without any constraints. Let us consider the following JavaScript example:

```
let data = 'Hello, world!';
data = 42;  // This is perfectly valid in JavaScript, but might not be what you intended.
```

Now, look at how TypeScript's type system can help structure this code:

```
let data: string = 'Hello, world!';
data = 42;  // TypeScript will throw an error, preventing a potential bug.
```

In the TypeScript example, the variable data is explicitly declared as a string. Any attempt to assign a non-string value to data will result in a compile-time error. This structuring ability helps developers catch potential bugs early in the development process.

In addition to this basic structuring, TypeScript's type system also allows more complex type structuring and extensions. For instance, it supports the definition of custom types using type aliases. This feature can be used to create complex, reusable type definitions, structuring the code in a more robust and maintainable way:

```
type StringOrNumber = string | number;
let data: StringOrNumber = 'Hello, world!';  // This is valid.
data = 42;  // This is also valid.
```

In this example, StringOrNumber is a type alias that represents either a string or a number. This kind of flexibility allows TypeScript's type system to be used for complex type structuring and extension, offering a balance between the dynamic nature of JavaScript and the need for more stringent type safety.

Interfaces

TypeScript interfaces act as contracts that define the structure and behavior of objects, covering everything from the basics to optional properties and interface extensions. We will look into how interfaces ensure type safety, promote code reusability, and make your code more maintainable.

Interface basics

In TypeScript, an interface is a contract that defines the structure of values, providing a way to ensure that a value adheres to a certain shape. Interfaces are particularly useful when dealing with objects as they allow you to define what properties and methods an object should have.

To start with, let us understand the concept of an interface through an example:

```
interface Person {name: string;   age: number;   greet(): void;
}
```

In the example above, we have defined an interface named Person with two properties, name and age, and a method called greet. Property name is of type string, age is of type number, and greet is a method that does not return anything (void).

When you create an interface in TypeScript, you are not creating a new data type but defining a shape for any data that claims to be of that interface type. This shape is a contract that objects claiming to be of type Person need to follow:

```
let person1: Person = {name: 'Alice', age: 30, greet() {
console.log('Hello, ' + this.name);
}
};
```

In the code above, person1 is an object that satisfies the Person interface. It has a name property that is a string, an age property that is a number, and a greet method. This greets method, when called, logs a greeting to the console but returns nothing (void).

If we attempt to create a Person that does not conform to the interface, TypeScript will throw a compile-time error. For instance, the following code will result in an error:

```
let person2: Person = {name: 'Bob',   // Missing 'age' and 'greet' will lead to an error.
};
```

This ability to enforce a certain structure for objects is especially useful when working with complex data structures, where you want to ensure that a particular object has specific properties or methods.

Interfaces can also be used to describe function types. This is done by defining a call signature within the interface. A call signature is similar to a function declaration with a parameter list and a return type. Here is an example:

```
interface AddFunction { (x: number, y: number): number;
}
```

In this example, AddFunction is an interface describing a function that takes two parameters, both of type number, and returns a number. We can now define a function that conforms to this interface:
```
let add: AddFunction; add = function (n1: number, n2: number) {
return n1 + n2;
};
```

Here, the function add matches the AddFunction interface, as it takes two numbers as parameters and returns a number.

Optional properties and methods in interfaces

While interfaces are powerful for ensuring adherence to a specific structure, there are scenarios where some properties or methods might not always be required. For instance, an object representing a Person might optionally have an email property. In TypeScript, you can specify such optional properties or methods using the? operator. Let us extend the Person interface from the previous example:

```
interface Person {
name: string;   age: number;   email?: string; // Optional property
greet(): void;   sayGoodbye?(): void; // Optional method
}
```

In this example, email and say Goodbye are optional. This means an object can still be considered a Person even if these properties do not exist:

```
let person: Person = {name: 'Alice',  age: 30,  greet() {
console.log('Hello, ' + this.name);
}
};
```

Optional properties and methods give you flexibility when defining your interfaces. They allow you to define properties that might not always be required, while retaining the benefits of TypeScript's type system. This flexibility is particularly useful when dealing with complex or dynamic data where not all properties might be always available. However, it is important to handle optional properties and methods carefully in your code, as they could be undefined.

Extending interfaces

Extending interfaces in TypeScript is a powerful feature that promotes code reusability and a robust design pattern.

It is a form of interface inheritance where an interface can inherit the properties and methods from another interface. The keyword extends is used to achieve this inheritance.

Consider the following example:

```
interface Person {name: string;  age: number;  greet(): void;
}
interface Employee extends Person {
employeeId: number;   department: string;   clockIn(): void;
}
```

In this example, the Employee interface extends the Person interface, thereby inheriting the name, age, and greet() properties and methods. Additionally, Employee defines its own unique properties and methods:

employeeId, department, and clockIn().

This ability to extend interfaces is a part of what makes TypeScript's type system so flexible and powerful. It allows developers to construct complex, hierarchical types that reflect the intricacies of real-world data models. When an object is typed as Employee, it must contain all the properties and methods from both Person and Employee interfaces, as shown here:

```
let employee: Employee = { name: 'Alice',   age: 30,   employeeId: 1234,   department: 'Sales',   greet()
{
console.log('Hello, ' + this.name);
},
clockIn() {
console.log(this.name + ' clocked in');
}
};
```

Classes
This section delves into TypeScript's object-oriented programming features, focusing on classes, constructors, inheritance, and encapsulation. Here, you will learn how classes act as object blueprints, how constructors make object initialization more efficient, and how inheritance enables code reusability.

We also cover encapsulation techniques that protect data integrity, enhanced by TypeScript's access modifiers. These concepts lay the foundation for developing robust and maintainable applications.

Class basics and constructors

Classes in TypeScript serve as the foundation for object-oriented programming (OOP), allowing developers to define blueprints for creating objects. A class encapsulates data and functions that operate on that data, simplifying code organization and reuse by grouping related properties and behaviours.

To declare a class in TypeScript, you can use the class keyword followed by the class name:

```
class Car {
brand: string;  model: string;  year: number;
}
```

Here, Car is a class with properties brand, model, and year. You can create an instance of the Car class using the new keyword:

```
let myCar = new Car();
myCar.brand = 'Toyota';
myCar.model = 'Corolla';
myCar.year = 2010;
```

However, this approach of setting properties one by one can be tedious, especially for classes with many properties.

This is where constructors come into play. A constructor is a special method within a class that gets called when an instance of the class is created. It is typically used to initialize class properties. The constructor method is defined using the constructor keyword:

```
class Car {
brand: string;  model: string;   year: number;
constructor(brand: string, model: string, year: number) {
this.brand = brand;    this.model = model;    this.year = year;  }
}
```

Now, you can create a new Car instance and initialize its properties in one line:

```
let myCar = new Car('Toyota', 'Corolla', 2010);
```

TypeScript further simplifies this with parameter properties, allowing you to declare and initialize a class property in one place:

```
class Car {
constructor( public brand: string,    public model: string,    public year: number )
{ }
}
```

This code is equivalent to the previous example. The public keyword indicates that the parameters are also class properties and should be accessible outside the class.

With classes and constructors, TypeScript enhances JavaScript's object-oriented capabilities, providing a more straightforward and efficient way of defining and working with complex objects. This concept is fundamental for working with TypeScript and lays the groundwork for more advanced features such as inheritance and encapsulation.

Inheritance in classes

Inheritance is a core principle of object-oriented programming, allowing for code reusability and organization by forming parent-child relationships between classes. In TypeScript, a class can inherit properties and methods from another class, creating a hierarchy of classes that share common characteristics.

The extends keyword is used to create a subclass, or child class, that inherits from a parent class:

```
class Vehicle {
speed: number;
constructor(speed: number) {
this.speed = speed;
}
move() {
console.log(`The vehicle is moving at ${this.speed} miles per hour.`);
}
}
class Car extends Vehicle {
wheels: number;
constructor(speed: number, wheels: number) {
super(speed);
this.wheels = wheels;
}   honk() {
console.log('Beep beep!');
}
}
```

In this example, Vehicle is the parent class, and Car is the child class. The Car class inherits the properties and methods of the Vehicle class, defines its additional property, wheels, and its own method, honk().

The super keyword is used to call the constructor of the parent class. It is required to use super before accessing the keyword this in the derived class which ensures that the parent class is properly initialized before the child class starts its own initialization.

Inheritance enables the creation of a hierarchy of classes that share common properties and methods, while also defining their unique characteristics. It promotes code reusability and organization, leading to cleaner, more maintainable code.

In TypeScript, you can also use the protected modifier to ensure that a method or property is available to subclasses but not outside the class hierarchy. This encapsulation is useful for preserving the integrity of your classes while still allowing for code reuse through inheritance.

Inheritance is powerful, but it should be used judiciously. Overuse of inheritance can lead to complex class hierarchies that are difficult to understand and maintain. Often, using composition and building classes out of smaller, simpler classes or objects, can be a more flexible and maintainable approach.

TypeScript also supports abstract classes: classes that cannot be instantiated directly but can be extended. Abstract classes can define abstract methods, which do not have an implementation in the abstract class and must be implemented in any concrete (non-abstract) subclass.

```
abstract class Shape {
abstract getArea(): number;
}
class Circle extends Shape {
constructor(public radius: number)
{
super();
}
getArea(): number {
    return Math.PI * this.radius ** 2;
}
}
```

In this example, Shape is an abstract class that defines an abstract getArea method. Circle is a subclass of Shape that provides an implementation for getArea.

Encapsulation: private, public, and protected modifiers

Encapsulation, one of the four fundamental principles of object-oriented programming, refers to the bundling of related data and behaviour into a single unit, a class, and controlling access to that data. TypeScript supports encapsulation through access modifiers applied to class members. There are three access modifiers in TypeScript: public, private, and protected.

Public modifier

In TypeScript, all class members are public by default. This means that they can be accessed from outside the class.

Consider the following Circle class:

```
class Circle {
radius: number;
constructor(radius: number) {
this.radius = radius;
}
getArea(): number {
return Math.PI * this.radius ** 2;
}
}
```

In this example, both radius and getArea() are public by default. It would be the same if you explicitly typed public radius: number or public getArea(): number.

Either way they can be accessed and called from an instance of the Circle class:

```
const myCircle = new Circle(3);
console.log(myCircle.radius);  // Outputs: 3
console.log(myCircle.getArea());  // Outputs: 28.27 (rounded)
```

Private modifier

To make a class member private, the private keyword is used. Private members cannot be accessed from outside the class or by any subclasses, they can only be accessed from within the class itself. This concept of controlled access is called encapsulation.

If we add the private modifier to the type annotation for radius, an instance would not be able to access, it is now only visible for methods inside that class, like getArea and getRadius in this example:

```
class Circle {
private radius: number;
constructor(radius: number) {
this.radius = radius;
}
getArea(): number {
return Math.PI * this.radius ** 2;
}
getRadius(): number {
return this.radius;
}
}
```

Here, radius is a private member of the Circle class and cannot be accessed directly outside of the class, now TypeScript throws an error if you try to do that. We added a getRadius method to return the value of radius, that defaults to public like getArea, so they are accessible outside of the class;
```
const myCircle = new Circle(3);
console.log(myCircle.radius);  // Error: Property 'radius' is private and only accessible within class
'Circle'.  console.log(myCircle.getArea());  // Outputs: 28.27 (rounded)
console.log(myCircle.getRadius());  // Outputs: 3
```

Protected modifier

The protected access modifier is similar to private, but with one key difference: a protected member can be accessed within its class and by subclasses. This is useful for cases where you want to allow subclasses to use certain properties or methods but still keep them hidden from the outside world.

```
class Shape {
protected area: number;
constructor(area: number) {
this.area = area;
}
}
class Circle extends Shape {
radius: number;
constructor(radius: number) {
super(Math.PI * radius ** 2);
this.radius = radius;
```

```
}
getArea(): number {
return this.area;
  }
}
```

In this example, area is a protected member of the Shape class. It cannot be accessed directly outside of the class or its subclasses. However, it can be accessed within the Circle class because Circle is a subclass of Shape.

These access modifiers help you control how and where your class members can be accessed, promoting encapsulation and improving code maintainability. By restricting access where appropriate, you can prevent external code from inadvertently modifying the internal state of your objects in ways that could leave them in an inconsistent or invalid state. This makes your code safe, easy to understand, and maintain. However, encapsulation should not be overused. In many cases, simple and transparent code is preferable.

Type compatibility and coercion

In this segment, we will delve into TypeScript's approach to type compatibility, the utility of type coercion and assertions, and the nuanced concepts of covariance and contravariance. TypeScript's type system is largely structural, making it flexible yet specific. We will look at how this impacts assignments and type conversions, as well as the implications for function parameters and return types. Understanding these elements is essential for leveraging TypeScript's full capabilities, while navigating its inherent complexities understanding type compatibility.

Type compatibility in TypeScript is a fundamental concept that dictates how types relate to each other, particularly when assigning values of one type to another. It is based on structural typing, a system that determines compatibility and equivalence by an object's structure or, in other words, by the properties it possesses. This is in contrast to nominal typing used in other languages like Java or C++, where compatibility and equivalence are based on the names of types or explicit declarations. Consider the following example:

```
interface Named {name: string;
}
let x: Named;
let y = {
name: "Alice", location: "Seattle"
};
x = y;
```

In the above code, y is assignable to x because y has at least the same properties as x. Even though y has an additional property (location), TypeScript considers y to be compatible with x because y has at least all the properties that x expects.

This kind of flexibility is one of the reasons TypeScript is so powerful at managing JavaScript's dynamic nature. It allows TypeScript to enforce type safety while still allowing JavaScript-like flexibility while working with objects. However, TypeScript's structural type system can sometimes lead to surprising results:

```typescript
interface Named {
name: string;
}
class Person {
name: string;
}
let p: Named;
p = new Person();
```

Even though Person does not explicitly implement Named, TypeScript considers Person to be compatible with Named because Person has a name property just like it does. This illustrates the flexibility, but also the subtlety, of TypeScript's type compatibility rules.

Type coercion and type assertions

Type coercion and type assertions are two important concepts in TypeScript's type system. They offer developers control over how types are converted and interpreted in different contexts.

Type coercion in TypeScript is quite similar to JavaScript, where the language automatically converts one type into another based on the context. For example, when adding a number and a string together, JavaScript (and by extension TypeScript) converts the number into a string before performing the concatenation:

```typescript
let result = "Hello, " + 42; // result is "Hello, 42"
```

In this case, the number 42 is coerced into a string by the JavaScript runtime. This is a typical example of implicit type coercion. It is worth noting that TypeScript, being a superset of JavaScript, does not remove or alter JavaScript's type coercion behaviour.

On the other hand, TypeScript introduces a feature that is not present in JavaScript: type assertions. Type assertions are a way for developers to explicitly tell the TypeScript compiler to treat a value as a certain type:

```typescript
let someValue: any = "this is a string";
let strLength: number = (someValue as string).length;
```

In the above example, someValue is of type any, but we know that it is a string. By using a type assertion someValue as string, we tell TypeScript to treat someValue as a string, allowing us to access the length property without any compile-time errors.

It is important to understand that type assertions are purely a compile-time construct and have no runtime impact. TypeScript does not perform any special checks or restructuring of data when a type assertion is used. It is simply a way to provide hints to the TypeScript compiler about how the code should be analysed.

Type assertions do not override the type checking process. If TypeScript determines that a type assertion is not valid, it will produce a compile-time error. For instance, you cannot assert that a string is a number if the original type does not have the properties or methods of the target type.

Covariance and contravariance in TypeScript

In TypeScript, a type A is a subtype of B if A can be used wherever B is expected without causing a type error. This principle is known as substitutability, and it is at the heart of TypeScript's structural type system. Covariance and Contravariance describe how subtyping relationships interact with complex types like function parameters and return types.

Covariance refers to the ability to use a more derived type (a subtype) in place of a less derived type (a supertype). In TypeScript, function return types and array types are covariant. This means you can assign an array of a subtype to a variable of a supertype array. Similarly, a function that returns a subtype can be assigned to a variable expecting a function that returns a supertype.

```
class Animal {
constructor(public name: string) {}
}
class Dog extends Animal {
constructor(name: string, public breed: string) {
super(name);
}
}
let animals: Animal[] = [new Dog('Rex', 'German Shepherd'), new Dog('Spot', 'Dalmatian')];
function getDog(): Dog { return new Dog('Fido', 'Poodle');
}
let animalGetter: () => Animal = getDog;
```

In the code above, Dog is a subclass of Animal, which means any Dog instance can be used where an Animal is expected. The function getDog returns a Dog object, but it is assigned to animalGetter, a function returning Animal. This again demonstrates covariance, but this time in function return types.

Contravariance, on the other hand, is a bit more complex. It applies in the reverse situation: you can use a less derived type (a supertype) in place of a more derived type (a subtype). In TypeScript, function parameter types are contravariant, but this is only enforced under the strictFunctionTypes compiler option.

```
class Animal {constructor (public name: string) {}
}
class Dog extends Animal {
constructor(name: string, public breed: string) {
super(name);
}
}
function useAnimal(animal: Animal) {
console.log(`Using animal: ${animal.name}`);
}
let dogUser: (dog: Dog) => void = useAnimal;
dogUser(new Dog('Buddy', 'Beagle'));
```

This code compiles under strictFunctionTypes because useAnimal can certainly work with a Dog, since it is a subtype of Animal. These concepts may seem abstract, but help maintain type safety when working with complex type structures.

Readonly and Partial types

TypeScript's utility types like Readonly and Partial offer flexibility while maintaining type safety. Readonly types ensure immutability, making it impossible to change object properties after they are set, useful for maintaining consistency in complex structures like arrays and objects. On the other hand, Partial types make it easier to work with potentially incomplete objects by making all properties optional yet ensuring that existing properties conform to the expected types. These utility types are valuable tools for enforcing code reliability and can be particularly effective in various programming scenarios.

Readonly types

When you are working with TypeScript, there will be times when you want to ensure that once a variable is assigned a value, it cannot be changed. This can be especially useful when working with complex structures, like arrays and objects, where you want to ensure that the structure's contents remain consistent. This is where TypeScript's Readonly type comes in handy. Let us consider a simple example. Suppose we have an interface Person:

```
interface Person {
name: string;
age: number;
}
```

We can create a Readonly version of Person like this:

```
type ReadonlyPerson = Readonly<Person>;
```

Now if we try to modify the properties of ReadonlyPerson, TypeScript will give us an error:

```
let john: ReadonlyPerson = { name: 'John', age: 25 }; // Error: Cannot assign to 'age' because it is a read-only property.
john.age = 26;
```

By making john a ReadonlyPerson, none of its properties can be changed. This can be very useful in situations where you want to ensure that an object remains constant after its creation.

However, Readonly is not limited to objects. It can also be used with arrays by using the ReadonlyArray type. Let us say we have an array of numbers:

```
let numbers: number[] = [1, 2, 3, 4, 5]; numbers[0] = 0; // doesn't throw an error
```
We can make this array read-only in TypeScript by changing its type to ReadonlyArray<number>:
```
let numbers: ReadonlyArray<number> = [1, 2, 3, 4, 5];
numbers[0] = 6;
// Error: Index signature in type 'readonly number[]' only permits reading.
```

We can even make the array readonly, meaning that we cannot add or remove elements from the array:

```
numbers.push(6); // Error: Property 'push' does not exist on type 'readonly number[]'.
```

To ensure immutability at every level, TypeScript offers a technique known as deep immutability. This can be achieved using the as const assertion. When you assign an object with it, all nested properties are immutable.

```
const person = {
name: 'John',   details: { age: 25, address: '123 Street'   }
} as const;
```

person.name = 'Doe'; person.details.age = 26;

Partial types

When building applications with TypeScript, you often encounter situations where you need to work with objects that may not yet be fully formed. For example, you may have a function that accepts an object of a certain type, but in some cases, you may only have some of the object's properties available. To handle these situations, TypeScript provides a built-in utility type called Partial.

The Partial type takes an existing type and produces a new type, where all the properties of the original type are optional. This can be very useful when you want to create an object that matches a certain interface, but you do not have all the necessary information available at once.

Let us consider an example. Suppose we have the following interface:

```
interface Employee {
id: number;
name: string;
department: string;
}
```

Now, let us say we have a function createEmployee, which takes an employee object and adds it to a database. However, in some cases, we may not have all the employee details at the time of creation. For instance, we might want to create an employee record with just the id and name, and add the department later. In this case, we can use the Partial type:

```
function createEmployee(employee: Partial<Employee>) {   // Implementation here
}
```

Now we can call createEmployee with an object that has any subset of the Employee properties:

```
createEmployee({ id: 1, name: 'John' });
createEmployee({ id: 2, department: 'HR' });
createEmployee({ name: 'Jane', department: 'Engineering' });
```

This gives us a lot of flexibility when working with objects that may not yet be complete. However, it is important to note that while Partial makes all the properties optional, it does not change their types. So, if a property is present, it must still have the correct type.

The Partial type is a great example of how TypeScript's type system can provide flexibility and safety at the same time. We can handle objects that may not have all their properties yet, while still ensuring that any properties that are present have the correct type. This can be very helpful in many real-world coding scenarios.

One important note to keep in mind is that Partial only makes the properties of the first level optional. Nested objects within the original type still have their properties as mandatory. This is referred to as shallow partial. If you need to make nested objects also partial, you will have to apply the Partial type to them individually.

Defining and using custom types

This section guides you through the nuances of defining and using custom types in TypeScript. From creating shorthand notations via type aliases to harnessing the power of union and intersection types, we cover the tools that make your code both flexible and type-safe. Additionally, we introduce type guards and type predicates, techniques that offer dynamic type checking, further strengthening your TypeScript applications.

Type aliases

TypeScript provides a feature called type aliases, which gives you the ability to create a new name for an existing type. Once a type alias is defined, you can use it anywhere you would use the original type. Let us look at a simple example. Suppose you are working on a program that handle coordinates in a 2D space. You might frequently use pairs of numbers to represent these coordinates. Instead of writing {x: number, y: number} every time you need to use such a pair, you could define a type alias. The syntax for creating a type alias is straightforward, you use the type keyword followed by the name of the alias, an equal to sign, and then the existing type:

```
type Point = { x: number;   y: number; }; // Now you can use 'Point' to represent coordinates let p:
Point = { x: 10, y: 20 };
```

Type aliases are particularly useful for simplifying complex types. For instance, you might be working with a function that returns a Promise containing an array of objects, each with several properties. Instead of writing out this complex type every time, you could use a type alias:

```
type User = {name: string;   email: string; }; // Alias for a Promise containing an array of Users type
UserPromise = Promise<User[]>; // Now you can use 'UserPromise' as a type let g
etUsers: UserPromise;
```

While type aliases can make your code more readable and manageable, it is important to use them responsibly. Overuse of type aliases can lead to a situation where the actual types being used become obscured, making the code difficult to understand. It is generally better to use type aliases when you have a complex type that is used frequently, or when the alias provides a clear semantic benefit.

Union and intersection types

Type aliases can also be used to create union types, intersection types, and even recursive types. They are a flexible feature that can help you to write cleaner, more maintainable code.

Union types

Union type is a type that can be any one of several types. This is expressed using the pipe (|) operator. Here is a simple example:

```
type StringOrNumber = string | number;
let variable: StringOrNumber;
variable = "hello"; // This is ok
variable = 42; // This is ok
variable = true; // Error: Type 'boolean' is not assignable to type 'StringOrNumber'
```

Union types are particularly useful when you are dealing with values that can come from multiple sources or have multiple valid types. They enable you to model these kinds of scenarios accurately in your type system.

Intersection types

Intersection types are a way of combining multiple types into one. This is expressed using the ampersand (&) operator. The resulting type has all the properties of the constituent types. Here is an example:

```
type HasName = { name: string };
type HasAge = { age: number };
type Person = HasName & HasAge;
let person: Person = { name: "Alice",   age: 30 };  // This is okay let invalidPerson:
Person = {name: "Bob"};  // Error: Property 'age' is missing in type '{ name: string; }' but required in type 'Person'
```

Intersection types are useful when you want to create a type that combines the properties of multiple other types. They are often used with interfaces or type aliases to build up complex types from simpler ones.

Type guards and type predicates

TypeScript has a feature known as type guards, which allow you to perform runtime checks that narrow down the type of a variable or parameter. Type guards are expressions that perform a check and return a boolean result. When a type guard is true, TypeScript will narrow the type within scope of the true branch.

Here is an example of a simple type guard using typeof:

```
function doSomething(value: string | number) {
if (typeof value === "string")
{
console.log(value.toUpperCase());
}
else {
console.log(value.toFixed(2));   }
}
```

In this example, typeof value === "string" is a type guard. If it is true, TypeScript knows that value is a string within the true branch of the if statement. TypeScript also supports a more advanced kind of type guard called a type predicate. A type predicate is a function that returns a Boolean, but with a special return type annotation that tells TypeScript that the function is a type guard.

Here is an example of a type predicate:

```
function isString(value: any): value is string {
return typeof value === "string";
}
function doSomething(value: string | number) {
if (isString(value)) {    // In this scope, TypeScript knows that `value` is a string
console.log(value.toUpperCase());
}
```

```
else {      // In this scope, TypeScript knows that `value` is a number
console.log(value.toFixed(2));
}
}
```

In this example, isString is a function that takes a value as an argument and returns a Boolean, but it also includes a type predicate in its return type. In this case, the type predicate value is a string adds additional type information about value under the condition that the function returns true. This information can be used by TypeScript's type checker in subsequent code, telling it that, when this function returns true, the type of value is string.

In TypeScript, type guards and type predicates bridge the gap between JavaScript's dynamic type checking and TypeScript's static type system. They exemplify how TypeScript augments standard JavaScript practices with type aware capabilities. By utilizing type guards and type predicates, developers harness the flexibility of JavaScript's runtime checks while benefiting from TypeScript's compile-time type assurances.

Type system limitations, trade-offs, and performance considerations

Although TypeScript offers robust type safety and better development experience, it is crucial to understand its boundaries and the implications for your workflow and code performance. Here we will discuss about the limitations, trade-offs and performance issues posed by TypeScript.

Understanding type system limitations

TypeScript's type system is a powerful tool that helps developers write safer, more reliable code. However, remember that it is not a silver bullet for all kinds of programming errors. There are certain limitations in TypeScript's type system that you need to be aware of to use it most effectively.

One of the major limitations of TypeScript's type system is that it is not sound. Type soundness means that a type system accurately represents the possible values that a variable can hold. In TypeScript, this is not always the case. For instance, TypeScript allows certain operations that are not type-safe, like indexing an array with a string. This is a conscious decision by the TypeScript team, as they prioritize productivity and ease of use over complete type safety.

Another limitation of TypeScript's type system is that it operates based on structural typing, this means that TypeScript focuses on the shape that values have. While this is often a strength, it also means that TypeScript sometimes cannot distinguish between two types that are structurally identical but semantically different.

Also, TypeScript's type system only operates at compile time and has no runtime manifestation. This means that all of the type checks happen when your code is compiled, and there is no type checking at runtime. For example, TypeScript cannot check that a value you receive from an API call or a user input matches a certain type. This is a limitation you have to be aware of, and it means that TypeScript cannot replace the need for runtime checks in your code.

Understanding these limitations is important to ensure that you use TypeScript's type system effectively. It helps you understand where TypeScript can provide safety guarantees, and where you have to take additional steps to ensure that your code is safe.

Type system trade-offs

As with any tool, TypeScript's type system comes with its own set of trade-offs that must be understood and managed effectively to reap its benefits.

Compilation step: TypeScript requires a compilation step, converting TypeScript code into JavaScript. This can be seen as a trade-off as it introduces an extra process into the development workflow. However, this step is crucial as it allows TypeScript to perform type checking and catch potential issues early in development.

Verbose and rigid: TypeScript's focus on type safety can sometimes be seen as verbose and rigid, especially for developers coming from dynamically-typed languages like JavaScript. Writing types for every variable, function, and class might seem tedious, but it ensures type safety and can significantly reduce runtime errors. This verbosity and rigidity are a trade-off for improved reliability and maintainability.

Restrictive: TypeScript's static type system can be restrictive at times. Developers might need to use type assertions, or the $_{any}$ type when they know some detail about the value that TypeScript cannot infer. While this gives more flexibility, it by passes TypeScript's type checking and should be used sparingly.

Not aligned with certain OOP concepts: TypeScript's structural type system might not align with certain OOP concepts. Two different types with the same structure are considered to be the same type. While this provides flexibility and compatibility with JavaScript, it might not align with OOP principles where two classes with the same structure but different names are considered different types.

These trade-offs do not diminish the value of TypeScript. Instead, they highlight the importance of understanding the tool you are working with. By understanding these trade-offs, developers can use TypeScript more effectively, leveraging its strengths and mitigating its weaknesses.

Performance considerations

Performance is a critical aspect to consider when writing software, and TypeScript is no exception. While TypeScript offers a myriad of features to improve code quality, readability, and maintainability, it is essential to understand the performance implications of using TypeScript.

However, there are a few things to keep in mind:

TypeScript compilation: TypeScript's type checking and down-compiling to JavaScript can add to the build time of a project. This time increases as the size of the codebase grows. It is not usually a problem for smaller projects, but for larger codebases, this can be noticeable. Various strategies can be used to minimize this, such as using the --incremental flag for faster subsequent builds or using project references to split your codebase into smaller, more manageable parts.

Autocompletion and IntelliSense: TypeScript's robust type system can make autocompletion in IDEs slower if the codebase is very large. However, the advantages of having autocompletion and type-checking often outweigh this minor inconvenience.

Memory usage: TypeScript's compiler uses memory to store type information and perform type checks. For small to medium-sized projects, this is rarely an issue. However, for very large codebases, TypeScript can consume a significant amount of memory during compilation.

Optimization: TypeScript cannot optimize your code for performance. That is still up to you, the developer. TypeScript's main job is to catch errors at compile-time and provide a better development experience.

Runtime type checking: TypeScript does not provide runtime type checking. Any type checking is done at compile-time only. If you need runtime type checking, you will need to implement it yourself or use a library that provides this feature.

Conclusion: The Art and Science of Structuring and Extending Types in TypeScript

TypeScript's ability to handle types dynamically, statically, and flexibly has made it the de facto choice for developers working on complex JavaScript-based applications. At its core, the process of structuring and extending types serves as a bridge between robust type safety and the expressive dynamism of JavaScript, allowing developers to strike a fine balance between predictability and creativity.

1. Evolution and Significance of Type Structuring

Structuring and extending types in TypeScript is more than just a toolset; it's a paradigm that reflects the evolution of programming languages toward enhancing developer productivity. Traditional JavaScript lacked the built-in safeguards that TypeScript offers, often resulting in runtime errors due to unchecked assumptions about object shapes, function arguments, and variable types.

TypeScript revolutionized this by introducing interfaces, type aliases, and a structural type system that infers types based on usage patterns rather than rigid nominal type definitions. This approach reduces the boilerplate associated with traditional type annotations and enables developers to create scalable systems that adapt well to changes.

For example, consider a scenario where an application's user model evolves from a simple object to a more complex structure due to new business requirements. TypeScript's ability to extend existing interfaces ensures minimal disruption while maintaining consistency across the codebase.

```
interface User {
  id: number;
  name: string;
}
interface ExtendedUser extends User {
  address: string;
  isAdmin: boolean;
}
```

Such extensibility empowers teams to adapt rapidly without compromising code reliability.

2. The Building Blocks of TypeScript's Power

2.1 Modular and Reusable Designs

One of TypeScript's greatest strengths is its modularity. By breaking down complex types into reusable components, developers can craft systems that are both easy to understand and extend. Structuring types into smaller, composable units allows for maximum flexibility.

For instance:

Interfaces: Provide a clear contract for object shapes, allowing better integration with third-party libraries.

Type Aliases: Allow union and intersection types that facilitate complex and conditionally applied structures.

Generics: Introduce the ability to create reusable components that maintain strict type safety while accommodating diverse use cases.

These tools, combined, form a robust mechanism to define and manage complex data flows in modern applications.

2.2 Balancing Strictness and Flexibility

Strict typing often raises concerns about potential over-restriction, particularly in JavaScript ecosystems known for their fluid and loosely defined constructs. TypeScript's structural type system avoids this pitfall by ensuring that objects are checked against shape rather than identity.

This structural approach means that if an object fulfills a contract (e.g., an interface), it can seamlessly integrate into the application, regardless of its source. It eliminates the unnecessary rigidity found in nominal typing systems and ensures that TypeScript remains accessible to developers transitioning from JavaScript.

2.3 Enhancing Maintainability and Scalability

As applications grow, maintaining consistency becomes a challenge. Poorly defined types can lead to fragmentation, where similar entities have subtle but incompatible type definitions. TypeScript mitigates this by allowing:

Inheritance of Types: Through extends for interfaces and intersections for type aliases.

Utility Types: Such as Partial, Required, Pick, and Omit, which reduce duplication and enforce consistency.

Mapped Types: To transform existing types dynamically based on specific needs.

These features collectively ensure that scaling a TypeScript application doesn't come at the expense of readability or maintainability.

3. Addressing Real-World Challenges with TypeScript

The real value of structuring and extending types emerges when applied to solve complex, real-world challenges:

3.1 Dynamic Data Modeling

APIs often return data with evolving structures. TypeScript's conditional and mapped types provide a flexible framework to define such dynamic models.

```
type ApiResponse<T> = T extends {success: boolean}? T & {timestamp: number}: T;
```

This allows applications to handle varying responses without sacrificing type safety.

3.2 Framework Development

Frameworks like Angular and NestJS rely heavily on TypeScript's type system to define reusable abstractions, ensuring type safety while preserving the flexibility needed for customization.

For example, React's props system often extends base interfaces to create more specific component contracts:

```
interface ButtonProps {
  label: string;
  onClick: () => void;
}
interface IconButtonProps extends ButtonProps {
  icon: string;
}
```

4. Best Practices for Structuring and Extending Types
Achieving mastery in TypeScript involves adhering to certain best practices:

Consistency Over Complexity: Opt for simpler structures unless the complexity is warranted by the application's needs.

Modularization: Divide type definitions into logical groups and modules, improving maintainability and collaboration in team settings.

Leverage Utility Types: Use built-in utility types like Omit and Pick to avoid redundant definitions and maintain DRY (Don't Repeat Yourself) principles.

Document Complex Types: Provide clear explanations for non-intuitive types to ensure future maintainability.

Test Types with Real Data: Validate type assumptions against actual data flows to prevent subtle bugs.

5. Future-Proofing Applications with TypeScript

The trajectory of TypeScript suggests continual enhancement, with features like template literal types, variadic tuple types, and more sophisticated inference mechanisms enriching the ecosystem. Developers should remain updated with these advancements to maintain competitive and robust codebases.

Future-facing practices include:

Using Strict Compiler Options: Enable options like strictNullChecks and noImplicitAny to catch errors early.

Adopting Evolving Patterns: Integrate new patterns such as discriminated unions for better type narrowing.
By doing so, developers ensure that their applications not only perform well today but also adapt seamlessly to tomorrow's demands.

6. Conclusion: Embracing the TypeScript Philosophy

Structuring and extending types in TypeScript is a testament to the language's philosophy of providing powerful tools that enhance developer productivity without introducing unnecessary friction. These capabilities align with modern software development principles, emphasizing clarity, modularity, and adaptability.

For developers, mastering these concepts translates to:

Fewer Runtime Errors: By catching issues during development.

Increased Code Reuse: Through modular and extensible type definitions.

Greater Confidence in Refactoring: Ensuring changes do not introduce unintended bugs.

As TypeScript continues to evolve, its ability to structure and extend types will remain a cornerstone of its success, enabling developers to build complex, scalable applications with confidence and ease. By embracing these principles, the global development community can harness the full potential of TypeScript, paving the way for a more efficient and reliable coding future.

9. Event Loop and Asynchronous Behaviour

Introduction

TypeScript, a superset of JavaScript, inherits its asynchronous nature, making it essential for developers to understand how the event loop works and how it handles asynchronous operations. Asynchronous behavior is foundational to building non-blocking, performant applications, especially for tasks like handling I/O operations, API calls, and real-time data streaming.

This article explores the event loop mechanism, asynchronous patterns, and TypeScript's capabilities to effectively handle asynchronous code while maintaining type safety.

1. The Event Loop: An Overview

The event loop is a core component of JavaScript's runtime environment. It enables non-blocking I/O by managing the execution of multiple tasks, such as code execution, pending operations, and handling events.

Key Components of the Event Loop

Call Stack

The call stack is a data structure that holds the execution context of functions. When a function is called, it is added to the stack, and once executed, it is removed.

Web APIs

These are provided by the browser or runtime (e.g., Node.js) to handle asynchronous operations such as timers (setTimeout), DOM events, or HTTP requests.

Task Queue (Callback Queue)

This queue stores callbacks from asynchronous operations. The event loop ensures these callbacks are moved to the call stack when it's empty.

Microtask Queue

Microtasks, such as promises, have higher priority than tasks in the callback queue. The event loop processes all microtasks before moving to the next task.

2. Event Loop in Action

Let's examine how the event loop manages tasks with an example:

```
console.log('Start');

setTimeout(() => {
  console.log('Timeout callback');
}, 0);
```

```
Promise.resolve('Promise resolved').then((value) => {
  console.log(value);
});
console.log('End');
```

Output:

```
Start
End
Promise resolved
Timeout callback
```

Explanation:

console.log('Start') and console.log('End') are synchronous and executed first.
setTimeout schedules a task in the callback queue.
The resolved promise queues a microtask in the microtask queue.
The event loop processes the microtask (Promise resolved) before the callback queue (Timeout callback).

3. Understanding Asynchronous Behaviour

Asynchronous programming in TypeScript allows the execution of non-blocking code, improving performance and responsiveness. The language enhances JavaScript's asynchronous capabilities by providing strong typing, making it easier to manage complex asynchronous workflows.

Asynchronous Patterns
Callbacks
Functions passed as arguments to other functions, executed upon completion of tasks.

```
function fetchData(callback: (data: string) => void) {
    setTimeout(() => {
      callback('Data fetched');
    }, 1000);
}
fetchData((data) => {
    console.log(data);
});
```

Promises

Promises represent a value that may be available now, or in the future, or never.

```
const fetchData = new Promise<string>((resolve, reject) => {
    setTimeout(() => {
      resolve('Data fetched');
    }, 1000);
});
fetchData.then((data) => console.log(data));
```

Async/Await

Introduced in ES2017, async/await simplifies working with promises and improves readability.

```
async function fetchData(): Promise<string> {
    return new Promise((resolve) => {
        setTimeout(() => {
            resolve('Data fetched');
        }, 1000);
    });
}
async function displayData() {
    const data = await fetchData();
    console.log(data);
}
displayData();
```

4. TypeScript Enhancements for Asynchronous Code

TypeScript's type system enhances the safety and maintainability of asynchronous operations.

Typing Promises

TypeScript allows you to define the type of data a promise resolve to.

```
const fetchData = (): Promise<string> => {
    return new Promise((resolve) => {
        setTimeout(() => resolve('Data fetched'), 1000);
    });
};
fetchData().then((data) => console.log(data));
```

Async/Await with Type Annotations

Using async functions with explicit return types improves clarity:

```
async function getData(): Promise<string> {
    return 'Data';
}
getData().then((data) => console.log(data));
```

5. Advanced Topics in Asynchronous Behavior

Concurrency and Parallelism

While JavaScript is single-threaded, it can achieve concurrency via the event loop. Tools like Promise. All allow parallel execution of asynchronous tasks.

```
async function fetchData(urls: string[]): Promise<string[]> {
    const promises = urls.map((url) => fetch(url).then((res) => res.text()));
    return Promise.all(promises);
}
```

```
fetchData(['url1', 'url2']).then((data) => console.log(data));
```

Error Handling in Async Code

Errors in promises or async functions can be caught using. catch or try...catch.

```
async function fetchData(): Promise<string> {
   throw new Error('Failed to fetch data');
}
fetchData()
   .then((data) => console.log(data))
   .catch((error) => console.error(error));

async function displayData() {
   try {
      const data = await fetchData();
      console.log(data);
   } catch (error) {
      console.error('Error:', error);
   }
}
displayData();
```

Debouncing and Throttling

Asynchronous tasks like API calls can be optimized using techniques like debouncing and throttling.

```
function debounce(func: Function, delay: number) {
   let timeoutId: NodeJS.Timeout;
   return (...args: any[]) => {
      clearTimeout(timeoutId);
      timeoutId = setTimeout(() => func(...args), delay);
   };
}
const logMessage = debounce((message: string) => console.log(message), 300);
logMessage('Hello');
```

6. Practical Use Cases

1. Real-Time Applications

Applications like chat systems or live dashboards require constant updates. WebSockets and async functions handle these effectively.

```
const socket = new WebSocket('ws://example.com');
socket.onmessage = (event) => {
   console.log('Message from server:', event.data);
};
```

2. API Integration

Asynchronous operations are crucial for making HTTP requests and handling their responses.

```typescript
async function fetchUserData(userId: string): Promise<any> {
    const response = await fetch(`https://api.example.com/users/${userId}`);
    return response.json();
}
fetchUserData('123').then((user) => console.log(user));
```

3. File Handling

Asynchronous file handling in Node.js ensures non-blocking execution.

```typescript
import {promises as fs} from 'fs';
async function readFile(filePath: string): Promise<string> {
    return await fs.readFile(filePath, 'utf8');
}
readFile('./data.txt').then((content) => console.log(content));
```

7. Debugging Asynchronous Code

Debugging asynchronous code can be challenging. Tools and techniques to simplify this include:

Async Stack Traces

Modern JavaScript runtimes preserve stack traces for async functions, aiding debugging.

Logging with Timestamps

Adding timestamps to logs helps track the sequence of events.

Browser DevTools

Use the "Async" stack view to trace asynchronous operations.

TypeScript Linters

Linters like ESLint can detect unhandled promises or other issues in async code.

Let's begin

This chapter introduces you to event loops and asynchronous behaviour. However, before you proceed with learning these topics, let's have a look at a hypothetical scenario to really understand how synchronous and asynchronous executions work.

Imagine a small bank that has a single teller. His name is Tom, and he's serving clients all day. Since it's a small bank and there are few clients, there's no queue. So, when a client comes in, they get Tom's undivided attention. The client provides all the necessary paperwork, and Tom processes it. If the process needs some kind of outside input, such as from a credit bureau or the bank's back-office department, Tom submits the request, and he and the client wait for the response together.

They might chat a bit, and when the response comes, Tom resumes his work. If a document needs to be printed, Tom sends it to the printer that's right on his desk, and they wait and chat. When the printing is done, Tom resumes his work. Once the work is completed, the bank has another satisfied client, and Tom continues with his day. If somebody comes while Tom is serving a client (which happens seldom), they wait until Tom is completely done with the previous client, and only then do they begin their process. Even if Tom is waiting on an external response, the other client will have to wait their turn, while Tom idly chats with the current client.

Tom effectively works synchronously and sequentially. There are lots of benefits of this approach to working, namely, Tom (and his bosses) can always tell whether he is serving a client or not, he always knows who his current client is, and he can completely forget all the data about the client as soon as the client leaves, knowing that they have been serviced completely. There are no issues with mixing up documents from different clients. Any problems are easy to diagnose and easy to fix. And since the queue never gets crowded, this setup works to everyone's satisfaction.

So far, so good. But what happens when the bank suddenly gets more clients? As more and more clients arrive, we get a long queue, and everyone is waiting, while Tom chats with the current client, waiting on a response from the credit bureau. Tom's boss is, understandably, not happy with the situation. The current system does not scale – at all. So, he wants to change the system somehow, to be able to serve more clients. How can he do that? You will look at a couple of solutions in the following section.

The Multi-Threaded Approach

Basically, there are two different approaches. One is to have multiple Toms. So, every single teller will still work in the exact same simple and synchronous way as before – we just have lots of them. Of course, the boss will need to have some kind of organization to know which teller is available and which is working, whether there are separate queues for each teller, or a single large queue, along with some kind of distribution mechanism (that is, a system where a number is assigned to each customer). The boss might also get one of those big office printers, instead of having one printer per teller, and have some kind of rule in order to not mix up the print jobs. The organization will be complex, but the task of every single teller will be straightforward.

By now, you know we're not really discussing banks. This is the usual approach for server-side processing. Grossly simplified, the server process will have multiple sub-processes (called threads) that will work in parallel, and the main process will orchestrate everything. Each thread will execute synchronously, with a well-defined beginning, middle, and end. Since servers are usually machines with lots of resources, with heavy loads, this approach makes sense. It can accommodate low or high loads nicely, and the code that processes each request can be relatively simple and easy to debug. It even makes sense to have the thread wait for some external resource (a file from the file system, or data from the network or database), since we can always spin up new threads if we have more requests.

This is not the case with real live tellers. We cannot just clone a new one if more clients come. The kind of waiting done by the threads (or by Tom) is usually referred to as busy waiting. The thread is not doing anything, but it's not available for any work, since it's busy doing something – it's busy waiting. Just like Tom was actually busy chatting with the client while waiting for a response from the credit bureau.

We have a system that can be massively parallel and concurrent, but still, each part of it is run synchronously. The benefit of this approach is that we can serve many, many clients at the same time. One obvious downside is the cost, both in hardware and in complexity. While we managed to keep the client processing simple, we'll need a huge infrastructure that takes care of everything else – adding tellers, removing tellers, queueing customers, managing access to the office printer, and similar tasks.

This will use all the available resources of the bank (or the server), but that is fine, since that's the whole point – to serve clients, as many and as fast as possible, and nothing else. However, there is another approach – asynchronous execution.

The Asynchronous Execution Approach

The other approach, the one taken by the web and, by extension, JavaScript and TypeScript, is to use just a single thread – so Tom is still on his own. But, instead of Tom idly chatting with a waiting client, he could do something else. If a situation arises where he needs some verification from the back office, he just writes down what he was doing and how far he got on a piece of paper, gives that paper to the client, and sends them to the back of the queue.

Tom is now ready to start serving the next client in line. If that client does not need external resources, they are processed completely and are free to leave. If they need something else that Tom needs to wait for, they too are sent to the back of the line. And so on, and so forth. This way, if Tom has any clients at all, he's processing their requests. He's never busy waiting, instead, he's busy working. If a client needs to wait for a response, they do so separately from Tom. The only time Tom is idle is when he has no clients at all.

The benefit of this approach is fairly obvious – before, Tom spent a lot of his time chatting, now he is working all the time (of course, this benefit is from Tom's boss' point of view – Tom liked the small talk). An additional benefit is that we know our resource consumption up front. If we only have one teller, we know the square footage that we will need for the office. However, there are some downsides as well. The most important downside is that our clients now have to know our process quite intimately. They will need to understand how to queue and requeue, how to continue working from where they left off, and so on.

Tom's work also got a lot more complicated. He needs to know how to pause the processing of a client, how to continue, how to behave if an external response is not received, and so on. This model of working is usually called asynchronous and concurrent. Doing his job, Tom will jump between multiple clients at the same time. More than one client will have their process started but not finished. And there's no way for a client to estimate how long it will take to process their task once it is started – it depends on how many other clients Tom processes at the same time.

From the early days, this model made much more sense for the web. For starters, web applications are processed on the device of the client. We should not make any technical assumptions about it – as we cannot be sure about the kind of device that the client might be using. In essence, a web page is a guest on the client's device – and it should behave properly. For example, using up all of a device's resources to show what amounts to a fancy animation is not proper behavior at all. Another important issue is security. If we think of web pages as applications that contain some code, we're basically executing someone's code on our machine whenever we enter a web address in the browser's address bar.

The browser needs to make sure that the code on the page, even if it's malicious, is restricted in what it can do to our machine. The web would not have been as popular as it is today if visiting a website could make your computer explode.

So, since the browser cannot know in advance which pages it will be used for, it was decided that each web page will only get access to a single thread. Also, for security reasons, each web page will get a separate thread, so a running web page cannot meddle in the execution of other pages that may execute at the same time (with features such as web workers and Chrome applications, these restrictions are somewhat loosened, but in principle, they still apply).

There is simply no way for a web page to spawn enough threads to swarm the system, or for a web page to get the data from another web page. And, since a web page needs to do lots of things at once, using the synchronous and sequential approach was out of the question. That is why all the JavaScript execution environments completely embraced the asynchronous, concurrent approach. This was done to such an extent that some common synchronization techniques are, intentionally, just not available in JavaScript.

For example, lots of other languages have a "wait some time" primitive, or a library function that does that.

For example, in the C# programming language, we can have this code:

```
Console.WriteLine("We will wait 10 s");
Thread.Sleep(10000);
Console.WriteLine("... 10 seconds later");
Thread.Sleep(15000);
Console.WriteLine("... 15 more seconds later");
```

This code will write some text to the console, and 10 seconds later, write some more text. During the 25 seconds of the wait, the thread this executes on will be completely non-responsive, but the code written is simple and linear – easily understood, easily changeable, and easily debuggable. JavaScript simply does not have such a synchronous primitive, but it has an asynchronous variant in the **setTimeout** function. The simplest equivalent code would be the following:

```
console.log("We will wait 10 s");
setTimeout(() => {
console.log("... 10 seconds later");
setTimeout(() => {
console.log("... 15 more seconds later");
}, 15000);
}, 10000);
```

It's obvious that this code is much more complex than the C# equivalent, but the advantage that we get is that this code is non-blocking. In the 25 total seconds that this code is executing, our web page can do everything it needs to do. It can respond to events, the images can load and display, we can resize the window, scroll the text – basically, the application will resume the normal and expected functionalities.

Note that while it's possible to block the JavaScript execution with some special synchronous code, it's not easy to do it. When it does actually happen, the browser can detect that it did happen and terminate the offending page:

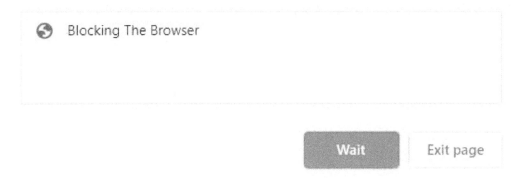

Page Unresponsive

You can wait for it to become responsive or exit the page.

🌐 Blocking The Browser

Wait   Exit page

Figure: Unresponsive page

Executing JavaScript

When a JavaScript execution environment, such as a node or a browser loads a JavaScript file, it parses it and then runs it. All the functions that are defined in a JavaScript file are registered, and all the code that is not in a function is executed. The order of the execution is according to the code's position in the file. So, consider a file having the following code:

```
console.log("First");
console.log("Second");
```

The console will always display this:
First
Second

The order of the output cannot be changed, without changing the code itself. This is because the line with **First** will be executed completely – always – and then, and only then, will the line with **Second** begin to execute. This approach is synchronous because the execution is synchronized by the environment. We are guaranteed that the second line will not start executing, until and unless the line above it is completely done. But what happens if the line calls some function? Let's take a look at the following piece of code:

```
function sayHello(name){    console.log(`Hello ${name}`); }
function first(){    second(); }
function second(){    third(); }
function third(){    sayHello("Bob"); }
first();
```

When the code is parsed, the environment will detect that we have four functions – **first, second, third,** and **sayHello**. It will also execute the line of code that is not inside a function (**first();**), and that will start the execution of the **first** function. But that function, while it's executing, calls the **second** function. The runtime will then suspend the running of the **first** function, remember where it was, and begin with the execution of the **second** function. This function, in turn, calls the **third** function.

The same thing happens again – the runtime starts executing the **third** function, remembering that once that function is done, it should resume with the execution of the **second** function, and that once **second** is done, it should resume with the execution of the **first** function.

The structure the runtime uses to remember which function is active, and which are waiting, is called a **stack**, specifically, the call stack.

The executing functions are put one on top of the other, and the topmost function is the one being actively executed, as shown in the following representation:

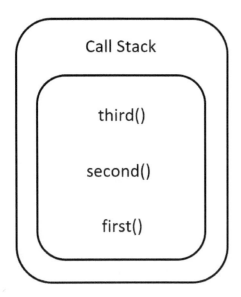

Figure: Stack

In the example, the **third** function will call the **sayHello** function, which will in turn call the **log** function of the **console** object. Once the **log** function finishes executing, the stack will start unwinding. That means that once a certain function finishes executing, it will be removed from the stack, and the function below it will be able to resume executing. So, once the **sayHello** function finishes executing, the **third** function will resume and finish in turn. This will trigger the continuation of the **second** function, and when that function is done as well, the **first** function will continue, and eventually finish. When the **first** function finishes executing, the stack will become empty – and the runtime will stop executing code.

It's worth noting that all of this execution is done strictly synchronously and deterministically. We can deduce the exact order and number of function calls just from looking at the code. We can also use common debugging tools such as breakpoints and stack traces. **Exercise 10.01: Stacking Functions** In this exercise, we'll define few simple functions that call each other. Each of the functions will log to the console when it starts executing and when it's about to finish executing. We will analyze when and in what order the output is mapped to the console:

Create a new file, **stack.ts**. In **stack.ts**, define three functions called **inner**, **middle**, and **outer**. None of them need to have parameters or return types:

```
function inner () { }
function middle () { }
function outer () { }
```

In the body of the **inner** function, add a single **log** statement, indented by four spaces:

```
function inner () {
console.log("Inside inner function");
}
```

In the body of the **middle** function, add a call to the **inner** function. Before and after the call, add a **log** statement, indented by two spaces:

```
function middle () {
console.log("Starting middle function");
inner();
console.log("  Finishing middle function");
}
```

In the body of the **outer** function, add a call to the **middle** function. Before and after the call, add a **log** statement:

```
function outer () {
console.log("Starting outer function");
middle();
console.log("Finishing outer function");
}
```

After the function declaration, create a call only to the **outer** function:

```
outer();
```

Save the file, and compile it with the following command:

tsc stack.ts

Verify that the compilation ended successfully and that there is a **stack.**

js file generated in the same folder. Execute it in the **node** environment with this command:

node stack.js

You will see the output looks like this:

Starting outer function
Starting middle function
Inside inner function
Finishing middle function
Finishing outer function

The output shows which function started executing first (**outer**), as that is the first message displayed. It can also be noted that the **middle** function finished executing after the **inner** function was already finished, but before the **outer** function was finished.

Browsers and JavaScript

When a web page is requested by the user, the browser needs to do lots of things. We won't go into the details of each of them, but we'll take a look at how it handles our code.

First of all, the browser sends the request to the server and receives an HTML file as a response. Within that HTML file, there are embedded links to resources that are needed for the page, such as images, stylesheets, and JavaScript code. The browser then downloads those as well and applies them to the downloaded HTML. Images are displayed, elements are styled, and JavaScript files are parsed and run.

The order in which the code is executed is according to the file's order in the HTML, then according to the code's position in the file. But when are the functions called? Let's say we have the following code in our file:

```
function sayHello() {
console.log("Hello");
}
sayHello();
```

First, the **sayHello** function is registered, and then when it's called later, the function actually executes and writes **Hello** to the console. Take a look at the following code now:

```
function sayHello() {    console.log("Hello"); }
function sayHi() {    console.log("Hi"); }
sayHello(); sayHi(); sayHello();
```

When the file with the preceding code is processed, it will register that it has two functions, **sayHello** and **sayHi**. Then it will detect that it has three invocations, that is, there are three tasks that need to be processed. The environment has something that is called the **task queue**, where it will put all the functions that need to be executed, one by one. So, our code will be transformed into three tasks. Then, the environment will check if the stack is actually empty, and if it is, it will take the first task off the queue and start executing it. The stack will grow and shrink depending on the execution of the code of the first task, and eventually, when the first task is finished, it will be empty. So, after the first task is executed, the situation will be as follows:

The execution stack will be empty.
The task queue will contain two tasks.
The first task will be completely done.

Once the stack is empty, the next task is dequeued and executed, and so on, until both the task queue and the stack are empty, and all the code is executed. Again, this whole process is done synchronously, in a specified order. **Events in the Browser**

Now, take a look at a different example:

```
function sayHello() {    console.log("Hello"); }
document.addEventListener("click", sayHello);
```

If you have this code in a JavaScript file that is loaded by the browser, you can see that the **sayHello** function is registered but not executed. However, if you click anywhere on the page, you will see that the **Hello** string appears on the console, meaning the **sayHello** function got executed. If you click multiple times, you'll get multiple instances of **"Hello"** on the console. And this code did not invoke the **sayHello** function even once; you don't have the **sayHello()** invocation in the code at all.

What happened is, you registered our function as an event listener. Consider that you don't call our function at all, but the browser's environment will call it for us, whenever a certain event occurs – in this case, the **click** event on the whole **document**. And since those events are generated by the user, we cannot know if and when our code will execute. Event listeners are the principal way that our code can communicate with the page that it's on, and they are called asynchronously – you don't know when or if the function will be invoked, nor how many times it will be invoked.

What the browser does, when an event occurs, is to look up its own internal table of registered event handlers. In our case, if a **click** event occurs anywhere on the **document** (that's the whole web page), the browser will see that you have registered the **sayHello** function to respond to it. That function will not be executed directly – instead, the browser will place an invocation of the function in the task queue. After that, the regular behavior explained previously takes effect. If the queue and stack are empty, the event handler will begin executing immediately. Otherwise, our handler will wait for its turn.

This is another core effect of asynchronous behaviour – we simply cannot guarantee that the event handler will execute immediately. It might be the case that it does, but there is no way to know if the queue and stack are empty at a specific moment. If they are, we'll get immediate execution, but if they're not, we'll have to wait our turn.

Environment APIs

Most of our interaction with the browser will be done in the same pattern – you will define a function, and pass that function as a parameter to some browser API. When and if that function will actually be scheduled for execution will depend on the particulars of that API. In the previous case, you used the event handler API, **addEventListener**, which takes two parameters, the name of an event, and the code that will be scheduled when that event happens.

In the rest of this chapter, you will use two other APIs as well, the environment's method to defer some code for later execution (**setTimeout**) and the ability to call on external resources (popularly called AJAX). There are two different AJAX implementations that we will be working with, the original **XMLHttpRequest** implementation, and the more modern and flexible **fetch** implementation.
setTimeout

As mentioned previously, the environment offers no possibility to pause the execution of JavaScript for a certain amount of time. However, the need to execute some code after some set amount of time has passed arises quite often. So, instead of pausing the execution, we get to do something different that has the same outcome. We get to schedule a piece of code to get executed after an amount of time has passed. To do that we use the **setTimeout** function. This function takes two parameters: A function that will need to be executed, and the time, in milliseconds, it should defer the execution of that function by:

```
setTimeout(function() {
console.log("After one second");
}, 1000);
```

Here it means that the anonymous function that is passed as a parameter will be executed after 1,000 milliseconds, that is, one second.

Exercise: Exploring setTimeout

In this exercise, you'll use the **setTimeout** environment API call to investigate how asynchronous execution behaves and what it does:

Create a new file, **delays-1.ts**.

In **delays-1.ts**, log some text at the beginning of the file:
```
console.log("Printed immediately");
```

Add two calls to the **setTimeout** function:

```
setTimeout(function() {
console.log("Printed after one second");
}, 1000);
setTimeout(function() {
console.log("Printed after two second");
}, 2000);
```

Here, instead of creating a function and giving it to the **setTimeout** function using its name, we have used an anonymous function that we have created in-place. We can also use arrow functions instead of functions defined with the **function** keyword.

Save the file, and compile it with the following command:

tsc delays-1.ts

Verify that the compilation ended successfully and that there is a **delays-1. js** file generated in the same folder. Execute it in the **node** environment with this command:

node delays-1.js

You will see the output looks like this:

Printed immediately
Printed after one second
Printed after two second

The second and third lines of the output should not appear immediately, but after 1 and 2 seconds respectively.

In the **delays-1.ts** file, switch the two calls to the **setTimeout** function:

```
console.log("Printed immediately");
setTimeout(function() {
console.log("Printed after two second");
}, 2000);
setTimeout(function() {
console.log("Printed after one second");
}, 1000);
```

Compile and run the code again, and verify that the output behaves identically. Even if the former **setTimeout** was executed first, its **function** parameter is not scheduled to run until 2 seconds have passed.

In the **delays-1.ts** file, move the initial **console.log** to the bottom:

```
setTimeout(function() {
console.log("Printed after two second");
}, 2000);
setTimeout(function() {
console.log("Printed after one second");
```

```
}, 1000);
console.log("Printed immediately");
```

Compile and run the code again, and verify that the output behaves identically. This illustrates one of the most common problems with code that behaves asynchronously. Even though the line was at the bottom of our file, it was executed first. It's much harder to mentally trace code that does not follow the top-down paradigm we're used to.

Create a new file, **delays-2.ts**.

In **delays-2.ts**, add a single call to the **setTimeout** function, and set its delay time to **0**. This will mean that our code needs to wait 0 milliseconds in order to execute:

```
setTimeout(function() {
console.log("#1 Printed immediately?");
}, 0);
```

Add a **console.log** statement after the call to **setTimeout**:

```
console.log("#2 Printed immediately.");
```

Save the file, and compile it with the following command:

```
tsc delays-2.ts
```

Verify that the compilation ended successfully and that there is a **delays-2. js** file generated in the same folder. Execute it in the **node** environment with this command:

```
node delays-2.js
```

You will see the output looks like this:

```
#2 Printed immediately.
#1 Printed immediately?;
```

Well, that looks unexpected. Both lines appear basically immediately, but the one that was in the **setTimeout** block, and was first in the code, came after the line at the bottom of the script. And we explicitly told **setTimeout** not to wait, that is, to wait 0 milliseconds before the code got executed.

To understand what happened, we need to go back to the call queue. When the file was loaded, the environment detected that we had two tasks that needed to be done, the call to **setTimeout** and the bottom call to **console.log** (#2). So, those two tasks were put into the task queue. Since the stack was empty at that time, the **setTimeout** call started executing, and #2 was left in the task queue. The environment saw that it has a zero delay, so immediately took the function (#1), and put it at the end of the task queue, after #2. So, after the **setTimeout** call was done, we were left with two **console.log** tasks in the queue, with #2 being the first, and #1 being the second.

They got executed sequentially, and on our console, we got #2 first, and #1 second.

AJAX (Asynchronous JavaScript and XML)

In the early days of the web, it was not possible to get data from a server once the page was loaded. That was a huge inconvenience for developing dynamic web pages, and it was solved by the introduction of an object called **XMLHttpRequest**. This object enabled developers to get data from a server after the initial page load – and since loading data from a server means using an external resource, it had to be done in an asynchronous manner (even if it has XML right in the name, currently, it will mostly be used for JSON data). To use this object, you'll need to instantiate it and use a few of its properties.

To illustrate its usage, we'll try to get data about William Shakespeare from the Open Library project. The URL that we'll use to retrieve that information is https://openlibrary. org/authors/OL9388A.json, and the access method that we will use is **GET**, as we will only be getting data.

The data received is of a specific format, defined by Open Library, so you'll start by creating an interface for the data that you will actually use. You'll display only an image of the Bard (received as an array of photo IDs), and the name, so you can define the interface like this:

```
interface OpenLibraryAuthor {
personal_name: string;
photos: number[];
}
```

Next, create the **XMLHttpRequest** object, and assign it to a variable called **xhr**:

```
const xhr = new XMLHttpRequest();
```

Now you need to **open** a connection to our URL:

```
const url = "https://openlibrary.org/.json";
xhr.open("GET", url);
```

This call doesn't actually send anything, but it prepares the system for accessing the external resource. Lastly, you need to actually send the request, using the **send** method:

```
xhr.send();
```

Since the request is asynchronous, this call will execute and finish immediately. In order to actually process the data once this request is done, you need to add something to this object – a callback. That is a function that will not be executed by us, but by the **xhr** object, once some event happens. This object has several events, such as **onreadystatechange**, **onload**, **onerror**, **ontimeout**, and you can set different functions to react to different events, but in this case, you will just use the **onload** event. Create a function that will get the data from the response and show it on the web page where our script is running:

```
const showData = () => {
if (xhr.status != 200) {
console.log(`An error occured ${xhr.status}: ${xhr.statusText}`);
}
else {
const response: OpenLibraryAuthor = JSON.parse(xhr.response);
const body = document.getElementsByTagName("body")[0];
const image = document.createElement("img");
image.src = `http://covers.openlibrary./${response. photos[0]}-M.jpg`;
```

```
body.appendChild(image);
const name = document.createElement("h1");
name.innerHTML = response.personal_name;
body.appendChild(name);
}
};
```

In this method, you will be using some properties of the **xhr** variable that was defined previously, such as **status**, which gives us the HTTP status code of the request, or **response**, which gives us the actual response. If we just call the **showData** method by ourselves, we'll most likely get empty fields or an error, as the response will not have finished. So, we need to give this function to the **xhr** object, and it will use it to call the **showData** back:

```
xhr.onload = showData;
```

Save this code as **shakespeare.ts**, compile it, and add it to an HTML page using the following:

```
<script src="shakespeare.js"></script>
```

Activity: Movie Browser Using XHR and Callbacks

As a TypeScript developer, you have been tasked with creating a simple page to view movie data. The web page will be simple, with a text input field and a button. When you enter the name of a movie in the search input field and press the button, general information about the movie will be displayed on the web page, along with some images relevant to the movie.

You can use The Movie Database as a source of general data, specifically its API. You need to issue AJAX requests using **XmlHttpRequest**, and use the data the site provides to format your own object. When using an API the data will rarely, if ever, be in the format we actually need. This means that you will need to use several API requests to get our data, and piecemeal construct our object. A common TypeScript approach to this issue is to use two sets of interfaces – one that exactly matches the format of the API, and one that matches the data that you use in your application. In this activity, you need to use the **Api** suffix to denote those interfaces that match the API format.

Another important thing to note is that this particular API does not allow completely open access. You'll need to register for an API key and then send it in each API request. In the setup code for this activity, three functions (**getSearchUrl**, **getMovieUrl**, **getPeopleUrl**) will be provided that will generate the correct URLs for the needed API requests, once the **apiKey** variable is set to the value you will receive from The Movie Database. Also provided will be the base HTML, styling, as well as the code used to actually display the data – all that is missing is the data itself.

Those resources are listed here:

display.ts – A TypeScript file that houses the **showResult** and **clearResults** methods, which you will call to display a movie and clear the screen, respectively.

interfaces.ts – A TypeScript file that contains the interfaces that you will use. All interfaces that have an **Api** suffix are objects that you will receive from The Movie Database API, and the rest (**Movie** and **Character**) will be used to display the data.

script.ts – A TypeScript file that has some boilerplate code that will start the application. The **search**

function is here, and that function will be the main focus of this activity.

index.html – An HTML file that has the basic markup for our web page.

styles.css – A style sheet file that is used to style the results.

The following steps should help you with the solution:

In the **script.ts** file, locate the **search** function and verify that it takes a single string parameter and that its body is empty.
Construct a new **XMLHttpRequest** object.
Construct a new string for the search result URL using the **getSearchUrl** method.
Call the **open** and **send** methods of the **xhr** object.

Add an event handler for the **xhr** object's **onload** event. Take the response and parse it as a JSON object. Store the result in a variable of the **SearchResultApi** interface. This data will have the results of our search in a **results** field. If you get no results, this means that our search failed. If the search returned no results, call the **clearResults** method.

If the search returned some results, just take the first one and store it in a variable, ignoring the other ones.
Inside the **onload** handler, in the successful search branch, create a new **XMLHttpRequest** object. Construct a new string for the search result URL using the **getMovieUrl** method. Call the **open** and **send** method of the constructed **xhr** object.

Add an event handler for the **xhr** objects's **onload** event. Take the response, and parse it as a JSON object. Store the result in a variable of the **MovieResultApi** interface. This response will have the general data for our movie, specifically, everything except the people who were involved in the movie. You will need to have another call to the API to get the data about the people.

Inside the **onload** handler, in the successful search branch, create a new **XMLHttpRequest** object. Construct a new string for the search result URL using the **getPeopleUrl** method. Call the **open** and **send** method of the constructed **xhr** object.
Add an event handler for the **xhr** object's **onload** event. Take the response, and parse it as a JSON object. Store the result in a variable of the **PeopleResultApi** interface. This response will have data about the people who were involved in the movie.

Now you actually have all the data you need, so you can create your own object inside the people **onload** handler, which is inside the movie **onload** handler, which is inside the search **onload** handler. The people data has **cast** and **crew** properties. You'll only take the first six cast members, so first sort the **cast** property according to the **order** property of the cast members. Then slice off the first six cast members into a new array.

Transform the cast data (which is **CastResultApi** objects) into our own **Character** objects. You need to map the **character** field of **CastResultApi** to the **name** field of **Character**, the **name** field to the **actor** name, and the **profile_path** field to the **image** property.

From the **crew** property of the people data, you'll only need the director and the writer. Since there can be multiple directors and writers, you'll get the names of all directors and writers and concatenate them, respectively. For the directors, from the **crew** property, filter the people who have a **department** of **Directing** and a **job** of **Director**. For those objects, take the **name** property, and **join** it together with an

& in between.

For the writers, from the **crew** property, filter the people who have a **department** of **Writing** and a **job** of **Writer**. For those objects, take the **name** property, and **join** it together with an **&** in between.
Create a new **Movie** object (using object literal syntax). Fill in all the properties of the **Movie** object using the data from the movie and people responses you prepared so far.

Call the **showResults** function with the movie you constructed.
In your parent directory (**Activity01** in this case), install dependencies with **npm i**.
Compile the program using **tsc ./script.ts ./interfaces.ts ./ display.ts**.
Verify that the compilation ended successfully.

Promises
Using callbacks for asynchronous development gets the job done – and that is great. However, in many applications, our code needs to use external or asynchronous resources all the time. So, very quickly, we'll get to a situation where inside our callback, there is another asynchronous call, which requires a callback inside the callback, which in turn needs a callback on its own.
It was (and in some cases, it still is) not uncommon to be a dozen levels deep inside the callback hole.

Exercise: Counting to Five

In this exercise, we'll create a function that, when executed, will output the English words one through five. Each word will appear on the screen 1 second after the last word was displayed:

Create a new file, **counting-1.ts**.

In **counting-1.ts**, add an array with the English number names up to and including five:

```
const numbers = ["One", "Two", "Three", "Four", "Five"];
```

Add a single call to the **setTimeout** function, and print out the first number after a second:

```
setTimeout(function() {
console.log(numbers[0]); }, 1000);
```

Save the file, and compile it with the following command:

```
tsc counting-1.ts
```

Verify that the compilation ended successfully and that there is a **counting-1.**

js file generated in the same folder. Execute it in the **node** environment with this command:

```
node counting-1.js
```

You will see the output looks like this:

```
One
```
The line should appear 1 second after the application was run.

In the **counting-1.ts** file, inside the **setTimeout** function, below **console.log**, add another, nested, call to the **setTimeout** function:

```
setTimeout(function() {
console.log(numbers[0]);
setTimeout(function() {
console.log(numbers[1]);
}, 1000);
}, 1000);
```

Compile and run the code again, and verify that the output has an extra line, displayed 1 second after the first:

One
Two

In the **counting-1.ts** file, inside the nested **setTimeout** function, above **console.log**, add another nested call to the **setTimeout** function:

```
setTimeout(function() {
console.log(numbers[0]);
setTimeout(function() {
setTimeout(function() {
console.log(numbers[2]);
}, 1000);
console.log(numbers[1]);
}, 1000);
}, 1000);
```

In the innermost **setTimeout** function, below **console.log**, add yet another nested call to **setTimeout**, and repeat the process for the fifth number as well. The code should look like this:

```
setTimeout(function() {
console.log(numbers[0]);
setTimeout(function() {
setTimeout(function() {
console.log(numbers[2]);
setTimeout(function() {
console.log(numbers[3]);
setTimeout(function() {
 console.log(numbers[4]);
}, 1000);
}, 1000);
}, 1000);
console.log(numbers[1]);
}, 1000);
}, 1000);
```

Compile and run the code again, and verify that the output appears in the correct order as shown:

One
Two

Three
Four
Five

In this simple example, we implemented a simple functionality – counting to five. But as you can already see, the code is becoming extremely messy. Just imagine if we needed to count to 20 instead of 5. That would be a downright unmaintainable mess. While there are ways to make this specific code look a bit better and more maintainable, in general, that's not the case. The use of callbacks is intrinsically connected with messy and hard-to-read code. And messy and hard-to-read code is the best place for bugs to hide, so callbacks do have a reputation of being the cause of difficult-to-diagnose bugs.

An additional problem with callbacks is that there cannot be a unified API across different objects. For example, we needed to explicitly know that in order to receive data using the **xhr** object, we need to call the **send** method and add a callback for the **onload** event. And we needed to know that in order to check whether the request was successful or not, we have to check the **status** property of the **xhr** object.

What are Promises?

Fortunately, we can promise you that there is a better way. That way was initially done by third-party libraries, but it has proven to be so useful and so widely adopted that it was included in the JavaScript language itself. The logic behind this solution is rather simple. Each asynchronous call is basically a promise that, sometime in the future, some tasks will be done and some result will be acquired. As with promises in real life, we can have three different states for a promise:

A promise might not be resolved yet. This means that we need to wait some more time before we get a result. In TypeScript, we call these promises "pending."

A promise might be resolved negatively – the one who promised broke the promise. In TypeScript, we call these promises "rejected" and usually we get some kind of an error as a result.

A promise might be resolved positively – the one who promised fulfilled the promise. In TypeScript, we call these promises "resolved" and we get a value out of them – the actual result.

And since promises are objects themselves, this means that promises can be assigned to variables, returned from functions, passed as arguments into functions, and lots of other things we're able to do with regular objects.

Another great feature of promises is that it is relatively easy to write a promisified wrapper around an existing callback-based function. Let's try to promisify the Shakespeare example. We'll start by taking a look at the **showData** function. This function needs to do a lot of things, and those things are sometimes not connected to one another. It needs to both process the **xhr** variable to extract the data, and it needs to know what to do with that data. So, if the API we're using changes, we'll need to change our function.

If the structure of our web page changes, that is, if we need to display a **div** instead of an **h1** element, we'll need to change our function. If we need to use the author data for something else, we'll also need to change our function. Basically, if anything needs to happen to the response, it needs to happen then and there. We have no way to somehow defer that decision to another piece of code. This creates unnecessary coupling inside our code, which makes it harder to maintain.

Let's change that. We can create a new function that will return a promise, which will provide the data about the author. It will have no idea what that data will be used for:

```
const getShakespeareData = () => {
const result = new Promise<OpenLibraryAuthor>((resolve, reject) => {
const xhr = new XMLHttpRequest();
const url = "https://openlibrary.org/.json";
xhr.open("GET", url);
xhr.send();
xhr.onload = () => {
if (xhr.status != 200) {
reject({error: xhr.status,
message: xhr.statusText})
}
else {
const response: OpenLibraryAuthor = JSON.parse(xhr.response);
resolve(response);
}
}
});
return result;
};
```

This function returns a **Promise** object, which was created using the **Promise** constructor. This constructor takes a single argument, which is a function. That function takes two arguments as well (also functions), which are by convention called **resolve** and **reject**. You can see that the function inside the constructor just creates an **xhr** object, calls its **open** and **send** methods, sets its **onload** property, and returns. So, basically, nothing gets done, except that the request is fired off.

A promise thus created will be in the pending state. And the promise stays in this state until one of the **resolve** or **reject** functions is called inside the body. If the **reject** function is called, it will transition to a rejected state, and we'll be able to use the **catch** method of the **Promise** object to handle the error, and if the **resolve** function is called, it will transition to the resolved state, and we'll be able to use the **then** method of the **Promise** object.

One thing that we should note is that this method does nothing that is UI-related. It does not print any errors on the console or change any DOM elements. It simply promises us that it will get us an **OpenLibraryAuthor** object. Now, we're free to use this object however we want:

```
getShakespeareData()   .then(author => {
const body = document.getElementsByTagName("body")[0];
const image = document.createElement("img");
image.src = `http://covers.openlibrary.org author. photos[0]}-M.jpg`;
body.appendChild(image);
const name = document.createElement("h1");
name.innerHTML = author.personal_name;
body.appendChild(name);
}).catch(error => {
console.log(`An error occured ${error.error}: ${error.message}`);
})
```

In this piece of code, we call the **getShakespeareData** data function, and then on its result, we're calling two methods, **then** and **catch**. The **then** method only executes if the promise is in the resolved state and it takes in a function that will get the result. The **catch** method only executes if the promise is in the rejected state, and it will get the error as an argument to its function.

One important note for the **then** and **catch** methods – they also return promises. This means that **Promise** objects are chainable, so instead of going in depth, as we did with callbacks, we can go in length, so to say. To illustrate that point, let's count to five once again.

Exercise: Counting to Five with Promises
In this exercise, we'll create a function that, when executed, will output the English words one through five. Each word will appear on the screen 1 second after the last one was displayed:

Create a new file, **counting-2.ts**.
In **counting-2.ts**, add an array with the English number names up to and including five:

const numbers = ["One", "Two", "Three", "Four", "Five"];

Add a promisified wrapper of the **setTimeout** function. This wrapper will only execute when the given timeout expires:

```
const delay = (ms: number) => {
const result = new Promise<void>((resolve, reject) => {
setTimeout(() => {
resolve();
}, ms)
});
return result;
}
```

Since our promise will not return any meaningful result, instead just resolving after a given number of milliseconds, we have provided **void** as its type.

Call the **delay** method with a parameter of **1000**, and after its resolution, print out the first number:

delay(1000) .then(() => console.log(numbers[0]))

Save the file, and compile it with the following command:

tsc counting-2.ts

Verify that the compilation ended successfully and that there is a **counting-2. js** file generated in the same folder. Execute it in the **node** environment with this command:

node counting-2.js

You will see the output looks like this:

One

The line should appear 1 second after the application was run.

In the **counting-2.ts** file, after the **then** line, add another **then** line. Inside it, call the **delay** method again, with a timeout of 1 second:

```
delay(1000) .then(() => console.log(numbers[0]))
.then(() => delay(1000))
```

We can do this because the result of the **then** method is **Promise**, which has its own **then** method.

After the last **then** line, add another **then** line, inside which you print out the second number:

```
delay(1000) .then(() => console.log(numbers[0]))
.then(() => delay(1000))
.then(() => console.log(numbers[1]))
```

Compile and run the code again, and verify that the output has an extra line, displayed 1 second after the first.

In the **counting-2.ts** file, add two more **then** lines for the third, fourth, and fifth numbers as well. The code should look like this:

```
delay(1000) .then(() => console.log(numbers[0]))
.then(() => delay(1000))
.then(() => console.log(numbers[1]))
.then(() => delay(1000))
.then(() => console.log(numbers[2]))
.then(() => delay(1000))
.then(() => console.log(numbers[3]))
.then(() => delay(1000))
.then(() => console.log(numbers[4]))
```

Compile and run the code again, and verify that the output appears in the correct order.

Let's compare this code with the code of the previous exercise. It's not the cleanest code, but its function is relatively obvious. We can see how we could expand this code to count to 20. And the major benefit here is that this code, while asynchronous, is still sequential. We can reason about it, and the lines that are at the top will execute before the lines at the bottom. Furthermore, since we have objects now, we can even refactor this code into an even simpler and more extensible format – we can use a **for** loop.

In the **counting-2.ts** file, remove the lines starting with **delay(1000)** until the end of the file. Add a line that will define a resolved promise:

```
let promise = Promise.resolve();
```

Add a **for** loop that, for each number of the **numbers** array, will add to the **promise** chain a delay of 1 second, and print the number:

```
for (const number of numbers) {
promise = promise.then(() => delay(1000)).then(() => console.log(number))
};
}
```

Compile and run the code again, and verify that the output appears in the correct order as shown:

One
Two
Three
Four
Five

Activity: Movie Browser Using Fetch and Promises

In this activity, we will be repeating the previous activity. The major difference is that, instead of using **XMLHttpRequest** and its **onload** method, we'll be using the **fetch** web API. In contrast to the **XMLHttpRequest** class, the **fetch** web API returns a **Promise** object, so instead of nesting our callbacks to have multiple API calls, we can have a chain of promise resolutions that will be far easier to understand.
The activity has the same files and resources as the previous activity.

The following steps should help you with the solution:

In the **script.ts** file, locate the **search** function and verify that it takes a single string parameter and that its body is empty.

Above the **search** function, create a helper function called **getJsonData**. This function will use the **fetch** API to get data from an endpoint and format it as JSON. It should take a single string called **url** as a parameter, and it should return a **Promise**.

In the body of the **getJsonData** function, add code that calls the **fetch** function with the **url** parameter, and **then** call the **json** method on the returned response.

In the **search** method, construct a new string for the search result URL using the **getSearchUrl** method. Call the **getJsonData** function with the **searchUrl** as a parameter.

Add a **then** handler to the promise returned from **getJsonData**. The handler takes a single parameter of the type **SearchResultApi**.

In the body of the handler, check whether we have any results and if we don't, throw an error. If we do have results, return the first item. Note that the handler returns an object with **id** and **title** properties, but the **then** method actually returns a **Promise** of that data. This means that after the handler, we can chain other **then** calls.

Add another **then** call to the previous handler. This handler will take a **movieResult** parameter that contains the **id** and **title** of the movie. Use the **id** property to call the **getMovieUrl** and **getPeopleUrl** methods to, respectively, get the correct URLs for the movie details and for the cast and crew.

After getting the URLs, call the **getJsonData** function with both, and assign the resulting values to variables. Note that the **getJsonData(movieUrl)** call will return a **Promise** of **MovieResultApi**, and **getJsonData(peopleUrl)** will return a **Promise** of **PeopleResultApi**. Assign those result values to variables called **dataPromise** and **peoplePromise**.

Call the static **Promise.all** method with **dataPromise** and **peoplePromise** as parameters. This will create another promise based on those two values, and this promise will be resolved successfully if and only if both (that is, all) promises that are contained within resolve successfully. Its return value will be a

Promise of an array of results.

Return the promise generated by the **Promise.all** call from the handler.

Add another **then** handler to the chain. This handler will take the array returned from **Promise.all** as a single parameter.

Deconstruct the parameter into two variables. The first element of the array should be the **movieData** variable of type **MovieResultApi**, and the second element of the array should be the **peopleData** variable of type **PeopleResultApi**.

The people data has **cast** and **crew** properties. We'll only take the first six cast members, so first sort the **cast** property according to the **order** property of the cast members. Then slice off the first six cast members into a new array.

Transform the cast data (which is **CastResultApi** objects) into your own **Character** objects. We need to map the **character** field of **CastResultApi** to the **name** field of **Character**, the **name** field to the **actor** name, and the **profile_path** field to the **image** property.

From the **crew** property of the people data, we'll only need the director and the writer. Since there can be multiple directors and writers, we'll get the names of all directors and writers and concatenate them, respectively. For the directors, from the **crew** property, filter the people who have a **department** of **Directing** and a **job** of **Director**. For those objects, take the **name** property, and **join** it together with an **&** in between.

For the writers, from the **crew** property, filter the people who have a **department** of **Writing** and a **job** of **Writer**. For those objects, take the **name** property, and **join** it together with an **&** in between. Create a new **Movie** object (using object literal syntax). Fill in all the properties of the **Movie** object using the data from the movie and people responses we've prepared so far.

Return the **Movie** object from the handler.

Note that we did not do any UI interactions in our code. We just received a string, did some promise calls, and returned a value. The UI work can now be done in UI-oriented code. In this case, that's in the **click** event handler of the **search** button. We should simply add a **then** handler to the **search** call that will call the **showResults** method, and a **catch** handler that will call the **clearResults** method.

Although we used **fetch** and promises in this activity, and our code is now much more efficient but complex, the basic function of the website will be the same and you should see an output similar to the previous activity.

async/await
Promises solved the problem of callbacks quite nicely. However, often, they carry with them lots of unneeded fluff. We need to write lots of **then** calls, and we need to be careful not to forget to close any parentheses.

The next step is to add a piece of syntactic sugar to our TypeScript skills. Unlike the other things in this chapter, this feature originated in TypeScript, and was later adopted in JavaScript as well. I'm talking about the **async/await** keywords. These are two separate keywords, but they are always used together, so the whole feature became known as **async/await**.

What we do is we can add the **async** modifier to a certain function, and then, in that function, we can use the **await** modifier to execute promises easily. Let's go once more to our Shakespearean example, and let's wrap the code we used to call **getShakespeareData** inside another function, simply called **run**:

```
function run() {
getShakespeareData().then(author => {
const body = document.getElementsByTagName("body")[0];
const image = document.createElement("img");
image.src = `http://covers.openlibrary.org author. photos[0]}-M.jpg`;
body.appendChild(image);
const name = document.createElement("h1");
name.innerHTML = author.personal_name;
body.appendChild(name);
}).catch(error => {
console.log(`An error occured ${error.error}: ${error.message}`);
}) }
run();
```

This code is functionally equivalent to the code we had previously. But now, we have a function that we can mark as an **async** function, like this:
```
async function run() {
```

Now, we're allowed to just get the result of a promise and put it inside of a variable. So, the whole **then** invocation will become this:

```
const author = await getShakespeareData();
const body = document.getElementsByTagName("body")[0];
const image = document.createElement("img");
image.src = `http://covers.openlibrary.org author. photos[0]}-M.jpg`;
body.appendChild(image);
const name = document.createElement("h1");
name.innerHTML = author.personal_name;
body.appendChild(name);
```

You can see that we don't have any wrapping function calls anymore. The **catch** invocation can be replaced with a simple **try/catch** construct, and the final version of the **run** function will look like this:

```
async function run () {
try {
const author = await getShakespeareData();
const body = document.getElementsByTagName("body")[0];
const image = document.createElement("img");
image.src = `http://covers.openlibrary.org { author. photos[0]}-M.jpg`;
body.appendChild(image);
const name = document.createElement("h1");
name.innerHTML = author.personal_name;
body.appendChild(name);
}
catch (error) {
console.log(`An error occured ${error.error}: ${error.message}`);
}
```

}

You will notice that the amount of code that is deeply nested is drastically reduced. Now we can look at the code, and have a good idea of what it does, just from a quick glance. This is still the same, deeply asynchronous code, the only difference is that it looks almost synchronous and definitely sequential.

Exercise: Counting to Five with async and await

In this exercise, we'll create a function that, when executed, will output the English words one through five. Each word will appear on the screen 1 second after the last one was displayed:

Create a new file, **counting-3.ts**.
In **counting-3.ts**, add an array with the English number names up to and including five:

```
const numbers = ["One", "Two", "Three", "Four", "Five"];
```

Add a promisified wrapper of the **setTimeout** function. This wrapper will only execute when the given timeout expires:

```
const delay = (ms: number) => {
const result = new Promise<void>((resolve, reject) => {
setTimeout(() => {
resolve();
}, ms)
});
return result;
}
```

Since our promise will not return any meaningful results, instead of just resolving after a given number of milliseconds, we have provided **void** as its type.

Create an empty **async** function called **countNumbers** and execute it on the last line of the file:

```
async function countNumbers() { }
countNumbers();
```

Inside the **countNumbers** function, await the **delay** method with a parameter of **1000**, and after its resolution, print out the first number:

```
async function countNumbers() {
await delay(1000);
console.log(numbers[0]);
}
```

Save the file, and compile it with the following command:

```
tsc counting-3.ts
```

Verify that the compilation ended successfully and that there is a **counting-3. js** file generated in the same folder. Execute it in the **node** environment with this command:

node counting-3.js

You will see the output looks like this:

One

The line should appear 1 second after the application was run.

In the **counting-3.ts** file, after the **console.log** line, add two more lines for the rest of the numbers as well. The code should look like this:

```
async function countNumbers() {
await delay(1000);
console.log(numbers[0]);    await delay(1000);    console.log(numbers[1]);    await delay(1000);
console.log(numbers[2]);    await delay(1000);    console.log(numbers[3]);    await delay(1000);
console.log(numbers[4]);
}
```

Compile and run the code again, and verify that the output appears in the correct order.

Since the code is completely identical for all the numbers, it's trivial to replace it with a **for** loop.

In the **counting-3.ts** file, remove the body of the **countNumbers** function, and replace it with a **for** loop that, for each number of the **numbers** array, will **await** a delay of a second, and then print the number:

```
for (const number of numbers) {
await delay(1000);    console.log(number);
};
```

Compile and run the code again, and verify that the output appears in the correct order:

One
Two
Three
Four
Five

Activity: Movie Browser Using fetch and async/await

In this activity, we will be improving on the previous activity. The major difference is that instead of using the **then** method of the **Promises** class, we'll use the **await** keyword to do that for us magically. Instead of a chain of **then** calls, we'll just have code that looks completely regular, with some **await** statements peppered throughout.

The activity has the same files and resources as the previous activity.

The following steps should help you with the solution:

In the **script.ts** file, locate the **search** function and verify that it takes a single string parameter and that its body is empty. Note that this function is now marked with the **async** keywords, which allows us to use the **await** operator.

Above the **search** function, create a helper function called **getJsonData**. This function will use the **fetch** API to get data from an endpoint and format it as JSON. It should take a single string called **url** as a parameter, and it should return a promise.

In the body of the **getJsonData** function, add code that calls the **fetch** function with the **url** parameter, and **then** call the **json** method on the returned response.

In the **search** method, construct a new string for the search result URL using the **getSearchUrl** method. Call the **getJsonData** function with **searchUrl** as a parameter, and **await** the result. Place the result into the **SearchResultApi** variable.

Check whether we have any results and if we don't, throw an error. If we do have results, set the first item of the **result** property into a variable called **movieResult**. This object will contain the **id** and **title** properties of the movie.

Use the **id** property to call the **getMovieUrl** and **getPeopleUrl** methods to, respectively, get the correct URLs for the movie details and for the cast and crew.

After getting the URLs, call the **getJsonData** function with both, and assign the resulting values to variables. Note that the **getJsonData(movieUrl)** call will return a promise of **MovieResultApi**, and **getJsonData(peopleUrl)** will return a promise of **PeopleResultApi**. Assign those result values to variables called **dataPromise** and **peoplePromise**.

Call the static **Promise.all** method with **dataPromise** and **peoplePromise** as parameters. This will create another promise based on those two values, and this promise will be resolved successfully if and only if both (that is, all) promises that are contained within resolve successfully. Its return value will be a promise of an array of results. **await** this promise, and place its result into a variable of type **array**.

Deconstruct that array into two variables. The first element of the array should be the **movieData** variable of type **MovieResultApi**, and the second element of the array should be the **peopleData** variable of type **PeopleResultApi**.

The people data has **cast** and **crew** properties. We'll only take the first six cast members, so first sort the **cast** property according to the **order** property of the cast members. Then slice off the first six cast members into a new array.

Transform the cast data (which is **CastResultApi** objects) into our own **Character** objects. We need to map the **character** field of **CastResultApi** to the **name** field of **Character**, the **name** field to the **actor** name, and the **profile_path** field to the **image** property.

From the **crew** property of the people data, we'll only need the director and the writer. Since there can be multiple directors and writers, we'll get the names of all directors and writers and concatenate them, respectively. For the directors, from the **crew** property, filter the people who have a **department** of **Directing** and a **job** of **Director**. For those objects, take the **name** property, and **join** it together with an **&** in between.

For the writers, from the **crew** property, filter the people who have a **department** of **Writing** and a **job** of **Writer**. For those objects, take the **name** property, and **join** it together with an **&** in between. Create a new **Movie** object (using object literal syntax). Fill in all the properties of the **Movie** object using the data from the movie and people responses we've prepared so far.

Return the Movie object from the function.

Note that we did not do any UI interactions in our code. We just received a string, did some promise calls, and returned a value. The UI work can now be done in UI-oriented code. In this case, that's in the **click** event handler of the **search** button. We should simply add a **then** handler to the **search** call that will call the **showResults** method, and a **catch** handler that will call the **clearResults** method.

Although we used **fetch** and **async/await** in this activity, and our code is now just as efficient but less complex compared with the previous activity, the basic function of the website will be the same and you should see an output similar to the previous activity.

Conclusion: Mastering Asynchronous Behaviour in TypeScript
The event loop and asynchronous programming in TypeScript form the backbone of modern web and server-side development. They enable efficient handling of tasks that would otherwise block execution, ensuring applications remain responsive and performant. This conclusion ties together the essential aspects of asynchronous programming, reinforcing the importance of understanding and implementing these concepts effectively.

1. Reiterating the Importance of the Event Loop

The event loop is the core mechanism that enables TypeScript (and JavaScript) to handle asynchronous operations seamlessly in a single-threaded environment. By managing the interaction between the call stack, Web APIs, and task/microtask queues, the event loop ensures that tasks are executed in the correct order, preserving the non-blocking nature of the runtime.

In practice:

Task prioritization ensures smooth performance by addressing microtasks (e.g., promises) before tasks in the callback queue (e.g., setTimeout).

Concurrency allows developers to write code that manages multiple asynchronous operations simultaneously, vital for real-time applications, API integrations, and I/O-heavy tasks.

2. Benefits of Asynchronous Programming in TypeScript

Adopting asynchronous techniques in TypeScript unlocks several advantages:

Improved Responsiveness: Applications can handle multiple I/O-bound operations without freezing the UI or halting the event loop.

Efficient Resource Utilization: Asynchronous operations maximize CPU usage by allowing tasks to run in the background while other operations proceed.

Scalable Architectures: TypeScript's type-safe asynchronous features enable developers to create scalable, maintainable systems capable of handling growing workloads.

3. Best Practices for Asynchronous Programming in TypeScript

To leverage asynchronous programming effectively, developers should adopt the following practices:

1. Prioritize Readability with async/await

Using async/await makes asynchronous code appear synchronous, enhancing readability and maintainability. Complex chains of promises can be refactored into straightforward workflows:

```
async function fetchAndProcessData() {
  try {
    const data = await fetchData();
    process(data);
  } catch (error) {
    console.error('Error fetching data:', error);
  }
}
```

2. Handle Errors Gracefully

Uncaught errors in asynchronous code can propagate silently, causing debugging challenges. Proper use of try...catch with async/await or. catch for promises ensures robust error handling.

3. Leverage Strong Typing

TypeScript's ability to enforce strict type checking extends to promises and asynchronous functions. This minimizes runtime errors and enhances code reliability:

```
async function fetchData(): Promise<string> {
  return 'Data fetched';
}
```

4. Optimize Performance with Promise.all

When multiple independent tasks must run concurrently, Promise.all reduces execution time by starting all promises simultaneously:

```
const [data1, data2] = await Promise.all([fetchData1(), fetchData2()]);
```

5. Use Throttling and Debouncing

To control the frequency of API calls or event handlers, implement throttling or debouncing techniques to balance performance with functionality.

4. Debugging Asynchronous Code

Understanding the asynchronous flow of execution is crucial for effective debugging:

Enable Async Stack Traces: Modern browsers and Node.js provide enhanced stack traces for debugging async functions.

Leverage Logging Tools: Adding timestamps and structured logs can reveal execution sequences and timing discrepancies.

Rely on Linting Tools: Use TypeScript-compatible linters like ESLint to catch common pitfalls in async programming, such as unhandled promises.

5. Challenges and Future Directions

While TypeScript's features enhance asynchronous programming, challenges remain:

Complexity in Error Propagation: Handling errors across multiple asynchronous layers can be intricate, requiring careful planning.

Balancing Concurrency and Resource Limits: Overloading the system with too many simultaneous tasks can degrade performance.

Ensuring Predictable Execution: Asynchronous behaviour introduces timing uncertainties, demanding thoughtful architecture to ensure predictability.

Looking forward, advancements in JavaScript and TypeScript runtimes, along with tools like Deno and new ECMAScript proposals, promise even more powerful and efficient asynchronous capabilities.

6. Final Thoughts

Mastering the event loop and asynchronous behaviour in TypeScript is essential for modern developers. By combining a deep understanding of these concepts with TypeScript's type-safe features, developers can write robust, efficient, and maintainable code. Whether building a real-time chat application, handling complex API integrations, or processing large datasets asynchronously, TypeScript empowers developers to tackle these challenges with confidence.

To excel in asynchronous programming:

Focus on understanding the event loop's mechanics.
Adopt async/await for clear and concise code.
Utilize TypeScript's typing system to ensure safety and predictability.
Continuously refine your practices to adapt to evolving tools and standards.

Asynchronous programming in TypeScript is not just a technical skill but a foundational ability that enables developers to create the responsive, high-performance applications demanded in today's digital landscape.

10. Object-Oriented Programming (OOP) and Aspect-Oriented Programming (AOP)

Introduction

TypeScript is a strongly typed superset of JavaScript, designed to enhance JavaScript with modern programming paradigms like Object-Oriented Programming (OOP) and Aspect-Oriented Programming (AOP). These paradigms enable developers to build scalable, maintainable, and reusable code. While OOP focuses on encapsulating data and behaviour into objects, AOP allows for the modularization of cross-cutting concerns, such as logging, security, and error handling.

This introduction explores the core concepts, syntax, and applications of both paradigms in TypeScript, highlighting their significance and how they complement each other.

Part I: Object-Oriented Programming (OOP) in TypeScript

1. What is OOP?

Object-Oriented Programming is a programming paradigm based on the concept of "objects," which are instances of classes. These objects encapsulate data (properties) and behaviour (methods). The four fundamental principles of OOP are:

Encapsulation: Bundling data and methods operating on the data into a single unit (class).
Inheritance: Reusing and extending functionality from existing classes.
Polymorphism: Writing code that works with objects of multiple types through interfaces or inheritance.
Abstraction: Hiding complex implementation details while exposing only the necessary features.

2. OOP in TypeScript

TypeScript provides robust support for OOP with features such as classes, interfaces, access modifiers, and abstract classes. Let's explore these in detail.

2.1 Classes and Objects

Classes are blueprints for creating objects.

```
class Animal {
  private name: string;
  constructor(name: string) {
    this.name = name;
  }
  public speak(): void {
    console.log(`${this.name} makes a noise.`);
  }
}
// Creating an object
const dog = new Animal("Dog");
dog.speak(); // Output: Dog makes a noise.
```

Constructor: Initializes object properties.
Access Modifiers: Control access to class members:
public: Accessible from anywhere.
private: Accessible only within the class.
protected: Accessible within the class and its subclasses.

2.2 Inheritance

Inheritance enables a class to extend another class.

```
class Dog extends Animal {
  constructor(name: string) {
    super(name); // Call the parent class constructor
  }
  public speak(): void {
    console.log(`${this.name} barks.`);
  }
}
const dog = new Dog("Rex");
dog.speak(); // Output: Rex barks.
```

2.3 Interfaces

Interfaces define the structure of an object or class, ensuring type safety.

```
interface Shape {
  area(): number;
}
class Circle implements Shape {
  constructor(private radius: number) {}
  public area(): number {
    return Math.PI * this.radius ** 2;
  }
}
```

2.4 Polymorphism

Polymorphism allows using different class implementations interchangeably.

```
function printArea(shape: Shape): void {
  console.log(`Area: ${shape.area()}`);
}
const circle = new Circle(10);
printArea(circle); // Output: Area: 314.159...
```

2.5 Abstract Classes

Abstract classes cannot be instantiated directly but can define common methods and properties for subclasses.

```typescript
abstract class Vehicle {
  constructor(protected name: string) {}
  abstract move(): void;
  public describe(): void {
    console.log(`This is a ${this.name}.`);
  }
}
class Car extends Vehicle {
  public move(): void {
    console.log(`${this.name} drives on roads. `);
  }
}
const car = new Car("Sedan");
car.describe(); // Output: This is a Sedan.
car.move();     // Output: Sedan drives on roads.
```

3. Benefits of OOP in TypeScript

Code Reusability: Promotes DRY (Don't Repeat Yourself) principles through inheritance and interfaces.
Scalability: Classes and objects provide a modular code structure.
Maintainability: Clear separation of concerns via encapsulation.
Type Safety: Interfaces and access modifiers enhance code reliability.

Part II: Aspect-Oriented Programming (AOP) in TypeScript

1. What is AOP?

Aspect-Oriented Programming focuses on separating cross-cutting concerns that span multiple parts of an application. Cross-cutting concerns, such as logging, error handling, and security, often require code to be repeated in multiple places. AOP aims to modularize these concerns, improving code maintainability and reducing duplication.

Key concepts of AOP include:

Aspects: Modular units encapsulating cross-cutting concerns.
Advice: Code that is executed at specific points (e.g., before or after a function call).
Pointcuts: Predetermined points in the application (e.g., method execution).
Join Points: Specific places in the code where advice is applied.
Weaving: The process of integrating aspects into the main program.

2. AOP in TypeScript

TypeScript supports AOP through decorators, which provide a way to modify class behaviour dynamically.

2.1 What are Decorators?

Decorators are special annotations that modify or extend the behaviour of classes, methods, or properties.

```
function LogMethod(target: any, propertyKey: string, descriptor: PropertyDescriptor): void {
  const originalMethod = descriptor.value;
  descriptor.value = function (...args: any[]) {
    console.log(`Method ${propertyKey} was called with args: ${JSON.stringify(args)}`);
    return originalMethod.apply(this, args);
  };
}
class Calculator {
  @LogMethod
  public add(a: number, b: number): number {
    return a + b;
  }
}
const calc = new Calculator();
calc.add(2, 3); // Output: Method add was called with args: [2,3]
```

2.2 Types of Decorators

Class Decorators: Modify or replace a class definition.
Method Decorators: Extend or wrap a method's behaviour.
Property Decorators: Define metadata or constraints on properties.
Parameter Decorators: Capture metadata about method parameters.

2.3 AOP Use Cases with Decorators

Logging:

```
function Log(target: any, propertyKey: string, descriptor: PropertyDescriptor): void {
  const original = descriptor.value;
  descriptor.value = function (...args: any[]) {
    console.log(`Executing ${propertyKey} with arguments:`, args);
    const result = original.apply(this, args);
    console.log(`Result of ${propertyKey}:`, result);
    return result;
  };
}
```

Error Handling:

```
function Catch(target: any, propertyKey: string, descriptor: PropertyDescriptor): void {
  const original = descriptor.value;
  descriptor.value = function (...args: any[]) {
    try {
      return original.apply(this, args);
    } catch (error) {
      console.error(`Error in ${propertyKey}:`, error);
    }
  };
}
```

Access Control:

```typescript
function Auth(role: string) {
  return function (target: any, propertyKey: string, descriptor: PropertyDescriptor): void {
    const original = descriptor.value;
    descriptor.value = function (...args: any[]) {
      if (/* check user role */ role !== "admin") {
        throw new Error("Unauthorized");
      }
      return original.apply(this, args);
    };
  };
}
```

3. Benefits of AOP in TypeScript

Separation of Concerns: Modularizes cross-cutting concerns into aspects.
Reusability: Centralizes common functionality (e.g., logging).
Maintainability: Reduces code duplication and improves readability.
Flexibility: Easily adapt or extend application behaviour without altering the core logic.

Combining OOP and AOP in TypeScript

OOP and AOP complement each other in TypeScript, creating robust and flexible applications. OOP structures the application into cohesive classes and objects, while AOP abstracts repetitive concerns, ensuring clean and maintainable code.

Example:

```typescript
class Payment {
  constructor(private amount: number) {}
  @LogMethod
  @Catch
  public process(): void {
    if (this.amount <= 0) {
      throw new Error("Invalid payment amount.");
    }
    console.log(`Processing payment of $${this.amount}`);
  }
}
const payment = new Payment(100);
payment.process();
```

Object Oriented Programming with TypeScript

Object-Oriented Programming (OOP) is one of the most popular programming paradigms that has been adopted across different programming languages. TypeScript as a superset of JavaScript, which means that it supports all the features of JavaScript and adds some additional features, including advanced OOP concepts.
With this in mind we will explore together OOP concepts with TypeScript.

Inheritance: One class can inherit the methods and properties of another class. A derived class can inherit properties and methods from a base class using the "extends" keyword.

```typescript
class Vehicle {
protected name: string;
constructor(name: string) {
this.name = name;
    }
   public move(distance: number): void {console.log(`${this.name} moved ${distance} km`);
    }
}
class Car extends Vehicle {
private color: string;
constructor(name: string, color: string) {
super(name);
this.color = color;
    }
public getColor(): string {
return this.color;
    }
}
const car = new Car("BMW", "blue");
console.log(car.getColor());
car.move(100);
```

Polymorphism: Capacity for an object to take on multiple forms is known as polymorphism; you can achieve polymorphism by using interfaces or abstract classes.

```typescript
interface Shape {
draw(): void;
}
class Circle implements Shape {
public draw(): void {
console.log("Drawing a circle...");
    }
}
class Square implements Shape {
public draw(): void {
console.log("Drawing a square...");
    }
}
function drawShapes(shapes: Shape[]): void {
shapes.forEach(shape => shape.draw());
}
drawShapes([new Circle(), new Square()]);
```

Encapsulation: Encapsulation involves hiding an object's implementation details from the outside world. TypeScript enables encapsulation through access modifiers such as public, private, and protected. These modifiers control the visibility and accessibility of class members, ensuring that internal details are not exposed unnecessarily.

```typescript
class BankAccount {
private balance: number = 0;
public deposit(amount: number): void {
this.balance += amount;
```

```typescript
    console.log(`Deposited ${amount}. New balance is ${this.balance}`);
    }
public withdraw(amount: number): void {
if (amount <= this.balance) {
this.balance -= amount;
console.log(`Withdrew ${amount}. New balance is ${this.balance}`);
    }
else {
console.log("Insufficient balance");
    }
  }
}
const account = new BankAccount();
account.deposit(1000);
account.withdraw(500);
account.withdraw(600);
```

Abstract Classes: Abstract classes are classes that cannot be instantiated and are used as base classes for other classes. In TypeScript, you can create abstract classes by using the "abstract" keyword.

```typescript
abstract class Vehicle {
protected name: string;
constructor(name: string) {
this.name = name;
    }
    public abstract move(distance: number): void;
}
class Car extends Vehicle {
private color: string;
constructor(name: string, color: string)
{
super(name);
this.color = color;
    }
    public move(distance: number): void {
console.log(`${this.name} moved ${distance} km`);
    }
}
const car = new Car("BMW", "blue");
car.move(100);
```

Interfaces: Interfaces are used to define a contract for objects that share similar properties and methods. In TypeScript, you can create interfaces by using the "interface" keyword.

```typescript
interface Employee {
id: number; name: string; age: number; department: string;
}
function printEmployeeInfo(employee:)
```

OOP concepts like inheritance, encapsulation, polymorphism, and abstract classes is crucial for becoming proficient in TypeScript, as these concepts play a significant role in structuring and organizing your code effectively.

Inheritance using TypeScript

Imagine a system designed to manage various types of vehicles, such as cars, trucks, and motorcycles. Each vehicle type shares common properties like make, model, year, and color, but they also possess unique properties and methods.

To represent these vehicles, a base class called "Vehicle" can be created, defining the shared properties and methods. Derived classes, like "Car," "Truck," and "Motorcycle," can then inherit from the "Vehicle" class while incorporating their distinctive properties and methods.

```typescript
class Vehicle {
constructor( public make: string,    public model: string,    public year: number,    public color: string
 ) {}
 public start(): void {    console.log(`Starting ${this.make} ${this.model}...`);
 }
 public stop(): void {    console.log(`Stopping ${this.make} ${this.model}...`);
 }
}
class Car extends Vehicle {
constructor(make: string, model: string, year: number, color: string, public numDoors: number
 )
{
super(make, model, year, color);
 }
public drive(): void {
console.log(`Driving ${this.make} ${this.model} with ${this.numDoors} doors...`);
 }
}
class Truck extends Vehicle {
constructor(make: string, model: string, year: number, color: string, public payloadCapacity: number
)
{
super(make, model, year, color);
}
public loadCargo(): void {
console.log(`Loading cargo into ${this.make} ${this.model} with ${this.payloadCapacity} lbs
capacity...`);  }
}
class Motorcycle extends Vehicle {
constructor(make: string, model: string, year: number, color: string, public hasSidecar: boolean)
{
super(make, model, year, color);
}
public popWheelie(): void {
console.log(`Popping wheelie on ${this.make} ${this.model}...`);
}
}
```

In this example, the "Vehicle" class serves as the foundation, outlining common properties and methods.

Derived classes like "Car," "Truck," and "Motorcycle" inherit these properties and methods, adding their own unique characteristics. For instance, the "Car" class introduces a "numDoors" property and a "drive" method, while the "Truck" class features a "payloadCapacity" property and a "loadCargo" method, and the "Motorcycle" class includes a "hasSidecar" property and a "popWheelie" method.

Using inheritance allows for the reuse of the shared properties and methods from the "Vehicle" class, preventing code duplication in derived classes. This approach facilitates code maintenance and minimizes the likelihood of errors.

In conclusion, inheritance is a strong OOP concept that enables code reuse and the establishment of related class hierarchies. It is particularly useful when classes share common properties and methods but also possess unique characteristics. The advantages of inheritance encompass code reuse, simplified maintenance, and error reduction.

Inheritance in a bank app

Suppose we are building a mini bank finance application and imagine we have various account types, such as savings accounts, checking accounts, and credit card accounts, in the context of a banking application.

```
class Account {
constructor(public accountNumber: string, public balance: number, public owner: string
)
{
}
public deposit(amount: number): void {
this.balance += amount;
console.log(`Deposited ${amount}. New balance is ${this.balance}`);
}
public withdraw(amount: number): void {
if (amount <= this.balance) {
this.balance -= amount;
console.log(`Withdrew ${amount}. New balance is ${this.balance}`);
}
else {
console.log("Insufficient balance");
   }
 }
}
class SavingsAccount extends Account {
constructor( accountNumber: string, balance: number, owner: string, public interestRate: number)
{
super(accountNumber, balance, owner);
}
public calculateInterest(): void {
const interest = this.balance * this.interestRate;
this.balance += interest;
console.log(`Calculated interest of ${interest}. New balance is ${this.balance}`);
}
}
```

```
class CheckingAccount extends Account {
constructor( accountNumber: string, balance: number, owner: string, public overdraftLimit: number
)
{
super(accountNumber, balance, owner);
}
public withdraw(amount: number): void {
if (amount <= this.balance + this.overdraftLimit) {
this.balance -= amount;
console.log(`Withdrew ${amount}. New balance is ${this.balance}`);
}
else {
console.log("Insufficient funds");
    }
  }
}
class CreditCardAccount extends Account {
constructor(accountNumber: string, balance: number, owner: string, public creditLimit: number)
{
super(accountNumber, balance, owner);
  }
public charge(amount: number): void {
if (amount <= this.creditLimit - this.balance) {
this.balance += amount;
console.log(`Charged ${amount}. New balance is ${this.balance}`);
}
else {
console.log("Credit limit exceeded");
    }
  }
}
```

Each type of account has its own special attributes as well as shared ones like account number, balance, and owner.
It is possible to define shared properties and methods for these accounts in a base class called "Account" to represent them.

Then, while incorporating their unique properties and methods, derived classes like "SavingsAccount," "CheckingAccount," and "CreditCardAccount" can inherit from the "Account" class.

The "Account" class in this illustration serves as the framework, outlining common properties and methods.
Derived classes like "SavingsAccount," "CheckingAccount," and "CreditCardAccount" inherit these properties and methods and add their own unique properties.

For instance, the "SavingsAccount" class adds the "interestRate" property and the "calculateInterest" method; the "CheckingAccount" class adds the "overdraftLimit" property and overrides the "withdraw" method; and the "CreditCardAccount" class adds the "creditLimit" property and the "charge" method. Using inheritance allows for the reuse of the shared properties and methods from the "Account" class, preventing code duplication in derived classes. This approach facilitates code maintenance and minimizes the likelihood of errors.

In conclusion, inheritance is an important OOP concept that enables code reuse and the establishment of related class hierarchies. It is particularly useful when classes share common properties and methods but also possess unique characteristics. The advantages of inheritance encompass code reuse, simplified maintenance, and error reduction.

Polymorphism using TypeScript

Imagine for a moment a program that works with a wide range of geometric shapes, some of which are squares, some of which are triangles, and each of which has a unique way of calculating area and perimeter.

How might one effectively represent these shapes and their distinctive characteristics in code?

```typescript
interface Shape {
calculateArea(): number;
calculatePerimeter(): number;
}
class Circle implements Shape {
constructor(public radius: number) {}
public calculateArea(): number {
return Math.PI * this.radius ** 2;
}
public calculatePerimeter(): number {
return 2 * Math.PI * this.radius;
  }
}
class Square implements Shape {
constructor(public side: number) {}
public calculateArea(): number {
return this.side ** 2;
}
public calculatePerimeter(): number {
return 4 * this.side;
  }
}
class Triangle implements Shape {
constructor(public base: number, public height: number, public sideA: number, public sideB: number)
{}
public calculateArea(): number {
return 0.5 * this.base * this.height;
}
public calculatePerimeter(): number {
return this.base + this.sideA + this.sideB;
}
}
```

A way to specify a set of shared attributes and operations between different classes. We can create derived classes like "Circle," "Square," and "Triangle" that implement this interface and provide their own unique method implementations by first defining an interface called "Shape" that outlines the necessary properties and methods (such as "calculateArea" and "calculatePerimeter").

We can then treat objects from these various classes as if they were of the same type thanks to the magic of polymorphism, in spite of their distinctive characteristics and behaviors. This keeps our code incredibly flexible and reuseable while also preventing the dreaded repetition of code.

```
const shapes: Shape[] = [new Circle(5), new Square(10), new Triangle(8, 5, 6, 7)];
shapes.forEach(shape => {
console.log(`Area: ${shape.calculateArea()}, Perimeter: ${shape.calculatePerimeter()}`);
});
```

The "calculateArea" and "calculatePerimeter" methods are called on each object in turn. However, what does this actually look like in practice? Imagine an array of shapes, all of different types. Without requiring knowledge of the precise type of each individual shape, the code outputs the area and perimeter of each shape. Fantastic, no?

In conclusion, polymorphism is an effective tool in any developer's toolbox, enabling increased flexibility, reuse, and decreased code error. We can effectively represent a wide variety of complex objects with comparatively little effort by implementing interfaces and derived classes with their own unique implementations.

Example of using polymorphism in a logistics app:
Suppose we are building a logistics application, in this example, the abstract class "Shipment" plays a vital role in the logistics application by defining the fundamental properties and methods such as "calculateWeight" and "calculateVolume." Meanwhile, the concrete classes, namely "Package," "Pallet," and "Container," extend this abstract class and provide their own implementation of these methods based on their specific properties.

The flexibility and reuse of the codebase are improved by using TypeScript's polymorphism to treat objects of various classes that extend the same abstract class as though they were of the same type.

```
abstract class Shipment {
constructor(public id: string, public description: string, public weight: number, public length: number,
public width: number, public height: number) {}
public abstract calculateWeight(): number;
public abstract calculateVolume(): number;
}
class Package extends Shipment {
constructor(id: string, description: string, weight: number, length: number, width: number, height:
number)
{
super(id, description, weight, length, width, height);
}
public calculateWeight(): number {
return this.weight;
}
public calculateVolume(): number {
return this.length * this.width * this.height;
  }
}

class Pallet extends Shipment {
constructor(id: string, description: string, weight: number, length: number, width: number, height:
number,    public numPackages: number) {
```

```typescript
super(id, description, weight, length, width, height);
}
public calculateWeight(): number {
return this.weight + this.numPackages * 2;
}
public calculateVolume(): number {
return this.length * this.width * this.height * this.numPackages;
}
}
class Container extends Shipment {
constructor(id: string, description: string, weight: number, length: number, width: number, height:
number,    public maxLoad: number) {
super(id, description, weight, length, width, height);
}

public calculateWeight(): number {
return this.weight + this.maxLoad;
}
public calculateVolume(): number {
return this.length * this.width * this.height * 100;
}
}
```

To further demonstrate, without knowing the precise type of each object, we can create an array of shipments and use the "calculateWeight" and "calculateVolume" methods on each object.

This sophisticated method of coding lowers errors, makes maintenance easier, and ensures effective code reuse.

```typescript
const shipments: Shipment[] = [
new Package("P001", "Small Package", 1.5, 10, 10, 10),
new Pallet("PL001", "Large Pallet", 50, 100, 100, 200, 10),
new Container("C001", "40-foot Container", 5000, 1200, 2400, 2400, 50000)
];
shipments.forEach(shipment => {
console.log(`Weight: ${shipment.calculateWeight()} kg, Volume: ${shipment.calculateVolume()} cm^
```

Encapsulation using TypeScript

Imagine a system that handles various employee types like managers, engineers, and sales reps. While each employee type has common attributes like name, age, and salary, they also possess unique properties and functions.

To represent these employees, we can establish a "Employee" class that outlines the shared properties and methods as protected or private. From there, we can form subclasses like "Manager", "Engineer", and "Salesperson", which inherit from the "Employee" class and access these properties and methods via public methods.

```typescript
class Employee {
constructor(protected name: string, protected age: number, private salary: number) {}
```

```
public getSalary(): number {
return this.salary;
}
public setSalary(newSalary: number): void {
    this.salary = newSalary;
  }
protected doWork(): void {
console.log(`${this.name} is working...`);
  }
}
class Manager extends Employee {
constructor(name: string, age: number, salary: number, public numReports: number) {
super(name, age, salary);
}

public getBonus(): number {
return this.getSalary() * 0.2;
}

public doManagerialWork(): void {
console.log(`${this.name} is managing ${this.numReports} reports...`);
this.doWork();
}
}
class Engineer extends Employee {
constructor(name: string, age: number, salary: number, public numProjects: number) {
super(name, age, salary);
}
public getBonus(): number {
return this.getSalary() * 0.1;
}
public doEngineeringWork(): void {
console.log(`${this.name} is working on ${this.numProjects} projects...`);
this.doWork();
  }
}
class Salesperson extends Employee {
constructor(name: string, age: number, salary: number, public numSales: number) {
super(name, age, salary);
}
public getBonus(): number {
return this.getSalary() * 0.15;
}
public doSalesWork(): void {
console.log(`${this.name} is selling ${this.numSales} products...`);
this.doWork();
  }
}
```

In this scenario, the "Employee" class safeguards common properties and methods as protected or private, promoting encapsulation and blocking direct external access. Subclasses such as "Manager", "Engineer", and "Salesperson" inherit from the "Employee" class and utilize public methods like "getSalary" and "setSalary" to access these properties and methods.

Through encapsulation, we can conceal the "Employee" class's implementation specifics and expose only the public interface, making the code sturdier and more secure. For instance, we can generate objects for different employee types and invoke their public methods without knowing each class's specific implementation details

```
const manager = new Manager("John Doe", 40, 100000, 5);
console.log(`Salary: ${manager.getSalary()}, Bonus: ${manager.getBonus()}`);
manager.doManagerialWork();
const engineer = new Engineer("Jane Smith", 30, 80000, 3);
console.log(`Salary: ${engineer.getSalary()}, Bonus: ${engineer.getBonus()}`);
engineer.doEngineeringWork();
const salesperson = new Salesperson("Bob Johnson", 45, 90000, 10);
console.log(`Salary: ${salesperson.getSalary()}, Bonus: ${salesperson.getBonus()}`);
salesperson.doSalesWork();
```

Abstract classes and interfaces

Imagine you're developing a game engine that supports a variety of game objects, such as sprites, sounds, and physics objects, each with their own unique rendering, playing, and interaction methods.

To represent these game objects, you can create an abstract class called "GameObject" that defines common properties and methods, like "x" and "y" coordinates, as well as "update" and "render" methods. Moreover, you can establish interfaces like "Sprite", "Sound", and "PhysicsObject" that outline specific properties and methods for each game object category.

```
abstract class GameObject {
constructor(public x: number, public y: number) {}
public abstract update(): void;
public abstract render(): void;
}
interface Sprite {
image: HTMLImageElement; width: number; height: number;
}
interface Sound {
audio: HTMLAudioElement;
}
interface PhysicsObject {
velocityX: number;   velocityY: number;   weight: number;
}
class SpriteObject extends GameObject implements Sprite {
constructor(x: number, y: number, public image: HTMLImageElement, public width: number, public
height: number) {
super(x, y);
}
public update(): void { // Update sprite animation or movement
}
public render(): void { // Draw sprite image on canvas
  }
}
```

```
class SoundObject extends GameObject implements Sound {
constructor(x: number, y: number, public audio: HTMLAudioElement) {
super(x, y);
}
public update(): void { // Update sound playback or volume
}
public render(): void { // No rendering for sound object
  }
}
class PhysicsObjectImpl extends GameObject implements PhysicsObject {
constructor(x: number, y: number, public velocityX: number, public velocityY: number, public weight:
number)
{
super(x, y);
}
public update(): void { // Update physics calculations based on velocity and weight
}
public render(): void { // Draw physics object on canvas based on position and weight
}
}
```

In this scenario, the "GameObject" abstract class sets out shared properties and methods, including "x" and "y" coordinates and the "update" and "render" methods.

Interfaces such as "Sprite", "Sound", and "PhysicsObject" detail particular properties and methods for each game object type.

Classes like "SpriteObject", "SoundObject", and "PhysicsObjectImpl" put these interfaces into action and provide distinctive implementations of "update" and "render" methods, tailored to their individual properties and necessities.

```
const gameObjects: GameObject[] = [ new SpriteObject(100, 100, spriteImage, 32, 32),
new SoundObject(0, 0, bgMusic),
new PhysicsObjectImpl(200, 200, 5, 10, 50)
];
gameObjects.forEach(gameObject => {
gameObject.update();
gameObject.render();
});
```

Utilizing abstract classes and interfaces ensures that every game object type adheres to a specific contract and includes necessary properties and methods. This approach results in more organized and maintainable code. For instance, we can generate an array of game objects and invoke their "update" and "render" methods without being aware of each class's specific implementation details.

Overall, abstract classes and interfaces are powerful OOP concepts enabling us to establish contracts for classes and confirm they implement required properties and methods.

Abstract classes facilitate defining a base class that can't be instantiated independently but can be inherited by other classes. They can outline both abstract and non-abstract methods, offering a default implementation for non-abstract methods. Abstract classes are helpful when wanting to establish a base class with shared functionality but allowing derived classes to implement specific methods.

On the other hand, interfaces allow us to define a set of properties and methods that a class must implement. They only define the class structure, not the implementation, functioning more like a contract that classes must adhere to. Interfaces are beneficial when defining a common structure for classes without a shared base class.

Abstract classes and interfaces offer benefits like code reuse, simpler maintenance, and fewer errors. By specifying a contract for classes, we can ensure they follow a certain structure and provide required properties and methods, leading to more organized and maintainable code, especially in large projects with numerous classes.

In the provided example, we used an abstract class to establish a base class for game objects and interfaces to detail specific properties and methods for each game object type. This approach made the code more organized and maintainable, and allowed treating different game object types as if they were the same, resulting in more flexible and reusable code.

Example that combines all OOP concepts in a single example:

Imagine you're building a music player app capable of supporting various audio file formats, including MP3, WAV, and FLAC. Each format has its own unique decoding, playing, and encoding methods.

To represent these audio files, you can create an abstract class named "AudioFile" that outlines common properties and methods like "name", "size", and "play". Additionally, you can design interfaces such as "Decoder", "Player", and "Encoder" that specify unique properties and methods for each audio file type.

```
abstract class AudioFile {
constructor(public name: string, public size: number) {}
public abstract play(): void;
}
interface Decoder {
decode(): void;
}
interface Player {
play(): void;
}
interface Encoder {
encode(): void;
}
class MP3File extends AudioFile implements Decoder, Player, Encoder {
constructor(name: string, size: number, public bitrate: number) {
super(name, size);
  }
  public decode(): void { // Decode MP3 file using specific algorithm
  }
public play(): void {  // Play MP3 file using specific player
  }
public encode(): void {  // Encode MP3 file using specific algorithm
  }
}
class WAVFile extends AudioFile implements Decoder, Player {
constructor(name: string, size: number, public bitrate: number)
{
super(name, size);
  }
  public decode(): void { // Decode WAV file using specific algorithm
  }
```

```
  public play(): void { // Play WAV file using specific player
  }
}
class FLACFile extends AudioFile implements Decoder, Player, Encoder {
constructor(name: string, size: number, public compression: number) {
super(name, size);
}
public decode(): void {  // Decode FLAC file using specific algorithm
}
public play(): void {  // Play FLAC file using specific player
  }
public encode(): void {  // Encode FLAC file using specific algorithm
  }
}
```

In this case, the "AudioFile" abstract class determines shared properties and methods like "name", "size", and "play". The interfaces like "Decoder", "Player", and "Encoder" detail distinct properties and methods for each audio file type.

Classes like "MP3File", "WAVFile", and "FLACFile" implement these interfaces and provide their custom implementations of the "decode", "play", and "encode" methods based on their specific properties and requirements. By utilizing inheritance, interfaces, abstract classes, and encapsulation, we can develop a flexible and expandable system for managing various audio file types. Each audio file type is represented by a separate class implementing the required interfaces and inheriting from the shared "AudioFile" base class. This approach results in more organized and maintainable code, particularly in large projects with multiple classes.

The advantages of using OOP concepts like inheritance, interfaces, abstract classes, and encapsulation include code reuse, simplified maintenance, and fewer errors. By establishing a standard structure for classes, we can ensure they adhere to a specific contract and provide the necessary properties and methods. This structure makes the code more organized and maintainable, especially in extensive projects with numerous classes.

In conclusion, by combining OOP concepts such as inheritance, interfaces, abstract classes, and encapsulation, we can create a flexible and scalable system for managing different object types. These concepts help guarantee that each object type follows a particular contract and includes the required properties and methods, making the code more organized and easier to maintain.

Example of a finance app that uses TypeScript concepts such as inheritance, polymorphism, and interfaces.
Imagine developing a finance app that handles various account types, like savings, checking, and investment accounts. Each account type has distinct interest rates, withdrawal limits, and account classifications. To represent these accounts, we can craft an abstract class named "Account" that lays out common properties and methods, such as "balance", "deposit", and "withdraw".

We can then create derived classes like "SavingsAccount", "CheckingAccount", and "InvestmentAccount" that inherit from the "Account" class and access these properties and methods using public methods. Additionally, we can establish an interface called "InterestCalculator" that specifies the unique method for calculating interest.

```typescript
abstract class Account {
|protected balance: number;
constructor(protected accountNumber: string, protected interestRate: number) {
this.balance = 0;
  }
public deposit(amount: number): void {
this.balance += amount;
  }
public abstract withdraw(amount: number): boolean;
public getBalance(): number {
return this.balance;
  }
}
class SavingsAccount extends Account implements InterestCalculator {
private withdrawalLimit: number;
constructor(accountNumber: string, interestRate: number, private monthlyWithdrawals: number) {
super(accountNumber, interestRate);
this.withdrawalLimit = 6;
  }
public withdraw(amount: number): boolean {
if (this.balance - amount < 0 || this.monthlyWithdrawals >= this.withdrawalLimit) {
return false;
}
this.balance -= amount;
this.monthlyWithdrawals++;
return true;
}
public calculateInterest(): number {
return this.balance * (this.interestRate / 12);
  }
}
class CheckingAccount extends Account {
private overdraftLimit: number;
constructor(accountNumber: string, interestRate: number, private overdraftFee: number) {
super(accountNumber, interestRate);
this.overdraftLimit = -500;
  }
public withdraw(amount: number): boolean {
if (this.balance - amount < this.overdraftLimit) {
this.balance -= this.overdraftFee;
return false;
}
this.balance -= amount;
return true;
  }
}
class InvestmentAccount extends Account implements InterestCalculator {
constructor(accountNumber: string, interestRate: number, private minBalance: number) {
super(accountNumber, interestRate);
  }
```

```typescript
public withdraw(amount: number): boolean {
if (this.balance - amount < this.minBalance) {
return false;
   }
this.balance -= amount;
return true;
}
public calculateInterest(): number {
return this.balance * (this.interestRate / 12) * 1.5;
  }
}
interface InterestCalculator {
calculateInterest(): number;
}
```

In this situation, the abstract "Account" class establishes attributes and methods like "balance," "deposit," and "withdraw."

Classes such as "SavingsAccount," "CheckingAccount," and "InvestmentAccount" derive from the "Account" class and access its properties and methods through public methods like "withdraw" and "getBalance."

Furthermore, the "SavingsAccount" and "InvestmentAccount" classes implement the "InterestCalculator" interface, which outlines the unique method for calculating interest.

By using inheritance and polymorphism, a versatile and adaptable system for handling various account types can be developed.

Each account type is represented by a distinct class that inherits from the general "Account" base class, providing its own implementation of interest calculation along with other exclusive features.

This strategy results in more organized and maintainable code, which is beneficial for web developers and programmers working with JavaScript and TypeScript.

Aspect Oriented Programming in TypeScript
Aspect-Oriented Programming (AOP) is a programming paradigm that focuses on separating cross-cutting concern from the main business logic of a program. TypeScript, a statically typed superset of JavaScript, supports AOP through the usage of decorators.

TypeScript's decorators enable developers to add metadata to classes, methods, properties, or parameters during compile-time. Decorators execute when the decorated element is declared, making them a practical tool for implementing AOP in TypeScript.

To utilize decorators for AOP in TypeScript, you must follow these steps:

Define the aspect: Define the cross-cutting concern that you want to apply to your code. For instance, logging is a common aspect that can be applied to multiple methods or classes.

Define the decorator: Define the decorator that will execute the aspect. A decorator is a function that takes the target (the class or method being decorated), the property key (the name of the method or property being decorated), and a property descriptor as its arguments. The decorator modifies the property descriptor to implement the aspect.

Apply the decorator: Apply the decorator to the class or method that you want to modify by using the @ symbol followed by the name of the decorator function. Here's an example of how to use decorators for AOP in TypeScript.

```
function log(target: any, key: string, descriptor: PropertyDescriptor) {
const originalMethod = descriptor.value;
descriptor.value = function (...args: any[]) {
console.log(`Calling ${key} with arguments ${args}`);
const result = originalMethod.apply(this, args);
console.log(`Result: ${result}`);
return result;
};
return descriptor;
}
// Apply the decorator class
MyClass {  @log  myMethod(arg1: string, arg2: number) {
console.log(`Executing myMethod with arguments ${arg1}, ${arg2}`);
return "myMethod result";
  }
}
// Usage const
myClass = new MyClass(); myClass.myMethod("hello", 42);

// Output:
// Calling myMethod with arguments hello, 4
// Executing myMethod with arguments hello, 42
// Result: myMethod result
```

In this example, the log function is the aspect that logs the method call and its arguments. The @log decorator is applied to the myMethod method of the MyClass class. When the myMethod method is called, the decorator intercepts the call and logs the arguments and the result.

AOP and decorators in a chat application:

```
// Define the aspect function
log(target: any, key: string, descriptor: PropertyDescriptor) {
const originalMethod = descriptor.value;
descriptor.value = function (...args: any[]) {
console.log(`Calling ${key} with arguments ${args}`);
const result = originalMethod.apply(this, args);
console.log(`Result: ${result}`);
return result;
};
return descriptor;
}
// Define another aspect function
retry(target: any, key: string, descriptor: PropertyDescriptor) {
const originalMethod = descriptor.value;
```

```
descriptor.value = async function (...args: any[]) { let retries = 3;
while (retries > 0) {
try {
const result = await originalMethod.apply(this, args);
return result;
}
catch (error) {
console.log(`Error calling ${key}: ${error}`);
retries--;
}
    }
    throw new Error(`Failed to call ${key} after 3 retries`);
  };
return descriptor;
}
// Define the chat service class

ChatService {
@log  @retry async sendMessage(message: string, recipient: string): Promise<void> {
// Send the message to the recipient
const response = await fetch("/api/send-message", {method: "POST", headers: {"Content-Type":
"application/json" }, body: JSON.stringify({ message, recipient }),
});
if (!response.ok) {
throw new Error(`Failed to send message: ${response.status}`);
    }
  }
}
// Usage const chatService = new ChatService();
chatService.sendMessage("Hello", "jane.doe").catch(console.error);
```

In this example, we have a ChatService class that sends messages to recipients using a web API. Our objective is to incorporate two aspects into this service: logging and retrying failed requests.

The log aspect logs the method call, arguments, and results. The retry aspect retries failed requests up to three times before throwing an error.

We apply the log and retry decorators to the sendMessage method of the ChatService class. When the sendMessage method is called, the decorators intercept the call and implement the aspects.

In the usage example, we create an instance of the ChatService class and invoke the sendMessage method with certain arguments. If the request fails, the retry aspect will attempt to resend the request up to three times before raising an error. The log aspect will log the method call, arguments, and results.

AOP and decorators in a CRM application

```
// Define the aspect function
log(target: any, key: string, descriptor: PropertyDescriptor) {
const originalMethod = descriptor.value;
descriptor.value = function (...args: any[]) {
console.log(`Calling ${key} with arguments ${args}`);
```

```typescript
    const result = originalMethod.apply(this, args);
    console.log(`Result: ${result}`);
    return result;
  };
  return descriptor;
}
// Define another aspect function
authorize(permission: string) {
  return function (target: any, key: string, descriptor: PropertyDescriptor) {
    const originalMethod = descriptor.value;
    descriptor.value = async function (...args: any[]) {      // Check if the user has the required permission
      if (!this.currentUser || !this.currentUser.permissions.includes(permission)) {
        throw new Error(`Unauthorized: user does not have permission ${permission}`);
      }
      // Call the original method
      const result = await originalMethod.apply(this, args);
      return result;
    };
    return descriptor;
  };
}
// Define the CRM service
class CRMService {
  private currentUser: any;
  @log  async getCustomer(id: string): Promise<any> {      // Get the customer from the API
    const response = await fetch(`/api/customers/${id}`, { method: "GET" });
    if (!response.ok) {
      throw new Error(`Failed to get customer: ${response.status}`);
    }
    const customer = await response.json();      return customer;
  }
  @log @authorize("create") async createCustomer(data: any): Promise<any> {
    // Create the customer via the API
    const response = await fetch(`/api/customers`, {
      method: "POST", headers: { "Content-Type": "application/json" },  body: JSON.stringify(data),
    });
    if (!response.ok) {
      throw new Error(`Failed to create customer: ${response.status}`);
    }
    const customer = await response.json();
    return customer;
  }
}
// Usage
const crmService = new CRMService();
// Set the current user
crmService["currentUser"] = {
  name: "John Doe", permissions: ["create", "read", "update", "delete"],
};
// Call the createCustomer method
crmService.createCustomer({name: "xyz xyz", email: "xyz.xyz@example.com" }).catch(console.error);
```

```
// Call the getCustomer method
crmService.getCustomer("123").catch(console.error);
```

In this example, we have a CRMService class that provides access to customer data via a web API. We want to add two aspects to this service: logging and authorization.

The log aspect logs the method call and its arguments, as well as the result. The authorize aspect checks if the current user has a specific permission before calling the original method. If the user does not have the required permission, an error is thrown.

We apply the log and authorize decorators to the createCustomer method of the CRMService class. The getCustomer method is only decorated with the log decorator.

In the usage example, we create an instance of the CRMService class and set the current user. We then call the createCustomer method with some data. If the current user has the "create" permission, the authorize aspect will allow the call to proceed. Otherwise, an error will be thrown. The log aspect will log the method call and its arguments, as well as the result.

Conclusion: Object-Oriented and Aspect-Oriented Programming in TypeScript

As we have seen, **Object-Oriented Programming (OOP)** and **Aspect-Oriented Programming (AOP)** are foundational paradigms that complement each other in building robust, scalable, and maintainable applications. **TypeScript**, being a superset of JavaScript, bridges the gap between these paradigms and practical application development by providing tools and constructs for modular design, reusability, and separation of concerns.

The Role of OOP in Application Design

OOP is pivotal in designing large-scale applications because it offers a structured approach to code organization. By encapsulating data and behavior into cohesive units (classes), OOP reduces complexity and fosters reusability. TypeScript enhances JavaScript's prototypal inheritance model by adding class-based constructs, access modifiers, and static typing, all of which make the development process more predictable and error-resistant.

The key advantages of OOP in TypeScript include:

Modularity: Classes and objects enable modular design, where each module focuses on a specific functionality. This leads to better separation of concerns, making applications easier to develop and maintain.

Reusability: Features like inheritance and polymorphism allow developers to reuse and extend code across multiple parts of an application.

Scalability: OOP structures make it easier to scale applications by adding new features or modifying existing ones without introducing bugs.

Type Safety: TypeScript's static typing system ensures that objects conform to their expected structures, reducing runtime errors.

For instance, when designing an e-commerce application, OOP principles help define core entities such as User, Product, Order, and Payment. Each class encapsulates data and operations specific to its role, ensuring clear responsibilities and reducing the likelihood of conflicts or redundancies.

The Role of AOP in Addressing Cross-Cutting Concerns

Aspect-Oriented Programming, though less common than OOP, plays a critical role in handling **cross-cutting concerns**—features that affect multiple parts of an application. These concerns, such as logging, authentication, error handling, and performance monitoring, often result in repetitive code scattered across the codebase. AOP eliminates this repetition by modularizing such concerns into **aspects**, which are applied dynamically to the main application logic.

TypeScript's **decorators** serve as a practical implementation of AOP. With decorators, developers can: Inject behaviour into classes, methods, or properties without altering their core logic.

Centralize shared functionality like logging or error handling, making the codebase cleaner and more maintainable.

Adapt application behaviour dynamically based on context (e.g., user role or runtime conditions).

For example, a logging decorator can uniformly apply logging to multiple methods, ensuring consistency and saving time during debugging. Similarly, authentication or authorization concerns can be handled with custom decorators that enforce access control across the application.

Balancing OOP and AOP

While OOP structures the core logic of an application, AOP enhances it by abstracting away repetitive tasks.

Both paradigms have distinct but complementary roles:

OOP focuses on the "what" and "how" of an application. It defines the core entities, their interactions, and the underlying operations. This is especially crucial for building domain-specific logic.

AOP focuses on the "where" and "when" of additional concerns. It determines where and when cross-cutting logic should be applied without cluttering the core code.

Together, they result in cleaner, more maintainable code.

For example, consider a financial application that processes payments:

The OOP layer would define core classes like Transaction, Account, and Bank. These classes encapsulate the business logic, such as computing interest or validating transactions.

The AOP layer would handle logging, monitoring, and security concerns. A logging aspect ensures every transaction is recorded, while a security aspect verifies user permissions.

Practical Benefits of OOP and AOP in TypeScript
Cleaner Codebase:

OOP reduces duplication by allowing inheritance and polymorphism.

AOP centralizes repetitive concerns, removing redundant code scattered throughout the application.

Improved Maintainability:

Changes in core logic (OOP) or cross-cutting concerns (AOP) can be made in a single place without affecting other parts of the application.

This modularity leads to faster debugging and easier feature addition.

Scalability:

With OOP, adding new entities (e.g., new classes) is straightforward.

AOP ensures new cross-cutting concerns can be introduced without modifying existing logic.

Enhanced Collaboration:

Teams can work independently on different aspects of the application. For example, one team might focus on implementing business logic using OOP, while another team develops reusable decorators for logging or security.

Future-Proofing:

TypeScript's static typing and support for modern paradigms ensure the code is robust and adaptable to future requirements.

Challenges and Considerations

While OOP and AOP bring significant advantages, they also introduce challenges:

Overhead:

Excessive use of OOP features, such as deep inheritance hierarchies, can make code difficult to understand and maintain.

Misuse of AOP (e.g., too many aspects or unnecessary advice) can lead to confusion, making the behavior of the application unpredictable.

Learning Curve:

Developers new to OOP may struggle with concepts like polymorphism or abstract classes.

AOP, being less common, requires familiarity with decorators and a deeper understanding of runtime behaviour.

Performance:

AOP adds a layer of abstraction, which can impact performance, especially if aspects are overused or applied inefficiently.

OOP, particularly when using inheritance, can lead to slower performance if not optimized properly.

Tooling and Debugging:

Debugging applications with heavy AOP usage can be challenging because aspects modify runtime behaviour.

Advanced debugging tools and techniques are often required to trace execution flow.

Despite these challenges, careful design and best practices mitigate these issues. For instance, avoiding over-engineering in OOP and using AOP sparingly for genuinely cross-cutting concerns can result in an efficient and maintainable codebase.

TypeScript's Unique Position

TypeScript stands out as a language that seamlessly integrates OOP and AOP:

Its class-based syntax makes it ideal for OOP, allowing developers to write expressive and type-safe code.
Its decorator feature aligns perfectly with AOP principles, enabling developers to modularize concerns effectively.

Additionally, TypeScript's interoperability with JavaScript ensures that legacy code can gradually adopt these paradigms without a complete rewrite. Its extensive ecosystem and support for modern development workflows make it a preferred choice for projects ranging from small-scale applications to enterprise-level systems.

Real-World Applications

Web Development:

OOP structures the core components of web applications, such as controllers, services, and models.
AOP handles cross-cutting concerns like logging HTTP requests or managing authentication.

Microservices:

OOP organizes individual microservices with clearly defined entities and behaviors.
AOP manages global concerns like monitoring, tracing, and service-level security.

Game Development:

OOP is essential for defining game objects, behaviours, and interactions.
AOP can dynamically adjust gameplay mechanics or log player actions for analytics.

Enterprise Software:

OOP provides a robust framework for implementing business logic.
AOP ensures compliance, logging, and error management across complex systems.

The Future of OOP and AOP in TypeScript

With TypeScript's growing popularity, the adoption of OOP and AOP is expected to increase. Future advancements in TypeScript, such as enhanced support for decorators or improved runtime performance, will further simplify these paradigms' implementation. Additionally, as the developer community matures, best practices and design patterns for combining OOP and AOP will become more standardized.

Emerging technologies like **serverless computing** and **AI-driven development tools** will also benefit from the modularity and maintainability provided by these paradigms. For instance, serverless architectures can use OOP for structuring functions and AOP for managing deployment pipelines or monitoring performance.

Final Thoughts

In conclusion, OOP and AOP are not merely programming paradigms but essential tools for managing complexity in modern application development. TypeScript's support for these paradigms enables developers to write clean, efficient, and maintainable code. While OOP structures the foundation of an application, AOP abstracts repetitive concerns, allowing developers to focus on core functionality.

By leveraging these paradigms together, developers can create applications that are not only powerful but also adaptable to evolving requirements. The synergy between OOP and AOP ensures that TypeScript remains a top choice for developers looking to build robust applications for the future.

11. Advanced Usage and Build

Introduction

TypeScript has become a cornerstone of modern JavaScript development, offering strong typing, enhanced tooling, and powerful constructs that improve code maintainability and scalability. While beginners may focus on the basics of types, interfaces, and classes, mastering advanced TypeScript usage and build processes unlocks the full potential of the language. This guide delves into **advanced concepts like utility types, conditional types, mapped types, decorators, and TypeScript-specific build tools.**

1. Advanced Type Features

1.1 Utility Types

Utility types in TypeScript simplify type manipulation, making code cleaner and more concise. These built-in types are crucial for advanced scenarios:

Partial<T>: Makes all properties of T optional.
Required<T>: Converts optional properties in T to required.
Pick<T, K>: Selects a subset of properties from T.
Omit<T, K>: Excludes specific properties from T.
Record<K, T>: Constructs a type with keys from K and values of T.
ReturnType<T>: Extracts the return type of a function.

Example:

```
type User = {
  id: number;
  name: string;
  email?: string;
};
type OptionalUser = Partial<User>;
type RequiredUser = Required<User>;
type EmailOnly = Pick<User, 'email'>;
type NoEmail = Omit<User, 'email'>;
```

1.2 Conditional Types

Conditional types enable dynamic type transformations based on conditions.

Syntax:

```
T extends U ? X : Y
```

Example:

```
type IsString<T> = T extends string ? 'Yes' : 'No';
type Test1 = IsString<string>; // 'Yes'
type Test2 = IsString<number>; // 'No'
```

They are pivotal for building generic utility types like Extract, Exclude, and NonNullable.

1.3 Mapped Types

Mapped types allow you to transform properties of an existing type into a new type.

Example:

```
type ReadonlyType<T> = {
  readonly [K in keyof T]: T[K];
};
type MutableType<T> = {
  -readonly [K in keyof T]: T[K];
};
type User = {
  id: number;
  name: string;
};
type ReadonlyUser = ReadonlyType<User>;
type MutableUser = MutableType<ReadonlyUser>;
```

1.4 Template Literal Types

Template literal types help define string-based types with embedded variables.

Example:

```
type Lang = 'en' | 'fr';
type Locale = `${Lang}-${'US' | 'FR'}`;
// Locale = 'en-US' | 'en-FR' | 'fr-US' | 'fr-FR'
```

1.5 Advanced Generics

Generics extend reusability. Advanced usage includes:

Generic Constraints:

```
function merge<T extends object, U extends object>(obj1: T, obj2: U): T & U {
  return { ...obj1, ...obj2 };
}
```

Default Generics:

```
interface Box<T = string> {
  value: T;
}
```

2. Advanced Concepts in TypeScript

2.1 Type Guards

Custom type guards ensure type safety during runtime.

Example:

```
function isString(value: unknown): value is string {
  return typeof value === 'string';
}
```

2.2 Decorators

Decorators are experimental but widely used in frameworks like Angular. They enhance classes and methods with metadata.

Example:

```
function Log(target: any, propertyKey: string) {
  console.log(`${propertyKey} was accessed`);
}
class MyClass {
  @Log
  greet() {
    console.log("Hello");
  }
}
```

2.3 Module Augmentation

Enhance existing modules by adding new functionality.

Example:

```
declare module 'express' {
  interface Request {
    user?: { id: string; name: string };
  }
}
```

2.4 Advanced Type Narrowing

Refined narrowing strategies using **in**, **instanceof**, and **custom guards**.

Example:

```
type Shape = Circle | Square;
if ('radius' in shape) {
  // Narrow to Circle
}
```

2.5 Symbol and Unique Symbols

symbol offers unique and immutable values. Use unique symbol for advanced type-safe keys.

Example:

const uniqueKey: unique symbol = Symbol('key');

3. Advanced Build Processes

3.1 Configuring tsconfig.json

Customizing the tsconfig.json file ensures optimized builds. Key settings:

strict: Enables strict type checking.
target: Specifies the ECMAScript version.
module: Defines the module format (e.g., CommonJS, ESM).
paths and **baseUrl**: Simplify module imports.

3.2 TypeScript Compiler APIs

Directly interact with TypeScript compiler APIs for custom tooling.

Example:

```
import ts from 'typescript';
const source = 'let x: string = "hello";';
const result = ts.transpileModule(source, { compilerOptions: { module: ts.ModuleKind.CommonJS } });
console.log(result.outputText);
```

3.3 Bundling with Webpack/Vite

Integrate TypeScript with modern bundlers:

Use the **ts-loader** or **esbuild-loader** for Webpack.
Leverage **Vite** for faster development and TypeScript support.

Example (Webpack):

```
module.exports = {
  entry: './src/index.ts',
  module: {
    rules: [
      {
        test: /\.tsx?$/,
        use: 'ts-loader',
        exclude: /node_modules/,
      },
    ],
  },
  resolve: {
    extensions: ['.tsx', '.ts', '.js'],
  },
```

```
};
```
3.4 Linting and Formatting

Enhance code quality with **ESLint** and **Prettier**.

Example (.eslintrc.json):

```
{
  "parser": "@typescript-eslint/parser",
  "extends": [
    "eslint:recommended",
    "plugin:@typescript-eslint/recommended"
  ],
  "rules": {
    "@typescript-eslint/no-unused-vars": ["error"]
  }
}
```

3.5 CI/CD with TypeScript

Automate testing and deployment with CI/CD pipelines. Steps include:

Type Checking:

tsc –noEmit

Linting:

eslint . --ext .ts
Testing: Run unit tests with frameworks like Jest or Mocha.

3.6 Performance Optimization

Use **incremental** compilation in tsconfig.json.
Utilize **composite projects** for large codebases.

3.7 Advanced Project References

Divide large projects into smaller, maintainable units using project references.

Example:

```
// tsconfig.json
{
  "files": [],
  "references": [{ "path": "./core" }, { "path": "./utils" }]
}
```

4. Future Trends in TypeScript

Native ESM Support: Improved compatibility with Node.js.

Gradual Typing: Interoperability with non-typed JavaScript.
Pattern Matching: Adding functional programming capabilities.
AI-Driven Tooling: AI-powered type inference and error suggestions.

Let's Begin,

In this chapter, we will use the types you've learned and combine them to solve advanced use cases, as a form of master class in TypeScript. For each type I will present, we will review the needs of the type, consider what types we have in our toolbelt that can address these needs, and then combine and build our advanced types step-by-step from the ground up together, so you can see how they're built and how to make the choices necessary when practicing TypeScript at an advanced proficiency.

We will start with the simpler of these advanced type challenges and use these to create types that in turn can be used to validate stages in the latter advanced types. And in finishing, I'll also list some places for further exploration of advanced types that can help you continue your learning journey and connect you to communities that can help you as you progress.

Now, on to the first advanced case!

Expect and IsEqual

If you've written runtime tests before, you'll be familiar with assertion libraries. The Mocha test framework uses the Chai assertion library; others such as Jest and Playwright use built-in assertion libraries. These provide the **equals** function you can use to assert that a value matches your expectations. So, as we'll be building the types in this section from ground up, let's start by making our own compile-time assertion library, to make it faster to test our types!

What we want is a type we can use like this:

```
type OurType<U> = { // Fancy TypeScript here to (eg.) convert a union into
// an array
}
type IntendedResult = [1, 2, 3];
type Result = IsEqual<OurType<1 | 2 | 3>, IntendedResult> ✓ type Result = IsEqual<number,
IntendedResult> ✗
```

Our desired IsEqual type

Unfortunately, the most straightforward conditional here will not work:

```
type IsEqual<A, B extends A> = A;
// It works!
type Result = IsEqual<1, 1>; ✓
// It works! type Result = IsEqual<1 | 2 | 3, "Invalid value">; ✗
 // It doesn't work type Result = IsEqual<1 | 2 | 3, 1>; ✓
```

A simple, but incomplete, approach to the IsEqual type

The problem is that in that last type, we want **IsEqual** to assert that the first and second arguments are equal types, not just that **B** is compatible with **A**. To solve this, break it into two parts: equality and then assertion.

The equality part is tricky. We can't use a simple conditional like the following because that'll do the same thing – only compare compatibility:

```
type IsEqual<A, B> =
  A extends B
    ? true
    : false;
type Result = IsEqual<1 | 2 | 3, 1>;
❯  type Result = true;
```

The problem with our simple approach

We're going to need to go a bit deeper here. To solve this, we're going to use a feature of how conditional operators are implemented internally in TypeScript (this is the Advanced Usage chapter, alright?): conditional types allow you to compare **extends** against generic functions and types; but to allow this, they would need to be able to compare the type parameters of the generics too, and these generic parameters are unknown so they cannot be compared. Instead, conditional operators internally defer the match and require the generic parameters and related types of both branches match each other directly. And this direct match is what we want to leverage for our **IsEqual** type. The result is this:

```
type IsEqual<A, B> =
  (<T>() => T extends A ? 1 : 2) extends
    (<T>() => T extends B ? 1 : 2)
// 1. ^ T is unknown, so extends requires it ^ is identical to this param.
// 2. And because it is identical, extends instead resolves
//    both sides down to be *f(A) extends f(B)* - which it
//    assumes can only be true if both X and Y are the -same- value.
    ? true
    : false;
```

Using deferred types to match cases exactly, rather than matching via extension.
Great! Now we have a type that checks types are equal. Now, we can use a type constraint to surface the true/false result:

```
type Assert<T extends true> = T;
type ResultN =
Assert<IsEqual<1 | 3 | 3, 1>>; ✘ // Yay, it works!
type ResultY = Assert<IsEqual<1, 1>>; ✔ // Yay, it still works!
```

Converting our true/false result type into a testable assertion for types

This has limitations – it won't work in some intersectional type cases. In most cases, this won't matter too much; but if it does, you'll need to go further than this chapter should cover, and you should use the extended implementation from the NPM type-plus package to do this detailed type comparison.
Compute

```
interface Employee {
    employeeNumber: number
    startDate: Date
}

interface Person {
    firstName: string
    lastName: string
    address: Address
}

interface Address {
    street: string
}
    ┌─────────────────────────────────────────────┐
    │ type EmployedPerson = Employee & Person       │
    └─────────────────────────────────────────────┘
type EmployedPerson = Employee & Person;
```

Figure TypeScript doesn't always show the most useful type

While accurate (and fast), this output is not very enlightening! So, our next type will be a type that instead displays the actual fields of a computed type, so we can see what's going on.

To do this, let's use a mapped type, to get all the fields from a target type defined in our generic parameters, and then pull all the fields onto our own type.

```
// For every key available across the whole of T, assign it
// to the same field's type (essentially copying type T into
// ourselves).
type Compute<T> = {
[Key in keyof T]: T[Key]
};
type EmployedPerson = Compute<Employee & Person>;
❯   type EmployedPerson = {
employeeNumber: number; startDate: Date; firstName: string; lastName: string; address: Address;
}
```

Copying the keys from a complex type (e.g., intersection) onto a new type in order to simplify them Great! But nested types (e.g., **address** field) are still obscured. To solve this, we can use a recursive intersection type to force computation of all the fields, as follows:

```
// We sort our unions by most-likely case first to allow TS to
// execute faster where possible. type Primitive =
    | string
    | number
    | null
    | undefined
    | boolean
    | bigint
    | symbol;
type Compute<T> = {
```

```
[Key in keyof T]: T[Key] extends Primitive | Date
? T[Key]: Compute<T[Key]>
};
```

Adding recursion for nested objects and arrays

However, in practice, this does exactly the same thing.

```
type EmployeedPerson = {
    employeeNumber: number;
    startDate: Date;
    firstName: string;
    lastName: string;
    address: Compute<Address>;
}

type EmployeedPerson = Compute<Employee & Person>;
```

Figure Our Compute type shows us more helpful information

What we need is to force TypeScript to process all the fields, and not take any shortcuts. One way to do this is to use an intersection type (**&**) – as discussed before, TypeScript merges all the fields from an intersection rather than overriding them, and to do this, it has to process them. We don't need to intersect to add any new fields, so we just intersect against a known empty type – the easiest built-in one being the **unknown** type:

```
type Compute<T> = {
[Key in keyof T]: T[Key] extends Primitive | Date
        ? T[Key]
        : Compute<T[Key]>
} & unknown;
type EmployeedPerson = Compute<Employee & Person>;
>   type EmployeedPerson = {
employeeNumber: number; startDate: Date; firstName: string; lastName: string;
address: {
street: string;
};
}
```

Intersecting triggers exact computation of all keys
JsonOf

Let's now use some more of our computed types to build the return type for this function:

```
function toPlainJsonObject<Value>(value: Value): ??? {
return JSON.parse(JSON.stringify(value));
}
```

Our target use case for a JsonOf<T> utility type
We will start with an example:

```
interface Person {
id: number
name: string
dateOfBirth: Date
address: {
street: string
postcode: string
movedInOn: Date
  }
}
const jenny = {
id: 1, name: 'Jenny', dateOfBirth: new Date(1990, 1, 1), address: {
street: '123 Some Street', postcode: '1234', movedInOn: new Date(2020, 1, 1),
},
} satisfies Person;
const result = toPlainJsonObject(jenny);
> const result = any;  // We can do better than this
```

Demonstrating the need for a type-safe approach to JSON.parse

It would be more helpful if the function had returned a result type more like this:

```
type JsonOf<Person> = { id: number     name: string     dateOfBirth: string
address: { street: string   postcode: string   movedInOn: string
  }
}
```

An example of the mapping we'd need in the result For JSON, we convert the following:

From	To

So, our result type is a mapped type of **Value**, with a conditional field type that translates following the aforementioned mappings:

```
type JsonOf<T extends object> = {
   [Key in keyof T]:
      T[Key] extends boolean | number | string ? T[Key]
      : T[Key] extends Date ? string
      : never
}
```

Mapping the fields to their serialized forms
But this isn't quite right:

```
type Result = JsonOf<Person>;
>   type Result = {id: number; ✓ // Yay, it worked!
name: string; ✓ // Yay, it worked!
dateOfBirth: string; ✓
address: { ✗ // Oh no, we forgot
```

```
        street: string; ✓ // nested objects
        postcode: string; ✓
        movedInOn: Date;  ✗
            };
    }
```

Don't forget nested types!

So, we need to recurse into the child value, like so:

```
type JsonOf<T extends object> = {
    [Key in keyof T]:
        T[Key] extends string | number | boolean ? T[Key]
        : T[Key] extends Date ? string: T[Key] extends object ? JsonOf<T[Key]>: never
}
type Result = JsonOf<Person>;
❯   type Result = {
id: number; ✓
name: string; ✓
dateOfBirth: string; ✓
address: {✓
street: string; ✓
postcode: string; ✓
movedInOn: Date; ✓ // Yay, it worked!
};
}
```

Adding recursion for nested types

But thinking more about it, why not allow JsonOf to be used on more than object types, as in practice, strings, numbers, objects, and arrays, all can be converted to JSON. So finally, let's invert our mapped type so that the conditional is topmost:

```
type JsonOf<T> =
    T extends string | number | boolean ? T
    : T extends Date | symbol ? string
    : T extends object ? {
        [Key in keyof T]: JsonOf<T[Key]>
    }
    : T extends (infer Item)[] ? JsonOf<Item>
    : never;
type A = JsonOf<string>; ✓
type B = JsonOf<number>; ✓
type C = JsonOf<Person>; ✓
type D = JsonOf<Person[]>; ✓
```

Supporting recursion over arrays

One last step to take now – when converting to JSON, all function values are set to **null** in arrays and are removed from objects. Setting to null is easy, but excluding functions is more tricky and needs a couple of utility types. Let's do that next:

```
// Utility type 1: Map the keys to their values, but may any
// key whose value is of type ExcludeValues to never type
ExtractKeysNotMatching<T extends object, ExcludeValues> = {
[Key in keyof T]: T[Key] extends ExcludeValues ? never : Key
}
interface Test {
foo: string    bar: number    baz: () => {}
} type Result1 = ExtractKeysNotMatching<Test, () => {}>
❯   type Result1 = {
foo: "foo"; bar: "bar";
baz: never;
// Mapped to never, now we need to exclude it
    }
// Utility type 2: Get all field value types of T as a union
// (any never values are excluded by TypeScript, because you
// can't have a union against never)
type ValuesAsUnion<T extends object> = T[keyof T];
type Result2 = ValuesAsUnion<
ExtractKeysNotMatching<Test, () => {}>>
❯   type Result2 = "foo" | "bar"
```

Excluding fields that are function types

Great! Now we have a way to exclude functions. Let's put the whole thing together:

```
type ExtractKeysNotMatching<T extends object, ExcludeValues> = {
[Key in keyof T]: T[Key] extends ExcludeValues ? never : Key
}
type ValuesAsUnion<T extends object> = T[keyof T];
type JsonOf<T> = T extends string | number | boolean ? T
  : T extends Date | symbol ? string
  : T extends Function ? null
  : T extends object ? {
    [Key in ValuesAsUnion<
        ExtractKeysNotMatching<T, () => {}>
      >]: JsonOf<T[Key]>
  }
  : T extends (infer Item)[] ? JsonOf<Item>
  : never;
```

The final code for our JsonOf type
Flatten

In our next advanced type, we want to represent the return type of the following function:

```
function fullFlatten<Values extends unknown[]>(values: Values): ??? {
const result: unknown[] = [];
```

```
function visit(x: unknown) {
if (Array.isArray(x)) {
        x.forEach(visit);
     }
else {
        result.push(x)
     }
   }
   values.forEach(visit);
return result;
}
const flattenedArray = fullFlatten([1, 2, [3, [4], 5], 6])
>   const flattenedArray = [ 1, 2, 3, 4, 5, 6 ]
```

Our target use case for our Flatten type

The current built-in return type for **Array.flat()** loses the result order for tuples, so we can also improve on this.

As a start, we know from the "Recursive Types" that in order to transform an array or tuple, we need to deal with one item at a time – by inferring the first (or "head") element of the array, transforming it, and then passing the remainder of the array into a recursion of our own type. So, we can start by writing the skeleton of our type like this:

```
type Flatten<T extends unknown[]> =
    T extends [infer Head, ...infer Rest]
        ? // Do something
        : [];
```

Using conditional types' pattern matching allows us to infer the types of the head and remaining elements.
Next, we know that we need to check if the head element is an array. If it is, then we need to instead call **Flatten** on it too and then spread that into our result array; otherwise, we can just add the value directly to our result array. Either way, this done, we can then recurse on the rest of the input array, as shown in the following code:

```
type Flatten<T extends unknown[]> =
    T extends [infer Head, ...infer Rest]
        ? Head extends unknown[]      // Is the head element  // an array?
            ? [
                ...Flatten<Head>,
                ...Flatten<Rest>,
]
: [
Head, Flatten<Rest>, ]: [];
type Result = Flatten<[1, 2, [3, [4], 5], 6]>;  >   type Result: [ 1, 2, 3, 4, 5, 6 ];
```
Recursively flatten the head element, and then repeat for the remaining elements.

UrlParameters

For this type, we want to provide the parameter type for the following method:

```
function interpolateUrl<Url extends string>(url: Url, parameters: ???) {
}
const result = interpolateUrl(
'api/person/:personId/address/:addressId',
{
// Here we want our function to type-check the arguments needed against the given Url.
personId: '123', ✓        addressId: '1', ✓      doesNotExist: 'foo' ✗
  }
);
```

> const result = 'api/person/123/address/1';

Our target use case for our UrlParameters type

To do this, we need to construct a record type for the parameters whose keys are dictated by the **:param** patterns in the URL string.

We can split up a URL string into parts using recursion across the string, matching it against template literals to extract pieces of the URL as types:

```
type SplitUrl<Url> =
Url extends `${infer Head}/${infer Rest}` ? [Head, ...SplitUrl<Rest>]: Url extends string ? [Url]
: never;
type Result = SplitUrl<'api/person/:personId/address/:addressId'>;
```

> type Result = ["api", "person", ":personId", "address", ":addressId"]

Using a conditional type, we can infer the pieces of the template literal and then use them to construct the result.

Now, we can convert the result tuple into a union using an indexer and then use **Extract** (the utility type, the opposite of **Exclude**) to get just those keys that match another string template type:

```
type Result = SplitUrl<'api/person/:personId/address/:addressId'>[number];
```

> type Result = "api" | "person" | ":personId" | "address" | ":addressId" type Result = Extract<
SplitUrl<'api/person/:personId/address/:addressId'>[number],
`:${string}`
>;

> type Result = ":personId" | ":addressId"

Filter the extracted pieces of the URL pattern to only those matching the pattern we're using for URL parameters.
Now we just construct a record with that type:
```
function interpolateUrl<const Url extends string>(url: Url,    parameters:
Record<Extract<SplitUrl<Url>[number], `:${string}`>, string> ) {
}
```

Our final result is a record using the keys we extracted for the URL parameters

UrlParameters with Optional Params

Let's improve our UrlParameters example to allow for optional parameters too, as shown in the following code example:

```
const result = interpolateUrl(
  'api/person/:personId/(address/:addressId)',
  {
    personId: '123',
  }
);
const result = 'api/person/123/';
```

Example how we could specify optional URL parameters

The type for parameters is now more like this:

```
type Result =
  Record<RequiredParameters, string>
  & Partial<Record<OptionalParamters, string>>;
>   type Result = {
personId: string
 addressId?: string
}
```

Our improved UrlParameters type: A combination of required and optional parameters. So now we need to split up our string into two groups of results. To do this, we return an object with known fields – one an array of required fields and the other an array of optional fields:

```
type SplitUrlWithOptionals<Url> =
Url extends `(${infer Head})/${infer Rest}`
    ? (
        {
          required: []
          optional: SplitUrl<Head>
        }
        & SplitUrlWithOptionals<Rest>
      )
  : Url extends `(${infer Head})`
    ? {        required: []
        optional: SplitUrl<Head>
      }
  : Url extends `${infer Head}/${infer Rest}`
    ? (
        {
          required: SplitUrl<Head> optional: []
        }
        & SplitUrlWithOptionals<Rest>
      )
  : Url extends string
    ? {
        required: [Url] optional: []
      }
  : never;
```

Collecting the required and the optional fields into separate fields of a result type

Unfortunately, this won't work. The intersections will end up trying to intersect subtypes such as the following, which we cannot index to extract a value for (it will index to return **never** because a value could not fulfill both variants):

```
type ComputedIntersection = {
required: ['a'], optional: ['b'],
} & {
required: ['y'], optional: ['z'] }
type Result = ComputedIntersection['required'][number];
> type Result = never;
```

The problem: non-intersecting fields are merged to a never type

Instead, we need to merge the subtypes instead of intersecting them, merging together the values in each array:

```
type MergeUrlParamSplits<A extends {
required: unknown[]
optional: unknown[]
},
B extends {
required: unknown[]
optional: unknown[]
}> = {
required: [...A['required'], ...B['required']]
optional: [...A['optional'], ...B['optional']] }
type SplitUrlWithOptionals<Url> =
Url extends `(${infer Head})/${infer Rest}`? MergeUrlParamSplits<
        {
          required: []
          optional: SplitUrl<Head>
        },
        SplitUrlWithOptionals<Rest>
  >    : Url extends `(${infer Head})`
      ? {
required: []
        optional: SplitUrl<Head>
    }
  : Url extends `${infer Head}/${infer Rest}` ? MergeUrlParamSplits<
        {
          required: SplitUrl<Head> optional: []
        },
        SplitUrlWithOptionals<Rest>
    : Url extends string
    ? {
        required: [Url]
optional: []
    }
  : never;
type Result =
```

```
        SplitUrlWithOptionals<"user/:userId/(dashboard/:dashboardId)/(:another)">;
>   type Result = {
        required: ["user", ":userId"];
        optional: ["dashboard", ":dashboardId", ":another"];
    }
```

Merging the array fields instead of intersecting them

That's looking better. Now we apply the same technique with the **Extract** utility type.

```
type UrlData = SplitUrlWithOptionals<"api/person/:personId/(address/:addressId)">;
type Result = Record<Extract<UrlData['required'][number], `:${string}`>, string>
& Partial<Record<Extract<UrlData['optional'][number], `:${string}`>, string>>
type P = {
        ":personId": string;
        ":addressId"?: string | undefined;
}
```

Applying our same Extract filter to include only the URL parameters

Nearly there. Now we reduce the **Record<Extract<...>>** repetition and rewrite the keys to strip the leading ':' using a mapped helper type, and we're done:

```
type RecordOfUrlParams<UrlParams extends string> = {
[UrlParam in Extract<UrlParams, `:${string}`> as ':'s
UrlParam extends `:${infer Param}` ? Param : never
]: string;
}
type UrlParamsOf<T extends string> =
RecordOfUrlParams<SplitUrlWithOptionals<T>['required'][number]>
& Partial<RecordOfUrlParams<SplitUrlWithOptionals<T>['optional'][number]>>
// Let's test it out:
type Result = UrlParamsOf<'api/person/:personId/(address/:addressId)'>
 type Result = {
personId: string;
addressId?: string | undefined;
}
function interpolateUrl<const Url extends string>(url: Url, params: UrlParamsOf<Url> ): string {
}
const url = interpolateUrl(
'api/person/:personId/(address/:addressId)',
{"personId": '123'} ✓ )
```

Our final version, making Record<Extract<...>> into a reusable type and cleaning up the field names at the same time.

Performance

We have mastered the language; now we must master the tool. As helpful as TypeScript is, it also represents a step between writing your code and running it in production. Large or complex code bases with numerous dependencies and intricate control flow can take some time to analyze and make this step slow.

Delays between writing code and running it are worth reducing. Aside from having small cost implications of dev time and CI/CD running expenses, there is a larger cost that is often overlooked: the human issue.

As humans, we love the creative process. Psychologically our desire to be creative, productive individuals means we bias toward the things we find most success in and err away from activity we experience friction from. Unfortunately, this means that if a build process is slow, we subconsciously avoid doing it. However, quality only occurs from feedback.

Static analysis helps raise quality by bringing large parts of the testing feedback cycle back within the creation process; but this feedback cycle is only of the code quality, not the quality of the UX flow or the suitability of the final product in market. Avoiding refining complex code can lead to it becoming even more complicated, or to it becoming less reliable. And so, far beyond being a simple convenience, it is in fact neurologically imperative to keep your team's build-measure-learn time to a minimum, to help speed up feedback cycles – learning loops – and thereby improve the quality of your product, as well as your team's detailed understanding of it.

There are several steps in the build-measure-learn cycle – and they should all be kept as short and integrated as possible. Other books will deal with other aspects of this – how to reduce test execution time, how to improve data collection rate, how to improve ideation process – but in mastering TypeScript, we should ensure we understand how to improve its performance too.

This section is therefore dedicated to how to optimize the performance of your TypeScript configuration. We will cover how to utilize caching to store and reuse previously computed types; ways to increase caching and reduce computationally expensive inferred types and intersection types; and code partitioning strategies to permit incremental build. Lastly you will discover how to debug and isolate compilation performance issues in CPU and memory using some built-in and community tools for TypeScript.

To be able to optimize wisely (without overstepping per Knuth's principle) also ensures we understand the how of what we have built and is an important step to being a TypeScript expert.

Through the concepts covered in this chapter, you will gain a deep understanding of how to optimize TypeScript code for performance. By implementing these best practices, you can ensure that your TypeScript applications are more efficient to build and therefore more humanly likely to better maintain and scale in your product.

Reducing Inline Types
The first step in reducing any complex computation (such as, but not limited to, static type analysis) is to not do it. Caching allows us to store and reuse previously computed types and therefore is our first point of call-in improving TypeScript performance.

Take the following code for example:
```
const bob: { firstName: string    lastName: string } = getPerson('1');
const fred: { firstName: string    lastName: string } = getPerson('2');
```

Simple identical anonymous types
In this code, you would've thought that TypeScript would be smart enough to recognize that the two pieces of code are the same and cache the anonymous type from the first piece of code to reuse for the second. But unfortunately, it doesn't – it will instead go ahead and recalculate the type anew for both

cases. This would be trivial in the preceding case, but when type computation starts to get complex involving intersections or inheritance, it starts to cost:

```
function renderName(employee: { firstName: string, lastName: string } &
Dto<EmploymentRecord> & AnotherComplexType): string {
return `${person.firstName} ${person.lastName}`;
}
function greet(person: { firstName: string, lastName: string } &
Dto<EmploymentRecord> & AnotherComplexType) {
console.log('Hello ' + renderName(person));
}
greet({ firstName: 'Bob', lastName: 'Smith', });
```

More complex identical anonymous types

In the preceding code, TypeScript will compute the arg types for **greet** and check if the "bob smith" variable can be passed in – and then it will do it again inside the **greet** function when calling the **renderName** function!

So, as convenient as inline types are, the way to solve this is to always name your types. Assigning the complex type to a type alias or interface, TypeScript can cache and reuse the computation more easily, and in cases like the aforementioned, it will instead bypass the check entirely.

```
type Employee = { firstName: string, lastName: string } &
Dto<EmploymentRecord> & AnotherComplexType;
function renderName(employee: Employee): string {
Reuse type computation
return `${person.firstName} ${person.lastName}`;
}
function greet(person: Employee) {
Reuse type computation
console.log('Hello ' + renderName(person));
Skip type assertion
}
greet({
firstName: 'Bob', lastName: 'Smith', });
```

Store anonymous inline types as type aliases, and then reuse them to reduce recomputation

Reducing Inferred Types

Another place TypeScript works extra hard is in inferred types. Take the following code for example:

```
function doSomethingComplex(x: any) {
if (subcomputation1(x)) {
return undefined;
}
if (subcomputation2(x)) {
return true;
}
const a = 1000;
if (subcomputation3(x)) {
return a + Number(x);
}
throw new Error(x);
```

```
}
const foo = doSomethingComplex(bar);
```

A function with a complex inferred return type

As a developer, if you were reading the code for **doSomethingComplex**, you can appreciate it would be hard to work out what the effective return type of a given value might be – and it's the same for TypeScript: it has to go through all the permutations in the function to work out the result. And doing it ourselves we can sympathize: it's fiddly, it takes time, and it uses up memory.

In contrast, if instead we explicitly set the function's return type, it would be easier to review the function and mentally check whether it conformed to the expected return value – and again it's the same for TypeScript: reviewing the function with a pre-known return type is simpler and involves less dynamic interpretation of return type, skipping recomputation of return type as each return permutation is calculated.

Adding the return type also can help development: it's simpler for the consuming developer to read and understand without digging through the function's body or subfunctions, and it can also help provide a simple form of TDD to stub out the function's return type before adding the body, allowing TypeScript to help ensure all return cases are met.

The following example shows how setting the return type allows us to skip reading the function body as well as helps with a TDD approach ensuring we write the correct body that conforms to our conditional type:

```
type SomethingComplexResult<X> =
    X extends undefined ? undefined
    : X extends (boolean | 'true' | 'false') ? true
    : X extends (NumericString | number) ? AsNumber<X>
    : never;
function doSomethingComplex<X>(x: X):
    SomethingComplexResult<X> {
if (subcomputation1(x)) {
    return undefined;
    }
    if (subcomputation2(x)) {
return true;
}
const a = 1000;
if (subcomputation3(x)) {
return a + Number(x);
}
if (subcomputation4(x)) {
return Date(x); ✗
}
throw new Error(x);
}
const foo = doSomethingComplex("123" as const);
const foo = 123;
```

Replacing inferred types with explicit types helps both the developer and the compiler

If you're still not sold on reducing inferred types (and, let's face it, they are pretty handy for avoiding maintenance friction), there's one last reason for ensuring return types on complex functions. And it has to do with future support for concurrency.

Take the following example code:
```
function parse(s: string, mode: 'mode1' | 'mode2' | 'mode3') {
switch (mode) {
case 'mode1':
        return parser1(s);
case 'mode2':
        return parser2(s);
case 'mode3':
        return parser3(s);
}
}
```

A simple function with an inferred result that depends on the result of further functions

To infer the return type, TypeScript has to process each of the **parser()** functions. If these also have inferred return types and internally call each other, then the processing gets harder and harder to parallelize until essentially TypeScript has to resolve their return types sequentially.

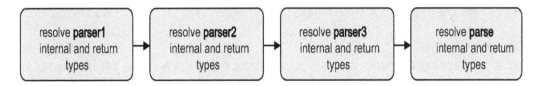

Figure Inferred return types mean parsing has to work sequentially

Instead, adding the return type means each function can be analyzed in parallel, as the type contracts for the subfunctions are already available.

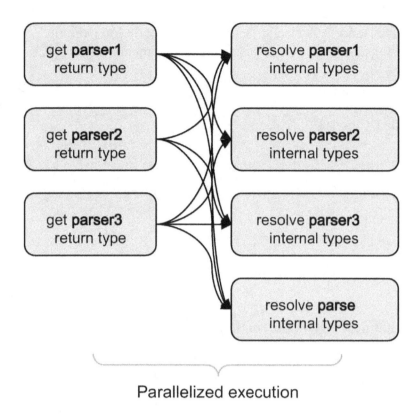

Parallelized execution

Figure Explicit return types mean parsing can be performed in parallel

Inline Caching Using Conditional Types

Another helpful technique to aid caching of static analysis is to use the **infer** keyword to act like a temporary type variable (like a generic parameter). Take the following type:

type Foo<T> = T extends string ? Concatenate<Some<Complex<Expensive<Bar, T>>>, '-'>: T extends number ? Concatenate<Some<Complex<Expensive<Bar, T>>>, '.'>: T;

A type with multiple recomputations of a complex subtype

In the preceding type, we have computed part of the same expensive result type twice. Can we improve this? Happily, yes – we can use the inline type created when inferring types during pattern matching to store our computed subtype like a variable to use elsewhere in the type:

type Foo<T> = Some<Complex<Expensive<Bar, T>>> extends **infer PrecomputedT**
Store complex type in a temporary type var
    ? (T extends string ? Concatenate<PrecomputedT, '-'>
      : T extends number ? Concatenate<PrecomputedT, '.'>
      : T
)
   : never;

Caching a complex subtype in a conditional type inference

Reduce Intersections

Intersections are one of the more expensive computed types, because they merge properties creating resultant properties with the common-denominator subtype that satisfies both. In addition to this, TypeScript also performs further checks when resolving a value as the type because the value has to be checked against both properties, ending in slightly more than double the amount of computation (or triple or more in the case of multi-intersectional types).

Intersections are useful to reducing maintenance and when creating complex types, but they can also add cognitive overhead, where the property-merge is not really needed. Take the following example:

```
interface Employee {
employeeNumber: number
firstName: string
lastName: string
postcode: number
}
interface Person {
name: string
postcode: string
}
type EmployeeRecord = Person & Employee;
type Postcode = EmployeeRecord['postcode'];
type Postcode = never;
```

Simple intersections can have undesirable results where fields overlap
In the preceding example, accidental overlap causes an error in the **postcode** field. To resolve this, you can use the **ShallowMerge** approach as shown in the following. But in the majority of cases, the overlap is better protected against rather than used as a feature.

```
`const result = { ...t, ...u };`
export type ShallowMerge<T, U> = Omit<T, keyof U> & U;
```

ShallowMerge type that avoids overlapping fields

Interfaces, on the other hand, require resolution of all conflicting fields pre-compilation. The inheritance hierarchy of interfaces is also slightly simpler than intersection types, because of the requirement to resolve conflicts pre-compilation, and therefore, the relationships between interfaces can often be cached to improve build performance. And beyond anything else, much like an intersection type, interfaces can extend from multiple types, as follows:

```
interface EmployeeRecord extends Person, Omit<Employee, 'postcode'> {}
type Postcode = EmployeeRecord['postcode'];
type Postcode = string;
```

Extending multiple types in an interface avoids the computation of merged fields that happens in intersections

Interfaces are therefore often safer and faster, and have less cognitive load, than intersection types. However, interfaces cannot extend types defined by their generic parameters, because they need to resolve all fields pre-compilation. So as a rule, use interfaces when combining known types, and use intersection types only when you need the property-merge effect and/or are combining types defined by generic parameters.

Reduce Union Types

Union types are incredibly important for avoiding invalid state, by attaching deeper values to otherwise simple enums. They come at a cost though, as values need to be checked against each value in the union to test that they are acceptable. This is fine with small enums, but when enums grow – especially via template literals – this checking can become exponentially heavy.

Therefore, reserve unions for where they are essential in your code, and consider using simple primitives (which are very fast to type-check) in cases where you are confident a union type has already effectively guarded.

Partition Using Packages and Projects

Partitioning Using Packages

Modern monorepo tooling, such as NX, allows common JavaScript patterns of multiple packages within the same repo to use caching between builds, reducing build (and even deploy) time greatly. This is the preferred approach to partitioning and is easiest to set up – just use the tool's built-in repo templating mechanism. See the "TypeScript Within a More Realistic Setup" section.

Partitioning Using Projects

Prior to monorepos becoming more popular, TypeScript added a feature called **project references**, which are still available today. Similar to packages, but in TypeScript only, project references allow you to organize your code base into smaller, manageable projects and establish build dependencies between them. With project references, you can build and reference multiple TypeScript projects as a single unit, allowing build caching of those individual projects where changes have not occurred.

The following is a simple example configuration of TypeScript project references:

```
// root/tsconfig.json:
{
   "compilerOptions": {
      "composite": true
   },
   "references": [
      { "path": './utils' },
      { "path": './app' },
   ]
}
// root/projects/utils/tsconfig.json:
{
   "compilerOptions": {
      "rootDir": "./src",
      "outDir": "../dist",
      "declaration": true
   },
   "include": [ "./src/**/*" ]
}
// root/projects/utils/src/index.ts
export function greet(name: string): string {
return `Hello ${name}!`; }
// root/projects/app/tsconfig.json:
{
```

```
  "compilerOptions": {
    "rootDir": "./src",
    "outDir": "../dist"
  },
  "references": [
    { "path": "../utils" }
  ],
  "include": [ "./src/**/*" ]
}
// root/projects/app/src/index.ts
import { greet } from 'utils';
const greeting = greet('James');
console.log(greeting);
// Outputs 'Hello James!'
```

Using TypeScript project reference to reduce recompilation
When you build the **app** project, TypeScript will automatically build the utils project first due to the project reference. The resulting JavaScript files will be output to the specified **dist** folders. Changes in the **app** project only will not require the **utils** project to be rebuilt.

Other Performance Tweaks

TypeScript's **tsc** compiler includes a **--incremental** CLI parameter (or **"incremental": true** tsconfig option), which, when enabled, will cause it to store the compilation state in a **.tsbuildinfo** file.
This file is used to determine the minimal set of files that may need to be re-evaluated or re-emitted since the last compilation, reducing the amount of build needed. You may also use the verbosely named **assumeChangesOnlyAffectDirectDependencies** suboption alongside this to even further reduce the recheck/rebuild effort of the compiler, at the expense of some exhaustivity.

Checking the .d.ts files within your node_modules packages is often pointless too, as – if you're using them – we'd assume they're bug-free. Therefore, TypeScript's **tsc** compiler includes **--skipDefaultLibCheck** and **--skipLibCheck** CLI parameters (**"skipDefaultLibCheck": true** and **"skipLibCheck": true** tsconfig options) to skip checking core libs (ECMAScript libs) and other node_modules packages, respectively.

Debugging Performance Issues
The preceding sections include a useful toolbelt of ways to ensure performance is good. But if it still isn't, then how do you find out the reason why?
Fortunately, TypeScript includes a suite of diagnostics that help us identify memory and CPU-intensive code. These diagnostics can be used to dump trace data during compilation, which can then be explored in a diagnostics viewer. To dump these diagnostics, use the CLI params as follows:
npx tsc --extendedDiagnostics --generateTrace ./trace-dir –noEmit

Command-line to save TypeScript extended diagnostics
Once the **tsc** process has completed, you will find it has created a folder called. **/trace-dir** and stored two files inside it: **trace.json** and **types.json**.

Traces are complex data blobs and need tools to view them. So, let's look at two tools we can use to do this.

Using the @typescript/analyze-trace NPM Package

We'll start with the easiest one. Run the following commands to install and run it:

npm install --no-save @typescript/analyze-trace npx analyze-trace ./trace-dir

Command-line to install and run TypeScript's analyze-trace tool
The tool will output a list of "hot spots" in your code where compilation is taking more than average effort, as well as the time taken for each spot. This should be enough for you to get started targeting your performance optimizations.

Hot Spots
├─ Check file \\demo\example-hot-spot.ts (3116ms)
│ ├─ Check variable declaration from (line 63, char 7) to (line 93, char 2) (1641ms)
│ │ └─ Check expression from (line 63, char 23) to (line 93, char 2) (1641ms)
│ │   └─ Check expression from (line 69, char 5) to (line 92, char 6) (1610ms)
│ │   ├─ Check expression from (line 70, char 21) to (line 80, char 10) (957ms)
│ │   └─ Check expression from (line 81, char 20) to (line 91, char 10) (653ms)
│ ⋮
⋮

Example output from TypeScript's analyze-trace tool
Using a Trace Viewer Within Your Browser
If you want to dig deeper, you can view the trace data in a trace viewer. Open a Chromium-based browser (such as Google Chrome or Edge), and enter **about:tracing** in the URL bar, and press enter. The browser will load a trace explorer view, where you can press the "Load" button shown in Figure and choose the **trace.json** file, and the browser will display the trace data.

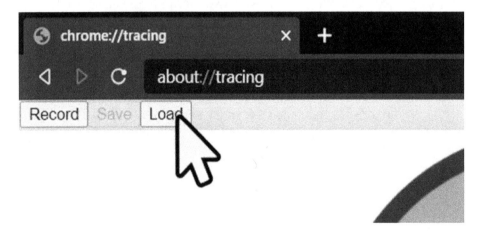

Figure Load your trace.json file by clicking this button

When the trace has loaded, it will show a flame graph of the build process effort (y axis) against time (x axis). You can click on the root of each flame to see which file was processed at each point in a view panel at the bottom of the graph – choose the widest ones to find the highest processing cost.

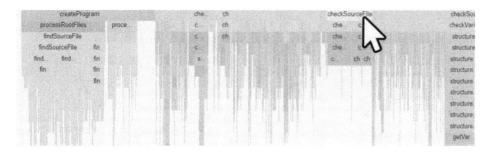

Figure The trace "flame graph" view

Clicking on the flame graph row segments below each file root will show the effort given the code processed within that file. Unfortunately, the quick-view panel for this is less helpful: the types are only given ids (source type and target type), not names, so you'll need to locate the corresponding id in the **types.json** file to find the correlative type name, compilation mode (union, object, etc.), and recursion depth. It's a slower process than using the NPM package, but it allows more fine-grained analysis of what is happening during compilation.

Build

We will cover the remaining aspects of the build process. TypeScript project configuration is essential to this process, and the heart of this configuration lies in the **tsconfig.json** file, located in the root of your project folder. We'll begin with an overview of the main options available in this file.

Understanding these options is crucial to successfully harness the full potential of the TypeScript compiler.
We will then cover what I would recommend you use as a sensible default for your **tsconfig.json** settings. Instead of overwhelming you with an exhaustive list of every option available, I'll highlight just the most important ones that will enhance your projects' code quality, maintainability, and compatibility.

After mastering the TypeScript compiler options, we explore additional tooling that can also help prevent errors available via linting. We will explore ESLint and its TypeScript ESLint supplement and again review what are a good go-to set of rules to leverage among the many available. By using the tsconfig and ESLint configurations in this chapter, you will have a robust tooling setup to catch the majority of common programming mistakes and improve code quality.

We will also look at another aspect of TypeScript compilation, which is support for the JSX format. You will see how JSX is just a syntactic sugar on top of normal JavaScript function calls and therefore how the type safety techniques you have learned in this book can be applied to JSX code also.

Finally, we will explore an essential aspect of the build and deployment process: modules. Understanding the different module formats, and how TypeScript resolves modules, is crucial for making informed choices and managing code organization, dependencies, and interoperability when performing post-compilation steps like bundling and chunking. With this knowledge, you'll be able to structure your projects efficiently and take full advantage of TypeScript's module system.

By the end of this chapter, you will have gained a comprehensive understanding of TypeScript's build configurations, linting options, and the way it interacts with modules. This knowledge will be the final piece of the puzzle in becoming a true TypeScript expert.

Compiler Options

TypeScript project configuration is provided by the presence of a **tsconfig.json** file in the root of the project folder. To create a boilerplate of this file, use the following command:
npx tsc –init

Creating a default tsconfig.json file
The **tsconfig.json** file includes settings for the following:

Compiler options: The tsconfig.json file allows you to specify various compiler options that control how TypeScript code is compiled. These options define the target ECMAScript version, module system, strictness level, output directory, and more.

Project structure: The tsconfig.json file helps define the structure of the TypeScript project. It specifies the root files or directories that should be included in the compilation process. It allows you to specify patterns for including or excluding files based on glob patterns.

Module resolution: TypeScript supports different module resolution strategies, such as Node.js, Classic, or
Custom. The **tsconfig.json** file lets you configure the module resolution strategy for your project, which affects how TypeScript resolves and imports module dependencies. For details of module types, see the "Module Types Explained" section, later in this chapter.

Declaration files: Declaration files (**.d.ts**) provide type information for external JavaScript libraries or modules. The **tsconfig.json** file allows you to specify the generation of declaration files, their output directory, and other related settings.

Build configurations: In larger projects, you may have different build configurations for development, production, or other environments. The **tsconfig.json** file enables you to define multiple configurations by creating different tsconfig.json files and specifying the desired options for each configuration.

Recommended tsconfig.json Settings
Rather than going through all the settings available, which are easy to find on the TypeScript official website, we will now go through those compiler options I recommend you use. In short, you should aim to use the following compiler options:

```json
{
   "compilerOptions": {
      "module": "ESNext",
      "moduleResolution": "NodeNext",
      "target": "ESNext",
      "lib": [ "esnext" ],
      // Prevent Optional Errors:
      "noEmitOnError": true,
      "strict": true,
      "strictNullChecks": true,
      "allowUnreachableCode": false,
      "noImplicitOverride": true,
      "noImplicitReturns": true,
      "noUncheckedIndexedAccess": true,
      "noUnusedLocals": true,
```

```json
      "noUnusedParameters": true,
      "noFallthroughCasesInSwitch": true,
      "isolatedModules": true,
      "allowJs": true,
      "checkJs": true,
      // Display Complete Errors:
      "noErrorTruncation": true,
      "downlevelIteration": true,
      "esModuleInterop": true,
      "allowSyntheticDefaultImports": true,
      "experimentalDecorators": true,
      "jsx": "react-jsx",
      // Project Structure and Build Output:
      "baseUrl": ".",
      "paths": {
        "src/*": [
          "src/*"
        ],
        "tests/*": [
          "tests/*"
        ],
      },
      "outDir": "dist",
  }
  "include": [
    "src/**/*.ts",
    "src/**/*.tsx",
    "src/**/*.d.ts",
    "tests/**/*.ts",
    "tests/**/*.tsx",
    "tests/**/*.d.ts",
  ],
  "exclude": [
    "node_modules"
  ]
}
```

Recommended tsconfig.json settings for modern TypeScript projects

The preceding configuration will target the newest browsers, save you from a range of optional errors, display complete errors, enable the widest range of safe interoperability, and lastly set your build project files structure to a standard configuration used by most projects. Phew – that's a lot! Let's go through these now to understand what they each do.

Targeting Modern Browsers

Why target only modern browsers? Don't we want a range of browsers or platforms to be able to load our code? Well, yes – we do. But the truth is that TypeScript isn't the best tool for this. It provides an acceptable output, but a much better output with easier definition can be achieved by using a post-build process such as **corejs** or **swc** against a **browserlist** aligned to your needs.

And for now, keep your TypeScript targeting only newer browsers, as follows:

module: "ESNext": Defines the module code generation for the emitted JavaScript. Using ESNext allows you to utilize ES modules, which offer better interoperability and support for tree shaking in modern JavaScript bundlers.

moduleResolution: "Node": Sets the strategy for resolving module dependencies. Choosing Node module resolution leverages the Node.js module resolution algorithm, which is widely adopted and works well for most scenarios. The alternative "Classic" strategy only remains for backward compatibility and can be ignored for modern development. For more details on how TypeScript resolves modules using the Node setting, see the "How TypeScript Resolves Modules" section.
target: "ESNext": Specifies the ECMAScript target version for the emitted JavaScript. By targeting ESNext, you can take advantage of the latest JavaScript features and syntax improvements, ensuring compatibility with modern environments.
lib:["esnext"]: Specifies the library files to include during the compilation. In this case, only the esnext library is included, providing access to the features introduced in the ESNext ECMAScript version.

Prevent Optional Errors

noEmitOnError: true: With this setting, the compiler won't emit JavaScript files if there are any errors in the TypeScript code. It helps enforce stricter error checking and prevents generating potentially broken output files.
strict: true: Activating strict mode enables a set of strict type-checking options. Setting this to true actually, enables a suite of different "sensible default" tests within TypeScript, including the following:

alwaysStrict: Ensures that your files are parsed in the ECMAScript strict mode and emit "use strict" for each source file
noImplicitAny: Prevents untyped cases where TypeScript would otherwise infer them as **any**. Ensures your devs explicitly set **any** when needed, which makes code review clearer.
noImplicitThis: Prevents untyped cases where TypeScript would otherwise need to infer **this** as **any**.

strictBindCallApply: Prevents cases where TypeScript infers the built-in **call**, **bind**, and **apply** methods are called with untyped arguments.
strictFunctionTypes: Ensures tighter type checks on function arguments.
strictNullChecks: Ensures **null** and **undefined** have their own distinct types, and so a type error will be provided if you try to use optional or nullable values without asserting the value's existence first.
strictPropertyInitialization: Ensures all properties are correctly initialized during class construction, preventing accidental **undefined**s.

useUnknownInCatchVariables: Ensures you correctly interrogate or cast caught errors to known types before using them. Enabling this default check suite provided by the TypeScript compiler helps catch common programming mistakes, enhances code quality, and improves maintainability.
strictNullChecks: true: When enabled, TypeScript enforces strict null checks, reducing the likelihood of null or undefined errors. It promotes safer programming practices by requiring explicit handling of nullable types.
allowUnreachableCode: false: Set to false, TypeScript raises errors for any code after a nonavoidable return statement. This protects against mistakes in logic paths that may unwittingly prevent subsequent code from running.
noImplicitOverride: true: Set to true, ensures subclass overrides do not mistakenly override their superclass counterparts, instead requiring them to have an explicit override keyword. This makes it easier to see intent and check for errors during code review.
noImplicitReturns: true: Without this, ECMAScript permits functions to have logic branches that include no return value, instead inferring a final return value of **undefined** when the end of the function is reached. Enabled, this option prevents this and ensures all code paths provide a suitable return value.

noUncheckedIndexedAccess: true: When accessing indexed types, it adds **undefined** as a union case to any field not explicitly declared (and therefore made type-safe) against the type.

noUnusedLocals: true: This option flags any unused local variables as errors during compilation. It helps identify and remove redundant code, leading to cleaner and more efficient programs.

noUnusedParameters: true: Similar to **noUnusedLocals**, this option treats unused function parameters as errors. It encourages writing focused and concise functions by highlighting unused arguments.

noFallthroughCasesInSwitch: true: Generates an error when a switch statement has cases that fall through without appropriate break, return, or throw statements. It improves code clarity and reduces the chances of unintentional fallthrough.

isolatedModules: true: When enabled, each file is treated as a separate module, without sharing a global namespace. It encourages better encapsulation and helps prevent unintentional variable conflicts.

allowJs: true: This setting allows TypeScript to compile JavaScript files (.js) alongside TypeScript files (.ts). It provides flexibility for gradually adopting TypeScript in projects with existing JavaScript code.

checkJs: true: This setting, in conjunction with allowJs, ensures TypeScript processes any types inferable within JavaScript files.

Display Complete Errors

noErrorTruncation: true: When enabled, this option ensures that TypeScript displays the complete error messages without truncation. It helps in understanding and diagnosing errors more effectively.

Enable Widest Range of Safe Interoperability

downlevelIteration: true: This option enables the compiler to emit code compatible with downlevel iterations. It's useful when targeting older JavaScript environments that lack native support for iteration constructs like for...of loops.

esModuleInterop: true: When using CommonJS modules, this option simplifies interoperability with ES modules that use default imports or named imports. It allows for more seamless integration between different module systems.

allowSyntheticDefaultImports: true: When set to true, TypeScript allows importing modules that don't have default exports as if they had one. This simplifies the interoperation with legacy CommonJS modules and libraries that weren't designed with ES modules in mind.

experimentalDecorators: true: Enables support for the experimental decorators' feature, which is used in conjunction with libraries like Angular or TypeScript transformers. This option allows using decorators for class and property declarations. jsx: "react-jsx": Enables support for JSX syntax (see the "JSX/TSX" section) using the modern, runtime-agnostic output format. Initially, JSX output in TypeScript was tied to React (or React-likes, such as Preact), but this newer approach outputs to a simple __jsx() function call, which can be defined by a wider range of runtime frameworks.

Project Structure and Build Output

baseUrl and **paths**: These options allow you to configure module resolution for custom module paths. "baseUrl" specifies the base directory used for resolving nonrelative module names, while "paths" define mappings from module names to specific directories or files. **outDir**: If you are not using a bundler and want TypeScript to output (a.k.a. "emit") JavaScript files, you'll need them saved somewhere. By default, the compiled files are emitted as siblings to each of their originating TypeScript files, which is actually pretty useless; **outDir** allows you to specify a more useful, specific, location for the resultant output.

However, if you are using a bundler, you may instead want to switch on **noEmit:true**, to use TypeScript for type checking only and rely on a different transpiler such as swc or babel (with corejs) to emit the output file(s).

include and **exclude**: **include** allows you to provide an array of globs of the entry point files you want to include in the compilation. Any files referenced from these files will also be included, so we can also **exclude** a "node_modules" glob to ignore traversing deeper into any packages we aren't creating ourselves.

Other Options

The only remaining options I would suggest considering would be the performance-related options **skipLibCheck**, **skipDefaultLibCheck**, and **incremental**, as well the diagnostic **diagnostics/extendedDiagnostics** options. These are all covered, in the "Other Performance Tweaks" and "Debugging Performance Issues" sections.

Linting

Linting is most often used as a way to enforce code style decisions across a team, or even just in your own code. But this isn't the true extent of what lint tools such as ESLint can bring to your development process.

Linting, simply put, is actually a static-analysis step that runs a suite of rules on your code. In this light, the TypeScript type checks themselves can be considered a lint ruleset. And using community-contributed tools such as ESLint, we can extend those type checks to include additional safety checks that haven't officially been made part of TypeScript yet.

ESLint comes with a suite of rules that it recommends as best practice. On top of these, the TypeScript team and the community have contributed a further suite of rules in the supplementary NPM package. We will review these in this chapter and list those ones that will assist with further type assertions.

Installing ESLint

First, to install ESLint and its TypeScript ESLint supplement, run the following command in the root of your project:
npm install --save-dev
  @typescript-eslint/parser
  @typescript-eslint/eslint-plugin   eslint
  Typescript

Installing ESLint and associated TypeScript plugins

The rules available in these tools are provided through ESLint plug-ins. To configure these, we now need to create a.**eslintrc.cjs** file in the root of our project and with the following code:

```
module.exports = {
extends: ['eslint:recommended',
'plugin:@typescript-eslint/recommended'],
parser: '@typescript-eslint/parser',
plugins: ['@typescript-eslint'],
root: true, };
```

A normal ESLint configuration for TypeScript

The preceding configuration will tell ESLint to use its own default "recommended" suite of rules, as well as the "recommended" ones provided in the **typescript-eslint** plug-in.

Ideal Ruleset

In many situations, devs will consider the aforementioned a sufficient coverage. But some of the rules included in the recommended sets are either better delivered by TypeScript itself or can be considered stylistic. Others are not included in the recommended sets yet because of the additional processing power they require, but are worth bringing into your project if possible. So, let's edit your. **eslintrc.cjs** now to the following more powerful setup:

```
module.exports = {
extends: [
    'eslint:recommended',
    'plugin:@typescript-eslint/recommended',
    'plugin:@typescript-eslint/recommended-requiring-type-checking'
  ],
parser: '@typescript-eslint/parser', parserOptions: {
project: './tsconfig.json', ecmaVersion: 2022,  sourceType: 'module', createDefaultProgram: true,
ecmaFeatures: {
tsx: true,
    },
},
plugins: [
    '@typescript-eslint'
  ],
root: true, rules: {
    '@typescript-eslint/default-param-last': 'error',
    '@typescript-eslint/no-array-constructor': 'off',
    '@typescript-eslint/no-empty-function': 'off',
    '@typescript-eslint/no-empty-interface': 'off',
    '@typescript-eslint/no-explicit-any': 'off',
    '@typescript-eslint/no-extra-non-null-assertion': 'off',
    '@typescript-eslint/no-extra-semi': 'off',
    '@typescript-eslint/no-implied-eval': 'error',
    '@typescript-eslint/no-inferrable-types': 'off',
    '@typescript-eslint/no-invalid-this': 'error',
    '@typescript-eslint/no-loop-func': 'warn',
    '@typescript-eslint/no-loss-of-precision': 'warn',
    '@typescript-eslint/no-misused-new': 'off',
    '@typescript-eslint/no-non-null-assertion': 'off',
    '@typescript-eslint/no-redeclare': 'error',
    '@typescript-eslint/no-shadow': [
      'warn',
      {
allow: ['_']
},
    ],
    '@typescript-eslint/no-unnecessary-type-assertion': 'warn',
    '@typescript-eslint/no-unsafe-argument': 'off',
    '@typescript-eslint/no-unsafe-assignment': 'off',
    '@typescript-eslint/no-unsafe-call': 'off',
```

```
      '@typescript-eslint/no-unsafe-member-access': 'off',
      '@typescript-eslint/no-unsafe-return': 'off',
      '@typescript-eslint/no-unused-vars': 'off',
      '@typescript-eslint/prefer-namespace-keyword': 'off',
      '@typescript-eslint/prefer-nullish-coalescing': 'warn',
      '@typescript-eslint/require-array-sort-compare': [
        'error',
        { ignoreStringArrays: true },
      ],
      '@typescript-eslint/require-await': 'warn',
      '@typescript-eslint/restrict-template-expressions': [
        'error',
        {
allowAny: false, allowBoolean: true, allowNullish: false, allowNumber: true, allowRegExp: false,
        },
      ],
      'constructor-super': 'off',
      'for-direction': 'off',
      'getter-return': 'off',
      'guard-for-in': 'warn',
      'no-async-promise-executor': 'off',
      'no-await-in-loop': 'warn',
      'no-caller': 'error',
      'no-class-assign': 'off',
      'no-compare-neg-zero': 'off',
      'no-console': [
      'warn',
        {
allow: ['warn', 'error']
},
      ],
      'no-const-assign': 'off',
      'no-control-regex': 'off',
      'no-delete-var': 'off',
      'no-dupe-args': 'off',
      'no-dupe-class-members': 'off',
      'no-dupe-keys': 'off',
      'no-eval': 'warn',
      'no-floating-decimal': 'warn',
      'no-func-assign': 'off',
      'no-implicit-globals': 'warn',
      'no-import-assign': 'off',
      'no-iterator': 'error',
      'no-labels': 'error',
      'no-multi-str': 'warn',
      'no-new-func': 'error',
      'no-new-symbol': 'off',
      'no-obj-calls': 'off',
      'no-octal-escape': 'error',
      'no-octal': 'error',
      'no-param-reassign': 'error',
```

```
        'no-proto': 'error',
        'no-redeclare': 'off',
        'no-return-assign': [
            'warn',
            'always',
        ],
        'no-self-compare': 'error',
        'no-sequences': 'error',
        'no-setter-return': 'off',
        'no-sparse-arrays': 'off',
        'no-template-curly-in-string': 'error',
        'no-this-before-super': 'off',
        'no-throw-literal': 'warn',
        'no-undef': 'off',
        'no-unreachable': 'off',
        'no-unused-vars': 'off',
        'no-useless-call': 'warn',
        'no-useless-rename': 'warn',
        'no-var': 'error',
        'no-warning-comments': 'warn',
        'no-with': 'off',
        'prefer-promise-reject-errors': 'warn',
        'symbol-description': 'error',
        'valid-typeof': 'off',
        'vars-on-top': 'warn',
    }
};
```

Recommended ESLint configuration for TypeScript

Phew! That's a lot of settings. Let's review these changes now and discuss each.

Additional Strict Errors@typescript- Default parameters are parameters that are assigned a specific default value when unspecified by a caller. Without enforcing **eslint/** defaults to be at the end, parameter assignment can be confusing.

defaultparam-last@typescript- Some JavaScript methods, such as setTimeout, allow a string rather than a function to be passed as their callback parameter. **eslint/** This can be a security concern, and therefore, we want to prevent it.

no-impliedeval@typescript- JavaScript follows a functional paradigm, and therefore, functions can be "bound" to a value and called. However, in most cases, **eslint/** this is just confusing, as this parameter is usually simpler to pass as a simple arg – directly or via a currying library if **no-invalid-** necessary. This rule enforces that functions do not use this keyword if not part of a class.

this@typescript- Ensures a stricter extension approach extending interfaces, ensuring that redeclared fields are of the same type and therefore **eslint/** not mistakenly overridden.

no-redeclare@typescript- In JavaScript, array's. **sort** method actually does a string comparison of each of the items – which is fine if your array is of **eslint/**strings, but otherwise will internally convert them to strings by calling. toString() on each value before comparison. The **require-**results are therefore usually undesired (e.g., number arrays become sorted lexicographically rather than by magnitude). To **array-sort-** avoid this, this rule ensures we specify a comparison function when sorting.

compare@typescript- JavaScript template literals can contain any value in their expressions, and on each a **.toString()** function is called before **eslint/**   incorporating into the template output. This is fine for many primitives, but values such as objects, or undefined, or symbols **restrict-** are instead included in an unhelpful way (e.g., "Hello [object Object]!"). This rule ensures we convert values beforehand, **template-**thereby avoiding errors.

expressions

no-caller ECMAScript's **arguments.caller** and **arguments.callee** make some code optimizations impossible and also complicate your code. This rule disallows the use of these values.

no-iterator Disallows the use of a legacy **__iterator__** property – if you wanted this, you should probably use the new ECMAScript iterables, for a simpler control flow.

no-labels Labels and their correlative **break** (goto) statements make control flow difficult to reason about, introducing an additional layer of statefulness that makes testing hard. This rule disallows the use of labels.

no-new-func To, simplify code readability, the **new** keyword should be restricted to use for constructing classes. This rule ensures this keyword isn't used against functions, which can make it difficult to debug and reason about the types returned by and used internally within those functions.

no-octal- Earlier versions of JavaScript required octal escape sequences for extended character sets. Many developers are not familiar **escape** with these and are more comfortable now with the more modern Unicode escape sequences. This rule ensures no octal escape **&** sequences are used.

no-octal

no-param- The use of parameters as reassign able variables inside functions can lead to confusing behavior, such as mutation of the inbuilt **reassign arguments** object and/or counterintuitive execution flow. This rule ensures no parameters are reassigned and is somewhat correlative to **no-var**, described later in this section.

no-proto the use of the inbuilt **__proto__** property has been deprecated since ECMAScript 3.1. This rule ensures this property is not used in your code.

no-self- Comparing a value to itself (e.g., **if (person === person))** is both pointless as well as usually a mistake. This rule **compare** ensures this is prohibited in your code.

no-sequences Comma operators in JavaScript allow multiple expressions to occur in a single line in some special situations. However, they are more confusing to reason about than simple control flows and therefore can lead to errors. This rule prevents the comma operator being used and thereby avoids these potential control-flow errors.

no-template- String templates use **${}** syntax to load in their template values. The use of this syntax in a nontemplate string (i.e., a string **curly-in-** delimited by "or 'characters) is usually a typo, and therefore, this rule protects you from these typos.

no-var The, original ECMAScript **var** keyword only respect's function scope and ignores scopes more often used in other languages such the scopes provided by the **while**, **if**, or **for** keyword. As a solution, **const** and **let** were brought into ECMAScript v6 onward, and so this rule disallows the **var** keyword in preference to these newer, safer approaches.

symbol- Anonymous symbols are hard to debug and locate in code. This rule ensures all your symbols are given descriptions when **description** constructing them.

Additional Strict Warnings

@typescript- This rule protects against bad closures within functions. Functions mistakenly enclosing vars (rather than scoped lets or **eslint/no-loop-** consts) can have these values updated outside their scope, and so protecting against these helps avoid unanticipated **func** errors.

@typescript- Numbers in JavaScript have a finite number of digits – which means that as you start to use large floats or high-precision **eslint/** floats beyond a certain number of columns, JavaScript will start to automatically round them! This lint check protects you **no-loss-of-** against this by ensuring high-precision values are stored in types that can handle it.

precision@typescript- Declaring a variable within a function that has the same name as a variable in the scope surrounding the function is called **eslint/no-** variable "shadowing." It doesn't cause errors, but reasoning in the code can become very difficult, especially when both **shadow** internal and external values are needed. This rule ensures you name your variables uniquely across scopes, preventing shadowing.

@typescript- This rule is included in the typescript-eslint recommended set but is set to "error", which is too severe. Setting it to warn **eslint/** allows you to use type assertions as you prefer but flags them as optionally removable if they are extraneous.

no-unnecessarytype-assertion@typescript- In JavaScript, you can coalesce falsy values using the || operator. As undefined and null are both counted falsy, it can be **eslint/** tempting to use the || operator to coalesce these too; but modern ECMAScript provides a dedicated operator **??** for this **prefer-** instead, making the code's intent clearer.

nullishcoalescing@typescript- There's no point marking a function with the **async** keyword if it doesn't include at least, one **await** statement – it's **eslint/require-** either an error or a false function signature. This rule ensures this is detected and flagged.

await guard-for-in	In JavaScript, it's possible to write a **for** statement with no exit clause. This is nearly always a mistake, as it provides an infinite loop. This rule protects against this in your code.
no-await-inloop	While you can call **await** inside a loop, it's usually better to instead use **Promise.all** to execute the operations in parallel. The main scenario where you'd want to use an await in a loop is in an async generator function that is looping over another async generator – and as this is so infrequent, then we protect against accidents by enabling this rule.
no-console	The **console.log** variants (log, debug, warn, error) are useful for investigating bugs and checking control flow. However, it's important to remove these before you ship your code to production, so this rule allows us to check for these calls. We have set our rule to allow warn and error logs though, which are rarely used explicitly when debugging, as these are more likely to be legitimate outputs in your code for logging nonfatal runtime conditions.
no-eval	The **eval** statement in JavaScript is widely considered a security risk, as it can allow accidental behavior injection that is hard to sanitize against. This rule prevents the use of **eval** to protect against these security errors.
no-floatingdecimal	ECMAScript permits floating decimals to be defined in code without a leading or trailing zero (e.g., **.8** instead of **0.8**, or **1** instead of **1.0**). However, without a leading or trailing zero, these decimal operators are hard to spot and can also be typos; and so this rule prevents these by flagging them as errors.

no-implicitglobals	Global variables are intrinsically hard to reason about, as every operation across your program can read and write to them. As such, they add statefulness to every function and so massively increase the complexity and undermine the exhaustive testability of your program. However, they are sometimes a necessary evil; but being such should need to be declared explicitly rather than implicitly and therefore potentially by accident. This rule ensures explicit statement of global vars and protects against this concern.
no-multi-str	The backslash character can escape special chars in strings. You can backslash apostrophes, quotes, tabs, and others to ensure they are included literally rather than interpreted as the string. One of the chars you can backslash (an undocumented feature) is the newline char itself (actual newline, rather than \n). This is usually seen as bad practice as it can confuse readability, and the \n approach is more canonical. This rule prevents the intentional or accidental use of escaped newlines.
no-returnassign	Assignments in JavaScript all actually return a value, and one of the quirks of this means that you can write **return x=y+1** validly in a function. However, this is rarely needed unless x is global, and in practice, usually it represents a typo of **return x===y+1**. This rule prevents this form of typos.
no-throwliteral	In JavaScript, any given value can be thrown – errors, strings, numbers, nulls, booleans – anything! Unpacking these values in a catch statement can therefore be very difficult. Narrowing the variance by enforcing that only errors (and subclasses of errors) can be thrown at least means that errors include a readable toString and some other expected error data.

no-useless-call- This is an edge case, but this prevents unnecessary calls to the inbuilt functional.call and **.apply** methods where a direct call would have the same effect. Admittedly in practice, you're unlikely to trigger this rule, but it'll keep unnecessary curly code at bay.

no-useless- When refactoring in an IDE, renaming a variable (F2 in VSCode) will, due to a limitation in the tooling, lead to unnecessary **rename** import statements such as **import { x as x } from 'x.js'**. This rule will protect against these.

no-warning- Conventional tags such as **fixme** and **todo** in comments will be flagged by this so that these human-recognized issues are **comments** logged with your other static analysis.

prefer-promise- Similar to **no-throw-literal**, this rule ensures that only Error classes are passed into **Promise.reject()** calls, **reject-errors** making try/catch handling simpler and more reliable.

vars-on-top- This is a backup to the **no-var** rule, ensuring that if you really do need to use vars, they are at least only in the outermost scope, which makes them slightly easier to reason about.

Removed Rules
In addition to switching on some additional rules in the preceding config, we also switched some of the "recommended" rules off. There are two groups of reasons for these. For those in the typescript-eslint plug-in, newer versions of TypeScript already provide safer checking than the ruleset does, and so we no longer need them. And for those in the ESLint config (further down in the following table), they are simply already covered by existing TypeScript error checks and type safety, so they are also no longer needed.

Further Rules

ESLint is a powerful tool to add to your build workflow, adding many checks that are not yet part of the TypeScript type-checking analysis. It represents an important aspect of your build process and should be part of every TypeScript project to augment and protect against errors.

As you may have noticed, in all the cases we've discussed in this section, we are focusing our lint checking on rules that prevent actual errors in our code. This type of static analysis is important to reduce the maintenance effort on your team. And if you wish to go further, additional suites of these error-prevention rules are also available in the following rulesets that ship with the **typescript-eslint** package:

plugin:@typescript-eslint/strict plugin:@typescript-eslint/strict-type-checked

Beyond these error-prevention rules, you may also wish to review stylistic rules across your organization or within your teams. However, in most cases, I'd recommend treading lightly with these stylistic rules, and instead let teams largely determine their own, as these stylistic settings relate more to opinion than runtime impact.

The **typescript-eslint** package also includes some further stylistic rulesets too (**stylistic** and **stylistic-type-checked**), which may also be helpful as they align to most coding practices in larger orgs, and you can (as we have for error checks) always customize further to define your own "sensible defaults."

JSX/TSX

JSX, which stands for JavaScript XML, is an extension to the JavaScript language. It allows the developer to write HTML-like syntax directly within JavaScript code, combining the power of JavaScript and the flexibility of HTML together, and is written in files with a **.jsx** file extension. TSX is an extension of JSX, bringing TypeScript type checking to JSX, and so it is written in files with a (you guessed it!) **.tsx** extension.

Here's an example of the JSX/TSX syntax:

const element = <h1>Hello, world!</h1>;

Example of JSX and TSX syntax

Most browsers and runtimes won't be able to run this directly, and so during build, this is actually transpiled to the following:

const element = _jsx("h1", { children: "Hello, world!" });

Whatever JSX runtime you have configured (the default is React) will have provided a function called **_jsx** to the global scope, and so the preceding code will call this function. This JSX runtime function will then essentially correlate your input arguments with an internal structure called a Virtual DOM and then use this to synchronize your changes to the actual browser DOM so that your **<h1>Hello, world!</h1>** is displayed as a real HTML H1 with text content in your browser.

For the curious, the reason your changes aren't written directly to the browser DOM is that changes to the browser DOM are relatively expensive in terms of processor and memory, as they involve layout, repainting, removing/attaching event handlers, and many other things. The Virtual DOM, on the other hand, can be cheaply mutated, and then only the changes are synchronized across.

Let's now see an example of adding our own component to the syntax. We do this by creating a function and naming it using Pascal case (i.e., its name needs to start with an uppercase first letter):

```
interface MyComponentProps {}
const MyComponent: React.FC<PropsWithChildren<MyComponentProps>> = (props) =>
{
return (
 <div>
{props.children}
    </div>
  )
} const element = <MyComponent>Hello, world!</MyComponent>
```

Creating and using a React component in TSX syntax

Now, take a look at what those compiles into:

```
const MyComponent = (props) => {
return (_jsx("div", { children: props.children }));
};
const element = _jsx(MyComponent, { children: "Hello, world!" });
```

Normal ECMAScript convention is to name functions and variables with a lowercase first letter (called camelCase, because it has a hump in the middle). Naming the function in Pascal case triggers the compiler to record the function as a JSX receiver. When the transpiler then spots the receiver in the JSX element name, it will use your function as an argument for the **_jsx** runtime function. Internally, the **_jsx** runtime function will then effectively do this:

```
function _jsx(component, props) {
const renderedComponent = component(props);
}
```

How the TSX _jsx runtime function works internally
You may also notice in the preceding example that the props being passed in are an object, and any JSX children's components are passed in via a property automatically named **children** by the transpiler.

Because we now know that all JSX components are simple function calls, then of course we can also define our own properties alongside the automatic **children** property:

```
interface MyComponentProps { imageSrc: string }
const MyComponent: React.FC<PropsWithChildren<MyComponentProps>> = (props) =>
{
return (
<div>
      <img src={props.imageSrc} />
        {props.children}
    </div>
  )
}
const element =  <MyComponent imageSrc="assets/greeting.png"> Hello, world!
```

```
</MyComponent>
```

Passing parameters to our component, which come through as function arguments

And we can even redefine the type of the **children** property and require only a specific type of children:

```
interface AnimalComponentProps {
name: string
type: 'amphibian' | 'bird' | 'fish' | 'mammal' | 'reptile'
}
const AnimalComponent: React.FC<AnimalComponentProps> = (props) => {
return (
<div>
{props.firstName} {props.lastName}
    </div>
  )
}
interface MyComponentProps {
imageSrc: string
children: ReactElement<AnimalComponentProps>[]
}
const MyComponent: React.FC<React.PropsWithChildren<MyComponentProps>> =
(props) => {
return (
<div>
        <img src={props.imageSrc} />
        {props.children}
      </div>
  )
}
const element =
   <MyComponent imageSrc="assets/animals.png">
     <AnimalComponent name="Garfield" type="mammal" />
     <AnimalComponent name="Nemo" type="fish" />
     <AnimalComponent name="Tweetie" type="bird" />
   </MyComponent>;
```

Defining types requiring specific children in our React component or to require a function as a child:

```
interface MyComponentProps {
imageSrc: string     children:
(args: { greetingName: string }) => ReactElement<AnimalComponentProps>[]
}
const MyComponent: React.FC<React.PropsWithChildren<MyComponentProps>> =
(props) => {
return (
<div>
        <img src={props.imageSrc} />
{props.children({ greetingName: 'World' })}
      </div>
  )
```

```
}
const element =
  <MyComponent imageSrc="assets/animals.png">
    {({ greetingName }) =>
        Hello, {greetingName}!
        <AnimalComponent name="Garfield" type="mammal" />
        <AnimalComponent name="Nemo" type="fish" />
        <AnimalComponent name="Tweetie" type="bird" />
    }
  </MyComponent>;
```

Defining our children as a more powerful function rather than a simple JSX node

Lastly, as components in JSX/TSX are simple function calls, we can also provide generic parameters to them (or have them infer generic parameters), much the same as normal function calls:

```
interface MyListProps<Item> {    items: Item[]
onPress: (item: Item) => void }
const MyList = <Item,>(props: MyListProps<Item>) => {
}
const items = useMemo(() => [1, 2, 3], []);
const onPressHandler = useCallback((item: number) => { /* ... */ }, []); const element =
<MyList<number>        items={items}
onPress={onPressHandler}
/>;
```

Using generics in TSX
Modules
Module Types Explained

Prior to ECMAScript Modules (ESM), modules were just conventions around closures in JavaScript files. As outlined in this book's introduction, these evolved from emerging needs over the course of time, and TypeScript has added output support for each of these as they were released. However, as the industry has grown, and additional techniques such as bundling, chunking, and zero-js delivery have emerged, the TypeScript team's development has necessarily focused more on type checking, the core team instead contributing to Babel's TypeScript "preset", in order to not lag on the pace of change. However, it is still worth having a basic appreciation of these underlying module types, as these are still part of the module resolution process and therefore part of TypeScript compilation and present in the **tsconfig.json** options.

To demonstrate, take the following example snippet of TypeScript code. In each following section, we will review the same code transpiled by TypeScript to each module system, so you can see how the closure conventions work in each case:

```
import { URL } from 'node:url';
export function createUrl(href: string) {
return new URL(href);
}
```

Example of a simple module written in TypeScript

CommonJS (CJS)

Created in 2009 to solve the lack of a native ECMAScript module system at that time and adopted by the
Node.js core team while still in its infancy. This format is still supported by many bundlers (e.g., Webpack, Rollup), but gradually the industry is moving away from. It defines a global var (var without a var keyword) called **exports** and attaches the module as a field within this var.

```
"use strict";
Object.defineProperty(exports, "__esModule", {value: true});
exports.createUrl = void 0; const node_url_1 = require("node:url");
function createUrl(href) {
return new node_url_1.URL(href);
}
exports.createUrl = createUrl;
```

Asynchronous Module Definition (AMD)

Created in 2011 as CommonJS remained unsupported by browsers as non-canon to ECMAScript standard, AMD – via the module loader RequireJS – became a way to simulate modules in browser JavaScript, largely deprecated nowadays. It uses a **define** function within RequireJS to manage loading a closure, which in turn (like CommonJS) adds the module to a global **exports** var.

```
define(["require", "exports", "node:url"], function (require, exports, node_url_1) {
"use strict";
Object.defineProperty(exports, "__esModule", { value: true });
exports.createUrl = void 0;
function createUrl(href) {
return new node_url_1.URL(href);
}
exports.createUrl = createUrl; });
```

Universal Module Definition (UMD)
Created later in 2011 as a way to host both CommonJS and AMD module conventions in a single JavaScript file, but not widely adopted by the industry as there was no clear market leader for a module loader for this more verbose practice.

```
(function (factory) {
if (typeof module === "object" && typeof module.exports === "object") {
var v = factory(require, exports);
if (v !== undefined) module.exports = v;
}
else if (typeof define === "function" && define.amd) {
define(["require", "exports", "node:url"], factory);
   }
})
(function (require, exports) {"use strict";
Object.defineProperty(exports, "__esModule", {value: true});
exports.createUrl = void 0;
const node_url_1 = require("node:url");
function createUrl(href) {
return new node_url_1.URL(href);
}
```

```
exports.createUrl = createUrl;
});
```

SystemJS

Not actually a module system but included here to avoid confusion when referencing tsconfig.json module options, SystemJS is actually a module loader that (like RequireJS) has a particular syntax and so required a specific module output format – and like RequireJS, it used a named function to manage asynchronous load and the modules, although it used a return value rather than a global var. This, as well as AMD and UMD, is now largely deprecated by the JavaScript community in favour of the ESM native module format.

```
System.register(["node:url"], function (exports_1, context_1) {
"use strict";
var node_url_1;
var __moduleName = context_1 && context_1.id;
function createUrl(href) {
return new node_url_1.URL(href);
}
exports_1("createUrl", createUrl);
return {
setters: [
function (node_url_1_1) {
node_url_1 = node_url_1_1;
}],
execute: function () {
    }
  };
});
```

ESM

ES modules, finally standardized in 2015, are the native implementation of modules. As TypeScript follows ECMAScript, the syntax for this is essentially identical (without the type notations) to what you will already be familiar with in TypeScript.

```
import { URL } from 'node:url';
export function createUrl(href) {
return new URL(href); }
```

Exports and Imports

By changing your tsconfig.json target, you can write code in ESM format and emit output in any of the aforementioned module formats. So, let's cover this ESM format now and explore how to use it.
The ESM file format is defined by the use of the **import** and **export** keywords. Any file that does not either import or export a value or type is inferred to be a classic JavaScript file, and the values and types therein are added to the global scope. This means they are available in all files without additional import.

Once you include either an **import** or **export**, the game changes. Your file is processed instead as an ESM module, and any values and types therein are only available to other values and types within the same file. To use them in other files (modules), you need to first **export** them from your file and then **import** them into the desired consuming module.

To export a value or type, just prefix the value or type with the **export** keyword:

```
// Export a constant or variable:
export const greeting = 'Hello world!'
// Export a function:
export function greet(name: string) {
return `Hello ${name}!`; }
// Export an interface:
export interface Person {
firstName: string
lastName: string
}
// Export a type alias:
export type PersonKey = keyof Person;
```

Exporting values and types from a module
You can also export them using an export statement:

```
const greeting = 'Hello world!'
interface Person {
firstName: string
lastName: string
}
export {greeting, Person};
```

Exporting values and types from a module using a single statement

To make compilation simpler (so that TypeScript doesn't need to work out which imports/exports to exclude during transpilation), you can also mark the exports with an optional **type** keyword hint to indicate they are type exports:

```
export {greet, type Person};
```

Using type hints on exports to help the compiler

Importing is similar, although you have two options: importing synchronously during module load and importing asynchronously and conditionally during runtime.

Importing synchronously during module load is the most common practice and has a similar syntax to exporting:

```
import {greet, Person} from './module.js';
console.log(greet('Dave')); // Outputs 'Hello Dave!'
```

Importing values and types from a module
Like when exporting, you can optionally add the **type** keyword as an optimization hint to the TypeScript compiler to help save it a few steps during compilation when working out whether to exclude imports from emitted code:

```
import {greet, type Person} from './module.js';
```

Using type hints on imports to help the compiler

Note that the module file name in TypeScript needs to be suffixed with the file extension of the emitted file, not the source file. The reason for this is to keep the highest parity with the final code, and the **allowImportingTsExtensions** tsconfig option only works when no code will be emitted for this very reason.

You can also alias imports using the **as** keyword as well as re-export imports, as shown in the following code:

```
import {greet as renderGreeting} from './module.js'; // Use alias
console.log(renderGreeting('Dave'));
import * as MyModule from './module.js'; // Import everything // from a module
console.log(MyModule.greet('Dave'));
export { type Person } from './module.js'; // Re-export the // type or value
```

Renaming imports using the as keyword

The imports covered so far are performed when the module is loaded. But if instead you want to conditionally import a module based on runtime logic, you can also import it via an inline import:

```
function async createGreetingAsync(name: string) {
let greeting = 'Hello'
if (features.translationEnabled) {
const translator = await import('./hugeTranslatorModule.js');
greeting = translator(greeting);
}
return `${greeting} ${name}`;
}
```

ESM supports conditional (runtime) asynchronous imports, as well as the normal bundle-time ones. The conditional import approach allows you to exclude some optional pieces of your code from your main bundle and deliver these in increments after your app is mainly up and running, to provide a faster, smoother, experience for the user.

How TypeScript Resolves Modules

Module "resolution" means the process TypeScript uses to find the file that an **import** statement refers to. TypeScript can be set to resolve in either "Classic" or "Node" mode. Classic mode is only included for compatibility with early versions of TypeScript and can be ignored; Node module resolution mode instead copies the resolution process that Node.js (and other compatible runtimes) uses and is now TypeScript's default module resolution mode.

This "Node" module resolution mode works as shown in Figure

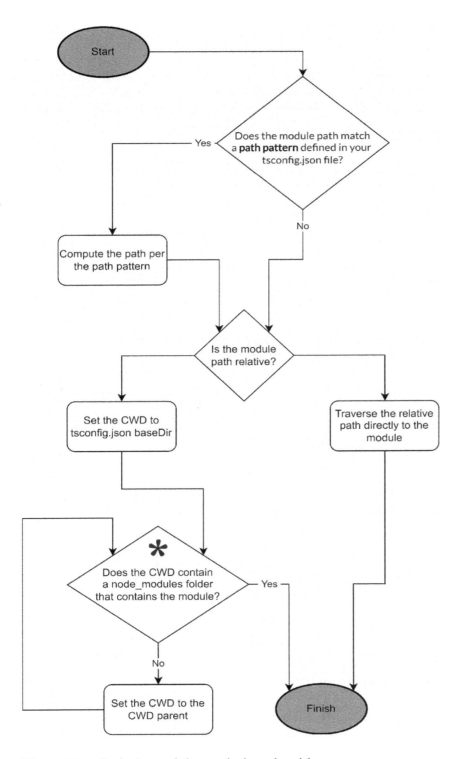

Figure TypeScript's module resolution algorithm

When TypeScript evaluates the step marked with an asterisk (*) in the preceding Node.js algorithm, there are a few substeps that are worth detailing. These begin by determining whether the module path requested is a path to a module folder only (e.g., "react"), or to a specific file within a module (e.g., "zod/lib/helpers/util.js").

If the path is to a module folder, the algorithm loads the package.json within that folder and traverses to the entrypoint specified in the package.json's "main" entry and the type definitions specified in its "types" entry. If these entries do not exist, then it'll check some default file names instead. If the path is to a specific module file, the algorithm instead tries to jump directly to that file.

However, in both the case of checking default file names and if jumping directly to a specific module file, if the file name in question has no extension specified, then lastly the algorithm will try the following possible extensions for this: .ts, .mts, .cts, .tsx, .mtsx, .ctsx, .d.ts, .js, .mjs, .mjsx, .cjs, and .cjsx.

As you can see from the aforementioned, there are quite a few options attempted when trying to resolve modules. Adding main/types to your package.json will help shortcut this, but let's review a hardest-possible resolution within a monorepo to illustrate the algorithm in action:

import { someValue } from 'my-custom-package';
Resolving:
  › 'my-custom-package' is not a relative module path ✗
  › 'my-custom-package' is not in path patterns in tsconfig.json ✗
  › **'/src/packages/myPackage/node_modules' exists** ✓
  › '/src/packages/myPackage/node_modules/my-custom-package' does not exist ✗
  › '/src/packages/node_modules' does not exist ✗
  › '/src/node_modules' does not exist ✗
  › **'/node_modules' exists** ✓
  › **'/node_modules/my-custom-package' exists** ✓
  › **'/node_modules/my-custom-package/package.json' exists** ✓
  › my-custom-package package.json does not contain a main entry ✗
  › '/node_modules/my-custom-package/index.ts' does not exist ✗
  › '/node_modules/my-custom-package/index.mts' does not exist ✗
  › '/node_modules/my-custom-package/index.cts' does not exist ✗
  › '/node_modules/my-custom-package/index.tsx' does not exist ✗
  › '/node_modules/my-custom-package/index.mtsx' does not exist ✗
  › '/node_modules/my-custom-package/index.ctsx' does not exist ✗
  › '/node_modules/my-custom-package/index.js' does not exist ✗
  › '/node_modules/my-custom-package/index.mjs' does not exist ✗
  › **'/node_modules/my-custom-package/index.cjs' exists** ✓
  › **Resolved 'my-custom-package'='/node_modules/my-custom-package/index.cjs'** ✓

Example steps when resolving a module

To debug your own imports, TypeScript includes a helpful **traceResolution** CLI parameter and tsconfig.json setting. Setting this to true will log to your STDOUT the results of its module resolution for every import in your project.
npx tsc --noEmit --traceResolution

Conclusion: Unlocking TypeScript's Full Potential
As TypeScript continues to shape modern software development, its advanced features and build processes empower developers to tackle complex challenges with greater confidence, precision, and efficiency. Moving beyond the fundamentals, mastering advanced TypeScript concepts and optimizing the build process are crucial for creating scalable, maintainable, and high-performing applications.

This conclusion reflects on the key lessons from exploring **Advanced Usage and Build in TypeScript**, elaborating on their significance, applications, and future outlook.

1. The Power of Advanced TypeScript Features

1.1 Streamlining Code with Utility Types

Utility types like Partial, Omit, and Record provide an intuitive way to manipulate and shape types. These tools reduce boilerplate code, ensuring that developers can focus on logic rather than repetitive type definitions. For instance, dynamically selecting or excluding properties of complex objects is a common need in APIs, and utility types make these operations seamless.

By mastering utility types, developers can create reusable and dynamic codebases that adapt to changing requirements without breaking the underlying structure.

1.2 Conditional and Mapped Types: Beyond Static Definitions

One of the most transformative aspects of TypeScript is its ability to derive types dynamically using **conditional** and **mapped types**. These features align with real-world scenarios where data structures evolve based on context. For instance:

A **conditional type** can dynamically infer whether a user-provided input meets specific conditions.

Mapped types allow for mass transformations of type properties, enabling consistency and avoiding manual adjustments.

Such flexibility enhances TypeScript's suitability for large-scale applications, especially in environments where type safety and adaptability are paramount.

1.3 Template Literal Types: Precision in String Handling

Template literal types simplify handling string-based constraints, such as managing internationalization or formatting patterns. For example, constructing types for localized strings (en-US, fr-FR) or defining URL patterns becomes straightforward with this feature. These types ensure correctness at compile time, preventing runtime errors caused by string mismatches.

By incorporating template literal types, developers can enforce stringent rules and patterns, fostering consistency across a project.

2. Building Robust Applications with TypeScript

2.1 Enforcing Runtime Safety with Type Guards

Type guards extend TypeScript's safety guarantees into runtime, ensuring applications behave predictably under all circumstances. By implementing custom type guards, developers can verify unknown or external data, such as API responses, at runtime. This minimizes potential errors, ensuring stability even in unpredictable environments.

2.2 Leveraging Decorators for Code Enhancement

Decorators, though still experimental, bring the power of metaprogramming to TypeScript. They enable developers to enhance classes and methods with additional functionality, such as logging, validation, and dependency injection. Frameworks like Angular heavily utilize decorators, showcasing their importance in building scalable, modular applications.

Mastering decorators empowers developers to extend their applications' capabilities while maintaining clean, modular code.

2.3 Scaling Applications with Module Augmentation

Module augmentation is invaluable for extending third-party libraries or customizing existing modules. This feature is particularly useful in enterprise-grade applications where developers often need to integrate or adapt libraries to meet specific needs.

For instance, augmenting the express module with custom request properties can streamline user authentication and session management, enhancing both performance and developer experience.

3. Optimizing the Build Process

3.1 Fine-Tuning tsconfig.json

The TypeScript configuration file (tsconfig.json) serves as the foundation for an efficient build process. Customizing options like strict, target, and module ensures compatibility with modern JavaScript environments while maintaining strict type safety. For complex projects, settings like paths and baseUrl simplify module resolution, improving code readability and maintainability.

3.2 Integrating TypeScript with Modern Toolchains

Integrating TypeScript with modern tools like Webpack, Vite, or Rollup facilitates seamless application bundling and optimization. These tools leverage TypeScript's static type-checking capabilities, producing high-quality builds with minimal overhead. For instance, ts-loader in Webpack or esbuild for Vite enables rapid builds and efficient dependency management.

Using these tools, developers can focus on building features rather than struggling with compatibility and performance issues.

3.3 Enhancing Code Quality with Linting and Formatting

Code quality tools like **ESLint** and **Prettier** ensure consistent coding standards, reducing technical debt over time. By incorporating TypeScript-specific rules, these tools prevent common mistakes, such as unused variables or incorrect type annotations. Automated formatting and linting pipelines further enhance productivity by eliminating repetitive tasks.

For teams working on large projects, these tools are indispensable for maintaining clean and consistent code.

3.4 Continuous Integration and Deployment

CI/CD pipelines are crucial for modern development workflows, and TypeScript integrates seamlessly with these processes. Automated type checking, linting, and testing ensure that changes meet quality standards before deployment. By leveraging tools like GitHub Actions, Jenkins, or GitLab CI/CD, developers can maintain robust delivery pipelines.

For instance, running tsc --noEmit in CI ensures all code is type-safe without generating unnecessary artifacts, saving time and resources.

4. The Strategic Advantages of Advanced TypeScript

4.1 Increased Developer Productivity

TypeScript's advanced features streamline complex workflows. With strong typing, developers can rely on autocomplete, intelligent error reporting, and refactoring tools, reducing the cognitive load and preventing errors before they occur.

4.2 Improved Maintainability

Codebases written with advanced TypeScript concepts are inherently easier to maintain. Strong typing provides clear contracts between components, reducing ambiguity and improving collaboration in teams. Techniques like modularization, project references, and custom types make scaling applications manageable.

4.3 Enhanced Application Performance

While TypeScript is a superset of JavaScript and doesn't directly affect runtime performance, its ability to catch bugs and enforce correctness improves overall application reliability. Optimized build processes and modern tooling ensure efficient deployment and execution.

4.4 Future-Proofing Applications

TypeScript's forward-compatible features, such as support for ECMAScript proposals and evolving standards, ensure that applications remain relevant as the JavaScript ecosystem grows. Developers who master advanced concepts are better equipped to adopt new paradigms and tools.

5. The Future of TypeScript Development

Looking ahead to 2024 and beyond, TypeScript will continue to evolve, addressing developer needs and industry trends. Key developments to watch include:

Enhanced ESM Support: TypeScript is poised to improve its integration with modern ECMAScript Modules, ensuring better compatibility with Node.js and browsers.

Pattern Matching: Borrowing ideas from functional programming languages, pattern matching in TypeScript could revolutionize conditional logic.

Improved Tooling: AI-driven enhancements in tooling may provide smarter error reporting, type suggestions, and automated refactoring capabilities.

Ecosystem Growth: With the increasing adoption of frameworks like Next.js and NestJS, TypeScript's ecosystem will expand, offering new libraries and tools for advanced use cases.

These trends highlight the importance of staying updated with TypeScript's advancements to remain competitive and effective in the software development landscape.

6. Call to Action

For developers looking to maximize their TypeScript proficiency, here are actionable steps:

Experiment with Advanced Features: Practice utility types, conditional types, and generics in real-world scenarios.

Optimize Build Processes: Configure tsconfig.json for your project's needs and integrate with modern bundlers like Vite.

Leverage Best Practices: Adopt tools like ESLint, Prettier, and CI/CD pipelines to maintain high code quality.

Stay Updated: Follow TypeScript's official updates and community resources to learn about new features and trends.

Final Thoughts

The journey into advanced TypeScript usage and build processes is a transformative experience for developers. It not only enhances technical skills but also fosters a deeper understanding of how to write better, more robust software. With its unparalleled type safety, developer tooling, and ecosystem support, TypeScript stands as a beacon of modern programming excellence.

By embracing TypeScript's advanced features and build optimizations, developers can elevate their projects, delivering scalable, maintainable, and high-quality applications. Whether you're a seasoned developer or just starting, TypeScript offers a rewarding path to mastering the art of software development in 2024 and beyond.

Thank You

As we conclude The Pragmatic TypeScript Programmer: Reshaping Modern JavaScript, I hope this journey through TypeScript has equipped you with the tools, knowledge, and confidence to approach modern development with clarity and purpose.

TypeScript is more than just a superset of JavaScript; it's a mindset—a commitment to writing code that is clean, maintainable, and scalable. By embracing TypeScript, you're not only improving the quality of your applications but also shaping the future of development in a world where strong typing and better tooling are becoming essential.

Remember, programming is a craft that evolves with every line of code you write. As you continue exploring, experimenting, and creating, let TypeScript be your ally in turning complex problems into elegant solutions.

Thank you for trusting me to guide you on this journey. Whether you're building web applications, diving into the backend, or exploring new technologies, I encourage you to push boundaries, stay curious, and keep reshaping the way you think about code.

Happy coding,

Mike Zephalon